A–Z of Corporate Environmental Management

Kit Sadgrove

EARTHSCAN
Earthscan Publications Ltd, London

To Alexandra

First published in the UK in 1997 by
Earthscan Publications Ltd.

A catalogue record for this book is available from the British Library.

ISBN: 1 85383 330 4

Typeset and page design by Oxprint
Printed and bound by Biddles Ltd, Guildford and Kings Lynn

Cover design by Andrew Corbett

For a full list of publications, please contact:
Earthscan Publications Ltd
120 Pentonville Road
London N1 9JN
Tel: 0171 278 0433
Fax: 0171 278 1142
email: earthinfo@earthscan.co.uk
http:/www.earthscan.co.uk

Earthscan is an editorially independent subsidiary of
Kogan Page Limited and publishes in association with WWF-UK and
the International Institute for Environment and Development.

Contents

List of Illustrations and Case Studies

Figures

Tables

Boxes

Case Studies

Acronyms and Abbreviations

ACCA	Chartered Association of Certified Accountants, UK
ADE	advection dispersion equation
ADI	acceptable daily intake
ADR	alternative dispute resolution
ADR	European Agreement on the Carriage of Dangerous Goods by Road
ALARA	as low as reasonably achievable
ALATA	as low as technically achievable
AONB	Area of Outstanding Natural Beauty
APES	alkyl phenol ethoxylates
BANANA	ban all new activities now and always
BAT	best available technique
BATNEEC	best available techniques not entailing excessive cost
BCSD	Business Council for Sustainable Development
BEO	best environmental option
BET	best environmental timetable
BOD	biochemical oxygen demand
BPEO	best practical environmental option
BPM	best practical means
BRE	Building Research Institute, UK
BREEAM	Building Research Establishment Environmental Assessment Method
BS	British Standard
BSI	British Standards Institution
BT	British Telecom
CAP	Common Agricultural Policy
CBI	Confederation of British Industry
CCEM	Centre for Corporate Environmental Management
CCGT	combined cycle gas turbine
CEFIC	European Chemical Industry Council
CEN	Comité Européen de Normalisation
CEO	chief executive officer
CERES	Coalition of Environmentally Responsible Economies
CFC	chlorofluorocarbon
CGL	Comprehensive General Liability
CHIP	Chemicals (Hazard Information and Packaging for Supply)
CHP	combined heat and power
CIA	Chemical Industries Association, UK
CIMAH	Control of Industrial Major Accident Hazard Regulations
CITES	Convention on International Trade in Endangered Species
CNG	compressed natural gas
CO	carbon monoxide
CO_2	carbon dioxide
COD	chemical oxygen demand
COMAH	Control of Major Accident Hazards
COSHH-UK	Control of Substances Hazardous to Health Regulations
CRT	cathode ray tube
CSI	Common Sense Initiative
CTBT	Comprehensive Test Ban Treaty
DDT	dichlorodiphenyltrichloroethane
DIY	do it yourself
DNA	deoxyribose nucleic acid

DoE	Department of the Environment, UK
DSD	Dualles System Deutschland
EA	Environmental Assessment
EA 95	Environment Act 1995, UK
EC	European Community
ECF	elemental chlorine-free
ECL	Eastern Counties Leather
EDI	electronic data interchange
EDTA	ethylene diamino-tetra-acetic acid
EEA	European Environmental Agency
EFTA	European Free Trade Agreement
EFW	energy from waste
EIA	environmental impact assessment
EINECS	European Inventory of Existing Commercial Chemical Substances
ELA	Environmental Liability Act, Germany
EMAS	Eco-Management and Audit Scheme
EMF	electromagnetic fields
EMS	Environmental Management System
ENDS	Environmental Data Services
EPA	Environmental Protection Act, US
EPA 90	Environmental Protection Act, 1990, UK
EPAQS	Expert Panel on Air Quality Standards, UK
EPR	environmental performance reporting
EQO	Environmental Quality Order
EQS	Environmental Quality Standards
ES	environmental statement
ESA	Environmentally Sensitive Area
ESAP	Environmental Self-Assessment Programme
EU	European Union
EVABAT	economically viable application of best available technology
EWMC	Environmental Waste Management Corporation, Toronto
FAO	United Nations Food and Agriculture Organization
FGD	flue gas desulphurization
FRN	Furniture Recycling Network
FSC	Forestry Stewardship Council
GDP	gross domestic product
GEMI	Global Environmental Management Initiative
GMO	genetically modified organism
HAZOP	hazard and operability
HCFC	hydro-chlorofluorocarbon
HMIP	Her Majesty's Inspectorate of Pollution
HMSO	Her Majesty's Stationery Office
HSWA	Hazardous and Solid Waste Amendments
ICC	International Chamber of Commerce
IEM	Institute of Environmental Managers
IMDG	International Maritime Dangerous Goods Code
IMO	International Maritime Organization
inco	incontinence products
IOD	Institute of Directors
IPC	Integrated Pollution Control
IPPC	Integrated Pollution Prevention and Control
IPCC	Intergovernmental Panel on Climate Change
IRBM	Integrated River Basic Management
ISO	International Organization for Standardization

IT	information technology
IUCN	International Union for the Conservation of Nature and Natural Resources
IWC	International Whaling Commission
kWh	kilowatts per hour
LAAPC	Local Authority Air Pollution Control
LAC	Local Advisory Committee
LCA	Life-Cycle Analysis
LDC	London Dumping Convention
LED	light-emitting diode
LGMB	Local Government Management Board
LULU	locally undesirable land use
MMF	man-made mineral fibres
MO	Material Organizations, UK
mpg	miles per gallon
mph	miles per hour
MRL	maximum residue level
NAAQS	National Ambient Air Quality Standard
NAPM	National Association of Paper Merchants, UK
NIMBY	not in my backyard
NO	nitric oxide
NO_2	nitrogen dioxide
N_2O	nitrous oxide
NRA	National Rivers Authority
NSA	Nitrate Sensitive Area
NTA	nitrilo-tri-acetic acid
NVZs	nitrate-vulnerable zones
OC	organochlorine
ODS	ozone-depleting substances
OECD	Organization for Economic Cooperation and Development
OP	organophosphate
OWP	Organic Waste Processing Ltd, UK
PAH	polycyclic (polynuclear) aromatic hydrocarbon
PBB	polybrominated biphenyl
PCA	polycarboxylate
PCB	polychlorinated biphenyl
PCN	polychlorinated napthalene
PCP	pentachlorophenol
PFA	pulverized fuel ash
PFC	perfluorocarbon
PHAST	Process Hazards Assessments Screening Tools Programme
PIC	products of incomplete combustion
POTW	publicly owned treatment work
ppb	parts per billion
ppm	parts per million
PR	public relations
PV	photovoltaics
PVC	polyvinyl chloride
RAC	Royal Automobile Club
RCEP	Royal Commission on Environmental Pollution
RCRA	Resource Conservation and Recovery Act
R&D	research and development
REPAC	Regional Environmental Protection Advisory Committee

RIBA	Royal Institute of British Architects
RICS	Royal Institution of Chartered Surveyors
RID	Regulations on the International Carriage of Dangerous Goods by Rail
RIDDOR	Reporting of Injuries, Diseases and Dangerous Occurrences Regulations 1985, UK
RME	rapeseed methyl ester
RSI	repetitive strain injury
RVM	reverse vending machine
SAC	Special Area of Conservation
SAGE	Strategic Advisory Group on the Environment
SARA	Superfund Amendments and Reauthorization Act, US
SBS	sick building syndrome
SCEEMAS	Small Company Environmental and Energy Management Assistance Scheme
SCS	Scientific Certification Services
SEA	Strategic Environmental Assessment
SEFRA	Self-Financing Regulatory Agency, UK
SEPA	Scottish Environmental Protection Agency
SMMT	Society of Motor Manufacturers and Traders, UK
SO_2	sulphur dioxide
SPA	Special Protection Area
SSSI	Site of Special Scientific Interest
TBT	tributylin compound
TBTO	tributyl tin oxide
TCDD	tetrachlorodibenzo-p-dioxin
TCE	trichloroethane
TCF	totally chlorine-free
TCP	toiletries, cosmetics and pharmaceutical industry
TDS	total dissolved solids
TEL	tetra-ethyl lead
TEQ	toxic equivalent value
TNT	trinitrotoluene
TQM	total quality management
TRI	Toxics Release Inventory, US
TSS	total suspended solids
UES	Uniform Emission Standard
UKAS	United Kingdom Accreditation Service
UNCED	United Nations Conference on Environment and Development
UNEP	United Nations Environment Programme
USABC	US Advanced Battery Consortium
UST	underground storage tank
UV	ultra violet
VAH	volatile aromatic hydrocarbon
VOC	volatile organic compound
WAZAN	World Bank Hazard Analysis Programme
WBCSD	World Business Council for Sustainable Development
WHO	World Health Organization
WICE	World Industry Council for the Environment
WMO	World Meteorological Organization
WPZ	water protection zone
WQO	water quality objectives
WWF	World Wildlife Fund

How To Use This Book

There are many ways in which you might use this book. Here are some of them.

If you want to ...	*See ...*
Do an environmental audit	See *Audit, environmental.**
Become more green in the office	See *Office* in the Reference Section.
Implement an environmental management system	See *Environmental management system* in the Reference Section.
Know what a term means (such as *LULU* or *Banana*)	See their respective entries.
Understand the impact of a particular substance (such as *organophosphates*, *HCFCs* or *formaldehyde*)	See each under its own heading.
Undertake a project (for example, packaging, liquid waste, or marketing)	See their respective entries.
Improve your organization's environmental performance	Begin with the following entries: • *Audit* • *Environmental management system* • *Policy* • *Strategy*.
Understand the wider issues, such as *Global warming*	See the entries listed under 'Issues' in the Reference Section.

Finding Out More

At the end of many entries you will find a 'See also' list of related entries. This leads you to more information about the subject. You should also look at the Reference Section at the back of this book, where major entries are grouped under 21 broad headings, from *Air pollution* to *Water and Water pollutants*. Under Air pollution, for example, you will find a number of related headings, such as Acid rain, Carbon monoxide and Diesel.

*Italics denote a main entry.

Inclusions and Omissions

To keep this book to a manageable size, some topics have had to be omitted. The omissions tend to be issues related to ecology or biology, rather than management. (With reluctance, the word *polychloromethylsulphonamidodiphenylether* has been excluded from the *A–Z*. It is a moth proofer which is dangerous to aquatic species. Not many people know that.) Nor has it been possible to include more than the most important of the environmental laws produced by the world's major countries. Likewise, health and safety matters, though linked to the environment, are not the main focus of this book.

References to legislation should not be taken as definitive, and you should seek qualified legal advice on environmental law.

Definitions

The goal of this book is to explain environmental management, rather than simply define words. For this reason, the *A–Z* avoids defining words in a legalistic way where it does not aid understanding. When there has been a conflict between detail and clarity, the entry usually opts for clarity.

A Note about Classification

Subjects are classified under the most important word. For example, you will find *Environmental policy* under *Policy*. This avoids too many headings starting with the word *Environment*.

Feedback and Consultancy

If you would like information about the consulting and training services available from the Business Institute, please contact Kit Sadgrove, The Business Institute, Honeycombe House, Bagley, Wedmore, Somerset BS28 4TD, UK. Tel: 01934 713563. Fax: 01934 713492. The author welcomes comments on the entries of this book.

List of Entries

1-3 Butadiene: *see Butadiene*

2,4,5-T

Toxic herbicide. A component of the notorious *Agent Orange* used in the Vietnam War to denude large areas of the countryside. 45,000 US Vietnam War veterans sued the manufacturers of *Agent Orange* and received US$180 million in compensation.

2,4,5-T is banned in nine countries including the US, and restricted in eight others. It is classified as 'moderately hazardous' by the World Health Organization (WHO). 2,4,5-T is sold under many trade names, including Farmon, Kilnet and Nettleban.

Best Practice

- Do not use.

2,4-D

Moderately toxic selective weed killer for lawns. Irritates eyes and skin, and is an *oestrogen mimic* which reduces male fertility. Possibly a carcinogen.

Best practice

- Avoid use.

See also: Black list; Phenoxy acid.

ACCA Guidelines

Guidelines by the UK's Chartered Association of Certified Accountants say that companies' environmental reporting should cover the following issues:

Qualitative

Company profile
Environmental policy
Targets and objectives
Community relations

Management

Environmental management system
Risk management
Site practices

Quantitative

Environmental indicators
Energy and natural resources
Regulatory compliance
Financial indicators

Products

Products
Processes
Contact personnel
See also: Report, environmental.

Accounting

Traditional accounting ignores any cost which does not appear on the balance sheet. As a result, environmental costs are not taken into account. Today, accounting bodies are seeking ways of measuring companies' full effects on the environment. The problem is how to value a view or a lake. Full-cost accounting would include the cost of pollution, and it would allow natural capital (such as clay) to be translated into man-made capital (such as bricks). Environmental accounting systems try to ensure a balance of 'intergenerational capital' (in other words, natural capital is not to be squandered).

Case Study 1: A Cost Sheet from Curtis Fine Papers

Curtis Fine Papers is part of Crown Vantage, a $1 billion business with 11 manufacturing sites in the US and Scotland and 4000 employees.

	£000 1994	*£000 1995 (projected)*
Sales turnover	40,000	–
Effluent plant-operating costs	337	345
Sludge disposal	53	83
Solid-waste disposal	20	25
Testing	15	38
Management time	77	83
Research projects	5	24
External audits	–	9
Training	10	10
Environmental report	–	25
Total environmental cost	517	642

Capital costs in 1991 and 1992 totalled £3 million.

See also: Costs, LCA, Technology

Acids, Acidity

Acid in the air can corrode buildings and kill trees; when it falls on lakes it makes them acidic, which harms fish and other aquatic species. Acid comes from the emissions of acidic oxides (*sulphur dioxide, nitrous oxide* etc) from power stations and car exhausts. Acid mine drainage also affects some water courses.

The scale of the acidity can be reduced by lessening these polluting emissions (through the use of filters, catalytic converters in cars, and through the use of renewable energy). The pH of acidified lakes has sometimes been reduced by lime, though this provides only temporary relief; stopping the pollution at source is the only long-term solution. The pH of acidic industrial waste water can be balanced by adding specific *chemicals*, such as sodium hydroxide.

See also: Acid rain.

Acid Rain

Sulphuric acid, nitric acid, other acids or ammonium, carried sometimes long distances by prevailing winds, and falling as rain, mist or dry particles. Technically, acid rain is acidic precipitation where the pH is less than 5.6, the normal equilibrium for *carbon dioxide* and water.

Acid rain is caused by *sulphur dioxide* emitted by coal-fired power stations, and *nitrogen oxides* from car exhausts. When it falls, acid rain makes lakes acidic, which kills the fish and other creatures. It damages trees (over half of Germany's forests are dying though acid rain), and stonework on buildings. It also causes irritation to people's airways, causing coughing or wheezing.

In the long term, acid rain is likely to diminish, as vehicles and power stations become cleaner.

Best Practice

- Companies can combat acid rain by conserving energy (thereby reducing the demand for energy from power stations).
- Power stations should filter their *sulphur dioxide.*

Acrylamide

Toxic substance used in the making of paper, dyes, artificial leather, photographic emulsion, and adhesives.

Activated Sludge

The treatment of *organic* waste (waste containing micro-organisms) by feeding it with compressed air and settled sludge. This technique converts a high proportion of the waste into stable inorganic matter, and is used in *sewage treatment* and industrial *liquid wastes.*

ADE

Advection Dispersion Equation. Used to model liquid flows, such as the dispersion of pollution in a river.

Adelphe

French packaging recovery organization for wine and spirit bottlers.

Adhesives

Adhesives are often applied with *solvents*, which are an environmental, fire, and health and safety hazard. Moreover, solvent adhesives may require solvent recovery systems and health and safety precautions. Some paper adhesives, such as those used in books, magazines and envelopes, cause difficulty in recycling.

Hot-melt adhesives do not use solvents but use a lot of energy. Water-based adhesives do not carry these disadvantages and may dry more easily.

Best Practice

- Investigate the feasibility of using adhesives that do not require solvents.

ADI

Acceptable Daily Intake. A measure used for *pesticide* residues in food.

See also: MRL.

ADR

(1) Alternative Dispute Resolution. *See:* Litigation.
(2) European Agreement on the Carriage of Dangerous Goods by Road. *See:* Transport of dangerous goods.

Adsorption

Process where a substance, usually a gas, accumulates on the surface of a solid and forms a thin film, often just a single molecule thick.

See also: Liquid waste.

Advertising: *see Marketing*

Aerobic

Containing air. Some processes for treating waste liquids, including *sewage* (such as activated sludge), require aerobic conditions.

Aerosols

Originally powered by *chlorofluorocarbons* (*CFCs*), many aerosols are now propelled by *propane* or *butane*, both dangerous and explosive gases. However, compressed air is now also being used, and this reduces *volatile organic compound* (*VOC*) emissions by 60 per cent. The steel and plastic aerosol containers involve a lot of packaging and are difficult to recycle.

After aerosols stopped using CFCs, some manufacturers began labelling them 'environmentally friendly', a claim which environmentalists thought was undeserved. This in turn led to the development of an independent EC *eco-label* for *hairsprays* and then *furniture care products*.

Best Practice

- Replace aerosols with trigger action sprays.
- If it is essential to use aerosols, choose ones powered by compressed air.

See also: Organic; Packaging.

Aerospace Industry

The aerospace industry's impacts are similar in style to those of the car industry. The impacts involved in the aircraft's manufacture (use of energy and non-renewable raw materials, such as metal and plastics) are small in comparison with the impacts during the plane's use, namely:

- the fuel and oils used;
- the de-icers sprayed on the wings before take-off in freezing weather;
- the noise of the aircraft's take-off and landing;
- The loss of habitats caused by *airport* construction (which is not strictly the aircraft's impact).

Today's aircraft are quieter and more fuel-efficient than before, and today's larger aircraft mean more people can be carried for the same take-off and landing impacts. Nevertheless, the problem of noise for those who live under the flight path is still considerable.

See also: Defence industry.

Agenda 21

An 800-page document issued at the *Earth Summit* in Rio de Janeiro in 1992. It contains guidelines for governments in everything from population strategies to disposal of *hazardous waste, recycling*, and the role of unions and women in the environment. The document urges cuts in energy and in wasteful *packaging*, and encourages *renewable energy*.

Agent Orange: *see Phenoxy Acid*

Aggregates: *see Quarrying Industry*

Agriculture

The farming industry has created the rural landscape, which many townspeople think has somehow developed without interference from man. After being encouraged for centuries to grow crops and livestock ever more productively, farmers began to be criticized by the environmental movement which developed in the 1970s.

Farmers have access to powerful herbicides and larger equipment which in turn necessitate bigger fields and fewer *hedges*; nevertheless, they are criticized by environmentalists who mourn the loss of habitats. Conservationists demand that farmers manage the countryside for the environmental benefit of all, while economics dictates that farms ignore green issues. Farming impacts include:

- the loss of hedges, ancient meadows and forests;
- draining of wetlands, loss of *wildlife habitats*;
- pollution of the water courses through *nitrates* and farm effluents;
- poisoning of *wildlife* through *pesticides*;
- *pesticide* residues appearing in soil, animals and crops;
- loss of species though the use of monocultures;
- routine use of antibiotics and growth hormones which produces resistant micro-organisms;
- cruelty to animals raised in intensive conditions;
- burning of crop residues (notably stubble and straw burning).

6000 km (3700 miles) of hedgerows (a valuable *wildlife* habitat) are removed every year in England by farmers who want bigger fields because they are easier to manage. Species are also lost when farmers get rid of wildflowers through spraying of herbicides.

From Orchard to Agribusiness

The consumer now demands fresh food irrespective of the season, and multiple retailers rely on large food processors to deliver big volumes of food. This means buying from big agricultural suppliers, and so even the humble apple travels long distances, often around the world. As a result of these developments, the UK is now only 35 per cent self-sufficient in apples, and is the second largest importer of apples in the world. Despite this, the UK removed 14 per cent of its eating apple orchards in 1995 to reduce EU overcapacity.

Case Study 2: Co-op Farms

Co-op Farms is the agricultural arm of the Co-op, one of Britain's biggest retailers, and has 38,000 acres (15,379 hectares) under cultivation. In Leicestershire, England, it has converted the 127-acre (51-ha) Stoughton Lodge Farm to organic methods of arable cropping. The Co-op does not use intensive methods for livestock, such as breeding sows or battery chickens. Nor does it allow any use of hormone implants to boost milk production. Hunting with hounds is not permitted over Co-op farmland.

Best Practice

Farmers should undertake the following measures to reduce their impacts:

- Grow a range of crops and species to maintain *biodiversity* and rotate them to improve pest control.

- Use minimum effective inputs of *fertilizer*, crop-protection *chemicals* and *fossil fuels*.
- Avoid polluting water courses, recycle crop wastes, minimize the effects of farming on others, and maintain good conditions for livestock.
- Move towards organic farming by practising less-intensive methods of husbandry.
- Protect *wildlife* in hedges and field corners, and provide habitats for natural predators such as ladybirds.
- Avoid burning crop residues, a practice which is illegal in some countries.
- Prevent slurry (animal excreta) from polluting water courses. Using anaerobic digesters, the slurry can be converted to *biogas* and useful soil conditioner.

Air-Conditioning

Air-conditioning uses considerable amounts of energy, while its production uses non-renewable fuels and causes pollution. Many air-conditioning units use the *hydro-chlorofluorocarbon* (*HCFC*) R22, an *ozone-depleting substance*. Older units may still use CFCs.

Air-conditioning is not environmentally sound because it uses a lot of energy. Some 'wet' systems can also cause *Legionnaire's Disease*. Shading, the building's position, windows that open, and intelligent building design can reduce the need for air-conditioning. Furthermore, while air-conditioning may be essential in the world's hottest climates, elsewhere the temperature may not require it.

Best Practice

- Establish whether the company has air-conditioning plants, who is liable for them, and whether they use *ozone-depleting substances*.
- Replace ozone-depleting substances with non-depleting ones.
- Do not set air-conditioning at too cold a setting. Ensure that it operates only on the hottest days.
- Provide controls in each office so that office users can alter the temperature.
- Fit blinds and awnings to reduce the temperature of the sun's rays.
- Occupy offices which have windows that open.
- Use offices whose design allows natural ventilation (fresh air) to remove hot air.
- Minimize the loss of CFCs and HCFCs from air conditioning units, through reclaiming and reusing refrigerant. Ensure contractors conform to this policy.

See also: Energy management; Heating; Office.

Aire and Calder Project

A project involving 11 companies in the north of England. The project demonstrated the financial benefits of waste minimization and clean technology. Most of the savings came from controlling inputs such as energy and water, but savings on effluent costs were also significant.

Air Pollution

The main sources of air pollution are:

1) *Combustion:* Air pollution is caused by combustion (the burning of fuel) especially from car engines, power stations, industrial processes and incinerators. Combustion produces dust, smoke, and poisons such as *carbon monoxide*. Smoke also combines with *volatile organic compounds* (*VOCs*) to produce ground-level *ozone*. Air pollution affects the weaker members of society, such as asthmatics, infants and the elderly. Combustion also produces the acids that create *acid rain*. The United Nations believes that air pollution from car and lorry exhausts makes living in cities 10–100 times more dangerous than working in a nuclear power plant.
2) *Hazardous chemicals:* Air pollution also comes from *chemicals* which are produced from industrial processes and *aerosols*. These include *solvents*, *chlorine* compounds and *formaldehyde*. More rarely, it can also come from accidental radioactive discharges from nuclear power stations.
3) *Ozone-depleting substances:* A third kind of air pollution comes from the use of ozone-depleting substances, such as *CFCs* and *HCFCs*. This attacks the ozone layer, which protects mankind from the sun's harmful ultraviolet (UV) rays.
4) *Greenhouse gases:* Though they do not cause visible pollution, greenhouse gases, such as *carbon dioxide*, trap the sun's heat inside the earth's atmosphere, which leads to an increase in world temperatures.

Legislation

Standards and government regulations relate to each kind of emission. The company should become familiar with its requirements and conform to them. In Europe, companies which produce polluting emissions are controlled under the *Integrated Pollution Prevention and Control Directive*, where each plant has a single licence governing emissions to air, water and land, rather than separate ones for each type of pollution. In the UK, emissions are controlled under *IPC* and *LAAPC*.

California passed stringent air emission rules in 1990. They require the following:

- Higher pollution control standards on all new vehicles since 1997.
- By 2003, all cars sold in the state must produce 70 per cent fewer hydrocarbons and other smog-forming chemicals than 1993 models.
- By 1998, 2 per cent of all cars in California must produce zero emissions, this figure rising to 10 per cent by 2003. At present, only electric cars meet this standard.

These rules may be matched by other states and countries in the future. Twelve other states, all in North-East US, have adopted or considered adopting air emissions standards similar to California's.

Air Pollution at Work

Workers are most liable to be exposed to fumes and dust. This can be reduced by changing the process, or by improving filtration and ventilation. In cold periods, the cleaned air can be fed back into the plant to reduce heating bills.

Gas leaks are expensive and some are hazardous. They can be identified by the use of detectors which pinpoint a leak with an audible alarm. Equipment can detect all gases, including hydrogen, methane and other hydrocarbons.

Best Practice

For power stations:

- Use clearer fuels and improve pollution control. Move to renewable energy.

For industry:

- Ensure that, as a minimum, emissions stay within legal requirements.
- Clean waste gases before emitting them to the atmosphere by using scrubbers and filters.
- Take special care with start-up operations, when emissions are likely to be highest. Minimizing the number of process interruptions reduces emissions to air.
- Reduce the use of hazardous *chemicals*.
- Adopt renewable energy where appropriate.

For commercial vehicles:

- Ensure vehicles meet *Euro II* emission standards or World Health Organization (WHO) air quality guidelines.
- Reduce the amount of vehicle movement by better route planning and distribution techniques.

For cars:

- Reduce pollution from car exhausts by improving engines, adding catalytic converters, improving maintenance, better driving, and introducing less-polluting vehicles.
- Encourage staff to use public transport where appropriate.

See also: Air quality; Cars; Carbon dioxide; CFCs; Energy; Environment Act; HCFCs; Indoor pollution; Nitrogen dioxide; Smog; Sulphur dioxide; Transport.

Airports

The major impacts are:

- Noise from aircraft take-off and landings. This can be reduced by altering the way the aircraft is flown (notably the glide slope), by reducing or avoiding night flights, and by the introduction of quieter aircraft.
- *Air-pollution* from leakage or jettisoning of aviation fuel, and from the use of ground-based vehicles. Effective maintenance and choice of less-polluting vehicles helps to reduce this problem.
- *Water pollution* from oil, aircraft fuel and de-icing fluids seeping into water courses.
- Solid waste from catering and offices, including *packaging* waste and aircraft maintenance wastes (metals, plastics, foams etc).
- Energy used mainly in heating, lighting and air conditioning in buildings. (This is discussed further under *Office*.)

- Ecological impacts; the loss of habitat from constructing runways and buildings. This can be mitigated by effective planting and landscaping, so that airports can become *wildlife* havens.
- Traffic congestion (from passengers and airport staff). Fostering public transport will reduce this.

Air Quality Directive

EC Directive 80/779/EEC requires member states to set air-quality limit values and guide values for *sulphur dioxide* and *suspended particulates*.

Air Quality

The advanced nations generally have air quality standards for *sulphur dioxide, particulates, carbon monoxide, ozone, nitrogen dioxide* and *lead* (the US Federal list).

Box 1: World Health Organization Air Quality Guidelines

	1 hour	*8 hours*	*24 hours*
Nitrogen dioxide	210ppb*	n/a	80ppb
Carbon monoxide	25ppm*	10ppm	n/a

*ppb: parts per billion
*ppm: parts per million

The UK's Department of the Environment has a classification system which groups concentrations into bands: from very good to very poor. For nitrogen dioxide (NO_2) it is as follows:

Box 2: NO_2 concentrations (UK DOE Classification)

	Very good	Good	Poor	Very poor
NO_2 concentration	50ppb	50–99ppb	100–299ppb	300ppb

Standards vary: for particulates (PM_{10}), the US Environmental Protection Agency (EPA) uses a daily average standard of 150μg/m^3, while the WHO has a guideline of 70μg/m^3. The UK's Environment Act 1995 provides for a national air quality strategy, with policies for managing air quality. The act aims to set national air quality standards. Local authorities are responsible for reviewing the air quality in their area, and if they are not being met, to designate 'air quality management areas'. This would involve a plan for reducing air pollution in the area. It could also mean the banning of vehicles from the area.

The UK is also setting standards for nine pollutants including: *1,3 butadiene, carbon monoxide, benzene, sulphur dioxide, ozone, particulates, PAHs,* and *lead*. Legislation will require local authorities to establish Air Quality Management

Areas, with remedial plans where quality targets are breached. They will also have to take air quality into account in their development, transport and pollution control policies.

See also: Air pollution.

ALARA

As Low As Reasonably Achievable. Refers to the quantity of a pollutant released into the environment.

ALATA

As Low As Technically Achievable. Refers to the quantity of a pollutant released into the environment.

Aldehydes

Organic chemicals prepared by the oxidation of alcohols. Common aldehydes are *formaldehyde* and acetaldehyde.

Aldicarb

Hazardous toxic *pesticide* made by Union Carbide. It is an *oestrogen mimic*. Used as an *insecticide* on root vegetables and brassicas. Banned in Sweden, Denmark, Luxembourg, Finland and Tanzania. In 1985, it was used inadvertently on water-melons in California. After receiving complaints of nausea, diarrhoea, trembling and sweating from people who ate the fruit, 10 million water-melons were ordered to be destroyed – one third of California's entire crop.

Best practice

- Do not use.

See also: Carbamates.

Aldrin

One of the '*drins*', aldrin is a persistent, toxic, carcinogenic *insecticide*. Used to protect seeds, it attacks many insects including benign ones and is thought to be partly responsible for a huge decline in the population of otters. Aldrin is banned in eight countries and severely restricted in 11 others. It is marketed as Alderstan, Adrex, and other names containing the letters 'aldrin'.

Alexander Kielland

Accommodation rig that turned over during storms in the North Sea in 1980, killing 123 of the 213 men on board. The rig housed oil workers from the neighbouring *Edda* rig. 130 mph winds produced high waves, buffeting the rig, which was burdened by a 200-tonne derrick on its deck, making it unstable. The fifth supporting leg of the rig snapped under the water line, and the rig tipped over. Within 15 minutes the 10,000-tonne structure was upside down in the freezing Norwegian water. Investigations revealed that another five rigs had the same flaws and could have suffered the same fate.

See also: Oil and gas industry; Piper Alpha.

Algae, Algal Blooms: *see Eutrophication*

Alkyl Phenol Ethoxylates (APE)

Toxic and persistent *detergents*, used in the wool industry, which have oestrogenic (sex change) effects on fish. APEs are poorly degraded in *sewage* works and cause foaming in rivers. These problems caused the *detergent* industry to stop using them in domestic cleaning products in the early 1980s.

Best Practice

- Do not use.

Aluminium

Widely used because of its many benefits: lightness, corrosion resistance, low cost, malleability and strength. Aluminium has superseded other materials in many applications, such as timber window frames. Aluminium is also used as a coagulant in water treatment plants to collect impurities suspended in the water.

Impacts

Aluminium is alleged to cause Alzheimer's Disease, a form of senile dementia, and dialysis encephalopathy, a brain disease. Some surveys have found high levels of ingested aluminium in sufferers. As a result, Norway has banned aluminium cooking pans. However, the World Health Organization (WHO) has pronounced aluminium safe. Research findings are inconclusive and contradictory at present.

Recycling

Aluminium is easy to recycle and cost effective. Aluminium cans are 20 per cent cheaper to recycle than to make, and require 5 per cent of the energy. Approximately 65 per cent of the US's aluminium is recycled.

Case Study 3: the Camelford Disaster

At 4.30 pm on 6 July 1988, a tanker driver dumped 20 tonnes of aluminium sulphate by mistake into the drinking-water treatment works at Camelford, Cornwall, England. At least 20,000 local people were given a toxic cocktail of metals: the aluminium was 3000 times EC permitted levels.

According to *The Observer* newspaper, the effects included diarrhoea, vomiting, nausea, headaches, skin complaints, mouth ulcers and memory loss. Some people's hair fell out and their skin changed colour. They became depressed and marriages broke down. There were suicide attempts. Worst of all, three teenagers got leukaemia, and one of them has died.

South West Water, which is responsible for water supplies, denies any link between the leukaemia and the *water pollution*. It took five days to admit that there was anything wrong, and the firm persistently told callers that the water was safe to drink. Local health authorities told people they would soon recover, and it took six weeks for the details of the accident to emerge. No clinical tests were ever made, so there is no conclusive evidence about the effects of the disaster.

Best Practice

- Collect used aluminium (if the organization uses it in quantity) for recycling.
- Minimize occupational exposure to aluminium.

Ammonia

A pungent toxic *gas*, being a compound of *nitrogen* and hydrogen. It is used to make refrigerants (especially as a replacement for *CFCs*), *fertilizers*, *nitric acid*, metal *degreasing* fluid, household cleaners, explosives and synthetic fibres. It is on the EC *Grey List* of substances dangerous in water.

Another source of ammonia is urine from intensive agriculture. This acidifies the soil, because bacteria in the soil convert the ammonia to *nitric acid*.

Best practice

- Avoid its use where possible.

See also: Nitrogen.

Amoco Cadiz

Oil tanker which ran aground in 1978 on rocks off the fishing village of Portsall in Brittany, France. Its entire cargo of 220,000 tonnes of crude oil escaped, and the oil spread all over the beaches, penetrating the sand to a depth of 19 inches (48 centimetres), so that it could not be scraped away. The spill killed 30,000 seabirds and 230,000 tonnes of fish and shellfish along 100 miles

(161 kilometres) of Brittany's coast. Eventually, the sea washed the oil away, and the threatened consequences to marine life seem not to have happened.

It is said that wrangling between the tug and the captain of the *Amoco Cadiz* over the contract delayed the salvage operation. The weather worsened, the line connecting the ship and the tug broke and the ship was holed. It was 12 hours after first hitting the rocks before the captain sent up distress rockets to alert the authorities.

See also: Oil and gas industry.

Amoco: *see Amoco Cadiz; Oil and Gas Industry*

Anaerobic

Without oxygen. *Organic waste* (such as *sewage*) can be decomposed in anaerobic digesters.

Animals: *see Nature Conservation*

Animal Testing, Animal Rights

Animal testing, animal rights and animal cruelty are ethical rather than environmental issues. However, they are often linked with environmental issues (for example when examining the impacts of a shampoo). In some cases, such as medicines and medical research, animal testing may be defensible. In other cases, government approvals still require the use of live animals. However, a much wider range of tests which do not involve animals are now available. It is also generally agreed that personal care products (soaps, toiletries, cosmetics and perfumes) should not be tested on animals. Many manufacturers and retailers specify that:

- Their products have not been tested on animals.
- No ingredient in their products has been tested on animals since 1988 (or some other cut-off date).

Best Practice

- Do not make or use beauty products that lack the above statements.

See also: Marketing.

Antarctica

The last great wilderness, an unspoilt ice-bound area with potential mineral reserves. In 1991, the United Nations banned development in Antarctica for 50 years.

See also: Whales.

Antimony

Highly toxic metal, used in enamel glazes, pewter, rubber, flameproof textiles, dyes, paints, and medicines. It can cause heart disease, skin disorders and irritation of the mucous membranes. Outside industry, exposure is low.

Best Practice

- Do not use.

Anti-Perspirants

The European Union (EU) may develop an *eco-label* for these products, following studies done by the UK Eco-Labelling Board.

AONB – UK

Area of Outstanding Natural Beauty. An area which has been considered sufficiently attractive to be protected from development. It has less protection than the more important National Park.

Aquariums

Popular tourist attractions, they are attracting the hostility of environmentalists for their treatment of orcas (killer whales) and dolphins. Anheuser-Busch, the world's biggest brewer, has faced a consumer boycott of its Bud beer. Its four US aquaria attract 13 million visitors a year and have a turnover of just under $1 billion. Environmentalists say that the white-painted circular tank reflects the orca's sonar as a mirrored room would reflect a human image, which would drive a human insane. But the company has said that the animals could not be safely released because they cannot fend for themselves.

See also: Fishing industry; Zoos.

Aquatex

Dry cleaning product, said by its makers to be an environmentally sound alternative to *perchloroethylene*.

Aquifer

Underground water source, containing water that has often accumulated over thousands of years. Our thirst for water, especially in cities and for irrigation, is depleting many aquifers. In the long term this is unsustainable, and some aquifers have dried up through overextraction. In other cases, the land above the aquifer is sinking as the water is extracted, leading to problems of subsidence.

See also: Water use.

Aral Sea

The Aral Sea, the world's fourth largest inland sea, has all but disappeared. It has lost 75 per cent of its volume through intensive Soviet irrigation projects. Since 1980 it has also lost half its surface area. In some places the shoreline has retreated 75 miles.

Irrigation projects designed to improve Uzbekistan's cotton production have increased the flow of water out of the sea. Other cotton irrigation projects have reduced the volume of water coming into the sea by 90 per cent. Windblown salt and sand from the sea have been deposited on surrounding land, reducing soil fertility. The use of thousands of tonnes of *pesticides* has led to lung complaints among the local people. Experts are now trying to stabilize the sea at its current level, and to understand the implications of this ecological disaster.

See also: Water use.

Arsenic

Arsenic is a semi-metal whose compounds include both beneficial and highly toxic substances. Elemental arsenic is not itself toxic, and some compounds are used to kill syphilis and sleeping sickness organisms. On the other hand, arsenical weed killers are deadly.

Arsenic is used in chemical manufacture, semi-conductors, glass production, *pesticides* and wood preservatives. It is also sometimes found in soil on rural green-field sites, where it is attributable to the spraying of *pesticides* over many years. Arsenic poisoning causes anaemia, liver and kidney damage, and death. It is not widely used in industry.

Best Practice

- Avoid toxic arsenic compounds.

Asbestos

A hazardous, carcinogenic material made of tiny fibres (less than five millionths of a metre in length), asbestos provides excellent protection against fire. This is why it became so widely used in flame-retardant materials and in the construction industry. There are three kinds of asbestos:

- crocidolite: blue asbestos;
- amosite: brown asbestos;
- chrystolite: white asbestos.

These colours refer to the appearance of the material when freshly mined. Age and heat can turn all asbestos a similar colour, and only scientific tests can determine the type.

Impacts: The fibres can get caught in the lung passages and cause cancer, especially mesothelioma. Great care should be therefore taken when working in old lofts and roof spaces, and around old boiler houses, in case asbestos is present. Asbestos removal must be carried out by a licensed company.

Best Practice

- Undertake a check for asbestos in old buildings if this has not already been done.
- If asbestos is found, professional advice should be taken concerning its isolation or removal.

See also: Liability.

Ash: *see Derelict Land; Glass; Waste Management*

Aspect

Term used in *ISO 14001* to mean environmental issue. According to the standard, it denotes an element of an organization's activities, products or services which can interact with the environment. This term is neutral, signifying that an aspect can be beneficial or harmful. *Packaging*, therefore is an aspect, while the solid waste from packaging is an *impact*.

While 'aspect' is a useful aid to environmental thinking, some organizations find it rather theoretical. Once they have determined the range of aspects, they concentrate on major impacts.

See also: ISO 14001; Register of Effects.

Assessment

(1) An audit by an outside organization, usually a *certifier*, to check whether the company's system confirms to *ISO 14001* or a similar standard.
(2) An *Environmental Impact Assessment (EIA)* is a specialized audit used when an organization plans a new development, especially the construction of a major new road or building.

Assessor

An auditor who works for a *certifier*. His role is to assess the client organization's environmental system, to see whether it conforms to a standard such as ISO 14001 or *EMAS*. The assessor has the power to award or withhold certification.

Assessors should not undertake consultancy services during the assessment; they should be trained in the standard and in management systems, and should understand the processes they are auditing. Assessors should meet the requirements of *ISO 14011* and *ISO 14012*, as well as the related ISO 10011.

See also: Auditor.

Atmospheric Emissions: *see Air Pollution*

Atomic: *see Nuclear Power*

Atrazine

A systemic *herbicide* which inhibits photosynthesis in sprayed plants. It persists for a long period, and in the UK is frequently found to exceed the drinking water limit. Atrazine is on the UK *Red List* of dangerous *chemicals*, and in 1992 the government withdrew approval for both it and *simazine* for non-agricultural uses. Non-agricultural uses account for 77 per cent overall, and this includes its role as a *herbicide*. Aerial spraying is also banned.

Best Practice

- Do not use.

Audit, Environmental

An analysis of an organization's effect on the environment. It involves gathering information about the company's impacts. Several different kinds of audit can be distinguished:

1. *Preliminary (or Preparatory) review:* This is the first audit undertaken by an organization, and provides information for the creation of an *environmental management system*.
2. *EMS (or system) audit:* This assesses whether the company is conforming to its *environmental management system*.
3. *Site audit (which looks at a specific corporate site):* This is relevant when the organization has only one site, or when each of the company's sites have different processes. It is less relevant to a retail-type company whose outlets are identical. It contrasts with a corporate audit, which examines all the organization's impacts. This kind of audit is known as an effects audit.
4. *Process audit:* This examines the production impacts involved in making a specific product.
5. *LCA (life-cycle analysis):* Long-term impacts are considered here. By contrast, a Product Audit would look at the product's more immediate impacts.
6. *Acquisition or divestment audit:* This assesses whether an organization (or an asset, such as land) should be bought or sold. For example, a potential purchase of contaminated land may incur future liabilities for remediation which would make it unprofitable.
7. *Supplies audit:* This examines the impacts of one or all of the organization's suppliers.
8. *Third-party audit, or assessment:* This is usually carried out by a *certifier* to assess whether the organization's management system conforms to *ISO 14001* or *EMAS*.

Purpose of the Audit

As can be seen, different audits produce different sorts of information. It is therefore useful to decide the goals of the audit, which may include some of the following:

1 *Develop strategy:* A preliminary audit is often used to guide the organization in creating its environmental policy and programme. This first audit provides the raw information which helps the company determine which issues should be given priority.
2 *Identify impacts:* An audit is often used to reveal the nature and scale of a company's impacts. The audit often reveals hitherto unexpected impacts and opportunities. One such audit revealed an unofficial regular bonfire on the site, where staff burned rubbish, an activity which management was unaware of.
3 *Assess compliance:* An audit can check whether the company is conforming to legislation. This can include checks on how waste is disposed of, and the levels of air emissions and water discharges.
4 *Verify compliance to a system:* Where a policy or an *environmental management system (EMS)* is in place, an audit can assess the extent to which it is being followed.
5 *Measure progress:* The effective organization will set objectives and targets, and an audit can check whether these are being met.

Characteristics of the Audit

The audit should be independent, objective, regular, systematic and documented.

Independent means using staff who are not involved with the work being audited. The production manager should not audit his factory.

Objective means making judgements based on fact not opinion. It means that the audit should be able to examine quantified records of waste, raw materials used, and so on.

Regular: the frequency of the audits depends on the scale of the hazard. Some operations (such as *hazardous waste* and the treatment of *effluent*) need more regular audits than other parts of the system.

Systematic means having a preset schedule of areas and processes to be audited. This ensures that nothing is overlooked.

Documented involves putting the audit findings in writing. The conclusions and recommendations should be clear and concise, and transmitted to line management for action.

To be fully comprehensive, the audit should follow the products and processes all the way from suppliers to the consumer, and then to their final disposal. The audit should include not only the impacts of normal operating conditions, but also those of abnormal or emergency situations. It should cover all relevant departments. Most impacts are often found in production and engineering departments. In addition, the audit may examine purchasing, R&D, design, sales and marketing, warehousing and distribution. It may also look at grounds management and catering. However, the audit should report only on significant impacts. This will ensure cost-effective action, and will concentrate management's mind on the important issues.

The audit should include not only the adverse impacts listed above, but also the positive contributions the organization is making by use of recycled materials, by the production of environmentally responsible products, and so on. The company can train some of its staff to carry out audits, employ outside consultants, or use a combination of the two. If consultants are used, the audit should serve to educate staff about the nature of environmental impacts and their solutions.

The results of the audit should be communicated to staff. The audit should make recommendations for reducing the company's impacts, and this should result in action. Over time, the audit produces fewer surprises. As the company's impacts become better known, the priority will shift from correcting errors to improving the processes and introducing an *environmental management system (EMS)*.

Audit Methods

Methods used in undertaking an audit include:

1 *Questionnaires:* Sometimes the auditor will ask the person responsible for environmental management to complete a questionnaire. This is used to gather data in advance about the organization charts, the existence of underground storage tanks etc. A more general questionnaire may be given out to line managers or supervisors about the impacts of their specific process or department.
2 *Interviews* with relevant personnel.
3 *Checklists* (to ensure that no issues are overlooked).
4 *Inspection of activities:* This may involve watching how processes are carried out, and may be used to see how the actual process compares with its written procedure.
5 *Measurement of activities* (for example, collating data for the first time).
6 *Examining records* (such as *air pollution* or *solid waste*).
7 *Benchmarking* (comparing the organization's performance against that of other comparable organizations, to identify best practice).

Topics for an Effects Audit

An effects audit sets out to identify the scale of environmental impacts in an organization. It will normally examine the following areas:

- emissions to air;
- use of water;
- discharges to rivers, drains or other waters;
- *solid waste*, whether to landfill or incineration; use of recycling;
- preparations for emergencies;
- effect on *wildlife* (for example, the destruction of habitats);
- the use of energy; use of non-renewable energy sources; *pollution* caused;
- noise pollution;
- visual and light pollution;
- odour;
- raw materials – these could include liquids, *gases* or solids, whether plastics, powders, metals, oils, or *chemicals*; the use of non-renewable resources; the use of non-recyclable or non-biodegradable materials; use of *toxic substances*;

- *transport*, including distribution of goods, transport of waste, suppliers' transport, company cars, and use of planes, rail and bicycle;
- *packaging*;
- management systems used to control environmental *impacts* (This part of the audit checks that written *procedures* are being adhered to. If the company writes *procedures* for key processes, such as waste disposal, an auditor can assess whether staff are following the rules);
- human resources: allocation of responsibility, extent of training and awareness;
- conformance to environmental legislation (The company should know what legislation it should confirm to. It does this by having a *Register of Legislation*);
- previous history of breaches of consents or prosecutions;
- product use by the customer, and the product's final disposal;
- new products planned;
- suppliers – their environmental awareness and systems.

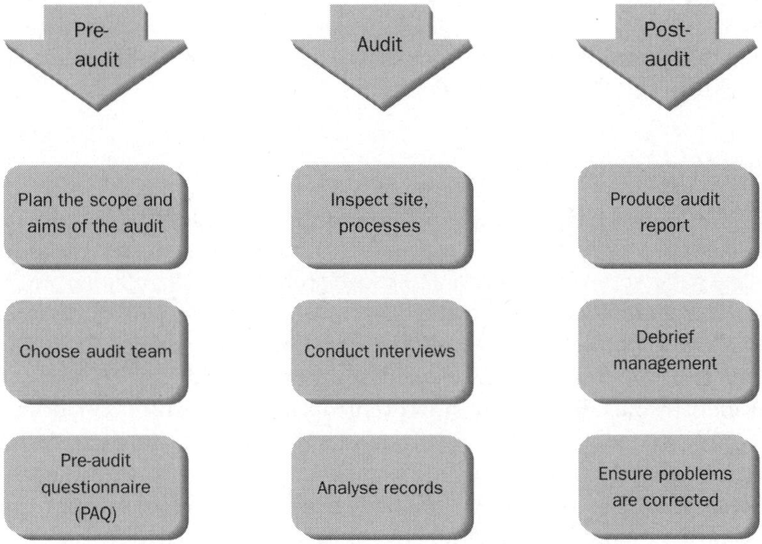

Figure 1: Plan for an Environmental Audit

See also: Auditor; EIA; EMS audit; Environmental management system; Preliminary review; LCA; Purchasing.

Auditor

Person who undertakes audits. The auditor usually works in the organization being audited (as distinct from an assessor who works for an independent certification body).

The auditor should be:

- independent of the area being audited (a supervisor should not audit his own production area);

- environmentally competent, which means understanding environmental issues;
- adequately trained in auditing (including auditing an *EMS*, if that is being audited;
- sufficiently experienced in the processes and industry which he is auditing;
- experienced in the relevant standard (for example, *ISO 14001*), if he is auditing to a standard.

Problems arise because the *EMS* auditor often has a *quality management system* (*QMS*) background and lacks detailed environmental knowledge; or is an environmentalist who lacks an understanding of management systems. Training and practical experience are needed to ensure that the audit is carried out professionally.

See also: Assessor.

Australia

See: Biogas; Genetically modified organisms; Leg-hold traps; Public relations; PVC; Solar energy; Wetlands; Whales.

Automotive industry

The industry's direct impacts include the consumption of large quantities of non-renewable raw materials (metals and plastics), the use of water, *liquid effluent* and *scrap*. The paint spray process can also cause problems of *air pollution* and health and safety hazards. Indirect impacts associated with the industry relate to the problems caused by vehicle use and road building: *air pollution*, congestion, the consumption of fuel and the destruction of the countryside.

The industry has slowly made improvements in fuel consumption, drag coefficient (wind resistance) and the use of recyclable parts. But the internal combustion engine is still the same pollution machine it was 100 years ago. Major advances will not be made until the arrival of mass-market vehicles that use renewable fuel. Until now manufacturers were hampered by restrictions on battery technology, which limited the speed a vehicle could travel at and the distance it could travel before needing recharging. However, advances in hydrogen technology indicate that major changes may not be distant.

Even when its use does not pollute, the private car will still cause congestion and car parks will continue to consume land; the problem is one that can only be solved by government support for other forms of transport.

Vehicle Repair and Maintenance

Paint spraying has consequences for vehicle repairers. The use of better spray guns, enclosed spray booths, and water-based paints can reduce this problem. Damaged car parts, such as bumpers, can be sent to the recycling industry.

See also: Cars; Renewable resources; Motor industry; Public transport.

Awareness, Environmental

A survey will assess whether staff are environmentally aware and motivated. Depending on the findings, a *training* programme can then be implemented. The training might need to focus on topics which need improvement, such as *waste disposal*.

Environmentally aware staff are less of a liability for the company, since they are less likely to make mistakes or cause pollution. It is therefore in the company's interest to ensure environmental awareness. For each relevant employee, awareness should include:

- the importance of conforming to policy and the *EMS* (if one exists);
- the significant impacts of their work;
- their role and responsibility in conforming to the system (including emergency preparedness and response);
- the consequences of departing from procedures.

See also: Human resources; Training.

Azinphos-Methyl

On the UK *Red List* of dangerous chemicals. A broad spectrum organophosphorus *insecticide*.

Best Practice

- Avoid use where possible.

Bagasse: *see Paper*

BANANA

Acronym for 'Ban all new activities now and always'. A BANANA is an extreme *NIMBY*.

Banking and Finance Industry

Impacts: Banks and finance companies have the same kind of impacts as other *office*-based organizations, such as *property*, *paper*, *energy* and *vehicles*. In comparison with manufacturing industry, they produce little pollution. The banks' lending policies provide their biggest threat and their biggest opportunity for positive action. Banks face three threats.

(1) They risk losing their collateral in cases where pollution reduces the value of a property held as security.

(2) The bank may also lose if the customer is unable to repay the loan, for instance if it faces litigation costs or because its production has been halted, again due to environmental problems.

(3) The bank risks being held liable for clean-up costs. In the US, court cases between 1986 and 1990 ruled that lenders could become liable if they foreclosed on a property or if they participated in the management of a facility.

The courts have rarely held banks liable for pollution, but the banks' deep pockets make tempting targets. If a bank becomes liable for remediation, the cost could greatly outweigh the income from the loan. In cases of bankruptcy or foreclosure in the UK and Ireland, the lender becomes a mortgagee in possession and therefore is potentially liable as the owner of the property. In continental Europe, ownership often devolves to the courts, which deprives the bank of its collateral. While this poses a general threat to banks, a project with the potential for major pollution would make a client's bankruptcy more possible.

This is encouraging banks to ask more questions about the environmental implications of a new project, to instigate site *audits*, and to work with environmental consultants and engineers. Some applicants are being turned down if the risk is too high. It can also lead to delays in starting work, as the bank makes a detailed assessment.

Banks and insurance companies should be able to target their environmental evaluation according to the scale of the risk – notably the size of the loan or policy, and the risks associated with the industry. Insurance companies face a similar situation. The costs of cleaning up after major oil spills or chemical pollution have caused them to rethink their insurance strategies. They are now much less likely to provide blanket cover for *pollution*, and in particular for pollution caused over a long period of time. The insurance companies are now sending *auditors* into manufacturers to assess their potential for environmental, health and safety problems. Insurance cover becomes conditional on carrying out the work required by the auditors.

70 companies in the industry have signed a Statement on the Environment and Sustainable Development, which was launched at the *Earth Summit* in Rio de Janeiro in 1992.

Best Practice

Banks and other financial services companies should:

- Assess the potential environmental impact their clients pose, and ensure that the revenue from each reflects the risk.
- Train their staff to understand the nature of environmental risk.
- Help corporate customers to reduce their impacts (Banco NatWest Espana SA has produced a product, EcoManager, to help Spanish business customers do environmental audits and control their impacts).
- Minimize the environmental impacts of their own business.

See also: Insurance; Liability.

Basel Convention

1994 agreement that prohibits the cross-border shipment of *hazardous waste* from *OECD* countries to non-member countries. Signed by 64 countries including the US.

See also: Transfrontier Shipment of Waste Directive; Waste, supervision and control of shipments.

Bathing Water – EU

EU Directive 76/160/EEC specifies the quality of bathing water. In 1993, the European Court of Justice ruled that the UK had failed to implement this directive. The case arose over the quality of bathing water in Blackpool and Southport, which failed to meet the standards.

BATNEEC

Best Available Techniques Not Entailing Excessive Cost. A formula applied by the EC (and hence national regulatory authorities) to reduce industrial pollution.

Companies with certain polluting processes have to adopt BATNEEC by using best possible techniques (including management and control as well as the right equipment). The clause 'not entailing excessive cost' prevents authorities from imposing an undue financial burden on a business.

Humorists have coined CATNIP (Cheapest Available Techniques Not Involving Prosecution), a formula that implies spending as little as possible.

See also: ALARA; ALATA; Best available technique; Best practical means; Best environmental timetable.

Batteries

Batteries are found in numerous consumer products, such as pocket calculators, mobile phones, hearing aids, watches and toys. They are also used commercially in payphones, electrical testers and hand-drills. Batteries are also used in cars and commercial vehicles.

Impacts

Batteries are said to consume 50 times more energy in their manufacture than they provide as a power source. Traditional batteries contain *mercury* and *cadmium*, both of which are *toxic* heavy metals. Virtually all are now *mercury* free, and some no longer contain *cadmium*. Disposable batteries are difficult to recycle, because of the lack of a market.

By eliminating the heavy metals and making longer-lasting batteries, manufacturers can reduce the amount of *toxic waste* dumped by consumers. Conservation and recycling of material in manufacturing also reduces pollution. In four years, Duracell reduced *hazardous waste* by 50 per cent and increased the volume of recycled materials by 45 per cent.

Alternatives

Among conventional batteries, cadmium-free batteries are better than those which contain *cadmium*. Rechargeable batteries are environmentally superior to throwaway batteries. Mains electricity uses fewer resources than rechargeable batteries, while solar power (or other renewable fuels) is better still.

Disposal

Mercury-free, alkaline, lithium and zinc air batteries are safe for disposal with ordinary waste. Old batteries should not be concentrated because it can bring them into electrical contact with each other, creating a safety risk. Some garages will take old car batteries for recycling.

Legislation

In Europe, batteries are governed by EU Directive 91/157/EEC on batteries and accumulators containing dangerous substances. This requires member states to prohibit the marketing of batteries containing dangerous substances, ensure that spent batteries and accumulators are collected separately for recovery or disposal, and to this end ensure that appliances containing them are marked. The marking system is published as Directive 93/86/EEC.

In the UK, the directive is implemented by the Batteries and Accumulators (Dangerous Substances) Regulations 1993.

Case Study 4: Varta

Thanks to a positive attitude towards the environment, Varta has achieved many advances and won numerous awards. It was the first company to launch mercury-free batteries in Britain, the first to introduce a free recycling scheme for rechargeable batteries, and the first to use plastic-free blister *packaging* (which eliminates 150 tonnes of non-biodegradable *PET* plastic).

Best practice

- Use mains electricity in preference to batteries, and rechargeable batteries to non-chargeable. Use solar power or other non-polluting energy source in preference to all of these.
- Ensure that batteries are disposed of in an environmentally sound way, especially through recycling.

Bauxite

The ore from which *aluminium* is produced.

BCSD

Business Council for Sustainable Development, an organization that merged with *WICE* to become WBCSD (World Business Council for Sustainable Development).

Benefits

The advantages of managing the organization's environmental impacts are listed below.

Financial

Increased profit resulting from reduced costs and increased revenue. Higher share price. Easier access to finance.

Production

Energy savings. Waste reduction. Higher productivity through increased employee motivation.

Marketing

More sales and greater market share by producing better products which provide more customer satisfaction, including the ability to command higher prices through improved products.

Corporate Image

Improved image among staff, the local community, customers, shareholders and environmentalists. Less risk of being targeted by conservationists.

Distribution

Reduced *packaging* and *transportation* costs.

Risk Management

Reduced risk of pollution incidents and legal action. Environmental management may serve as a legal defence: written procedures and records of inspection could be a defence in any future legal action.

Benomyl

Garden and agricultural fungicide, used on vegetables. A possible *carcinogen* and *oestrogen mimic*. Benomyl is the chemical used in Benlate, manufactured by US chemical giant Du Pont, which was held to be responsible for causing a child to be born without eyes. John Castillo, whose mother had lived near a Florida fruit farm, was awarded US$4 million (UK£2.7 million) in damages. This 1996 case was the first to link a birth defect with an airborne *pesticide*. Du Pont maintains that the child's condition was genetic. Benlate is not on sale in the UK.

Best Practice

- Do not use.

Bentazone

A contact *herbicide* used on a variety of crops, including maize, beans and peas. In 1994, the UK's National Rivers Authority (NRA) found that 15 per cent of groundwater was contaminated with Bentazone.

Best Practice

- Do not use.

Benzene

A liquid *hydrocarbon* compound made from oil or coal tar. It is highly flammable, and is used by the chemical industry to make detergents, nylon and *insecticides*. It is an excellent solvent for resins, and it is the chief component of the solvent known as naphtha. It is also found in exhaust fumes and coal tar distillation.

The vapour is highly toxic and a *carcinogen*. Benzene combines with ground-level ozone in sunlight to produce smog. This is especially a problem in cities in the summer. The UK government has set an air quality standard of five parts per billion, measured as a running annual average.

Best Practice

- Ensure that the organization's emissions do not exceed five parts per billion.

See also: Air pollution; Filling stations.

Benzidine

Dangerous *chemical*, whose import, export, marketing and use in the EC is controlled (Regulation EC 3135/94).

Best Practice

- Do not use.

Beryllium

One of the most toxic of all metals, beryllium is used in alloy manufacturing and the manufacture of fluorescent lights, in copper alloys and ceramics. It is also found in high-beryl coal. It causes serious lung disease.

Best Practice

- Do not use.

Best Available Technique (BAT)

Defined by the EU as 'the most effective and advanced ... activities and methods ... for providing ... emission limit values ... to prevent and, where that is not practicable, to reduce emissions and the impact on the environment.' The techniques should take into consideration 'the costs and advantages', should have been developed so as to allow 'implementation in the relevant industrial sector', and should be 'reasonably accessible to the operator'.

Many industries have guidance notes setting out what BAT or *BATNEEC* means for its companies. Sometimes these notes are aimed at larger firms, those with high environmental standards, or those which have ISO 9000, the quality standard. In other words, they are not suitable for every firm. In the US, BAT refers to Best Available Technology, a term introduced in the 1972 *Clean Water Act*. US firms were required to adopt BAT for the prevention of water pollution by 1989.

See also: BATNEEC; BPEO; BPM.

Best Practical Means (BPM)

Techniques for managing industrial processes so as to minimize pollution. Now replaced by *BATNEEC*. BPM is similar to BPT (Best Practical Control Technology) introduced in the US 1972 *Clean Water Act*, which required industry to introduce *BAT* (Best Available Technology) by 1989.

BET

Best Environmental Timetable. This is achieved by extending the timetable for reducing pollution so that costs become sufficiently low so as to justify the measure. For example, the application of BET to the elimination of lead from petrol in the UK gave industry seven years to adapt. BET was discussed in the UK's Royal Commission on Environmental Pollution in 1983 and 1984.

Bhopal

Town in India: location of a Union Carbide plant which produced *carbaryl*, an *organophosphate insecticide* used in cotton production. One of its ingredients was *methyl isocyanate*, which is partly derived from phosgene, the gas used in the trenches in World War I. Workers and local residents were not warned about the fatal effects of the chemical. Safety instructions stipulated that, in the event of a leak, workers were to run upwind.

At 1.00 am on 3 December 1984, a valve burst from overpressure, and a 45-tonne tank of methyl isocyanate was released into the air. It formed a cloud over the town and sirens went off. As the workers ran upwind, they found themselves barred by a high concrete wall topped with barbed wire. People choked, convulsed, vomited and went blind. At least 3000 died immediately, and total deaths may be as high as 10,000. Another half a million people suffered visible after effects, including disfigurement, blindness and ill health.

Even after the accident, the Union Carbide chief medical officer telephoned the local hospital to tell staff that the chemical was merely an irritant, and should be washed off with water. The Indian government launched a claim for UK£1800 million for compensation on behalf of the victims. Union Carbide made an interim payment of UK£150 million. Nevertheless, Union Carbide denied negligence and alleged sabotage. Others pointed to cost-cutting, inefficiency and the pursuit of profit at the expense of safety.

In 1992, Indian magistrates ordered the seizure of the property of Warren Andersen, Union Carbide's former chairman. They declared that the company was an 'absconder' for failing to reply to various court summonses in the criminal proceedings following the disaster. Criminal immunity had been granted as part of the settlement, but was quashed following the Indian Supreme Court's ruling in 1991 approving a US$470 million settlement between India and the company.

An amendment to India's 1991 Public Liability Insurance Act requires insurance companies to pay the victims of industrial accidents at hazardous chemical plants immediate compensation before a final settlement for damages is reached. However, the insurance industry has refused to provide cover for such accidents.

See also: Hazardous substances; Methyl isocyanate; Seveso.

Bicycles

The majority of journeys in the UK and many other countries are less than ten kilometres. This means that the bicycle is an ideal method of transport. Bicycles cover four billion kilometres every year in Britain with no pollution at all. Companies can help by encouraging the use of bicycles. They can, for example, provide interest-free loans or subsidies for buying bikes. Staff should be encouraged to come to work by bicycle through the provision of:

- bicycle lanes on company property;
- showers so that staff can wash and change their clothes before starting work;
- secure covered storage for bicycles.

Organizations should offer a cycling mileage allowance (at the same rate as for cars) to encourage staff to use bikes. Large sites should consider providing company bicycles, if this will reduce the amount of car usage around the plant.

Best Practice

- Evaluate the possibility of encouraging more bike travel, and the actions required by the organization to achieve that.

Binapacryl

Dangerous chemical whose import, export, marketing and use in the EC is controlled (Regulation EC 3135/94).

Best Practice

- Do not use.

Bioaccumulative

The build-up of certain *toxins* (such as *PCBs*) in the bodies of fish and other animals. At the top of the food chain is mankind, which ends up eating the toxins. *See also:* Persistent.

Biocides: *see Pesticides*

Biodegrade

To decompose. Most things eventually biodegrade. Glass, for example, takes 6000 years. There are two levels of biodegradability. The first is primary biodegradability (breaking down to the point where the product loses some characteristics, such as foaming). The second is ultimate biodegradability, which occurs when the product is broken down into elements such as carbon dioxide and water. There are OECD and EU tests and standards for biodegradation.

Biodiversity

Maintaining biological diversity; preserving a range of species. Biodiversity is threatened by intensive farming, which uses few strains of crop (a monoculture) and maximizes output by increased applications of *pesticides* and *fertilizers*. This destroys a range of *wildlife*. The destruction of tropical rainforest and other habitats threatens the future of other species, such as the giant panda.

Species are becoming increasingly harmonized, propelled by man. All over the world, starlings, cattle, trout and ants are becoming less different. In part this is due to farmers using the most productive species, and in part by man intruding into formerly enclosed communities with technology, viruses and aggressive species. Putting Nile perch into Lake Victoria killed off half the 300 species of fish in the lake. Extinction is a natural process – species have always died out while others have evolved. But today's harmonization poses a threat to the future.

Biodiversity is important because a future virus could wipe out the few types of cereal that are currently grown, while a traditional or rare species might be able to withstand the attack. Huge numbers of plant species have not been recorded or analysed, yet they are likely to hold the solution to future diseases. A Biological Diversity Convention was signed by 152 heads of state at the *Earth Summit* in Rio de Janeiro. This commits states to developing plans to conserve biological diversity.

Case Study 5: Species Loss – the Water Vole

In the UK, the water vole population has declined by 70 per cent since 1900, and could sink to as little as 6 per cent by the year 2000. This would put it on a par with the rhinoceros and the tiger.

Characterized as Ratty in *The Wind in the Willows*, the water vole has a useful role in wetlands where it can clear up to 20 per cent of the vegetation that threatens to clog open water. The water vole's greatest threat has been mink, which were introduced into Britain from North America in 1929 for mink farms, and have bred successfully in the wild for more than 40 years. Mink enjoy eating water vole. Other causes of loss are habitat degradation following intensified agriculture, loss of wetland, and increased use of *herbicides*. Now the UK government plans to spend £80 million over 15 years to help the water vole and 116 other threatened species.

Best Practice

National governments should:

- Prevent loss of habitat through excessive development.
- Avoid the introduction of foreign species into vulnerable populations.
- Maintain rare or 'old fashioned' species in captivity, in seed banks or in a DNA blueprint.
- Conduct impact assessments on projects that threaten biological diversity.
- Accept access to and equitable sharing of benefits from research and marketing of genetic resources.

See also: Earth Summit.

Bio Fuel

A fuel made from plants, such as *RME*.

Biogas

Gas, such as methane, produced from biological treatment of waste or landfill operations. Biogas can be used to provide electricity or heat.

Case Study 6: Biogas in Action

A 1200-head pig farm run by Charles IFE in Ballarat, Victoria, Australia, produces 210,000 litres of slurry a day. Bio-treatment of this waste now produces 3840 kilowatts per hour (kWh) of electricity a day, and 28,800 megajoules of energy a day in the form of hot water, in addition to 100,000 litres of *liquid fertilizer*.

Biological Diversity: *see Biodiversity*

Biological Treatment

The introduction of bacteria into organic waste, breaking down hazardous material into harmless substances.

See also: Liquid waste; Sewage.

Biome

An ecological region, of which Unesco has defined 14 types. They include tropical humid forest, tundra and temperate grasslands. Biomes show what would grow in an area if mankind had not built on it (for example, much of Europe would be temperate broadleaf forest).

Biosphere

The part of the earth and its atmosphere that has living organisms.

Birds: *see Wild Birds Directive*

Black List

Dangerous substances listed by the European Union and originally published as List I in EC Directive 76/464/EEC. Limits are set on their discharge. *Grey List* substances (List II) are of a lower toxicity. The Black List comprises:

- organohalon compounds;
- *organophosphorus* compounds;
- *organotin* compounds;

- substances which have proven *carcinogenic* properties in or via the aquatic environment;
- *mercury* and its compounds;
- *cadmium* and its compounds;
- persistent mineral oils and *hydrocarbons* of petroleum origin;
- persistent synthetic substances which may interfere with any use of the waters.

List I Chemicals

- *mercury*;
- *cadmium*;
- hexachlorocyclohexane;
- *carbon tetrachloride*;
- *DDT*;
- *pentachlorophenol*;
- '*drins*': aldrin, dieldrin, endrin and isodrin;
- hexachlorobutadiene;
- *chloroform*;
- chlorinated hydrocarbons: *aldrin*, dieldrin, chlordane, chlorobenzene, dichlorobenzenes, chloronaphthalene, chloroprene, chloropropene, chlorotoluenes, chlorotoluidene, *endosulfan*, endrin, heptachlor, *hexachlorobenzene*, hexachlorobutadiene, *hexachlorocylohexane*, *hexachloroethane*, *PCBs*, tetrachlorobenzenes, trichlorobenzenes;
- chlorophenols: monochlorophenols, 2,4-dichlorophenol, 2-amino-4-chlorophenol, pentachlorophenol, 4-chloro-3-metholphenol, trichlorophenol;
- chloroanilines and nitrobenzenes: monochloroanilines, 1-chloro-2,4-dinitrobenzene, dichloroanilines, 4-chloro-2-nitrobenzene, chloronitrobenzenes, chloronitrotoluenes, dichloronitrobenzenes;
- polycyclic aromatic hydrocarbons: anthracene, biphenyl, naphthalene, *PAH*;
- inorganic chemicals: *arsenic* and compounds, *cadmium* and compounds, dibutyl tin compounds, *mercury* and compounds, tetrabutyltin;
- solvents: *benzene*, *carbon tetrachloride*, chloroform, *dichloroethane*, dichloroethylene, dichloromethane, dichloropropene, dichloropropanol, dichloropropane, ethylbenzene, *toluene*, *tetrachloroethylene*, *trichloroethane*, *trichloroethylene*;
- others: benzidine, benzyl chloride, benzylidene chloride, chloral hydrate, chloroacetic acid, chloroethanol, dibromomethane, dichlorobenzidine, dichloro diisopropyl ether, diethylamine, dimethylamine, epichlorohydrin, isopropylbenzene, tributyl phosphate, trichlorotrifluoroethane, vinyl chloride, xylenes;
- pesticides: *azinphos*, ethyl and methyl, coumaphos, cyanuric, chloride, *2,4-D* and derivatives, *2,4,5-T* and derivatives, *DDT*, demeton, dichlorprop, *dichlorvos*, dimethoate, disulfoton, fenitrothion, fenthion, linuron, malathion, MCPA, mecoprop, methamidiophos, mevinphos, monolinuron, omethoate, oxidemiton-methyl, parathion, phoxim, propanil, pyrazon, *simazine*, triazophos, *tributyl tin oxide*, trichlorofon, trifluoralin, triphenyltin compounds.

See also: Grey List; Red List.

Bleach, Bleaching

A process for whitening clothes, paper or other substances. One of the best known bleaches is *chlorine*, which has a severe impact on the environment. Oxygen bleaches are also used.

In clothes washing, only one in four domestic washes contains whites, so a lot of bleach (75,000 tonnes a year in the UK) goes down the drain each year to no purpose. Detergents without bleaches do not need stabilizers and activators, which is another reason for excluding bleach if possible.

See also: Chlorine; ECF; Paper, board and pulp industry; TCF.

Blue Angel

A label used in Germany to denote environmentally sound paper. The paper must be 100 per cent recycled, of which 51 per cent has to consist of post-consumer waste.

BOD

Biochemical Oxygen Demand. A measure of dissolved pollutants in a water course, BOD is the potential for organic matter to deoxygenate water. Measured in milligrams per litre or kilograms per day, or total discharge per year of polluting substances (eg 500 tonnes a year). BOD measures the level of *organic* pollution (especially from agriculture, sewage and food processors) in a water course. The test involves incubating a sample for five days at 20°C, and measuring how much oxygen is used up. The result is expressed in mg/l^{-1}.

A regulatory authority may set a consent level of (say) 50 kg/day, which the plant may not exceed. The plant may reduce the BOD of its effluent by oxidizing it, by treating it biologically with bacteria, or by concentrating it into a solid form through sedimentation.

See also: COD; Eutrophication, Liquid waste; Suspended solids; Water pollution.

Bodenschutz

The principle, developed in Germany, that soil is a scarce, valuable material which needs to be preserved for the future. This is done by controlling its present use.

See also: Contaminated land.

Body Shop: *see Packaging; Refillables; Toiletries; Cosmetics and Pharmaceutical Industry*

Boilers

A source of pollution through combustion. See *combustion plant*.

BPEO

Best Practical Environmental Option. Also known as BEO (Best Environmental Option). A plan that minimizes total environmental damage. Environmental management is complex and a solution to one problem may cause another. For example, switching from landfill to incineration will reduce *solid waste* but may increase *air pollution*. So whatever plan is adopted should be the one that has least overall impact on the environment.

See also: BATNEEC.

BREEAM – UK

Building Research Establishment Environmental Assessment Method. A scheme introduced by the UK's Building Research Institute (BRE) for environmentally sound new offices and subsequently, new homes.

Office Scheme

The BREEAM scheme checks global, neighbourhood and indoor issues. Criteria include *global warming*, *ozone depletion*, *rainforest* destruction, *Legionnaire's Disease*, wind, reuse of an existing site, *lighting*, indoor *air quality* and *hazardous* materials, thermal values and windows that open.

The scheme provides building owners with a 35-point certificate. This can be put on display and used in the marketing of the building. Unlike other certification schemes, it is not a 'win or lose' situation. Each building gets a certificate showing how many points it achieved. Even one credit on the certificate indicates that the building will be environmentally superior compared to normal practice. However, applicants are expected to get a significant number of credits. Today, 16 per cent of all new office designs in the UK are being assessed for environmental impact using BREEAM.

Housing Certificate

In the housing certification scheme, credits are given for:

- low energy running costs;
- use of renewable materials;
- avoidance of *toxic chemicals*;
- provision of space for the storage of materials that can be recycled.

Brewing and Distilling Industry

This industry uses substantial amounts of water and can produce waste water with a high *BOD*. It also produces *solid waste* from the raw materials. Numerous strategies exist to reduce pollution. Waste can be converted into by-products (for example, the use of distiller's grain produces methane which can be used as a fuel, and hypha albumen, which can be sold as fodder). Cooling water can be recycled, and CO_2 produced from fermentation can be used to produce liquid CO_2. Raw material losses can also be reduced through better control over buying and improved storage. Improved maintenance and housekeeping can also reduce leaks and spills.

British Steel: *see Dust and Fumes; Oil and Gas Industry*

Broke: *see Mill Broke*

Brominated Flame Retards: *see PBB*

Bromine

A halogen, like *chlorine* and *fluorine*. Bromine is a constituent of *halons*, which are *ozone-depleting substances*. Bromine is very poisonous and corrosive to the skin. It is used in dyes, organic synthesis and the production of bromides.

Best Practice

- Do not use if possible.

Brownfield Site

A run-down inner-city site. Not the first choice of developers for development, but building in the city has several environmental advantages. It reduces the extent of commuting, reduces the pressure on the green belt, and prevents urban sprawl and ribbon development.

See also: Green belt; Nature conservation.

BS 7750

A management system, devised by the British Standards Institution (BSI), for managing a company's impacts. It is based on BS 5750 (also known as BS EN ISO 9000).

As the first national environmental standard, BS 7750 influenced the development of *ISO 14001*, and was withdrawn when ISO 14001 was recognized as an international standard by CEN (the European standards body). BS 7750 is compatible with the European Union's *EMAS*, and companies can convert from BS 7750 to EMAS by producing a *Statement* that is validated by an accredited EMAS verifier.

A number of Japanese companies have also been certified to BS 7750, after Japan's Audit and Certification Organization for Environment was accredited to award BS 7750 certificates. The firms include household names such as Hitachi, Matsushita, NEC, Sony and Toshiba.

Reasons for Choosing BS 7750 (or any other environmental management system)

- The firm becomes more efficient and less wasteful of fuel and materials.
- It may reduce the company's legal liability by demonstrating 'due diligence' – should an environmental incident occur.
- It improves staff morale by demonstrating commitment.

- It fits with existing quality systems (such as ISO 9000).
- External verification by the certification body will endorse the company's claim to be 'environmentally responsible'.

See also: Audit; CEN; EMAS; ISO 14001; Programme; Register of effects; Register of legislation.

BSI

British Standards Institution. The body that sets national standards in Britain. A member of *CEN* and *ISO*, it has no formal commitment to adopt ISO standards, but where CEN adopts an ISO standard as a European standard, BSI must withdraw any conflicting standard and use the CEN one. This was the case with *BS 7750*, one of the world's first standards for *environmental management systems*, which was withdrawn in favour of *ISO 14001*.

Building Design

Designers and clients should produce buildings that use minimal energy, do not clash with the landscape or other buildings, are functional, and use low impact materials. To do this, they should adopt the following principles.

Design, Siting and Appearance

The development should match the local area and be built on a human scale. It should incorporate any existing buildings of architectural or historical merit. It should also be located in an area well served by public transport, to minimize the need for private cars.

Out-of-town developments (such as shopping and leisure facilities) should be avoided on the grounds of non-accessibility, loss of open space and traffic generation. New sites should incorporate green open spaces, or outdoor leisure facilities. The building should ideally be built on land previously developed. This helps conserve the green areas. Obtrusive signs should be avoided.

Energy and the Use of Natural Light

The siting and construction of the building should take advantage of passive solar energy. This could save the UK£230 million by the year 2035, and four times that figure in the later decades of the next century. Areas of solar gain can be used to warm the building, with shades used to minimize glare and overheating. Day lighting is popular with residents, and reduces energy demand.

South-facing walls should have large glazed areas, which should be free from overshadowing. North-facing walls should have less glazing. Perimeter day lighting uses glass in the outside walls. The light is then distributed evenly through baffles or light shelves. Core day lighting uses roof apertures, atria and courtyards to bring light into the interior of the building.

Buildings should be designed to cope with a fuel crisis in the early twenty-first century, with fuel shortages in 15 to 20 years' time leading to energy taxes and rocketing fuel bills, according to a report by the Royal Institute of British Architects (RIBA), the Royal Institution of Chartered Surveyors (RICS) and the UK's Department of the Environment (DOE).

Over 25 per cent of the fuel costs in buildings could be saved by combining wall insulation, double glazing with low emissivity glass, and more efficient central heating boilers with electronic control.

Building Services

Building services incorporate heating, lighting, ventilating and plumbing. The prime impacts are the use of energy and water, and to a lesser extent the use of non-renewable metals and plastics. Companies should train engineers and staff to understand environmental issues. This will enable them to modify their practices so as to minimize the environmental impact of building services.

Air Conditioning

The lowest energy offices are naturally ventilated, while those with high energy costs are fully air conditioned. So before the building is built, decide whether air conditioning is really necessary. Though a growing sophistication in the market might encourage it, there are many strategies for reducing a building's heat without the need for electrical assistance. For example, windows should be openable to increase natural ventilation.

Air conditioning plant should not use *ozone-depleting* refrigerants. There should be a maintenance programme to prevent Legionnaire's Disease; and local areas should have timed switches capable of overriding the air conditioning.

Heat

- Group heat-emitting machinery such as photocopiers in one well-ventilated room.
- Use low energy lighting to reduce heat gain. Use shades and blinds and window size to reduce solar heat.
- Heaters should be fitted with thermostats. The heating system should be computer controlled and it should be powered by an energy-efficient system. Hot water should not be dependent on central boilers, unless they need to be on throughout the year. Consider fitting point-of-use electric water heaters.

Materials

Use natural materials where possible. They can be more expensive than their man-made substitutes, but they may also last longer. They also biodegrade harmlessly.

The building should use timber from sustainably managed sources, and it should avoid the use of materials that release *formaldehyde* (eg chipboard). No asbestos should be used and extinguishers should be halon free.

Surface treatments should avoid the use of toxic *pesticides* or dangerous wood preservatives, including *lindane* or *tributylin* oxide, and insulation materials that have been blown with *ozone-depleting substances*. Consider adopting the following guidelines:

- Avoid *asbestos* or asbestos-containing products, which are carcinogenic.
- Avoid urea *formaldehyde* foam or materials which may release *formaldehyde* in quantities which may be hazardous.

- Do not use materials comprised of mineral fibres which have a diameter of three microns or less and a length of 200 microns or less. These may be *carcinogens*.
- Do not use material with a high alumina content.
- Avoid calcium chloride admixtures for use in reinforced concrete.
- Avoid the use of insulation materials or air conditioning plant that contain *ozone-depleting substances*.

Refurbishment and Maintenance

When refurbishing a building, check whether it is used by bats or birds and protect the habitat. Retain architectural features where possible when refurbishing. Check what substances are being used in building maintenance. Avoid *toxic* materials.

Ensure that buildings are properly maintained, to minimize decay and heat and water loss.

Landscaping and Wildlife

The building should be designed or sited so as to retain existing landscaping. It should also keep natural features, such as ponds or mature trees. Trees should be planted as screens to shut out noise or visual impact from the company's operations. Shrubs and other vegetation should be planted to bring *wildlife* to the area. The development should incorporate bat boxes and owl nesting sites.

Waste Management

New developments should contain their own recycling and waste treatment facilities where practical.

See also: Air conditioning; BREEAM; Construction industry; Energy management; Office.

Building Industry: *see Construction Industry*

Buildings: *see Building Design; Construction Industry; Office*

Bunding

The construction of a secure wall around a tank containing polluting or hazardous liquids, including fuel oil. This catches any leaks or spillages and thereby prevents pollution. Known as secondary containment.

See also: Drum storage; Liquid waste.

Butadiene

A highly reactive colourless, flammable gas made from *butanes* and *butenes*. It is used to make synthetic rubber, and is on the EU's *Black List*. 1-3 butadiene is an air pollutant associated with fuel combustion and causes ground level ozone (when mixed with nitric oxide in sunlight).

In the UK, the Expert Panel on Air Quality Standards (EPAQS) has recommended a government limit for 1-3 butadiene of one part per billion (ppb), measured as a running annual average.

Best Practice

- Ensure that corporate emissions do not exceed one part per billion.

Butane

A colourless flammable gaseous alkane, found in crude oil. It is used to make synthetic rubber, and in its liquid form it is used as a fuel. It is commonly employed to power aerosols and contributes to low-level atmospheric pollution.

See also: Hydrocarbons.

Cadmium

A toxic heavy metal used in electroplating (in which it forms a bright, corrosion-resistant finish), in plastic stabilizers, nickel cadmium batteries, dyes and signs, in brazing and soldering, scrap metal refining, and metal manufacture. It is obtained as a by-product of zinc refining.

Cadmium gets into the air from nickel and copper smelting, from the combustion in scrap metal recovery, from incinerators, and from cigarette smoke. Once in waste streams, cadmium can contaminate foodstuffs. It is on the EU *Black List* of dangerous substances, and an EU directive sets limits on cadmium use and bans polymers. In the UK, the Environmental Protection Act (controls on injurious substances etc) 1993 restricts its use.

Cadmium's toxicity was first realized after people living on the Jintzu River in Japan developed *Itai-Itai* ('Ouch Ouch') Disease. This was caused by a lead-zinc mining and smelting operation upstream from where the victims lived. Inhabitants absorbed the cadmium by air pollution from cadmium-containing fumes and particulates, and from water pollution (via rice grown in the paddy fields flooded by the river that contained cadmium). It caused severe lumbago-type pain, progressing to severe bone damage with multiple fractures of softened bones, followed by death, though this is unusual for cadmium poisoning.

Cadmium poisoning normally causes high blood pressure, enlarged hearts, and in some cases heart attacks. In breeding rats it causes major congenital abnormalities.

Case Study 7: Eliminating Cadmium

West Middlesex Plating of Uxbridge, England, managed to eliminate cadmium from its waste water by removing the cadmium residue electrolytically and reusing it, and then recycling the rinse water. It has also installed a system to monitor cadmium loss. From 16,000 grams of cadmium a year, the plant now discharges none. This has resulted in water charges being reduced by UK£35,000 a year.

Best Practice

- Avoid the use of cadmium where possible.
- Electroplaters should prevent cadmium from entering drains.
- Battery manufacturers should not discharge cadmium in waste waters.
- Emissions from zinc smelters must be closely controlled.
- Incineration of material containing cadmium (yellow plastic bags, plastic products, paints, car tyres, discarded vehicles and so on) should be carefully controlled.

California: *see Air pollution; Aldicarb; Liability; Litigation; Motor Industry; Oil and Gas Industry; Paper, Board and Pulp Industry; Perchloroethylene; Roads; Tradeable Permits*

Camelford: *see Aluminium*

Capadafol

Dangerous chemical whose import, export, marketing and use in the EC is controlled (Regulation EC 3135/94).

Best Practice

- Do not use.

Carbamates

Used as *insecticides*. They include aldicarb and carbofuran.

Best Practice

- Do not use.

Carbaryl

Toxic *pesticide* used to treat head lice, apples, lawns and domestic pests. Affects the nervous system. In 1995, the UK government announced that carbaryl, which had been used for 40 years, causes cancer. Carbaryl was being made at the *Bhopal* plant when it exploded.

Best practice

- Do not use.

Carbofuran

A hazardous *carbamate insecticide*.

Carbon Black: *see Indoor Pollution*

Carbon Dioxide (CO_2)

The main *greenhouse gas*. It is caused by burning fossil fuels, namely coal, gas and oil. There has been a big growth in the concentration of CO_2 in the atmosphere during the twentieth century, from around 290 parts per million (ppm) at the beginning of the century to around 350 ppm at the end.

Impacts

An increase in the *greenhouse gases* causes the earth's temperature to rise. This causes the polar ice caps to melt, bringing a rise in sea levels, which causes flooding in low lying areas. Even small temperature rises can have a major effect on the weather which, in turn, affects *agriculture* and people's livelihoods.

Best Practice

- See Greenhouse gas.

Carbon Monoxide (CO)

An invisible, odourless poisonous gas, 85 per cent of which, in the UK, comes from petrol engine exhausts. It is produced from the incomplete combustion of fossil fuels (such as oil or natural gas). Carbon monoxide reduces the blood's ability to carry oxygen to the brain and other organs. It particularly affects people with cardiovascular and respiratory problems.

Table 1: Air Quality Standards and Guidelines for Carbon Monoxide

Organization	Limit, in parts per million (ppm)	Sampling method
EPAQS* Recommended UK standard	10	8-hour running average
US EPA	35	1 hour
	9	8 hours
World Health Organization	25	1 hour mean
	10	8 hour mean

*Expert Panel on Air Quality Standards

See also: Air pollution.

Carbon Tax – EU

A proposed EU tax, now abandoned. It was first mooted in 1992, supported by Germany, and aimed at fulfilling the EU's commitment to reducing CO_2 emissions, in line with its *Earth Summit* commitment. In 1995, the EU accepted defeat following disagreement by member states and opposition by the UK, and removed references to it from EU policy guidelines. The EU's policy remains that of stabilizing CO_2 emissions at 1990 levels by the year 2000.

Carbon Tetrachloride

A colourless, non-flammable liquid that gives off poisonous fumes and is used as a *solvent*. It is an *ozone-depleting substance* and is controlled under the *Montreal Protocol*. It is on the EU *Black List* of dangerous substances and subject to an EC directive (86/280/EEC). It is also known as carbon tetrachloromethane.

Best Practice

- Do not use.

Carcinogen

A substance that causes cancer.

Cars

Cars give people the freedom and flexibility to travel as they wish, and they are also less polluting than they once were. According to the UK's Society of Motor Manufacturers and Traders (SMMT), new cars emit half the fumes and use up to 30 per cent less fuel compared with vehicles built a decade ago. They also emit only one third of the noise. With the increased use of *catalytic converters*, pollution will continue to fall.

Most people find it difficult to do without their cars. According to the polling organization MORI, two-thirds of people in Britain want the government to cut exhaust fumes, but only 17 per cent are prepared to use public transport to reduce pollution.

Impacts

1 *Air pollution:* Road transport accounts for 85 per cent of *carbon monoxide*, 45 per cent of *nitrogen oxides* and 30 per cent of hydrocarbon atmospheric emissions in Britain.
2 *Use of non-renewable resources: Cars* are big users of *fossil fuels*.
3 *Congestion:* Growing *car* numbers have led to pollution and congestion especially in cities. In 1989 there were 23 million cars in Britain, which could double to 50 million by the year 2025. Governments and cities have considered or adopted various solutions, including 'congestion charging' whereby cars are charged for entering a city centre.
4 *Other pollutants* in cars include used oil (which is a suspected *carcinogen*), anti-freeze and brake fluid, *solvents*, lead and *cadmium* in the car paint, and the use of other non-renewable and non-biodegradable resources (notably in plastics).
5 *Drivers' behaviour* also has an effect on the environment. Excessive use of the accelerator and brake uses more fuel and increases pollution.

A Global Problem

From around 60 million vehicles in 1950, the world car fleet reached 500 million in 1990. In the Third World, where roads are full of bikes and pedestrians, roads cannot cope with the increase in *cars* and lorries. The construction of roads leads to a loss of land needed to feed a growing population, and many countries are seeing an increase of fuel imports, most of which comes from the politically unstable Middle East.

Vehicle Developments

All the tinkering with the internal combustion engine does little to affect its inherently polluting nature. In the short term, alternatives include less polluting cars (such as the use of *catalytic converters* to absorb the pollution), stricter legal controls over poorly maintained cars, and the fostering of *public transport*. In the longer term, the *motor industry* is trying to develop battery-powered, hybrid (*battery* and combustion) and hydrogen cell vehicles.

Diesel versus Petrol

The relative merits of petrol versus diesel engines are less clear-cut than they were once thought to be. This is due to improvements in petrol cars and a growing awareness of the problems of particulates in diesels. However, City Diesel, which produces 85 per cent less particulates, 99 per cent less *sulphurous oxides*, and 30 per cent less *carbon monoxide*, is environmentally more sound than ordinary diesel.

Oxygenated Petrol

A 1990 amendment to the US *Clean Air Act* required the winter use of a less-polluting gasoline in the cities most affected by smog. This reformulated fuel emits less *carbon monoxide* which is more toxic in cold weather.

Consumers complained that the new fuel gave them headaches and was expensive. In 1995 the Environmental Protection Agency (EPA) agreed that ordinary petrol could be sold in the Milwaukee area where complaints had been more numerous.

Greener Company Cars

Persuading company staff to change their car habits is difficult and should be handled with care. Sales people in particular obtain their status from the size of car they drive. Fleet owners can adopt the following solutions:

- Reduce or peg the mileage allowance for larger company cars, or provide a flat allowance for all cars. This encourages the use of fuel-efficient cars, while overgenerous allowances encourage staff to travel long distances. The UK's Department of the Environment allows a proportionately more generous allowance for cars below two litres. Cars over two litres receive an allowance 22 per cent below what it should be.
- Consider banning the purchase of any company car over three litres or whose miles per gallon (mpg) is below a certain figure. This would leave the majority of staff unaffected, and would show that the directors, who will be most affected, are committed to a green policy. Many prestigious cars come in a smaller-engined variant.
- Consider adding the cost of the car to the salary, and let people buy their own cars. People generally buy a smaller car and pocket the difference.
- Foster car sharing (to reduce the number of car journeys made).
- Adopt flexible working hours, or home working, so that employees do not have to travel in the rush hours, which wastes fuel. Many companies operate flexi-time.

- Keep company cars longer. As today's cars become increasingly more reliable, there is less need to replace them so often. Avoid routinely replacing vehicles when they are three years old or have done 60,000 miles (97,000 km). Judge the replacement of each car on its own merits.
- Limit the engine size of hire cars. This will save money as well as reduce pollution.
- Discourage driving in congested areas, where stationary cars pour out pollution. This will require better timing of meetings or trips, or the use of *public transport*, or fax and telephone and teleconference.
- Use a vehicle management system which allows the company to compare mileage and mpg for every driver. A monthly report can be sent to every departmental manager, comparing actual mpg with the manufacturer's predicted mpg. This will show up excessive fuel consumption as well as fraud. The company should set targets to improve mpg.
- As and when non-polluting cars (such as fuel cells or *battery*-powered vehicles) become more widely available, the company should encourage staff to use them.

Key Issues In Vehicle Purchase Or Leasing

1 *Fuel economy:* This is largely dictated by engine size. Fuel-efficient cars use less non-renewable resources and are likely to be less polluting. According to the RAC, every 100 cc reduction in engine size gives roughly a 3 per cent reduction in *carbon dioxide* emissions. That means a 1.4-litre engine causes 33 per cent less pollution than a 2.5-litre engine.
2 *Recyclability:* Some car makers (such as Mercedes) are using an increasing amount of recycled material in their vehicles, and are using coded plastic parts to ease recycling.
3 *Safety:* Figures from insurance companies and the government show that some cars are inherently safer than others.
4 *Distance from point of manufacture:* It makes more sense to buy a locally made car than to ship one from the other side of the world.
5 *Car life:* Longer-lasting cars are better for the environment because they reduce the amount of scrap in the world, and extend the life of valuable materials. Some cars, such as Volvo, have a longer life than their competitors.

Staff driving habits

The organization should encourage staff to drive carefully and should discourage speeding. Some executives routinely travel on motorways at speeds in excess of 100 mph, which wastes fuel. Cars travelling at 70 mph use 30 per cent more fuel than those going at 50 mph; and driving any faster is illegal in many countries. Companies should discourage employees from breaking the law.

Case Study 8: Car Pooling

Encourage car pooling. Try getting staff to share cars, especially in the journey to work. Set aside space on a notice board for car-sharing arrangements. An RAC survey showed that 81 per cent of people thought more could be done to encourage car pooling, while a Lex report showed that 80 per cent of drivers were willing to consider car pooling.

However, car pooling sometimes fails. Car sharers are unreliable, they reduce flexibility and there are personality clashes. Also, many people enjoy the privacy that their car gives them.

On some journeys, the car is often the only logical choice, especially where the destination is far from a railway station or where a journey involves several stops during the day (as a sales rep might make). But other routes are less suitable for car travel. They include city-to-city journeys and long-distance journeys. Other journeys are simply unnecessary. Car driving also stops the executive reading or writing. Time spent in the car is often wasted, though the mobile phone has improved executives' productivity.

Best Practice

- Create a green car policy for the company. Publicize it internally.
- Provide a company car only where it is essential for the job or necessary to attract or retain staff.
- Discourage fast or inconsiderate driving. This may require a change in corporate values.
- Produce regular reports on mpg achieved by each company car user.
- Encourage staff to use the *railway*.
- Discourage staff from making unnecessary journeys.
- Encourage the greater use of the telephone, fax and teleconferencing.
- Provide pool cars (or even pool bikes). This will discourage people from feeling obliged to drive to work in case they need a car during the day. Lease modest-sized pool cars.

See also: Air pollution; Diesel; Distribution, physical; Fuel cells; Motor industry; Railways; RME; Roads.

Cartridges, Copier and Printer

Over 13 million printer cartridges are dumped in Europe each year. Hewlett Packard alone sells 800,000 printers a year, each of which contains a cartridge. Throwing away cartridges is wasteful since they normally contain not just the toner cartridge but also the photo-conductive drum or the print head. Users can buy remanufactured cartridges which have been refilled with toner, or refill the cartridge themselves. Either solution saves money and benefits the environment. Many companies now sell recycled cartridges and will accept used ones.

Buying a remanufactured cartridge can save up to 50 per cent of the cost. BT uses 17,400 replacement cartridges annually and recycles 25 per cent of them. Alternatively, users can buy a printer whose photo-conductive drum is separate from the toner cartridge. This reduces the waste of resources when the toner is finished.

Remanufactured cartridges do not invalidate the printer warranty (though printer companies often warn users against them, largely because cartridges are a profitable business). However, users should check that the cartridge supplier provides a warranty against damage to the printer by the use of the cartridge.

Best Practice

- Use reconditioned printer cartridges.

See also: Office.

Catalytic Converter (Catalyser)

A device, fitted to the exhaust of petrol engined cars, which removes harmful emissions. Through a chemical reaction, it converts *nitrogen dioxide*, *carbon monoxide* and *hydrocarbons* into relatively harmless compounds such as nitrogen, water and carbon dioxide. In time, cars without catalytic converters may be banned from the roads because they will fail emission tests. However, a catalyser merely prevents pollution from escaping into the atmosphere. It does not stop its creation.

See also: Cars; Motor industry.

Catering and Hotel Industry

The industry's impacts include:

- Energy used in cooking, heating and air conditioning, hot water, laundry, lighting and vacuuming.
- *Packaging* from fast food wrappers, food packaging and litter from fast food outlets.
- Other solid waste, especially putrescibles (food that rots).
- Development, such as the visual intrusion caused by inappropriate buildings.
- Fixtures and fittings; hotels and restaurants are prone to use finishes such as tropical hardwoods to attract their clients.
- Discharges to water; the laundry, dishwashing and bathing water is probably no more than would be used by individuals at home. However, by fitting spray taps and other equipment which use less water, environmental and financial savings can be made.

Many of these impacts can be reduced, and a competitive advantage won, by the introduction of an environmentally sound policy. For example, in 1992 the 1000-room Park Plaza Hotel in Boston, US, saved (through 65 separate initiatives) the following costs:

- 10,000,000 gallons of water;
- 29,000 gallons of fuel oil;

- 100,000 sets of plastic dishware;
- 2,000,000 plastic bathroom amenity sets (potentially).

There are many other examples. Continental Hotels has 100 environmental targets, while Westin aimed to reduce electricity consumption by 25 per cent by progressively introducing energy-efficient lighting. In the UK, Forte Hotels' energy-efficient plants have a payback of less than two and a half years.

Case Study 9: McDonalds

Fast food restaurants have a young clientele who are environmentally aware. In the past, McDonalds has been beset by unfounded criticisms that it contributed to rainforest destruction by buying beef that was raised in rainforest clearances. The packaging waste generated by diners also reminds them about the environment. It is crucial, therefore, that fast food restaurants are seen to protect the environment. Yet at a time when competitors were introducing recycled card packaging, McDonalds retained its polystyrene packaging for several years longer than rival firms, on the grounds that it kept the food warmer for longer. While this was undeniable, it also meant that the polystyrene impact was regularly put in front of customers.

In its UK in-restaurant publicity material, McDonalds concentrates on two headings: *solid waste* and sponsorship. The sponsorship takes the form of educational materials for school and support for litter initiatives. Other important issues, such as the company's use of energy, its emissions to air and water, construction impacts, nature conservation, and the use of environmental impact assessments (EIA), are not discussed.

See also: Tourism industry.

Cat Litter

There are around 40 million cats in Europe, and their owners dispose of nearly one million tonnes of cat litter each year. As a result, the EC has proposed that there should be an *eco-label* for the product. The Dutch eco-labelling board has been studying the problem.

Best Practice

- Make or use only eco-labelled products, when available.

CBI

UK's Confederation of British Industry, which has issued many reports on the environment. Its Agenda for Voluntary Action is a seven-point charter which companies can adopt and which involves:

- Designating a board-level director with responsibility for the environment. If there is no board then the most senior representative should be nominated.
- Publishing a corporate environmental statement.
- Setting clear targets and publishing objectives for achieving the policy.
- Measuring current performance against targets.
- Implementing improvement plans.
- Communicating company environmental policy and objects to employees, seeking their contribution to improvement and providing appropriate training.
- Reporting publicly on progress in achieving the objectives.

The CBI has an Environment Business Forum, membership of which imposes certain requirements. They include:

- Submitting a plan outlining how the company will meet the terms of the Agenda for Voluntary Action (see above).
- Producing an environmental policy.
- Reporting annual progress.

The CBI agenda and its forum allow companies to set their own levels of environmental performance, which means that standards may be lower; but the information is open to public scrutiny which discourages *'greenwash'*.

See also: Charters, environmental; ICC.

CCGT

Combined Cycle Gas Turbine. A type of power station that burns gas. For each unit of electricity produced, such stations are said to use two-thirds the fuel of a coal fired station, produce 55 per cent less *carbon dioxide*, no *solid wastes*, and an 80 per cent reduction in *nitrogen oxides*.

See also: Electricity-generating industry; Energy.

CEFIC

European Chemical Industry Council. It has developed guidelines for environmental reporting and the presentation of emissions data. Members are supposed to report emissions for various substances if they exceed a given level. The substances include *nitrogen oxides*, *sulphur dioxide*, *volatile organic compounds (VOCs)*, *heavy metals*, and *phosphorus*. CEFIC's common format for environmental reporting covers:

- the organization;
- products;
- production processes;
- company plans;
- *environmental management systems*.

In their reports, member companies are supposed to supply information on:

- energy;
- safety;
- environmental expenditure;
- community activities;
- complaints.

See also: Chemical industry; Report, environmental.

Cement Industry

Cement kilns burn *fossil fuels*, and thereby contribute to the problems of *greenhouse gas* and *acid rain*. Too low a temperature in the kiln adversely affects the quality of the cement, while the higher the temperature the more *sulphuric* and *nitrogen oxides* are produced. This calls for accurate temperature control and feedback of information about airborne pollutants such as *nitrogen oxide* and *carbon monoxide*. Controlling temperature requires computerized systems to optimize the rate at which material is fed into the kiln, the kiln rotation speed, the quantity of fuel supplied, and other parameters. Optimizing these variables reduces the amount of fuel used, improves the quality of cement clinker, increases the kiln life, and reduces air pollution.

Cement works can also produce large amounts of alkaline toxic dust. The dust can be removed by the use of electrostatic dust precipitators.

On the other hand, the manufacture of cement blocks can use pulverized fuel ash from power stations to reduce the amount of new cement. As shown below, cement companies are investigating what else can be burnt in their kilns.

Case Study 10: Cement Works or Toxic Waste Incinerators?

Some cement works have turned to burning waste material as fuel. The Castle Cement works at Clitheroe, England, has been criticized for burning hazardous material, such as *chlorinated solvents* and heavy metals (*mercury*, lead and thallium). It is also thought that the combustion process has produced dioxins. In addition, the plume frequently grounds in the valley, producing respiratory problems.

Burning waste gives the company the advantage of being paid for its fuel, rather than having to buy coal. Supported by the UK's Environment Agency, the company says that the emissions are no worse than burning coal, and the health authority admits that it has no formal evidence that the process causes health problems. However, the House of Commons Environment Committee has recommended that cement kilns burning hazardous waste should be treated like waste incinerators, which require more stringent controls. Others say that hazardous waste should not be burnt in kilns which were not designed for that task.

See also: Energy from waste; Incineration; Indoor pollution.

CEN

European Committee for Standardization (Comité Européen de Normalisation). Its members comprise the national standards bodies of European countries. It developed *EMAS* and is responsible for recognizing *ISO 14001* as a European standard.

See also: BSI; ISO.

Ceramic Tableware

The Portuguese and UK *eco-labelling* boards have undertaken a joint study into the impacts of ceramic tableware. Following this, the EU may launch an eco-label.

Ceramic Tiles: *see Floor and Wall Tiles*

CERCLA – US

CERCLA (the Comprehensive Environmental Response, Compensation and Liability Act) is the controversial Superfund law, passed in 1980. The law is designed to identify toxic waste sites, decontaminate them, and make the owners pay for the clean-up. The law followed the outcries over *Love Canal* and other illegal toxic dumps.

Of the 1300 identified sites, only 79 have been cleared up to EPA standards. Each site has cost on average US$30 million, and the federal government has spent US$13 billion on the programme. The fund is paid for by taxes on crude oil, on 50 chemicals, and a corporate environmental tax. It is also supposed to receive reimbursements from polluters. Between 1987 and 1991, this produced just 3 per cent of the fund's total revenue.

The programme has since been bogged down in legal wrangles over responsibility, and the law has been much criticized for its cost, ineffectiveness, and the high standards that have been imposed. Superfund supporters say that the law is paying for the pollution created between the 1940s and the 1960s. It is a question of paying to clean up the mess now, they say, rather than requiring our children to do it.

The Republican US Congress has sought to repeal some of the Superfund provisions, namely retroactive liability for all waste and substance disposals that took place before 1987. Environmentalists see this as letting polluters off the hook.

See also: Contaminated land; Fleet factors; SARA.

CERES Principles

A set of environmental principles drawn up by CERES (Coalition of Environmentally Responsible Economies) after the *Exxon Valdez* disaster. Over 80 organizations, almost all American and including Polaroid, General Motors and Sun, have subscribed to them. Companies which sign up to the principles must undertake an annual self-evaluation, and must publish an annual public report. The principles are as follows:

1 *Protection of the biosphere:* We will reduce and make continual progress towards eliminating the release of any substances that may cause environmental damage to air, water or the earth or its inhabitants. We will safeguard all habitats affected by our operations and will protect open spaces and wilderness, while preserving *biodiversity*.

2 *Sustainable use of natural resources:* We will make sustainable use of renewable natural resources, such as water, soils and forest. We will conserve non-renewable natural resources through efficient use and careful planning.

3 *Production and disposal of waste:* We will reduce and where possible eliminate waste through source reduction and recycling. All waste will be handled and disposed of through safe and responsible methods.

4 *Energy conservation:* We will conserve energy and improve the energy efficiency of our internal operations and of the goods and services we sell. We will make every effort to use environmentally safe and sustainable energy sources.

5 *Risk reduction:* We will strive to minimize the environmental, health and safety risks to our employees and the communities in which we operate through safe technologies, facilities and operating procedures, and by being prepared for emergencies.

6 *Safe products and services:* We will reduce and where possible eliminate the use, manufacture or sale of products and services that cause environmental damage or health and safety hazards. We will inform our customers of the environmental impacts of our products or services and try to correct unsafe use.

7 *Environmental restoration:* We will promptly and responsibly correct conditions that we have caused that endanger health, safety or the environment. To the extent feasible, we will redress injuries we have caused to persons or damage we have caused to the environment and will restore the environment.

8 *Informing the public*: We will inform in a timely manner anyone who may be affected by conditions caused by our company that might endanger health, safety or the environment. We will regularly seek advice and counsel through dialogue with persons in communities near our facilities. We will not take any action against employees for reporting dangerous incidents or conditions to management or to appropriate authorities.

9 *Management commitment*: We will implement these basic principles and sustain a process that ensures that the board of directors and chief executive officer are fully informed about pertinent environmental issues and are fully responsible for environmental policy. In selecting our board of directors, we will consider demonstrated environmental commitment as a factor.

10 *Audits and reports:* We will conduct an annual self-evaluation of our progress in implementing these principles. We will support the timely creation of generally accepted environmental *audit* procedures. We will annually complete the *Ceres Report*, which will be made available to the public.

Though not being legally binding, the principles have been shunned by companies which are opposed to public communication. Some companies also fear that the principles make an open-ended financial commitment for environmental compensation and restoration. However, the companies who adhere to the principles believe that they simply reflect their current practices. By adopting an externally produced policy, such as the Ceres Principles, companies avoid the problems of bias or self-serving statements.

Best practice

- The organization should sign up to the Ceres Principles.

See also: ICC; Policy, environmental.

Certification and Labelling Schemes

Many independent schemes have been developed to provide an objective proof of a company or product's environmental performance. This follows the 1980s rise of company's own claims, which were sometimes seen as *'greenwash'*. The main schemes are as follows.

International Management Standards

- *ISO 14001*
- *EMAS*

General Labels

- European Union *eco-label*

Paper Labels

- ABCD scheme
- *Blue Angel*
- *HMSO* Points
- *NAPM* seal of approval
- *Nordic Swan*

Packaging Recovery Labels

- for example, Germany's *DSD* system

Energy Labels

- *Energy Star*
- *Energy Label*

Product Certification Schemes

- *BREEAM*
- *Green Mark*
- *Scientific Certification Services*
- *Wood mark*

See also: Labelling; Marketing.

Certifier; Certification Body

An independent organization which checks that a company's *environmental management system (EMS)* conforms to a specific standard (such as *EMAS* or *ISO 14001*). In ISO 14001, such a body is called a certifier. In EMAS, the body is called a *verifier*.

Certifiers should be treated like any other supplier, bearing in mind that, no matter how lofty they may seem, they are in business to make money. Assess, therefore, which certifier is best for your business. Decide which certifier is the most suitable – in terms of size, experience of your industry, or international credibility. Get estimates from several.

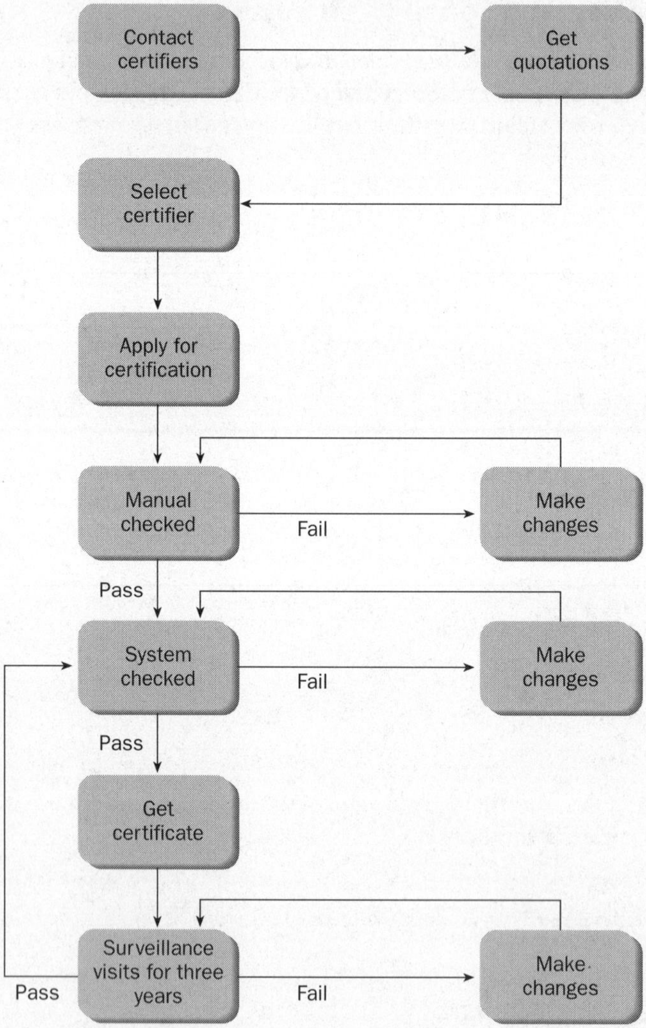

Figure 2: The Process of Gaining Certification to ISO 14001.

Once you have selected a certifier and have applied for certification, the certifier may start by checking your EMS manual. If it is lacking, the certifier may require you to improve the manual before carrying out a site *audit*. If the system, when checked, conforms to the standard, you will be awarded your certificate. This is normally followed by surveillance visits – of lesser intensity – for three years, after which you may have to undergo a major audit once again.

It is wise to choose a certification body (as it is known for the quality standard ISO 9000) which has been accredited by a government agency or other impartial organization (in the UK, *UKAS*).

CFCs

Chlorofluorocarbons are synthetic gases containing *chlorine*. They are used as a refrigerant, as a propellant in aerosols, and as a blowing agent for polystyrene foam. During the 1980s it was found that CFCs damaged the earth's *ozone*, a layer of gas that keeps out the sun's harmful ultraviolet rays. CFCs also act as *greenhouse gases*. A molecule of CFC-12 is 10,000 times more effective as a greenhouse gas than a molecule of *carbon dioxide*.

Under the *Montreal Protocol*, 93 countries agreed to phase out the production of CFCs. A subsequent meeting in Copenhagen brought forward the final phasing to 1996, and the EU later brought the date forward to the end of 1994. Consumption of CFCs should be 50 per cent below the 1986 level by 1999. However, millions of *cars* in the US alone contain CFCs in their air conditioning. CFCs are also found in fridges and office *air conditioning* systems, and their use will remain legal for some time. Also, CFCs have a long life, as shown below, so any reduction in CFC emissions will have little effect in the medium term.

Table 2: Lifetime of CFCs in Years

CFC	*Lifetime*
CFC-11	77
CFC-12	139
CFC-113	92
CFC-114	180
CFC-115	380

CFC emissions will eventually fall over time, and the chemicals in the atmosphere will disperse, which will allow the hole in the ozone layer to become smaller. Scientists predict that the stratosphere will be CFC-free within 60 to 100 years.

In some cases, CFCs have been replaced by hydro-chlorofluorocarbons (HCFCs), some of which can still damage the environment, if not to the same extent (especially R502, which causes one third of the damage). These, too, are being phased out. *Hydrocarbons* and *ammonia* are now being used as refrigerants.

Best Practice

- Replace CFCs used in *air conditioning* systems.
- Avoid the use of *packaging* which has been blown using CFCs or *HCFCs*.
- Dispose of equipment containing CFCs in a manner approved by your waste disposal authority.

Disposal: Seek advice from your waste disposal authority on the correct method of disposing of old refrigerators, freezers and air conditioning systems.

See also: Carbon tetrachloride; HCFCs; Halons; IT; Methyl chloroform; Ozone; Ozone-depleting substances; Ozone layer; Packaging; Refrigerants.

Charters, Environmental

Trade associations, business forums and similar organizations have produced a range of environmental charters to which companies may subscribe. Some are specific to a particular industry (such as chemical or oil companies) or country, while others are applicable to all organizations. They vary greatly in their requirements. Some have been seen as an attempt to ward off legislation or shareholder demands for higher standards. Others, such as *CERES*, are more stringent and as a result attract fewer signatories. Some, such as the *CBI's* Environment Business Forum, contain a full programme of activities, or are verifiable, while others (such as the *ICC* Charter) are neither of these things.

A local authority's environmental policy is also usually called a charter, though it is more akin to a policy produced by private industry than the type of charters issued by the bodies mentioned above.

Best Practice

- Identify the appropriate charter(s) and sign up to it or them.

See also: Policy, environmental.

Chemical Industry

Impacts: There is a wide variation of impacts within the industry due to the range of products produced, depending on the feedstock used and the process involved. Having been tightly regulated for many years, the chemical industry is now less polluting than many other sectors such as farms, dairies, power stations or *sewage treatment* companies. Certain parts of the industry use hazardous substances such as *chlorine*, and pump heavy metals into water courses; but for most companies it is the threat of major incidents rather than routine pollution that is the major issue.

Potential impacts relate to the danger from toxic, inflammable or explosive raw materials, as well as the possibility of water or air pollution caused by accidental release or process failure.

Case Study 11: New Uses for Solid Waste

P T Tifico, an Indonesian producer of polyester, found that its solid waste, known as RG-Residue, could be sold as an additive in the production of sheet carpet for roofing. This saved substantial amounts of incineration, which in turn was costly and produced air pollution. The company also tackled its waste water problem: by using an activated sludge process, it reduced the COD levels from 10,000 parts per million (ppm) to just 20 ppm. At least 32 per cent of its waste water is now reused in the process, reducing the need for fresh water by 2450 litres per minute.

The 3Es Project

In 1994, the UK's pollution inspectorate (now the Environment Agency) challenged the chemical industry to participate in a 3Es project. This was intended to assess the impact on process *emissions*, *efficiency* and *economics* of applying the culture of 'operator responsibility' that it is seeking to encourage. Allied Colloids, in working with Her Majesty's Inspectorate of Pollution (HMIP), identified savings of UK£1.5 million in its 18 processes which are controlled by law. Emissions of methyl chloride increased 80 times during changeover between products. Similarly, half the total mass release to air from one plant occurs when the plant is shut down. One third of the down time, which cost the company UK£1 million in lost profit, was caused by inefficient inventory control. The 3Es programme reflects the US *Environmental Protection Agency*'s 'Common Sense Initiative'.

Best Practice

- Adopt formal *HAZOP* studies at the design stage of new plant.
- Install control equipment to minimize emissions of gas, vapour and particulate.
- Install spill containment and capture systems.
- Ensure effective and ongoing staff training, including major incident training and practice.
- Implement a formal plant modification procedure to control risks from plant or raw material changes.
- Adopt a comprehensive Permit to Work system to control all engineering and maintenance work.
- Regularly test all safety-critical systems.

See also: CEFIC; Chemicals; CHIP – UK; Dangerous substances/preparations; Emergencies; HAZOP; Responsible care.

Chemical Release Inventory – UK

An inventory of polluting substances from industrial processes. The inventory aggregates the data from public registers created by the *Environmental Protection Act* (EPA) 1990. The inventory is based on the US *Toxics Release Inventory* (*TRI*).

The UK Department of Environment aims to list nearly 1000 substances, broken down by substance type, industrial sector and local authority area. However, it will not identify the actual sites or companies, for which it has been criticized by Friends of the Earth. By identifying companies, the TRI has had a major effect in reducing toxic emissions (down 43 per cent since the act was passed), according to the EPA.

Chemicals

According to the European Council of Chemical Manufacturers Federations, over six million chemicals have been created, of which 95,000 are in commercial use. Chemicals are used in every industry, from forestry and fishing through manufacturing industry, to service industries. Synthetic materials have replaced wood, paper, cotton and steel in *cars*, construction and consumer goods.

Overall the risks from chemicals are small compared with the quantity and frequency of use. The key potential impacts of any chemical can be measured by three factors:

1. *Toxicity:* measure of the chemical's ability to cause harm.
2. *Persistence:* the time taken for the chemical to disperse or decompose.
3. *Bioaccumulation:* its potential to become concentrated in the tissues of living things.

As an example, DDT is high in all three measures.

Storage

Chemicals should be stored according to the hazards they present. The risk of fire or explosion requires one type of storage, while toxicity in water may require another.

Disposal of Chemical Wastes

- The life of process chemicals should be extended as far as possible, through filtration, adsorption, etc (see *Liquid waste*).
- Used or redundant chemicals should be disposed of according to *best environmental practice*.

Information and Control of Risk

In the past, the control of chemicals in the work place has focused on health and safety issues, such as the threat to the worker from toxic fumes or corrosive chemicals. As a result, data sheets contain health and safety information but are less likely to have environmental information.

While health and safety data is essential, companies should augment this with information about the impacts caused by spillage or emissions to air, and the steps to be taken to prevent this. Staff should be made aware of this information. Any organization which uses sizeable quantities of chemicals should keep a database or inventory to control their impacts. Chemicals can be identified by the following factors:

- trade name, chemical name, chemical family;
- area or process involved;

- quantity on hand, volumes used;
- levels of atmospheric emission, etc;
- hazards to humans and the environment;
- safety measures and action to be taken;
- first aid;
- method of disposal;
- vendor;
- whether a data sheet is on file.

The database should be kept on computer and regularly updated. It should use standard words, and relevant sheets should be displayed in areas where a chemical is used. Since introducing such a system in 1991, Flachglass AG has entered more than 600 substances and methods of preparation in its database, which conforms to the German Directive on Chemicals.

Best Practice

- Introduce a database to manage and control chemicals.
- Avoid chemicals which are toxic, persistent or bioaccumulative.

See also: Chemical industry; Dangerous substances; Hazardous substances; Emergencies; HAZOP.

Chemical Sensitivity

The long-term effect on vulnerable people who have been exposed to low levels of *pesticides* or other pollutants, and suffer debilitating health effects as a result. In particular, they end up lacking some of the body's protective detoxifying enzymes. The term 'chemical sensitivity' is going out of favour and may be replaced by 'immunological dysfunction'.

Chernobyl

Site of a nuclear power plant, 80 miles (129 km) north of Kiev in the Ukraine, which exploded on 5 April 1986. Engineers had shut down the *RBMK* boiling water reactor for tests. The power level in the reactor was allowed to fall beneath its stable safety point, which led to a power surge. The surge disintegrated the nuclear fuel rods, which in turn evaporated the water into steam, causing a violent explosion. The reactor cracked, and 30 fires erupted. With temperatures reaching 2000°F (1093°C) and flames 15 metres high, 100 million curies of radiation were released into the air.

Evacuation was slow, and the 40,000 inhabitants of Chernobyl were not moved for six days. The radioactivity spread as far away as Wales, where the UK government stopped all sheep movements in certain areas after discovering that sheep were contaminated. Some 250,000 people died over the following years, while the effects on Russian agriculture are still unknown. Western nuclear experts say that the Chernobyl plant was a design not used in the West, though ageing and poorly maintained plants elsewhere in the former Soviet Union and Eastern Europe still pose a threat. The disaster alerted the West to the global threat posed by ill-maintained and ageing Soviet nuclear technology.

See also: Nuclear power; Three Mile Island.

Chester Network: *see Impel*

CHIP – UK

Chemicals (Hazard Information and Packaging for Supply) Regulations 1994 (known as 'Chip 2'). It implements EU directives on the packaging and labelling of *Dangerous substances*.

Chip 2 updated Chip (the 1993 regulations of the same name) by implementing new EC directives and applies not just to chemicals but to any substance that is dangerous (whether explosive or corrosive). The basic system of classifying, labelling and *packaging* chemicals remains the same.

Suppliers must provide safety data sheets containing specified information (for example, on first aid, handling and storage). The substances must be packaged according to regulations and must be labelled in specific ways (using terms like 'R55: toxic to fauna').

See also: Chemicals; Chemical industry.

Chloracne

Skin disease associated with exposure to chlorinated organic compounds. It was one of the results of the *Seveso* disaster.

See also: Chlorine.

Chlor-Alkali Industry

Produces *mercury*, whose discharge is governed in Europe by EC Directive 82/176/EEC.

Chlorinated Phenols

Chlorine and *phenol* compounds, which are known to produce toxic *dioxins*.

Best Practice

- Avoid their use.

Chlorinated Solvents

Family of *chlorine* and hydrogen compounds used in liquid form to dissolve materials, as a degreaser and cleaning chemical. Trichloroethylene, for example, is used in *dry cleaning*. Some chlorinated solvents are *carcinogens*. In the EU, they are controlled by Directive 94/60/EC.

See also: Degreasing.

Chlorine

Chlorine is an important but dangerous element. There are hundreds of chlorine-based compounds and some, like *dioxins* and chlorinated hydrocarbons, are highly toxic. The chlorine compound phosgene was used as a poisonous gas in World War I.

Chlorine kills germs, and is therefore used as a disinfectant in swimming pools and drinking water supplies, and as a toilet cleaner. It is also a *bleach*, which serves to remove colour from a dye. Its uses include household bleach and a whitening agent for paper. Chlorine is also used as a catalyst. Among the non-chlorinated products it produces are polyurethane, resins, plastics, dyes, drugs, and ingredients for paint, toiletries and agrochemicals. It is also used in *PVC* products and in some electrical insulation. Today, 85 per cent of pharmaceutical products contain chlorine or use it in the manufacturing process.

A study by Ecotec, a research group, showed that 60 per cent of Western Europe's chemical-industrial output depends on chlorine. This implies that banning chlorine (which has been discussed by governments) would carry a large economic cost.

Impacts

The commercial use of chlorine chemistry has resulted in chlorine compounds entering the sea, air and land in damaging quantities, according to the *Financial Times*. Many chlorine compounds are deadly. As a gas it can be poisonous. As an insecticide, it can (by definition) kill living things. It attacks most metals and many non-metals. *CFCs*, which are chlorine compounds, are responsible for damaging the *ozone layer*.

Best Practice

- Use substitutes wherever possible. For example, polypropylene pipes are environmentally more sound than PVC pipes.

See also: Bleaching; Bhopal; DDT; Dioxins; ECF; Furans; PVC; Paper, board and pulp industry; TCF.

Chlorofluorocarbons: *see CFCs*

Chloroform

Used in industry as a *solvent*. Chloroform is on the EC *Black List* of dangerous substances. It is a suspected *carcinogen*.

Best Practice

- Avoid its use where possible.

CHP: *see Combined Heat and Power*

Chromium

Toxic heavy metal, used in tanneries and metal processing. Its hexavalent form is more toxic than its trivalent form. Statutory authorities normally limit the quantity that may be discharged to water.

Best Practice

- Convert processes to trivalent chromium wherever possible, and minimize use.

Chronology

1952 The London smog killed 4000 people and led to clean air legislation.

1962 Publication of Rachel Carson's *Silent Spring*, an exposé of environmental problems. The book brought attention to the threat posed by industrial and agricultural pollution, especially *DDT*, and the potential extinction of many species such as the bald eagle. The book established the persistence of many toxic chemicals and led ultimately to the passing of US environmental laws.

1970 First Earth Day celebrated in US. President Nixon creates *Environmental Protection Agency (EPA)*. Congress passes *Clean Air Act*.

1972 DDT banned in USA.

1976 *RCRA* authorizes the EPA to regulate the disposal and treatment of municipal solid and hazardous wastes.

In Seveso, Italy, an explosion at a *herbicide* plant owned by Hoffman La Roche released toxic gas into the air. The town centre is uninhabitable to this day.

1977 The UN calls for a convention to protect the *ozone layer*. The call is ignored for another decade.

1978 Residents of *Love Canal* are evacuated when they are found to be living on top of a *chemical* waste dump.

1979 The *Three Mile Island* nuclear power plant in Pennsylvania, US, came close to exploding. If this had happened, the disaster could have destroyed Washington, DC.

1980 USA creates the *Superfund*, to clean up abandoned toxic waste dumps.

1981 *Lekkerklerk*, Netherlands: residents evacuated from 250 houses built on top of an illegal toxic waste dump. The site was cleared at a cost of UK£156 million.

1984 At least 3000 die in *Bhopal*, India, when a poisonous gas escapes from the *Union Carbide* plant.

Famine in Africa, magnified by military conflict, deforestation, overgrazing and desertification.

1985 Under pressure from conservationists, the International Whaling Commission (IWC) enacts a global moratorium on commercial whaling.

In Villach, Austria, scientists assembled by the UN and the World Meteorological Organization warn that the world's climate might be warming.

British Antarctic Survey finds a hole in the protective *ozone layer*. This leads to international agreement two years later to ban *CFCs*.

1986 *Chernobyl* nuclear power plant, north of Kiev in the Ukraine, explodes, casting doubts on the wisdom of nuclear energy.

The River Rhine is heavily polluted by a *chemical* spillage. This causes a rethink on environmental protection and major hazards throughout Europe.

1987 Signing of the *Montreal Protocol*, which committed countries to phase out production of the CFCs that damage the protective ozone layer.

1988 Scandals about illegal transportation of toxic waste across national boundaries. Attention focuses on the Karin B tanker. Governments start to search for a better strategy on waste.

1989 Oil tanker *Exxon Valdez* runs aground off the coast of Alaska, spilling millions of gallons of oil, leading to an expensive mop-up operation by the company.

1990 The 1000 scientists of the Intergovernmental Panel on Climate Change (IPCC) forecast sea level rises and major climate change due to *greenhouse gases*.

1991 International treaty bans development in Antarctica for 50 years.

The Iraqi army, retreating from Kuwait, damages nearly 800 Kuwaiti oil wells, poisoning 300 miles (483 km) of coast and 600 square miles (966 square km) of the Persian Gulf. Between 60 to 120 million barrels of oil were released, causing havoc among the fragile eco-systems of the Gulf. The first act of international eco-sabotage.

1992 *Earth Summit* in Rio, attended by more than 170 nations. The Convention on Climate Change is signed whereby the industrial nations commit themselves to curbing emissions of greenhouse gases. The conference also signs a Convention on *Biodiversity*.

1994 Congress rejects all but one major new environmental bill, as Republicans fight to reduce the scale of government.

1995 All around the world, climatic extremes continue. At least 700 people died in a Chicago heatwave, while the Caribbean faces its second most active hurricane season since records began in 1871. In Northern Europe, floods kill 26 people and cause 250,000 people to be evacuated. Britain has its driest summer for two centuries.

CIMAH – UK

Control of Industrial Major Accident Hazard Regulations 1984; amended in 1994 to include waste disposal sites. The law implements the 'Seveso' Directive of 1982 (82/501/EEC). The directive sought to reduce the threat of fire or explosion posed by *chemical* companies to their surrounding district.

Firms to Which the Regulations Apply

The legislation sets threshold limits for materials present on the site. The presence of more than a threshold quantity of material imposes a duty to take adequate steps to prevent major accidents and to limit the consequences of an accident. If a second, higher threshold quantity is reached, the company must prepare a safety report (known as a Safety Case) on the hazard posed by the substances used on the site, and the way in which the processes are safely managed.

The plant must also supply on-site and off-site emergency plans. The company must give those members of the public likely to be affected information about the hazards. That includes the names of substances involved, the types of hazard involved, arrangements for warning and action in the case of an incident.

The authorities have reported that many assessments concentrate on the health and safety risks rather than damage to the environment. Likewise, many firms are reported to be poor at assessing low-frequency/high-impact incidents.

Best Practice

For companies:

- Incorporate environmental risks into assessments and emergency plans.
- Identify sensitive features when surveying the site and its surroundings. This may include *wildlife habitats*, rivers or coasts, or vulnerable agricultural land.

See also: COMAH; Risk assessment; Seveso.

CITES

Convention on International Trade in Endangered Species, signed by 21 nations in Washington, DC, in 1973. Pronounced 'Site-ease', the treaty restricts trade in certain plants, animals and animal products between member countries, now 125 in number.

Non-member countries (such as Honduras, Argentina and Mexico) have undermined the success of the treaty by becoming centres for smuggling wild animals. Other countries such as Paraguay have signed the treaty but do not enforce it. Though CITES is known for its protection of animals, 21,000 of the 24,000 listed species are plants.

Among the treaty's successes is the listing of the African elephant as an endangered species, thereby halting the ivory trade. Items which may not be imported include elephant ivory, tortoiseshell, certain coral, spotted cats' fur (such as coats made from jaguar or leopard), oriental medicines made from products such as rhino horn, certain orchids (such as the Mexican living rock cactus), and skin from many reptiles such as crocodiles.

The US is the world's largest consumer of wildlife, receiving around 250 catchments a day, a quarter of which may be illegal. Japan is the world's largest trader in endangered species. With the help of France, Japan has decimated the rare musk deer from Nepal. In the first nine months of 1987, Japan imported more than 1700 pounds of musk, to be used as an aphrodisiac. This required the slaughter of 80,000 deer in that period alone.

As long as the demand remains constant, smuggling will continue. The rewards are high and the penalties slight. An ocelot coat can fetch UK£6000, while tiger penis soup can cost up to UK£200 a serving in Korea – because male diners think it will increase their potency (the Siberian tiger can copulate every 20 minutes).

Best Practice

- Ensure that the business does not sell animals listed in the convention, nor products made from them.
- Ensure that the business does not trade with companies that contravene CITES.

See also: Endangered Species Act; Nature conservation; Wildlife.

Cities

As a country industrializes, its cities grow, causing pollution and congestion. In the West, developers have sought to build on the outskirts of cities, leading to urban sprawl and the loss of green space.

As a focal point, the city provides good communications with the rest of the country and is the natural centre for government, commercial and industrial decision-making, although working in the city can be less effective, due to the noise, pollution and the time spent commuting. Companies are encouraging more employees to work from home while connected to their office by modem. Known as teleworking, this reduces the pollution caused by travel, but is more suited to senior staff whose work does not need to be supervised, or staff whose productivity can be quantified (such as sales people who can be judged by their orders).

Many city authorities are seeking to improve the environment by banning cars from the centre, by improving public transport, and by preventing development in 'green belt' areas just outside the city.

Case Study 12: Moving from the Country to the Town

In 1800 only 5 per cent of the world lived in cities, but the proportion has now risen to 40 per cent. This concentration is putting immense strain on the environment. The planet has difficulty coping with the pollution of air, water and land, while society has difficulty providing water, homes and *transport* for the two billion now crowded into cities.

The rich cities of Tokyo (19 million), New York (16 million) and London (10 million) face congestion and noise, but the West is able to cope better than the poorer countries with urbanization. Moreover, the West's growth has been gradual. The problems are therefore greatest in developing nations, where people move from the countryside to cities because of landlessness, mechanization of agriculture and job losses, as well as opportunities.

Simplistic action to make the agriculture of former communist and developing countries more 'efficient' (and less labour intensive) could result in the displacement of two billion people, according to some observers.

Best practice

- *Teleworking:* In the West, computer technology is leading to a reduced need for people to live in cities. The development of teleworking may reduce the growth of Western cities.
- *Agricultural policies:* In developing countries, government action to improve rural conditions and incomes, including the price of agricultural produce, will stem the outflow from rural areas.
- *Urban policies:* In the cities, giving people the right to own the land they are squatting on encourages them to improve their homes by providing them with a longer-term perspective.
- *Aid:* Flows of aid from rich to poor nations can improve conditions.
- *New towns:* To take the pressure off the big cities, many developing countries have built new towns, such as Brasilia in Brazil and Tenth Ramadan in Egypt.

See also: Population growth.

Civil Liability for Damage Caused by Waste

EC directive relating to clean-up of pollution from old landfill sites etc, where a secured lender (such as a bank) could be liable.

See also: Fleet factors.

Claims, Advertising: *see Marketing*

Clean Air Act – US

Enacted in 1970, the act sets emissions standards for 189 pollutants that cause smog. Factories and power stations require filters to prevent the release of polluting particles into the air. They also have to minimize emissions of *sulphur dioxide* by changing fuel or installing other anti-pollution controls. By 1994, toxic air emissions of 112 substances had been cut by 90 per cent.

The act also required car makers to install catalysts to reduce exhaust fumes. Oil companies had to remove lead from petrol. The act was amended in 1990 to include more stringent vehicle emission tests – a measure which several states refused to implement. The amendment also required more sophisticated testing of exhaust emissions and cut the permitted levels of factory emissions of 112 substances.

By 1990, 20 years after the law went into effect, the emission of particulates in the US had fallen from nearly 25 million tonnes to under ten million. Lead emissions from petrol had fallen from 200,000 tonnes to 10,000. The 1990 amendments also introduced an *acid rain* programme, which aimed to reduce emissions of SO_2, focusing on the top 111 facilities that are larger than 100 megawatts. The programme introduced the marketing of SO_2 allowances. Amendments also required states to administer a permit programme for the operation of plants which emit air pollution. States can collect fees from polluters to pay for the administration of the programme.

Also included in the 1990 amendments was a national policy for phasing out *ozone-depleting substances.*

Cleaner production

The goal of reducing industrial pollution, typically by:

- better house keeping;
- changing the process;
- changing the raw materials;
- reusing or recycling wastes;
- changing attitudes of staff and management.

See also: Closed loop; Pollution; Sustainable development; Zero discharge.

Cleaning Agents

The chemicals in cleaning agents have for a long time been accused of causing environmental damage. The problem is partly due to their widespread use: every household cleans dishes and washes clothes. Criticism has focused on the use of *nitrates* and *phosphates* in laundry *detergents*, though their impact is small compared with the quantity released by agricultural *fertilizers.*

The EU has produced proposals for an *eco-label* for hand and machine dish-washing detergents. There is a similar label for *laundry detergents*, and all have been prepared by Germany.

Best Practice

- Make or use only eco-labelled products when available.

Clean Water Act – US

Ground-breaking 1972 US law governing *water pollution*. The law requires industry, utilities and *sewage treatment works* to curb their output of *liquid waste*, and requires them to obtain permits to emit effluent. Notably, it bans the dumping of raw sewage into lakes and rivers in most of the US. Three-year prison sentences and fines of up to US$25,000 a day can be imposed for violation of the law. The act also provides limited protection for wetlands by hindering development.

Climate Change: *see Global Warming*

Climax Community

The trees and plants that would develop in the absence of human intervention. Much of Europe, therefore, would be broadleaved forest were it not for mankind's activities, including agriculture.

Clinical Waste

Waste resulting from medical activities. Such waste includes human tissue, body fluids, hypodermic needles, used dressings, and drugs. Such waste must be disposed of in a legally approved manner, usually by incineration.

Closed Loop

Reusing water (or some other input) in the manufacturing process, rather than disposing of it and using fresh water for the next batch of work. This reduces the volume of water used and avoids the discharge of *liquid waste* to drains.

Canada's biggest photo finisher, Black Photo Corporation, used to discharge 265,000 litres of waste water daily, but now discharges only 750 litres, following the introduction of a closed-loop system. This has helped to ensure regulatory compliance and given the company an improved image in the market.

Best Practice

- Assess whether closed-loop systems could be introduced into the organization.

See also: Cleaner production; Food processing industry; Photographic industry; Water pollution; Zero discharge.

Coal Mines: *see Mining and Quarrying*

COD

Chemical Oxygen Demand. A measure of pollution from liquid organic waste. Can be reduced by various means, including passing the waste through an *activated sludge* process.

See also: BOD; Sewage.

Co-disposal of Waste

The disposal of industrial hazardous wastes and household waste in one landfill site. It is intended that the biodegration of the household waste should break down the hazardous waste, making it harmless. However, it creates the possibility of toxic cocktails.

The EU *Landfill of Waste Directive* banned co-disposal of waste except in countries where it was practised (such as the UK), which were exempted for five years.

COMAH

The Control of Major Accident Hazards. This EC directive will replace the Seveso Directive (and in the UK, *CIMAH*) by the end of the century. Major plants will have to gain a consent to operate. And instead of merely accepting a plant's safety report (or safety case), the responsible authority (in the UK, the Health and Safety Executive) will have to systematically investigate and approve it (known as 'permissioning').

Combined Heat and Power (CHP)

A method of generating energy in which the waste heat is used to provide space heating or hot water. CHP increases the efficiency of heat and power generation from around 35 per cent to 80 or 90 per cent. This leads directly to lower energy costs and lower emissions of pollutants.

CHP is particularly attractive to companies in the food and paper producing industries which consume large amounts of electricity and gas. Surplus power is often sold to the electricity company or to other large industrial or commercial users. It is not unusual for companies to halve their annual fuel consumption and achieve payback in months rather than years by installing CHP.

Case Study 13: Museum of Science and Industry, Manchester

A water-cooled lean-burn gas engine drives the Museum of Science and Industry in Manchester. The museum is the largest of its kind in Europe, spreading over eight acres and comprising five groups of historic listed buildings, including the world's oldest railway station.

In 1995 the engine cost UK£3.20 an hour to run and provided electricity worth UK£4.86. As a by-product, it gives hot water for radiant heating and air conditioning. When a second CHP engine is installed, CHP will provide savings on running costs of UK£40,000 a year. In addition, it is likely to save 180 tonnes of *carbon dioxide* from being released into the atmosphere, compared with that from conventional heat and power generation.

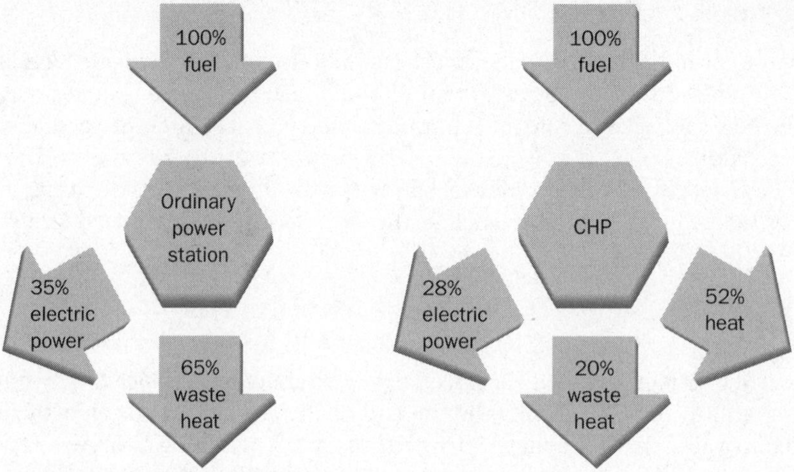

Figure 3: Comparison Between an Ordinary Power Station and CHP

Best Practice

- Investigate the possibility of using CHP if it is not already in use.

Combustion Plant

Because they produce *air pollution* (*carbon dioxide*, *particulates*, oxides of *nitrogen* and other pollutants), combustion plants (ie boilers or incinerators) are regulated. Regulations usually apply to plants over a certain size. Different requirements may hold for 20 to 50 megawatt plants compared with a plant that is greater than 50 megawatts. The method of combustion (eg oil, gas or coal) will also have an effect on the type and extent of potential pollution.

The regulatory authority is likely to have process guidance notes that demonstrate best practice. New plants may have to meet higher standards than existing plants which often have to be gradually upgraded to reduce pollution.

Best Practice

- Large plant: consider appointing a contractor to manage the plant.
- Get process guidance notes to determine best practice.
- Adopt appropriate *energy management* and control skills.
- Continuously monitor *air pollution*.

Common Agricultural Policy (CAP)

An agreement between member states of the European Union which protects farmers' incomes by fixing the floor prices of farm goods. The resulting overproduction has been reduced by lowering the prices and by introducing measures which pay farmers not to grow crops. This is also reducing the pressure on the environment from intensive farming (through *fertilizers* and *pesticides*, etc).

Common Sense Initiative: *see Environmental Protection Agency (EPA)*

Communication

It is vital to communicate the company's environmental policy and progress to interested groups, including employees, shareholders, trade unions, environmental groups and local residents. Major organizations also take into account the views of a wider audience, including national and specialist press, and other national opinion formers, such as elected national representatives, environmentalists and the media.

The amount of communication needed depends on the scale of the company and its impacts. At a minimum, the appropriate information should be available for anyone who asks. The company should also deal with complaints quickly and positively. A company with a major potential to pollute may issue a regular newsletter to local householders, or even set up a community committee. It may also hold open days, or operate an open-door policy for those who want to inspect the site. Some companies also engage in PR activities, such as sponsoring community activities or providing expertise or facilities to local groups. Internal communications include the use of notice boards, employee newsletters, environmental committees, and team briefings.

Box 3: Purpose of Communication

- To demonstrate management commitment to the environment.
- To demonstrate progress made in reducing the organization's impacts.
- To motivate and gain commitment to the organization and to improve its image.
- To provide information required by law.

Best Practice

- Undertake a communications *audit*, examining the comprehensiveness and effectiveness of the company's environmental information.

See also: Marketing; Public relations; Pressure groups.

Commuting

Every city has thousands of slow-moving *cars*, each with one occupant clogging the roads every day. Commuting causes congestion, pollution and uses non-renewable resources. While many of the solutions lie in the hands of transit authorities, employers can also help.

Best Practice

- Employees can be encouraged to work partly or wholly from home.
- They can also be helped to share cars.

- Companies should not encourage employees to drive large cars. Flat-rate travel expenses will encourage employees to drive a smaller car.
- Companies should provide bike stands and (on large sites) cycle and pedestrian paths.
- Companies can provide transport to and from the nearest railway or bus station at the start and end of each day.

See also: Cars; Cities; Teleworking; Transport.

Competent Body

Organization, appointed by a member state of the European Union, to register individual *EMAS* sites by receiving and approving EMAS statements which have been checked by a *verifier*. In the UK, the competent body is the Department of the Environment.

See also: Certifier; EMAS; Verifier.

Complaints

Complaints by the public must be taken seriously, because for every person who complains several hundred people may be angry but silent. Also, properly handled, complaints turn the complainant into a defender of the company. Badly handled complaints may result in expensive and time-consuming legal procedures, bad publicity, or action by the *regulatory authority*.

Environmental complaints often relate to *noise*, *odour* or *air pollution*. The impacts are likely to be governed by legal regulations, so such complaints should not be ignored. Companies seeking *ISO 14001* are likely to need a complaint handling procedure, in that the standard requires the company to commit itself to continuous improvement, to manage non-conformances, to maintain proper records, and to communicate with outside parties. Senior management should receive a regular summary of complaints, together with action taken.

Best Practice

- Analyse the number and nature of complaints received in the last 12 months.
- Set up a formal complaint-handling procedure.
- Implement a plan to overcome recurring complaints.

Compliance

Conforming to legislation or corporate policy. The word is often used to denote that a company is keeping its *emissions* and discharges within limits set by the regulatory authority. This is also known as conformance.

Legal compliance is the lowest common denominator, and should be just the starting point; many companies set standards much higher than legal compliance. Setting higher standards should be part of the company's striving for excellence, continuous improvement or total quality management. Whatever words the company uses, compliance is the minimum.

Best Practice

- The company should set as a target 100 per cent compliance with its environmental *consents*.
- It should then set new standards progressively higher than legal compliance.

See also: Conformance; Duty of care; Liability.

Composting

Commercial composting is one way of reducing the amount of *organic* waste material (waste containing micro-organisms) by converting it into soil conditioner or fertilizer. Everything from vegetable peelings to nappies can be composted. Compost temperatures can reach 150°F (66°C) which kills pathogens.

Palm Beach County, Florida, succeeded in reducing by two-thirds the quantity of rubbish going to landfill by creating a composting plant, as well as greater emphasis on recycling.

Best Practice

- Develop a composting programme if the organization produces enough *putrescibles* to warrant it.

Comprehensive Environmental Response, Compensation and Liability Act: *see CERCLA – US*

Compressed Natural Gas: *see Public Transport*

Computers

Given the quantity of equipment produced, computers impose a relatively light burden on the environment. The use of solvents for washing computer-printed circuit boards was an important impact which is now much reduced. One of the biggest remaining impacts is the use of consumables, notably printer *cartridges*, which can be reduced by the use of recycled cartridges. The disposal of old equipment results in quantities of solid waste.

Computers also have a positive impact on the environment by having the potential to reduce the use of *paper* (for example, through computer-based information retrieval systems), and cutting the need to travel (through computer networks).

Disposal

As technology advances, even quite recent equipment becomes out of date. As a result, disposal becomes an important issue. Companies can offer their old computer equipment to a skills-training project, or to a charity that will give it to the Third World. Charities and schools may also welcome equipment which is still in working order. Alternatively, the equipment can be sold or the supplier may take it back for recycling. Some companies like IBM operate a non-profit making take-back policy where they will recycle and safely dispose of old computers.

A company that gets rid of its equipment in any of these ways may need to carry out a safety check and signify on the equipment that it has done so. Taking reasonable steps to ensure that the equipment is safe will be a defence in any court action. If the equipment is disposed of as waste, ensure that the equipment goes to properly authorized waste contractors.

Best Practice

- Use systems that can be upgraded, because they result in less *solid waste*.
- Use low-power systems.
- Use networks and telecommunication systems to reduce business travel.
- Implement a programme to ensure that the *IT* system uses as little paper as possible.

See also: Cartridges; Furniture; IT industry; Office equipment; Paper; Printers.

Conformance

A term, borrowed from quality management, which means complying with written procedures or policies. The term 'compliance' is also used. In an organization which lacks written procedures, employees cannot be expected to know whether they are doing the right thing. In other words, they cannot know whether they are conforming to what is expected of them.

See also: Compliance; Environmental management system.

Congestion Charging: *see Cars*

Consents

Pollution limits set by a regulatory authority for an individual factory. A consent is a permit to pollute.

Conservation

Saving energy, *wildlife* or *raw materials*.

Conservation of Natural Habitats Directive: *see Habitats Directive*

Construction Industry

The industry converts natural capital – timber and clay – into man-made capital, with most of its products designed to last for hundreds of years. The industry also has the ability to create a more attractive and pleasant environment, and by building in a sensitive manner it can enhance people's lives.

Impacts

- The construction industry consumes non-renewable resources, such as stone and aggregates, and bricks and blocks made from clay. Some of the processes used in its products are energy intensive, especially brick-making.
- The industry uses *timber*, mostly from managed sources. Despite being grown as a crop, there are wide variations in the environmental controls applied by forestry companies. The industry also uses tropical timber, albeit a small part of its total timber use, though in countries such as Japan it is even used to make plywood. Much of the harvesting of tropical timber causes the destruction of nature and loss of habitats.
- The creation of *roads* leads to an increase in car use, with its attendant impacts.
- *Noise, dust* and vibration are another impact, as are the loss of scenic views.

Consumer Attitudes

Consumers are less likely to put up with the polluting effects of noise and dust than before. In 1991, residents in the London Docklands launched a claim for compensation against the London Docklands Development Corporation for the disturbance of living in what amounted to a building site. At the time, it was estimated that if the 10,000 people in the area received UK£10,000 each, the total claim would amount to UK£100 million.

Case study 14: The Use of Recycled Material

A considerable amount of old construction material is sent to landfill – from road resurfacing and the demolition of old buildings. Much of this can be reprocessed. In Liverpool, UK, City Centre Commercials Ltd recycles concrete and bricks, which are crushed, graded and sorted before being reused in new buildings. However, the lack of approved standards for recycled materials hinders their reuse.

Construction companies argue that they have little say in how a building is made, and are often given a mere five weeks to tender for a road which has been discussed for 30 years. Given these restrictions, the companies should seek to play an active part in preventing environmental damage, rather than 'acting under orders'.

In Copenhagen, Denmark, 80 per cent of one multi-occupancy building has been made from recycled material. This includes the main construction material (prefabricated concrete that has recycled concrete as aggregate). The house is clad with recycled bricks, much of the roof uses recycled timber, and the roof tiles are also recycled. The windows, however, are new, since regulations require them to be double glazed. The cost of the house was about the same as one made from normal raw materials.

Best Practice

For construction companies:

- Undertake an *environmental impact assessment* before finalizing plans.
- Consult with environmentalists and local residents, and adapt plans accordingly.
- Produce a 'Method Statement'. This defines how the work is to be carried out and how nuisance and environmental damage will be minimized.
- Retain mature trees, ponds and water courses.
- Avoid building in areas of special scientific interest (SSSIs).
- Give preference to refurbishment rather than new building, since it causes fewer impacts.
- In demolition and refurbishment, ensure that old building materials are recycled.
- Ensure that new buildings harmonize with their surroundings.
- Use recycled materials where possible.
- Use traditional and natural materials, such as timber and glass, where possible, recognizing that even traditional materials such as bricks have impacts.
- Avoid the use of toxic and *hazardous substances*.

See also: Building design; EIA; Road building; Utilities.

Consultancies, Environmental

The organization should use its own staff to manage its environmental impacts where possible. This helps staff to learn new skills and makes their jobs more interesting. However, there are times when consultants should be used. This the case when the company:

- lacks specialist skills or equipment (for example, when assessing contaminated land);
- lacks the time (when the company has a small core staff).

Before selecting consultants, the company should ascertain whether they have:

1. *Qualifications:* What qualifications do they need? Are they members of an association?
2. *Experience:* What other work have they carried out? Can they provide references? Environmental consultants often specialize in different aspects of the environment. They may have skills in ecological studies (for *EIAs*), *environmental audits* or management systems. Or they may have technical specialities (especially *waste water, air pollution* or *solid waste*).
3. *Proper equipment:* Can they measure *air pollution* or *noise* levels? Avoid being side-tracked by technical issues. Remember also that, because jobs are varied, even the largest consultancies rely on outside laboratories. For a consultancy to maintain a large staff of scientists and equipment may add an unnecessary overhead.
4. *Enough staff:* Does the company have many sites or a large organization? Many consultants are one-man bands. Some have specialities (such as air pollution).

According to ENDS, the market for environmental consultancy has slowed down. It believes that 'too many organizations are chasing a share of the available income'. Similarly, Denton Hall, a London City law firm, has noted that the number of environmental lawyers in the UK has grown from 40 to 1200, since 1990, 'despite the fact that there has not been a similar rise in the number of environmental cases.'

Typical projects undertaken by consultancies are:

- environmental *audit*;
- tackling specialist problems connected with the pollution of air, land or water (for example, soil remediation);
- introduction of *environmental management systems*.

Best Practice

When using consultants:

- Establish the objectives of the project clearly. Define what you are hoping to get out of it.
- Brief the consultants properly. This will ensure that you get the information you need.
- Set an agreed fee for each part of the assignment. Ensure that it is presented as a set number of work days. Make sure that it includes visits to all relevant sites and meetings with all relevant personnel.
- Ask for a plan of campaign from the consultancy. Agree a timing plan, including a date for presentation material. Ask for the information to be presented personally – this will give you a clearer understanding than pages of documentation.
- Consider carrying out work on a small part of the organization first. This will let you evaluate the consultants and absorb some extra knowledge.

Consumer

Today, 80 per cent of US citizens call themselves environmentalists, and an estimated 200 million people around the world took part in the twentieth anniversary of Earth Day in 1990. The consumer prefers to buy green products, all other things being equal. In 1993, at the height of the recession, the research company BMRB found that only 3 per cent of UK consumers were unaffected by environmental considerations, and 68 per cent of consumers were still prepared to pay a little more for 'green' products.

The percentage of UK consumers prepared to 'pay more for environmentally friendly products' rose strongly in the late 1980s and dropped back from 49 per cent to 40 per cent between 1990 and 1994. This may reflect a plateauing effect, or the fact that leading brands now seem 'green' because they provide environmental information. In the same survey, the proportion who disapproved of 'the effect of aerosols on the atmosphere' fell from 65 per cent to 49 per cent in the same period, reflecting a perhaps unjustified belief that the aerosol problem has been solved.

However, consumers are also contradictory. While they want green products, they are unwilling to tolerate any reduction in their product's performance. And while they claim to be willing to pay more, their purchase behaviour denies it. When consumers buy green products, it is often because of the economic benefits. They buy unleaded petrol if the government makes it cheaper, and they buy lavatory paper made from recycled paper because it, too, is cheaper. For example, Tesco, the UK supermarket chain, found that 60 per cent of its customers wanted an *eco-label* that indicated environmentally superior products. It also found that consumers would not pay more for them.

Unlike the older generation, young people are being taught about environmental issues at school, making them much more environmentally aware. The media also report environmental issues much more readily than before. This means that future consumers will be more aware of green issues than their parents.

Best Practice

- Identify the consumer (or customer's) environmental needs and attitudes.
- Assess the extent to which the organization is fulfilling those needs, and take corrective action if necessary.
- Ensure that the organization is consistently ahead of consumer expectations, rather than behind them.

See also: Marketing; Public relations.

Contaminated Land

Land which is a threat to health or the environment as a result of its current or previous use. In other words, it is land which has been contaminated by pollutants. Typical locations are *waste disposal sites*, *gas* works, filling stations, power stations, iron and steel works, petroleum refineries, *chemical* works, textile plants, leather tanning plants and timber treatment works.

At least 10,000 contaminated sites have been identified in the US, 50,000 in Germany and 4000 in the Netherlands. Major sources of soil contamination (including past uses) are *asbestos* manufacturing; explosives, pyrotechnics and propellants manufacture; fine *chemicals*; rubber processing; metal waste recycling; and gas works. The UK's Department of the Environment has issued profile notes explaining the various types of soil contamination.

Contaminated land can be remediated by chemical treatment, by the removal of topsoil, or by the planting of certain types of vegetation. Physically removing topsoil is an expensive process which merely takes the pollution from one site to another. Other activities may involve planting vegetation which absorbs and locks up the pollution.

Environmental Data Services (ENDS), a firm of analysts, found that in the UK advising on contaminated land clean-up was the biggest single category of work for consultants, accounting for 15 per cent of their turnover.

Legislation: the law varies in different countries, but regulatory authorities are keen to remediate contaminated land, though the costs (to the landowner) are high.

In the US, the costs of clean-up are shared between the current and previous owners, those who have dumped waste at the site, and those who have transported it there. Some money is also provided by the *Superfund*. Legal arguments about liability have hindered the clean-up. According to the *Financial Times*, if the Superfund rules on liability for contaminated land were fully enforced, much of the US banking and insurance sectors would be wiped out. As a result of the uncertainty, many firms remain unclear about their liabilities.

UK Legislation

In the UK, local authorities have power, under the Environment Act 1995, to enforce the remediation of contaminated land. This can happen where 'significant harm' is or has occurred, or where the contamination is causing water pollution. Local authorities must identify contaminated land in their area and decide whether it should be designated a 'special site', that is, one where serious pollution of controlled waters is happening or is likely to happen. If the land is thus designated, it comes under the control of the Environment Agency. Otherwise, responsibility remains with the local authority.

If the regulator (whether local authority or Environment Agency) decides that things are being done to improve the site, a Remediation Statement, recording what improvements will take place, must be produced by the person responsible. If, on the other hand, the regulator is not satisfied, it will issue a Remediation Notice, defining what work must be carried out and by whom. The maximum fine for failing to comply with a Remediation Notice is UK£20,000, but there can also be an additional fine of UK£2000 a day if the organization fails to comply. The agency can also refer the proceedings to the High Court if it believes that it is necessary to secure compliance.

The regulator may also carry out the work itself and recover the costs from the polluter.

Case Study 15: Paying for the Past

The US *Environmental Protection Agency* (*EPA*) has been pursuing Fleming Investment Trust for US$130 million to clean up pollution caused by a factory it sold in 1902. Under US *Superfund* law, the EPA has the power to come after polluters, even if the pollution took place in accord with the laws of the time, and even if the company was involved only tangentially, irrespective of how long ago the pollution occurred.

Flemings once owned a creosote business that polluted a nearby lake. The company has pointed out that:

- No one knows how much damage was caused during its ownership between 1882 and 1902.
- The creosote business had various owners, including billion-dollar American companies, until it stopped producing creosote in the 1970s.
- The creosote was produced expressly for railroad sleepers (known in the US as ties) which were critical to the economic success of the United States.

Sites which get registered as contaminated will be difficult to sell, so it is important for landowners and developers to identify contamination and clean it up. Legislation may become more stringent in future, which is another reason to act sooner rather than later.

Due to the high costs of removing contaminated land, it is sometimes better to clean up a site rather than pay for the removal of the spoil.

Best Practice

- Identify all the company's land holdings.
- Assess which, if any, have been contaminated.
- Obtain proposals for clearing up the contamination.
- Implement a remediation plan.
- Ensure that no future contamination takes place on company land.
- Ensure that no waste is stored on the company's sites.
- Commission an *environmental impact assessment* prior to purchasing any land.

See also: Derelict land; Gas industry; Landfill; Waste management.

Continental Tyres: *see Tyres*

Continuous Improvement

Some environmental management standards, notably *EMAS* and *ISO 14001*, require a commitment to continuous improvement. *Certifiers* will not expect to see improvement in every area each year. Therefore, management can select specific areas for improvement.

Management should use its *auditing programme* to identify areas for improvement. These areas for improvement should be discussed at the *Review*, and be implemented in the *Programme*. It can also harness the knowledge of its employees (through a suggestion scheme and better two-way communication), and improve standards by training and motivating the workforce. Involving the workforce in setting standards and targets may also be helpful.

Improvement may require investment (for example, in reducing pollution from *waste water*). On other occasions, it may require better quality assurance (to reduce scrap levels). It may also require better housekeeping (to reduce spills).

Best Practice

- Identify areas in which the organization does not perform well (such as *solid waste*).
- Introduce measures to improve these areas.
- Set environmental *indicators* as a base line.
- Monitor the indicators over time to check for improvement.

See also: Policy; Programme.

Contractors

Choosing contractors who demonstrate environmental awareness reduces the company's risk. There is less chance that the contractor (or other business partner) will make errors or cause pollution which could embarrass the company or make it liable for costs.

This includes work done on site (for example, maintenance or refurbishment work), as well as off-site, such as *waste disposal* or new building work. Contracts should include specifications concerning raw materials and solid and *liquid waste*, and disposal methods.

Best Practice

- Choose contractors who demonstrate environmental awareness.
- Include environmental specifications in contracts, or require contractors to provide an environmental plan for the work to be undertaken.

See also: Construction industry; Purchasing.

Controlled Waste – UK

Wastes subject to the Control of Pollution Act 1974. They are divided into three categories: household, commercial and industrial. They do not include explosives, wastes from mines or quarries, or agricultural wastes.

Conventions: *see Biodiversity; Earth Summit*

Copper

While essential for all forms of life, copper is toxic at high concentrations, causing liver and brain disease and early death. It is on the EC's *Grey List* of dangerous substances. Copper refining can produce atmospheric emissions of *cadmium* and *lead*.

COSHH – UK

Control of Substances Hazardous to Health Regulations, which implement the Health and Safety at Work Act. They control hazards that could affect the health of employees and others (such as visitors). The regulations require all employers to:

- produce a written assessment of the risks to health arising from exposure to *hazardous substances*;
- prevent or control exposure to these substance;
- monitor exposure and health 'where requisite' (ie where the risk is high);
- inform and train employees.

Wolverhampton Metropolitan Borough Council was prosecuted under the regulations for allowing an apprentice to spray (rather than brush) a fungicide on to the ceiling of a council property. The employee was exposed to high levels of the fungicide, and this was not the most effective method of work.

Other prosecutions involved two employees of another employer who were overcome by *carbon monoxide* poisoning from a petrol-driven generator used in a stairwell. Another employee was exposed to trichloroethylene after going into a degreasing tank with incorrect respiratory protection.

See also: Hazardous substances.

Cost-Benefit Analysis

Comparing the costs and advantages of an action, especially an investment. In general, an organization would only invest if the revenues outweighed the costs.

This process is now increasingly applied in government control of pollution. Under the *Environment Act* 1995, the UK's *Environment Agency* must show the likely costs and benefits of any action it is proposing to take.

For industry, cost-benefit analysis is complicated by the many unknowns in the future, such as the extent of greater legislation, and therefore the cost of *retro-fitting* pollution-control equipment.

See also: Accounting; Costs; Environment Agency; Environment Act 95.

Costs

Some environmental investment reduces costs (for example, draught-proofing reduces energy costs). Other investments (such as pollution-control equipment) are made in order to comply with legislation and do not necessarily produce a return. However, such investment may be necessary to gain government consent to carry out the process. If all companies are required by law to reduce their pollution, this creates a level playing field, and history shows that firms have been able to adapt to higher operating standards against their own expectations.

Traditionally, accountants measured investment in terms of payback. Some companies, such as DuPont, no longer apply those arguments to environmental investment. This is partly because some environment issues are difficult to cost. The company may decide to invest because it is unwilling to face protests from pressure groups, or because rising environmental standards may, in ten years' time, make a less-sophisticated plant obsolete. Furthermore, it may be difficult to separate environmental investments from investments which would happen naturally, though being able to state a figure can enhance the company's environmental credentials. Most new plants have much greater levels of environmental protection built in to them.

According to the UK Chemical Industries Association, spending on environmental improvements averaged 12 per cent of total investment.

See also: Accounting; Cost-benefit analysis.

Cotton Industry

Like any other crop, cotton is normally grown with the aid of artificial *fertilizers* and *pesticides*. Defoliant sprays are also used, and mechanically picked cotton is chemically dusted. It is possible to grow cotton organically, using natural compost, and in conformance with agricultural *eco-labelling* standards.

Cotton processing also has impacts. The spinning and knitting process involves large amounts of dust, which can be a health and safety hazard. Dyes can also be an environmental problem, though water-soluble dyes are available. High-pressure dyeing reduces *water use* and *air pollution*.

Chloride bleaches, traditionally used in the industry, can be replaced with hydrogen peroxide. Formaldehyde is also used in the drying process, but drying can be done mechanically with hot air (which can be recycled). Making up the cotton (cutting and sewing) is also a dusty process, and dust extraction should therefore be used.

Finally, dyes and phosphorus can be removed from the *waste water* through precipitation with lime and iron salts. *Activated sludge* then purifies the water.

See also: Textile industry.

Cradle to Grave

A product's total impact on the environment, at all stages of its life. This includes its raw materials and their impacts, the energy it uses and its disposal. It is usually carried out as a *Life Cycle Analysis*. Also known jocularly as 'from the sperm to the worm'. The term 'cradle to cradle' is now used to signify that a substance should be constantly reused (as in *closed loop* and *zero discharge systems*).

To evaluate a product's impacts, it is necessary to consider its whole life history. How was it made? What are its impacts during use? How will it be disposed of? For example, *PVC* looks like a harmless plastic. But its manufacture involves *chlorine*, which damages the environment. If incinerated at the end of its life, it can give off dangerous emissions. This means asking suppliers what materials they use and taking responsibility for the whole product, from design to recycling.

The cradle-to-grave assessment on p88 shows the energy and resources used at various stages of the paper industry, along with the outputs and waste produced. Companies producing their own cradle-to-grave analysis should quantify the actual amounts involved.

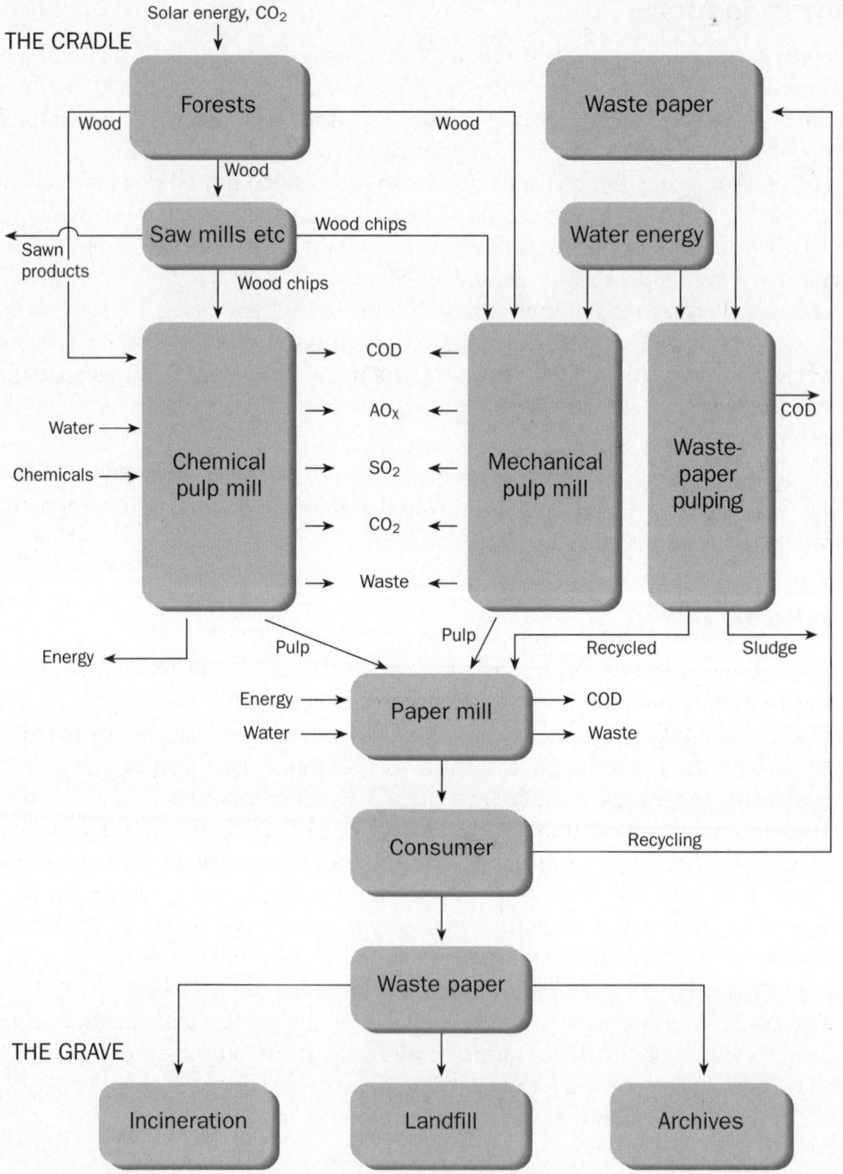

Source: UK Eco-labelling Board (1996) (adapted)

Figure 4: Cradle-to-Grave Assessment; Timber and Paper Industry

See also: Life cycle analysis; Sustainable development; Zero discharge.

Creosote

A *carcinogen*, some of whose components do not readily degrade and are poisonous to certain organisms. It is controlled in the EU by Directive 94/60/EC.

Best Practice

- Do not use.

See also: Contaminated land.

Crocidolite

Asbestos, whose import, export, marketing and use in the EC is controlled (Regulation EC 3135/94). A deeply hazardous product.

Best Practice

- Do not use.

CSA Z750 – 94 – A

Canadian standard for an *environmental management system*, similar to *ISO 14001*. It is a guidance document and does not contain elements that can be assessed.

Cups

Plastic cups are sometimes the subject of recycling initiatives, which in turn often fail due to higher-than-expected collection costs. Many companies have also found that plastic cups are not a major *environmental impact*. However, a professional approach can produce useful information, as the following case history shows. *LCA* research by the Australian Conservation Foundation indicated that china cups were environmentally better than plastic or polystyrene ones. Disposal of plastic or polystyrene cups was costly and inefficient, reusage was costly and unhygienic, and recycling was costly and ineffectual. Pilkington Australia therefore decided to give every employee their own personalized china mug, which has a projected life of three years. Each mug carries the employee's name, together with the company's vision. The cost of the mugs was cheaper than 12 months' supply of polystyrene mugs.

See also: Register of effects.

Cutting Oils: *see Metal Industry*

Cuyahoga River

River that runs through the heavily industrialized city of Cleveland, Ohio, US. The Cuyahoga caught fire in 1969, which caused local businesses to stop dumping waste in the river and led to improved *liquid waste* treatment in Cleveland and other US cities.

See also: Water pollution.

Cyanides

On the UK's *Grey List* of *hazardous substances*. Used in processing gold from its ore and in plating processes.

Best Practice

- Avoid use wherever possible.

See also: Gas industry.

Cyclamed

French *packaging*-recovery organization for the pharmaceutical industry.

Cyclohexane

An explosion of cyclohexane caused the Flixborough disaster in England on Saturday, 1 June 1974, in which 28 people died, 53 were injured and 3000 were evacuated. The Nypro plant at Flixborough in Lincolnshire produced caprolactam for use in the production of nylon, and its raw materials were *phenol* and cyclohexane. The explosion had the force of 15 to 45 tonnes of *TNT*, and had it occurred on a working day, the death toll would have been much greater. The Flixborough disaster was a turning point in the UK's approach to major hazards. It led to legislative control of such sites.

See also: Hexacyclohexane.

Cytotoxic

Substance which can damage cells.

Dams

Once heralded as the source of free, non-polluting and everlasting power, dams are now condemned by many conservationists. They are criticised for uprooting people, killing *wildlife* and flooding hundreds of square kilometres. Each dam is also thought to become less effective as it silts up.

Malaysia hopes to build one of the world's biggest dams in the middle of its rain forests in the Sungai Rajing Valley, in Sarawak State. The dam will produce 2400 megawatts of electricity, most of which will be sent via a 670-kilometre cable to peninsular Malaysia. The High Court ordered work to stop on the dam in June 1996, and required the project managers to submit an *environmental impact assessment* because an earlier report had not taken the views of residents into account. The project will involve clearing 170,000 acres (69,000 ha) of forest land and moving 9,000 tribal residents from the site. Eventually the dam will flood an area the size of Singapore.

See also: Defence industry; Energy; Water power.

Dangerous Substances/Preparations – EU

Several EU Directives (94/48/EC, 92/32/EEC, 90/492/EEC, 89/667/EEC, 88/379/EEC, 76/769/EEC and 76/464/EEC) control the classification, packaging and labelling of dangerous substances. They specify concentration levels for certain substances; preparations containing substances exceeding those levels are classified as harmful.

The 1994 Directive covers the use of 'whoopee' cushions, silly string aerosols, imitation excrement, artificial cobwebs and stink bombs. In the EU, Regulation 3135/94 controls the import and export of selected dangerous *chemicals*. In the UK, the directives are implemented by the Planning (Hazardous Substances) Act 1990, and the *CHIP Regulations*.

The UN has published Recommendations on the Transport of Dangerous Goods (known as the Orange Book).

See also: Black List; Chemical industry; Chemicals; Grey List; Hazardous substances; Transport of dangerous goods by road.

DBBT

Dangerous *chemical*, whose import, export, marketing and use in the EC is controlled (Regulation EC 3135/94).

Best Practice

- Do not use.

DDT

A *chlorine*-based *insecticide* whose use included combating malaria by killing locusts. DDT is said to cause cancer, sterility and hormone mutations. It does not biodegrade and therefore builds up in the birds and animals that feed on poisoned insects. This in turn becomes a threat to humans.

In the USA, DDT threatened the survival of the US bald eagle, the country's national symbol, along with other important US species, such as the whooping crane and brown pelican. The US banned DDT in 1972, and this and other measures have revived these species. DDT is on the EC *Black List* of dangerous substances, and is subject to EC Directive 86/280/EEC.

Best Practice

- Do not use.

See also: Chlorine.

Case Study 16: Does DDT Simply Not Go Away?

In 1996, the waters of Lake Maggiore, one of Italy's top holiday resorts, were found to contain 20 times the permitted level of DDT. An unconfirmed report said that trout examined in a public health laboratory contained 49 times the legal limit of DDT. Enichem Syntesis, the only chemical factory on the shores of the lake, and which makes DDT, was banned from discharging chemicals into the lake for 90 days.

DDT was banned from sale in Italy since 1978, but the firm uses it as an intermediate chemical for use in a fruit *pesticide* called Dicofol. Enichem said that its discharges were within the law, and some observers believe that the remaining DDT is simply the accumulation of pollution which began in the 1950s and stopped 20 years ago.

Defence Industry

Each kind of armament has a different impact on the environment. *Landmines* affect large areas of land by preventing them from being cultivated. *Chemical and biological* materials have the potential to wipe out crops and poison drinking water, but the difficulty of controlling them once released makes many governments cautious (though Iraq has fired poison gas into its own villages to curb opposition). At the end of the scale, *nuclear weapons* threaten the future of mankind.

The disposal of toxic old munitions is a threat, in many cases being dumped in the sea, where they either kill aquatic species or build up in the food chain. In Russia, spent nuclear materials lie on rotting naval quay sides.

The defence industries are keenly supported by national governments, often through dubious deals. For example, the British government helped pay for the environmentally damaging Pergau *Dam* in Malaysia in return for an arms contract. In recent years, armed forces have repositioned themselves as guardians of the environment, pointing out that land used for tank manoeuvres and firing ranges has not been treated with chemicals, and hence is a flourishing haven for *wildlife*.

Nuclear weapons

The seven Asian states of South East Asia have declared themselves a nuclear weapon-free zone. The states comprise Thailand, Indonesia, Malaysia, the Philippines, Singapore, Brunei and Vietnam. Also included were Burma, Cambodia and Laos, which are likely to become full members. America and China have expressed reservations because the treaty could interfere with the movement of their ships and submarines in the area. France was condemned throughout the world in 1995 for detonating nuclear bombs under the Pacific, while America is aiming to get an international Comprehensive Test Ban Treaty (CTBT) signed.

Many states are on the threshold of developing the capability of nuclear warfare. They include India and Pakistan. Meanwhile, India has refused to sign the Nuclear Non-Proliferation Treaty which it claims discriminates in favour of the old nuclear powers, such as the US.

See also: Nuclear power.

Deforestation: *see Timber Industry – Tropical*

Degreasing: *see Ammonia; COSHH–UK; Metal Industry; Trichloroethylene*

De-Inking: *see Paper, Board and Pulp Industry*

Deodorants

The EU may develop an *eco-label* for these products.

Derelict Land

Derelict land is ground that is so damaged by industrial or other development that it cannot be used without treatment. At least 0.2 per cent of land in England is derelict – some 42,000 hectares. Of this, 5 per cent is *contaminated* land.

Much of the dereliction is caused by *mining* and *quarrying* industries. Attempts have been made to reclaim it with varying success. 'Hard uses', such as housing, have often been unsuccessful, since the sites are located in depressed industrial landscapes. Soft uses, such as *agriculture* and public open spaces, have been more successful.

Minespoils are often very acidic, and there is a lack of plant nutrients such as *phosphorus*, while the reduced activity of the soil bacteria slows decomposition of organic matter. Minespoil can be covered with topsoil, which is a partial solution, but the transportation costs are high. The spoil can also be limed with limestone, though this is also expensive. Applying fertilizer is expensive and can be leached away. *Sewage* sludge has proved to be inexpensive and is in constant supply. Minespoils can also be treated with alkaline industrial wastes, including material from old industrial spoil heaps.

A low cost solution is to plant minespoils with *nitrogen*-fixing plants such as the common alder. Pulverized fuel ash (PFA) from power stations can also correct nutritional deficiencies, reduce bulk density and improve water-holding properties.

See also: Contaminated land; Solid waste; Waste management.

Desertification

Growth of desert areas, caused by overcropping, soil erosion and other factors. One third of the world's land surface is now threatened with desertification. Each year six million hectares of productive land become desert. A further 21 million become useless for growing crops or keeping animals. This is caused by several factors, including climate change, overgrazing, or the destruction of rainforest for its *timber*. When trees (especially in tropical rainforests) are cut down and a clearing made, the top soil often becomes eroded and a desert starts to grow. The indigenous people then have no shelter, firewood or any other crops, and a crisis can develop.

Design, Environmental

Designers can make sure their products are environmentally sound by adopting the following strategies:

- Use recycled or renewable raw materials or components.
- Use biodegradable raw materials or components.
- Avoid toxic, polluting or hazardous materials.
- Make sure the product can be dismantled and its components reused.
- Make sure that the components are easily serviceable or replaceable if they fail.
- Use good-quality components to ensure longevity of the product.
- Ensure that all plastic parts are coded for recycling.
- Provide instructions for recycling or disposal.

Each project can be scored on relevant environmental measures and a ranking obtained. The ranking will form part of the internal approval process for new products.

See also: Labelling; LCA; Packaging; Strategy; Technology.

Desulphurization: *see FGD*

Detergents: *see Cleaning Agents; Laundry Detergents*

Dewater

To remove water from *sewage* sludge or industrial *liquid waste* in order to reduce its weight and volume, resulting in savings in *transport* costs. Dewatering can be achieved by allowing the material to dry out, or by mechanically forcing the water out through pressure or vacuum.

Dichloroethane

Hazardous *chemical* mainly used as an intermediate in vinyl chloride manufacture. Also used as a *solvent* and a grain fumigant. On the EU *Black List* and the UK government's *Red List* of dangerous substances.

Best Practice

- Avoid its use.

Dichlorvos

Used as a *pesticide* on mushrooms, glasshouse crops, domestic pests, and in fish farming. Very toxic. Affects nervous system. Possibly carcinogenic. Irritates eyes and skin.

Best Practice

- Do not use.

Diesel

Diesel *cars*, buses and lorries produce only 10 per cent of the *carbon monoxide* produced by petrol engines, and they do not produce lead. They also last longer. However, they also emit *particulates*, which can carry carcinogens such as *PAHs* to the lungs. Diesel is smelly, foams up and any spillage is difficult to clear up.

German workers exposed to high levels of diesel fumes in confined spaces over long periods have suffered increased rates of bladder and lung cancer. However, studies have also found that the effects on the general public are negligible. Diesel does, however, produce city grime, *acid rain*, smells and smoke, and helps to form ground-level *ozone*.

Following an EC directive, diesel fuel sold in the EC after 1 October 1996 must not contain more than 0·5 per cent sulphur, compared with a previous limit of 2 per cent. This is expected to reduce acid rain considerably.

City diesel, which contains 0.001 per cent sulphur, has many environmental advantages. They include fewer *particulates*, virtually no *sulphur* oxides, and less carbon monoxide and *carbon dioxide*, all of which leads to a cleaner, healthier environment. In Sweden, due to tax incentives, city diesel accounts for 95 per cent of the market, and hostility towards diesels for inner-city traffic has greatly reduced. In the UK, city diesel accounts for 30 per cent, due to its lack of availability and higher price.

Best Practice

- Companies should monitor news of diesel pollution tests and product development, and use it to guide their strategy.
- Use city diesel in preference to standard diesel.

See also: Cars; Particulates.

Diethylene Dioxide (Dioxan)

Toxic substance used in paint manufacture and paint strippers.

Best Practice

- Avoid where possible.

Dilute and Disperse

A philosophy of getting rid of waste by dispersing gases in the atmosphere (through tall chimneys) and diluting *liquid waste* in the oceans (using long outflow pipes). The 'dilute and disperse' philosophy assumes that the planet is sufficiently vast to accommodate our pollution. This philosophy has been found wanting through evidence of *global warming*, the hole in the *ozone layer* and fish that have accumulated *PCBs* in their bodies.

Nowadays, dilute and disperse is less relevant, since most governments impose limits on what may be emitted. In addition, many charge industry for the right to pollute, and in doing so are encouraging companies to reduce or eliminate their pollution. Thirdly, some pollutants are now banned.

See also: Incineration; Landfill; Waste management.

Dinoseb

Dangerous *chemical* whose import, export, marketing and use in the EC is controlled (Regulation EC 3135/94).

Best Practice

- Do not use.

Dioxins

Family name for 75 compounds (dibenzo-p-dioxins) which result from some incineration processes, as well as products and industrial processes that involve *chlorinated phenols*.

Dioxins are extremely toxic, *teratogenic* and *fetotoxic*. Dioxins are stable, which means they persist, and can only be killed by high temperature incineration. Dioxins were produced at *Seveso*.

In 1994, the US *Environmental Protection Agency* (*EPA*) drafted a report which concluded that the greatest known source of dioxins was waste incineration, and added its weight to the view that dioxins cause cancer in humans. Cases involving dioxins have met with a mixed response in the courts. In 1996 Coalite Products were fined UK£150,000 and ordered to pay costs of UK£300,000 when they were found guilty of emitting dioxins from their incinerator at Bolsover, Derbyshire, England. This resulted in raised dioxin levels in milk from cows in the area, leading to a government ban on the sale of such milk. However, in a 13-month case which also ended in 1996, a farmer in Bonnybridge, Scotland, failed to prove that the death of his cows had been caused by emissions from an incinerator owned by Re-Chem. The judge decided that the connection between the incinerator and the cow's ill-health was unproven, and the main problem was an unrelated condition called 'fat cow syndrome'.

Best Practice

- Avoid the use of products and processes which produce dioxins.

See also: Cement industry; Chlorine; Furans; Incineration; Organochlorines; PVC; Seveso; Solid waste.

Directives and Regulations – EU

Directives passed by the European Union (EU) must be implemented by member countries while regulations do not have to be implemented by national parliaments because they already have legal force in member states.

Pan-European legislation is useful because it replaces 12 or more pieces of national legislation with one law. It also ensures a 'level playing field' for manufacturers across Europe. The major environmental directives and regulations are listed in the Reference Section of this book.

Discharges to Water: *see Liquid Waste*

Dishwashers: *see Cleaning Agents; Washing Machines*

Distribution, Physical

Impacts include *pollution* and *greenhouse gas* from exhausts; consumption of *fossil fuel*; the effects of road construction; and contribution to congestion.

Companies should take environmental issues into account when planning distribution. This includes the modal choice (road, rail, sea, air), with rail making more environmental sense than road for many trunking operations. Companies should also evaluate the environmental advantages of using a carrier compared with an in-house fleet. A carrier may produce fewer emissions by using resources more efficiently.

When choosing a carrier, include environmental awareness as a criterion. Does the company have an environmental *policy* and does it adhere to it? Does its fleet conform to best environmental practice, with body kits and spray guards, for example? The company that manages a fleet should consider commissioning a logistics study. This optimizes the warehousing and distribution strategy. It takes into account lorry sizes and drop sizes, check routes, distances travelled, and the frequency of deliveries. Routes should be planned so as to minimize wasted fuel. A logistics study also provides information about distribution volume and costs, and the data are often broken down by post code. It will reveal the most efficient way of distributing goods and should pay for itself by reducing costs. More efficient distribution means lower costs for the company, and less damage to the environment.

It is important to choose optimal vehicle size. Larger lorries produce fewer movements but can cause more vibration and visual impact. They also need large loads to be cost-effective and environmentally sound.

Energy Conservation

Energy conservation in transport can be achieved by:

- reducing the vehicle's speed (through driver training, motivation or through speed regulators);
- introducing better maintenance in order to improve engine efficiency.

Best Practice

- Determine best modal choice.
- Select environmentally aware carriers.
- Commission a logistics *audit* to minimize environmental *impact*.
- Use body kits to reduce drag and thereby improve fuel consumption.
- Fit anti-spray guards and air brake silencers to further reduce the environmental impact.
- Cover lorries with a tarpaulin if they are carrying loose material such as soil, sand or coal.
- Use speed regulators to reduce speeds and reduce fuel consumption.
- Take return loads to ensure that vehicles do not travel empty.
- Introduce driver training to reduce accidents and fuel consumption. Drivers are seen by retail customers, so they have an important PR role to play. Careful driving is one element of that.
- Adopt an efficient *maintenance* programme, and monitor exhaust emissions to reduce pollution.

See also: Cars; Maintenance; Roads; Waste transportation.

Documentation

Documentation refers to the key documents within an *environmental management system* (EMS). They may be held on the computer or other media. Typically they include:

- description of the main elements of the system (*auditing*, *record* keeping, etc);
- key roles and responsibilities of staff;
- policy, objectives, targets;
- programme;
- procedures (work instructions) for processes that have an environmental impact.

The EMS should specify which documents are part of the system and where they are located. Only current versions should be in circulation. Documentation should be periodically reviewed and revised.

Environmental documentation may be integrated into the organization's existing systems (such as ISO 9000).

Best Practice

- Determine which documents are essential to the operation of the EMS (or – in the absence of an EMS – documents which are essential to controlling the organization's impacts).
- Develop a procedure for controlling the issue, revision and withdrawal of these documents.

See also: Environmental management system.

Dolphins

Until recently, huge numbers of dolphins have drowned in the long so-called 'wall of death' tuna nets, now banned by the United Nations (dolphins swim with tuna, for unexplained reasons, hence their capture). In 1990 the US administration, followed by European nations, barred tuna imports from nations that failed to protect dolphins. This ban affected 80 per cent of the canned tuna market.

By 1995, the number of dolphins killed by tuna fishermen, whose nets encircle the dolphins, had fallen to 5000 world wide. Supported by the World Wildlife Fund (WWF) and the Environmental Defense Fund, the industry now adopts procedures which allow dolphins to escape. However, the use of encircling nets is criticized by other groups such as Earth Island Institute, the Sierra Club and Friends of the Earth. Nevertheless, attempts to abandon the nets might lead South American nations to return to their old ways, resulting in the death of more dolphins.

Case Study 17: Hong Kong

Chinese white dolphins have become threatened since the new Hong Kong Airport began to be developed. Dolphin numbers have fallen within the area from an estimated 200 to 400 in 1989 to around 80 in 1995. Related causes for the decline in the dolphin population include pollution, dredging, reclamation work, overfishing and shipping. Hong Kong says that a ban on harmful fishing activities is likely to be passed. The government is funding a study of the dolphins and its recommendations will form the basis for future action.

See also: Fishing industry.

Dow Chemical: see *Benymol; Freon; Montreal Protocol; PERI*

Drinking Water Directive – EU

EU Directive 80/778/EEC sets limits for *lead* and other substances in tap water. The limit is likely to be reduced by a factor of five, in line with World Health Organization (WHO) recommendations. The cost of replacing lead piping in domestic plumbing and mains would be substantial, though the new limits would be phased in over 15 years. The directive also specifies a number of parameters for various substances, including one part per billion for single *pesticides*.

In 1991 a UK survey by Friends of the Earth claimed that water supplies in many areas of the Thames Basin around London were contaminated with a number of pesticides by up to 16 times the permitted levels, and that illegal levels of pesticides were found in 70 per cent of supply zones of the Thames Water company. Friends of the Earth suggested that six million consumers were affected.

In January 1992, the European Court found that Britain had failed to fulfil its obligation by not transposing the drinking water quality objectives into British law by 1982. It also found that *nitrate* limits for drinking water were exceeded in East Anglia, and 800,000 residents were drinking water with an illegally high nitrate level. Ten other member states have been the subject of legal action for failing to meet the directive's requirements.

See also: Lead; Pesticides; Water pollution.

Drins

Common group name for *aldrin*, dieldrin, endrin and isodrin. They are on the EC *Black List* of dangerous substances.

Drum storage

Drums containing liquids are liable to leak or spill when used. Special care should be taken to store them in a way that prevents contamination of land. This may involve the use of pans which collect spills. Some drums pose different hazards, such as fire or explosion, and should be stored accordingly. Such products often give rise to large amounts of empties which may have to be disposed of as hazardous waste.

Best Practice

- Ensure that any leaks are caught in trays.
- Make sure that drum storage protects staff from fire or explosion.
- Investigate the possibility of using returnable drums or refillable containers, which would obviate the need for waste disposal.

Dry Cleaning Industry

The industry's main impact is its use of *chlorinated solvents*, which are said to be air pollutants and possible carcinogens (though the industry says the carcinogen link is unproven). Dry cleaners originally used *tetrachloromethane*, which has since been substituted (following health fears) with *trichloroethylene, perchloroethylene* and *trichloroethane*.

In Germany, dry cleaning shops may not be located near food stores, while in the UK they are often located inside supermarkets. Aquatex is said to be an environmentally sound, water-based alternative dry cleaning product, though dry cleaners are unconvinced by its performance.

DSD

Dualles System Deutschland. German *packaging* recovery system. A levy on manufacturers pays for the retrieval of packaging for recycling. It requires packaging manufacturers and retailers to return used bottles, cans, cartons and other packaging. Manufacturers and retailers are responsible for collecting all re-usable packaging, which is marked with a green dot. The system is intended to reduce Germany's household garbage from 30 million to 18 million tonnes a year.

See also: Eco-emballage; Packaging and Packaging Waste Directive; Packaging recovery system.

Dust and Fumes

An environmental *impact* in many industrial processes. Dust and fumes can be removed by the use of filters or electrostatic air cleaners. Some organizations (such as quarries, ore processors or steel works) store dusty material outside, such as coal, limestone or ores. Windblown dust can be a problem here. The stockpiles may be sprayed with water or the surface may be sealed. British Steel sprays a crusting agent on to its piles of ore, making the surfaces proof against erosion. On open land inside its works, the company is spraying a mixture of surface sealant, coarse grass seed and nutrient. The sealant retains the seed on the ground until it has taken root, after which the grass prevents erosion.

Vehicles exiting from dusty plants should be sprayed to remove the dust before entering the public highway. Dust should be monitored in plants where it is likely to be a problem.

Best Practice

For dust-producing plants:

- Define the source of the dust.
- Determine the best way of minimizing the dust and implement the solution.
- Install dust monitoring equipment.
- Seek to continuously reduce the amount of dust being produced.

See also: Indoor pollution; Welding and brazing.

Duty of Care – UK

Legal requirement for companies to monitor what happens to their *solid waste*. A concept enshrined in the UK's *Environmental Protection Act* 1990, covering companies who produce waste (as well as those who treat it, transport it or dispose of it). They have a duty to prevent its escape and to ensure that it is transferred to an authorized contractor. Among other things, it means that companies should provide employees with adequate equipment, training and supervision. The larger the organization, the more is expected of it in terms of knowing about the arrangements for the disposal of its waste.

Best Practice

- The organization should check that it is using a registered waste carrier, and that the waste is being delivered to a suitable disposal site.

EA: *see Environmental Impact Assessment*

Earth Summit

A United Nations Conference on Environment and Development (UNCED) which met in Rio de Janeiro in 1992. One hundred and fifty-three nations signed the Convention on Climate Change, where industrial nations committed themselves to curbing emissions of *carbon dioxide* and other *greenhouse gases*. Energy taxes were seen as a tool which would reduce the consumption of *fossil fuels*. In practice, countries have been reluctant to introduce taxes which would harm output and competitiveness.

The conference also signed a Convention on *Biodiversity*. This involves a national commitment to improved protection of wild animals and plants.

See also: Agenda 21; Global warming.

Eastern Counties Leather – UK

An important court case in which the House of Lords ruled that Eastern Counties Leather (ECL) was not liable to the Cambridge Water Company for losses suffered as a result of solvent ECL spilled during the 1950s and 1960s.

The House of Lords ruled that, to recover damages, it would have to have been foreseeable that harm would be done. Had the spillages happened in the 1990s, harm could have been foreseen, given the greater awareness of environmental issues in recent years.

See also: Rylands versus Fletcher.

Eastern Europe

Environmental damage was one of the legacies of communism. Poland has found it necessary to close down 100 of the country's 800 industrial plants which have been identified as causing dangerous levels of pollution. This included the notorious Polam lighting factory at Rzeszow. In 1991 the Polish Inspectorate for Environmental Pollution reported major problems of *groundwater* contamination with oil, threatening drinking water supplies.

Following the amalgamation of East and West Germany, the country set about improving standards in former East Germany. There are plans to renovate 278 power stations, to construct 27 new water treatment plants and renovate almost 60. Major improvements to the sewerage system were also planned. It is also planned to convert the disused salt mines of Saxony and Thuringia into toxic waste depositories to alleviate the chronic lack of secure waste sites in East Germany.

See also: Russia.

ECF

Elemental Chlorine-Free. A term used to describe environmentally improved virgin paper. ECF paper has been bleached with oxygen, chlorine dioxide or other *chemicals* rather than pure *chlorine*. Such processes do not form chlorinated compounds such as *dioxins*, furans and chlorophenols (which are produced with chlorine gas).

ECF is not as environmentally sound as *TCF*, which in turn is not as good as recycled paper.

Best Practice

- Use recycled rather than ECF paper.

See also: Paper; Paper and pulp industry; TCF.

Eco-Composites

A combination of renewable materials, such as natural fibre (for example, coconut) backed with natural plastic (made, for example, from vegetable oil). Eco-composites avoid the use of petroleum-based materials.

See also: Renewable resources.

Eco-Emballage SA

French *packaging* recovery organization for consumer goods. Companies pay a scaled contribution depending on the quantity of packaging they put on to the market. They identify this packaging by a green spot (two concentric arrows in a circle, as used by the German *DSD* system). Failure to comply with the decree is a criminal offence.

Eco-Label

An environmental claim that appears on a product's *packaging*. 'Eco-label' usually refers to a label awarded by a third party (such as the European Union's eco-label system), though it can also refer to an unverified claim made by the producer (for example, the term *Dolphin* Friendly). The international standard *ISO 14020* is a guide to the use of eco-labels.

The EU scheme

The EU scheme was set up to counter the many products which claimed to be 'environmentally friendly'. The eco-labels are an independently verified sign of environmental excellence and encourage manufacturers to make greener products.

The eco-labels are based on *life cycle analysis*, which examines the product's impacts 'from *cradle to grave*'. The pass mark is set at a level attainable by 10 to 20 per cent of brands or products on the market, and eco-label standards may rise over the years. Twenty-two products were initially planned to have labels, not all of which were subsequently developed. These and later ones are listed in Table 3.

Table 3: Eco-Label Standards

Product group	Lead country
Anti-perspirants/deodorants	UK
Batteries (likely to be delayed)	France
Building materials (dropped in favour of floor and wall tiles)	Italy
Cat litter	Netherlands
Ceramic floor /wall tiles	Italy
Ceramic tableware	Portugal/UK
Cleaning agents	Germany
Detergents	Germany
Fine paper	Denmark
Furniture care products	UK
Growing media	UK
Hairsprays	UK
Hairstyling aids	UK
Insulation materials	Denmark
Laundry detergents	Germany
Light bulbs	UK
Mattresses	Greece/France
Paints and varnishes	France
Packaging materials	Italy
Refrigerators	Italy
Shoes	Netherlands
Shampoos	France
Soil improvers	UK
Textiles (T-shirts, bed linen)	Denmark
Toilet rolls/kitchen towels	Denmark
Tourist services	Greece
Washing machines	UK

The second set of products includes:

- batteries;
- converted paper products;

- dishwasher detergents;
- floor cleaning products;
- rubbish bags;
- sanitary cleaning products;
- shampoos.

Each category has a set of criteria (such as the maximum amount of air or water pollution) to which the product must conform.

Each EU member state appoints its own 'competent body' (in the UK, it is the Ecolabelling Board) which can award an eco-label to individual products. A label awarded in one country is valid in all the others. It will therefore be recognized by Europe's 340 million consumers. The scheme is voluntary, self-financing and excludes food, drink and pharmaceuticals.

Gaining an Eco-Label

To gain an eco-label, the manufacturer or importer has to submit evidence to the 'competent body' that its product meets the criteria set for its category. An accredited laboratory will usually need to validate the test results. A product either passes or fails the criteria – there are no degrees of success or 'stars'. After the competent body indicates its intention to award an eco-label, there is a 30-day notice period during which other member states may object to an award, in which case it will go to arbitration.

Why Apply for an Eco-Label?

An eco-label gives a manufacturer a competitive advantage. It tells consumers that the product is environmentally sound, and so an eco-label should boost the product's sales.

Best Practice

- Assess whether the company makes any products that have (or are likely to have) an eco-label. If so, ensure that the products meet the criteria and obtain a label.
- Where an eco-label exists, use only products which meet its specifications.

See also: Cradle to grave; Energy label; Lifecycle analysis.

Eco-Mark

Japanese environmental label.

Ecosystem

A community of interdependent organisms and the environment they inhabit.

Ecotoxic

Harmful to the environment. The substance need not harm living organisms to be ecotoxic. For example, *CFCs* are non-flammable and non-poisonous but still cause substantial harm to the *ozone layer*.

EDTA

Ethylene diamino-tetra-acetic acid is a *bleach* activator used in washing powders. It is a complexing agent (see *NTA*).

Effect, Environmental

Another, more polite, word for environmental *impact*.

Effects Register: *see Register of Effects*

Effluent: *see Liquid Waste*

EIA: *see Environmental Impact Assessment*

EIA Directive

The Directive 337/85/EEC requires that an assessment be carried out on development projects which are likely to have significant effects on the environment before consent is granted. Developers must supply certain information, and the public and certain authorities must be consulted. The directive is implemented in the UK under the Town and Country Planning (Assessment of Environmental Effects) Regulations 1988. The activities are listed as follows.

Projects Subject to Mandatory Environmental Assessment

These projects include:

- crude oil refineries, installations for gasification and liquefaction of 500 tonnes or more of coal or bituminous shale per day;
- thermal power stations and other combustion installations with a heat output of 300 megawatts or more, nuclear power stations, nuclear reactors (except research installations with less than one kilowatt continuous thermal load);
- permanent storage or final disposal installations for radioactive waste;
- integrated works for the initial smelting of cast iron and steel;
- certain installations for the extraction and processing of *asbestos*;
- integrated *chemical* installations;
- construction of motorways, express roads, long-distance railway lines, airports with runway length of 2100 metres or more;
- ports and inland waterways for vessels of over 1350 tonnes;
- waste disposal installations for the incineration, chemical treatment or landfill of toxic and dangerous wastes.

Projects Subject to Voluntary Environmental Assessment (Annex II)

The following categories each have their own subcategories, which are listed in the annex to the directive:

- *agriculture*;
- extractive industry;
- energy industry;
- processing of metals;
- glass manufacture;
- chemical industry;
- food industry;
- textile, leather, wood and paper industries;
- rubber industry;
- infrastructure projects;
- miscellaneous projects;
- modification to development projects included in Annex I and projects in Annex I undertaken exclusively or mainly for the development and testing of new methods or products and not used for more than one year.

An amendment to the directive means that the following extra types of development (among others) now also require an EIA:

- construction or widening of 10 kilometres of dual carriageway;
- incineration or chemical treatment of non-hazardous wastes (with a capacity of more than 100 tonnes a day);
- waste water treatment plants for a population of over 150,000;
- intensive rearing of poultry and pigs over certain thresholds;
- pulp and paper factories;
- quarries and open cast mining (over 25 hectares);
- overhead power lines (over 15 kilometres);
- *dams* (with a capacity exceeding 10 million cubic metres).

EINECS

The European Inventory of Existing Commercial Chemical Substances (*chemicals* that were used between 1971 and 1981).

See also: Evaluation and control of risks of existing substances.

Electrical and Electronic Equipment Industry

Until recently, the industry's impacts included the use of *ozone-depleting substances* in washing components, but this has now been substantially reduced. Other impacts include tin/lead plating, *acids* used in etching and *solid waste* from scrap.

Different parts of the industry have their own impacts: in an assembly operation the impacts are little more than the disposal of faulty products, while a manufacturing plant is likely to use toxic materials and non-renewable resources, and is likely to produce emissions to air and discharges to water.

Outdated or faulty electronic equipment can be stripped down and its parts separated into groups of recoverable products. Old transformers are likely to contain toxic *PCBs*, which must be disposed of carefully. Precious metals can be cropped off or dissolved. Plastics can be granulated and reprocessed into specific materials. Ferrous and non-ferrous metals can be separated and processed.

Cathode ray tubes (CRTs) may also be reprocessed using micro-organisms to digest the heavy and rare earth metals found in CRT coatings. Sulphate-based plating, which produces waste water contaminated with lead and fluoroborate, can be substituted with pure tin.

See also: Computers; IT industry.

Electricity-Generating Industry

The industry's impacts are as follows:

- The use of *fossil fuels*. This can be reduced if the industry turns to *renewable* sources of energy.
- The production of *carbon dioxide*, the main *greenhouse gas*, from power stations.
- The production of *acid rain* from the *sulphur dioxide* and *nitrogen dioxide* emitted to air.
- Visual impact of high-voltage wires. Underground wires are sometimes suggested as a solution, though this can lead to problems over land use.
- Oil contamination: oil can leak from transformers. This is usually resolved by building *bunds* around them. If the bunds are not fully leak-proof, the oil can leak into watercourses. Interceptors can be built into the drainage system as an additional oil trap.
- Presence of hazardous *PCBs* in transformers.
- Noise from overhead lines caused by bad weather, excessive electrical load on the wires or dirty wires.
- Electromagnetic fields (EMF) generated under high voltage lines as well as from other electrical equipment, such as a television set. The higher the voltage, the more intense the field. Despite public concern, many governments believe that no link has yet been found between cancer and EMF.
- Loss of energy during transmission: energy is lost as voltage is stepped up and down, on its passage to and from the high voltage wires.

Best Practice

For industry:

- Invest in *renewable energy* (such as solar power).
- Fit the optimum pollution control technology to existing power stations (for example, flue gas desulphurization).
- Burn low-sulphur fuels in existing power stations.
- Assist consumers to fit low energy lights and insulation and other energy-saving devices.
- Consider adopting underground cable laying. This can reduce the visual intrusion, though burying cables uses five to 14 times more energy and reduces the range of land uses.

See also: CCGT; Electromagnetic radiation; Energy; FGD; Register of effects.

Electromagnetic Fields (EMF): *see Electricity Generating Industry*

Electromagnetic Radiation

Common household appliances, such as vacuum cleaners and food mixers, are thought to emit enough electromagnetic radiation to cause cancer, coronary artery disease, and Parkinson's and Alzheimer's diseases, according to some reports.

Electroplating: *see Plating*

EMAS

Eco-Management and Audit Scheme. A system launched in 1993 by the European Union (in Regulation 1836/93/EEC). It aims to promote good environmental management by manufacturing industry. EMAS is similar to *ISO 14001* except that:

- EMAS applies only to manufacturers (though in the UK it has also been adapted for *local authorities*).
- EMAS requires the company to provide a public report.
- EMAS requires a preliminary review and a Register of Legislation (though it would be difficult to get ISO 14001 without them).

Companies can upgrade from ISO 14001 to *EMAS*, though *CEN* (the association of European standards bodies) is adopting ISO 14001 as a European standard, which may reduce the distinctiveness and attractiveness of EMAS. Uptake of EMAS has been fairly slow. By spring 1996, only seven UK firms had registered. The numbers are likely to grow, however, as more companies develop *EMSs*.

EMAS will be useful for organizations which need to demonstrate environmental performance to their stakeholders. It was at one point the only environmental standard recognized throughout Europe, which was another of its benefits. But as ISO 14001 develops and becomes a formal European standard, EMAS may lose this uniqueness.

ISO 14001 has the elements shown in the outer circle in Figure 5. EMAS has the same elements plus those shown in the central box. Therefore, both standards require a written policy, while only EMAS requires an initial review. That said, it is difficult to construct an ISO 14001 EMS without doing the first three activities shown in the EMAS box – the initial review, registers and control of suppliers.

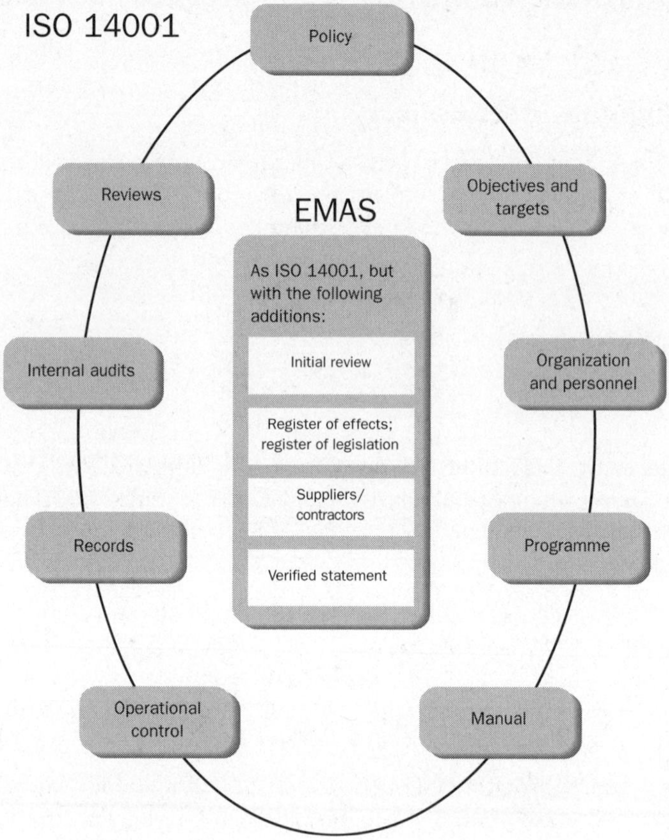

Figure 5: Comparison of EMAS and ISO 14001

How to Gain EMAS

To gain EMAS, the company should carry out seven steps:

- Produce an environmental *policy*.
- Carry out an environmental *review* of the site.
- Develop an environmental *programme*.
- Set up an *environmental management system*.
- Carry out an environmental *audit* (at least every three years).
- Publish an annual environmental *statement*.
- Commission an independent check by an outside body (called a *verifier*). This process is called *validation*. The verifier will inspect the company's environmental policy, programme, management system, audit procedure, and statement.

Once the company has successfully completed these steps, it can apply for EMAS registration. Each EC member state has its own competent body which handles this process. In the UK it is the EMAS Registration Office at the Department of the Environment.

Issuing a public statement may be difficult for some organizations. Many companies do not have site-specific environmental information. As companies increasingly record environmental data, the ease of capturing this information will grow and EMAS registration is likely to increase. In some industries, data are already generally available, notably the chemical industry, whose Responsible Care Programme has prepared companies for some aspects of EMAS.

Environmental performance reporting (EPR) may also be difficult for firms unused to public disclosure. Many will feel uncomfortable sharing information about their pollution with the public.

EMAS was initially devised by *CEN*, and instituted by the EC as Regulation 1836/93. This means it is directly applicable in all member states, but is applied voluntarily by companies to their individual sites.

EMAS Structure

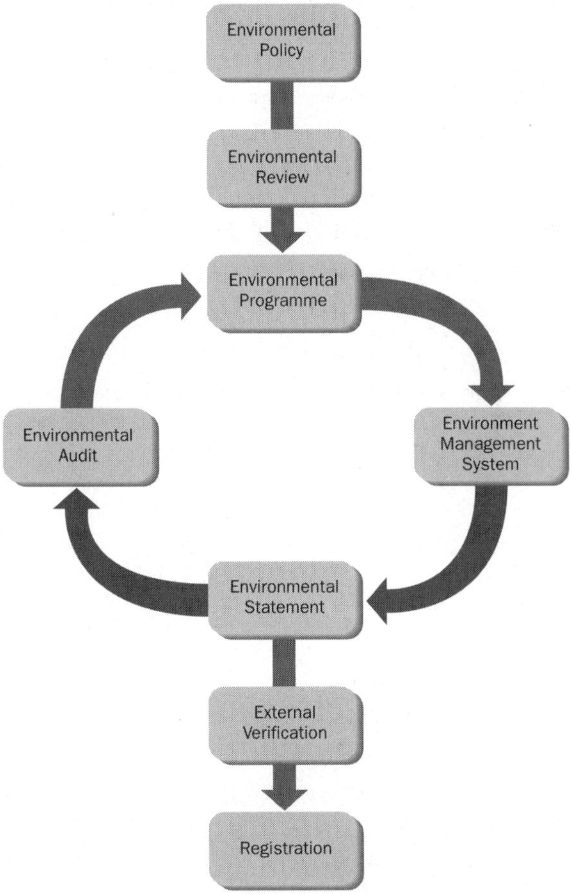

Figure 6: The EMAS Structure

See also: BS 7750; Environmental management system; ISO 14001; SCEEMAS; Statement.

Emergencies

Even the best run plant can suffer an emergency, which is why an emergency plan is essential. Some environmental problems (such as seepage) are gradual and often go unnoticed for years. If they contaminate land or water courses they may result in major litigation. However, the kinds of problems that create emergencies are those that are instantaneous and visible, such as the accidental release of chemicals into a river, causing a fish kill. This is often caused by corroded pipes, faulty couplings, the failure of effluent control equipment, or employee error. The emission of air pollution is also included in this category, often caused by a process error or the failure of filtration equipment.

A third kind of emergency involves fire or explosion, which is mainly a health and safety problem, though it will have environmental consequences as well.

The Emergency Plan

The organization should define its likely emergencies and should produce a plan to prevent them and to handle them should they occur. The plan should involve liaison with the municipal authority and the emergency services (such as fire and ambulance), and other statutory organizations (such as the water authorities).

The plan should outline the steps to be taken in the event of an emergency. It should allocate roles and responsibilities, and ensure that an emergency can be handled at any time of the day or night, including holidays and weekends. Some companies set up a crisis centre, which is the focal point for information and decisions. It helps to insulate the managers from day-to-day issues and improves communication.

The company should practise emergency procedures regularly, which will include simulating a serious incident. Furthermore, the plan should be revised regularly, to take into account changes in processes, procedures and the outside world.

What Constitutes a Crisis?

It is often difficult to determine whether a crisis really exists. Therefore, the emergency plan should define the word 'crisis'. This might entail:

- a threat to the long term reputation of the business;
- a potential cost equal to a proportion of annual turnover (say, 25 per cent), whether in sales decline, the costs of a recall, or in clean-up costs;
- the risk of widespread litigation;
- an interruption of business of a given time period (say, a week);
- effluent levels exceeding a given toxicity;
- the number of accidents reaching a certain level (forecasting a more major problem).

The company should have a management information system which indicates when these indicators reach critical limits.

Four Steps To Take In a Crisis

(1) Stop the problem. This could mean ceasing production of the product or turning off a valve.

(2) Instigate emergency procedures quickly – institute the emergency plan. This might involve mop-up operations.
(3) Liaise with media, customers and the authorities. Set up a hot line if appropriate. Be honest with people and communicate fully.
(4) Restart the business; get production flowing again, possibly using subcontract facilities.

Best Practice

When planning for a crisis:

- Carry out scenario planning: determine what kinds of emergencies could happen.
- Develop an emergency plan for each potential crisis area.
- Ensure that major threats are controlled by fail-safe alarm and shut-down systems.
- Nominate an emergency planning manager.
- Assign other roles and responsibilities. Ensure that the roles are understood.
- Test the plan: practise emergency procedures regularly.
- Implement a management system to prevent emergencies.
- Manage the media: build a good long-term rapport against the possibility of a future emergency.

Emergency Planning and Community Right-to-Know Act – USA

The 1986 Act requires the introduction of local emergency planning procedures to cope with *chemical* emergencies. This includes a requirement for companies to lodge information about their hazardous chemicals with responsible local officials.

The act also mandated the development of a national inventory of the release of toxic chemicals from manufacturing plants (the *Toxics Release Inventory*). This is designed to provide the public with information about the chemicals to which they may be exposed.

Emissions: *see Air Pollution*

EMS Audit

There are two stages to an EMS (environmental management system) audit.

1 *Adequacy audit:* This checks that the organization's manual conforms to the standard.
2 *Compliance audit:* This follows the adequacy audit and checks that staff are complying with the procedures contained in the manual.

The audit is less concerned with protecting the environment than ensuring that procedures are being adhered to. It is also worth noting that an EMS audit is not the same as 'surveillance' or 'inspection'.

If the company wants to be formally registered to a standard, such as *ISO 14001*, the EMS will have to be audited by an independent *certifier*. It also follows that the *certifier* cannot fault the company or its staff for failing to do something that is not in the manual (providing that the manual conforms to the standard). In other words, the audit will check that the system conforms to 'planned arrangements'. For example, if the manual does not require the company to recycle its *solid waste*, the auditor cannot criticize the lack of recycling initiative.

Objectives

The first task is to define the objectives of the audit, for example:

- determine whether the manual complies with the standard;
- see whether the system is being effectively maintained;
- identify areas for improvement;
- evaluate the EMS of an organization where you want to create a relationship (for example, with a potential supplier).

Roles

When undertaking an audit, there are four main roles:

1. The lead auditor: who has overall control of the audit. In allocating responsibilities, the auditor may concern himself with the strategic issues (such as the adequacy of the Register of Effects or the objectives).
2. *Auditors:* These are members of the audit team and may be given specific areas to audit.
3. *Auditee:* the manager whose department is being audited. The auditee will liaise with the lead auditor and make arrangements for interviews. He will provide information and receive the audit report.
4. *Client:* the organization which is being audited. The client is personified by a senior manager, who approves the audit plan.

Checking Procedures and Other Elements

The company's procedures should cover processes which have major environmental impacts. Typically, they include:

- use of raw materials, especially scarce or hazardous ones;
- liquid waste;
- disposal of *solid waste*;
- *air emissions*.

The auditor will also check whether the other elements of the EMS are working properly. He will check whether:

- the policy is understood by staff and acted upon;
- records are kept properly;
- reviews have been carried out and the findings acted upon;
- personnel are deployed as stated in the manual and can perform their environmental responsibilities;
- the management programme is being carried out as indicated in the manual;
- non-conformances from previous audits have been cleared up;
- no hitherto unobserved impacts are taking place.

It is sensible to amalgamate audits for different systems (notably *ISO 9000* and *ISO 14001*). This reduces the amount of auditing time and discourages the development of two paper mountains. This implies that in-house auditors need to be trained to carry out environmental, health and safety and quality audits. It also implies the need for checklists so that nothing is missed.

Best Practice

- Ensure that the organization has written procedures for all processes that have environmental impacts.
- Make sure that EMS audits regularly check conformance to these procedures.

See also: Environmental management system; ISO 14001; EMAS; Process; Procedures.

EMS: *see Environmental Management System*

Endangered Species Act – US

1973 law protecting endangered species. The act made it illegal to kill, injure or harass any species which is listed in the act as being endangered or threatened (species at less risk). The law limited the development of public and private land containing threatened plants and animals. Nearly 900 creatures are now listed and a further 4000 are under review for possible inclusion.

The law helped many species recover, notably the bald eagle – symbol of the US. Likewise, the number of alligators has recovered, after being severely reduced by excessive hunting. After effective state enforcement, the alligator now provides an important source of income through hunting and exports.

The act, however, is controversial because it hinders loggers, mine companies, oil companies, farmers and developers from using the land. When the northern spotted owl was added to the list, loggers had to reduce their harvest in Washington and Oregon. As unemployment spread in the industry, loggers said that the owl was being given priority over people's livelihoods.

See also: Extinction.

End of Pipe

The goal of controlling pollution after it has been created, for example by filtration. It is better to prevent the creation of pollution in the first place by using a different process or different raw materials.

Endosulfan

Broad spectrum organochlorine *insecticide*, on the UK government's *Red List* of dangerous chemicals.

Best Practice

- Avoid use if possible.

Energy

Energy comes from two types of fuel: renewable and non-renewable.

- Non-renewables include gas, coal and oil (the *fossil fuels*).
- *Nuclear energy* is a non-renewable fuel with a different set of environmental issues.
- Renewable fuels include solar energy (from the sun), water power (including tidal barriers) and wind power.

Impacts

When burnt, fossil fuels cause global warming through their emissions of *carbon dioxide*, the main *greenhouse gas*, as well as *acid rain* from emissions of *sulphur dioxide*.

Emissions

Of the non-renewable energies, coal produces the greatest amount of carbon dioxide (as Table 4 shows).

Table 4: Relative Emissions to Air, through Industrial Boilers

	SO_2	NO_x	CO_2
Coal	100	100	100
Oil	12	51	83
Gas	1	24	67

Environmentally, coal is the dirtiest of the *fossil fuels*, though technology can reduce the air pollution it causes. Fluidized bed plants and flue gas desulphurization use limestone to remove the sulphur, which in turn reduces *acid rain*. Coal is safe in transit, storage and combustion, unlike oil (which is renowned for its tanker pollution), gas pipelines and spent nuclear fuel. It is also in plentiful supply.

Renewable Energy

Renewables do not cause pollution because they harness natural forces to produce an electric current, which may be stored in a battery. However, renewables have the following impacts:

- Wind turbines may be visually intrusive and can be noisy.
- Hydroelectric power can cause the loss of *wildlife* habitats through *dams*, flooding and the silting of waterways.

Uses: energy is used to provide *transport* (in *cars* and planes), to power equipment (such as computers), to provide heating, lighting and hot water.

Best Practice

- Companies should have an environmentally sound energy policy and practices.

See also: Electricity generating industry; Energy; Energy management; Fossil fuels; Fuel cells; Nuclear energy; Renewable resources.

Energy from Waste (EFW)

Reclaiming the energy value of a product though incineration. Switzerland recovers energy from 72 per cent of its municipal *solid waste*, while the UK recovers only 5 per cent.

Energy from waste is seen as an alternative by those who believe that *recycling* is good and incineration is bad. Proponents of incineration say that recycling inexpensive materials (such as plastics) can never be truly cost-effective.

There are 50 EFW plants world wide, three of which are in the UK. At St Leonards-on-Sea in the UK, Reprotech processes 75,000 tonnes of waste from local homes, for which it has a long-term contract from the municipal authority, East Sussex County Council. Each year the company recovers up to 25,000 tonnes of light plastic, paper and cardboard which it manufactures into waste-derived fuel pellets and sells to power stations for conversion into electricity. It also recovers and sells 2500 tonnes of tin cans and 150 tonnes of aluminium.

See also: Cement; Incineration; Recycling; Waste management.

Energy Label

A European-wide label that applies an energy rating (*A* for the most efficient to *G* for the least efficient) to 'white goods', such as washing machines and fridges. It carries information about the machine's energy consumption, temperature and noise levels where appropriate.

See also: Eco-label.

Energy Management

Conserving energy has four benefits:

(1) It saves money (one company saved £4 million a year, representing 15 per cent of its annual *energy* bill. The previous year it had saved a further £6 million).
(2) Energy conservation reduces *acid rain* caused by power station emissions.
(3) It reduces *global warming* by cutting the amount of *carbon dioxide* emitted by power stations.
(4) It slows the consumption of non-renewable resources (eg oil) and reduces the pollution caused by their extraction (eg oil pollution).

Low-Cost Measures in Buildings

There are many low-cost measures that organizations can adopt to save energy in buildings. These often provide the greatest cost/benefit results:

- Insulate buildings (particularly roof *insulation*, draft proofing, heating pipes and the use of double glazing). Automatic doors also reduce energy loss.
- Install low energy lights, or install energy-saving lights which only operate in response to movement.
- Purchase low energy appliances.
- Improve maintenance of boilers.

- Improve building maintenance (for example, repair of broken windows which let in draughts).
- Install thermostatic controls on radiators.
- Educate and train staff to conserve energy by switching off unnecessary lights and equipment).

Higher Cost Investment

- Install new energy-efficient boilers.
- Install *combined heat and power systems* which reuse waste heat.
- Design new buildings so as to use minimum energy.
- Install automatic energy management systems which monitor temperature and humidity, and provide the right heating and ventilation.

Plant and Equipment

Energy conservation in plant and equipment can be gained by:

- using energy-efficient equipment, especially when replacing old equipment;
- preventing energy losses, especially steam losses and heating lost from pipes which have not been insulated.

Best Practice

To reduce its energy use, management should take the following steps:

- Create an energy policy.
- Commission an energy *audit*.
- Set targets for energy use.
- Monitor consumption.
- Introduce an energy management programme, using the low and higher cost measures mentioned above.

See also: Distribution, physical; Heating; Insulation.

Energy Star

An energy conservation label set up by the US government's Environmental Protection Agency in 1993. The award is given to PCs and monitors which consume less than 30 watts in standby mode, and printers which consume less than 30 to 45 watts depending on their type.

See also: Energy label.

Engineering Industry

Not so much a single industry as a set of related disciplines. Engineering has the capability to either pollute or protect the environment (depending, for example, on whether it is used to build a *fossil fuel* power station or one using *renewable energy*).

Many branches of engineering have comparatively little impact on the environment (such as electronics engineering), but below we consider three main disciplines that have impacts: mechanical, electrical and civil.

Mechanical Engineering

This branch of the industry is often concerned with the production of manufactured goods, as well as vehicle (automotive, aerospace and naval) design and maintenance. Its impacts include those associated with:

- *welding* and brazing;
- *metal working* and anodizing;
- *liquid waste*;
- *noise*;
- *heating* and *air conditioning*; refrigeration;
- industrial gases;
- production control;
- lubricants.

Electrical Engineering

This part of engineering is related to power generation (including the production of electricity) and to the use of electricity in buildings and vehicles. Its impacts concern:

- the choice of fuels (whether *fossil fuel*, *nuclear* or *renewable energies*);
- battery technology;
- environmental controls (for *heating* and energy conservation);
- power lines;
- electrical and battery powered vehicles;
- ovens and welding.

Civil Engineering

This branch of engineering is concerned with the construction of projects on the land, such as roads and bridges. Its areas of impact are as follows:

- highways, airports, railways;
- water supply issues (*water pollution*, *water conservation*);
- construction industry issues (site management, use of materials).

Best Practice

- Engineers should reduce their burden on the environment, by designing systems that use the least energy and materials, that produce the least noise, that create the least waste, and that result in the least air and water pollution. The use of environmental *audits* or *EIA*, and the application of an *EMS*, will help to ensure that this is achieved.

See also: Design, environmental; Electricity supply industry; Liquid waste; Markets for environmental technology; Motor industry; Technology; Waste management.

Envirometrics

The measurement of an organization's impacts on the environment (through *performance* measures or indicators).

Environment

The surroundings in which an organization operates, including air, water, land, plants, animals, humans and their interrelation. It was once thought that we could pollute the world without penalty. This was the theory of '*dilute and disperse*' – the idea that the oceans were big enough to absorb our waste. Now we are learning that our past will come back to haunt us, sometimes in surprising ways. The hole in the *ozone layer*, which can result in skin cancers, was caused by *chemicals* which for decades were thought to be harmless. Tall chimneys carry acidic emissions far away, but they kill the forests of distant nations. *Global warming*, produced by human activity all over the world, could end up altering the surprisingly fragile weather system, with consequences for food production and the flooding of low-lying areas.

See also: Extinction; Nature conservation; Pollution; Sustainable development.

Environment Act 1995 – UK

The Environment Act 1995 (EA 95) created the Environment Agency; a contaminated land regime; more power to control *water* and *air pollution*; and a *producer-responsibility* programme. EA 95 also includes provisions for abandoned mines, the regulation of National Parks, national waste management plans, and the protection of hedges.

Under EA 95, local authorities must assess their contaminated land and they can enforce their remediation. This can happen where:

- significant harm has occurred or is occurring; or
- the contamination is causing water pollution.

See also: Environment Agency; Contaminated land.

Environment Agency

Many countries in the West have given responsibility for controlling all kinds of pollution to an environment agency, including the original US *Environmental Protection Agency*.

The EU has also set up an agency, the *European Environmental Agency*, which is not, however, an enforcement agency.

UK Environment Agency

The UK's Environment Agency (*SEPA* in Scotland) was set up in 1995 and brought together the functions of the National Rivers Authority (NRA) (*water pollution*, land drainage and flood defence), the waste regulation authorities (waste disposal), and Her Majesty's Inspectorate of Pollution (*solid waste* and *air pollution*).

The agency applies standards by giving authorizations, licences and consents for emissions to air, water and land. It also monitors compliance and enforces the law, including prosecution. The agency is charged with:

- compiling information on pollution;
- assessing the effects of pollution;

- reporting on the options for preventing or reducing pollution;
- conserving the beauty of waterways and associated land;
- conserving water resources;
- maintaining fisheries.

See also: Contaminated land; European Environment Agency; Environmental Protection Agency.

Environmental Audit: *see Audit*

Environmental Choice

Canadian environmental label.

Environmental Impact Assessment (EIA)

Review of the potential impact of a new development, particularly for a new building or a road. It is also known as an EA (Environmental Assessment). An EIA does the following:

- assesses the existing environmental features;
- considers the adverse impacts of the new venture;
- analyses any mitigating factors (such as the preservation of large trees or the creation of a pond);
- adds a non-technical summary.

The EIA assesses the impacts upon *wildlife* and people. It also assesses the impacts from noise, visual intrusion, dust and additional traffic. Note that the term 'environmental impact assessment' is used only to denote an *audit* relating to land development.

The effect of an EIA varies by country. In the US, environmental impact assessment litigation has often favoured conservationists. In the UK, the courts have rarely used assessments to block development. EIAs are also of varying quality and (in the UK) rarely suggest that the venture should not proceed, since the assessments are usually paid for by the developer. A common failing is a lack of detail or a failure to provide a non-technical summary, as required by the regulations. Nevertheless, the EIA may encourage the developer to make environmental improvements that he might not otherwise have considered.

Legislation

In EU member states, all planning applications for major developments must be accompanied by an EIA. This is described above under *EIA Directive*.

SEA

There have been moves in the EU to produce legislation on Strategic Environmental Assessment (SEA). This would require government bodies to assess the impact of their policies, plans or programmes, whether national, regional or local. This is because many projects, such as quarries or roads, often stem from earlier high-level plans. Carrying out a SEA would help to integrate environmental considerations into policies from the outset.

Best Practice

- Companies should commission an EIA on all projects which might affect the local environment.
- Before commissioning an EIA, companies should assess a consultant's ability by examining its previous reports.

See also: Audit, environmental; Construction industry; Consultancies, environmental; Contaminated land; Dams; EIA directive; Extinction; Nature conservation; Oil and gas industry; Statement, environmental.

Environmental Impact: *see Impacts, Environmental*

Environmentally Friendly

This is a vague and therefore meaningless term unless it is qualified. It is better to make specific claims, such as 'made from 100 per cent recycled paper', or 'elemental chlorine free'. Products are rarely 'environmentally friendly' because their production involves the use of *energy*, raw materials, *packaging* and *waste*. The terms 'environmentally responsible' and 'environmentally sound' are sometimes used and are less sweeping terms. The term 'environmental probity' is also used to describe an ethical attitude.

See also: Marketing; Public relations.

Environmentally Sensitive Area – UK

Designated areas of environmental importance where farmers who adopt environmentally friendly methods are given grants. This could include repairing dry stone walls.

Environmental Management System (EMS)

A system for managing a company's environmental *impacts*. The system should be comprehensive, systematic, planned, regular, and documented. The best-known models for an EMS are *ISO 14001*, *EMAS*, and *BS 7750*. An EMS involves the following elements:

- Written objectives and targets for managing environmental impacts.
- Documented (written) procedures to control processes that impact on the environment. These written systems act like the company's bible. Without them, employees may start creating their own ways of doing things, or they may neglect to carry out certain checks.
- Allocation of roles and responsibilities. This ensures that people know who is responsible for what. It is often shown as an organization chart or through written job descriptions.

- Measurements and *audits*. These will reveal the scale of the company's impacts and whether procedures to control them are being followed.
- Reviews of the system (which often look at the results of the audit) to see where it can be improved.

Much of what is contained in an EMS is no more than good business sense, and many of the requirements will already be carried out by the company.

The final stage of implementing an EMS is to have it assessed and registered with an independent *certifier*. This registration demonstrates that the system conforms to the relevant standard (for example, ISO 14001), and is sometimes required by corporate customers.

Why Have an EMS?

An EMS reduces the organization's environmental risk by controlling its impacts in a comprehensive and systematic manner. It can be used to demonstrate legal compliance to regulatory authorities. The EMS also contributes to continuous improvement and cost reduction. An independently verified EMS demonstrates the organization's environmental probity to the outside world and can help to win contracts.

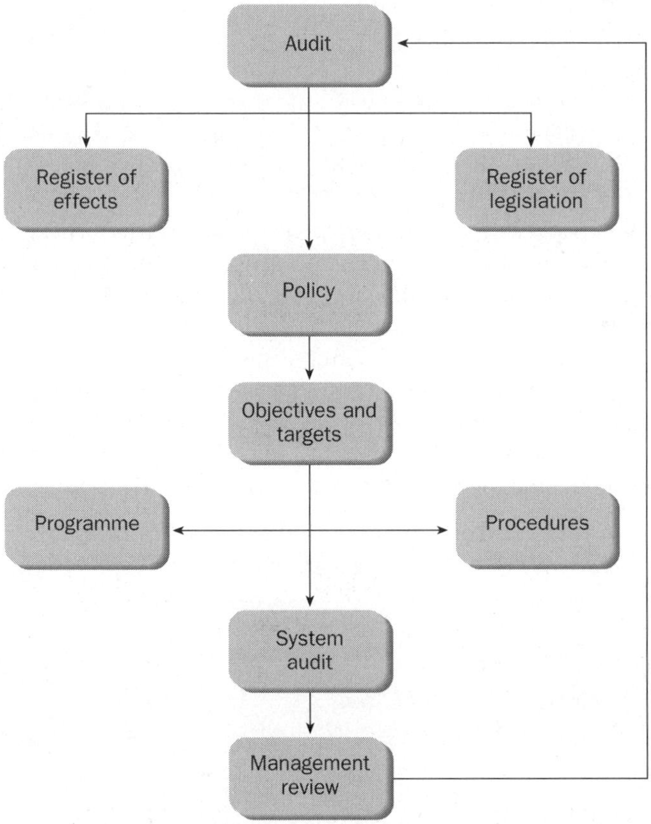

Figure 7: Structure of a Typical Environmental Management System

If the company already has a quality management system (such as ISO 9000), it makes sense to incorporate the environmental EMS inside it. This avoids duplication of meetings and audits. This in turn requires coordinating quality and environmental management. Elements that can usefully be combined are:

- document control;
- *operational control* and work instructions;
- information systems (computer information);
- *training*;
- organizational structure;
- measuring and monitoring;
- *reporting* and *communication*.

To officially gain ISO 14001 or EMAS, the company has to submit to an *audit* by an outside *certifier* (also known as a *verifier*). This audit, which is usually carried out every six to 12 months, ensures that the company is not letting its standards drop.

Is It Worthwhile?

Some companies reject the certified EMS approach adopted by ISO 14001 and EMAS, believing that it is too rigid and adds bureaucracy. Such organizations believe that by adopting 'rudimentary gauging' (NatWest Bank), they can control 80 to 90 per cent of their waste. The bank believes that the time and cost of controlling the remainder would yield little extra environmental advantage. It holds that sophisticated measurement systems are not appropriate for service industries such as financial services, whose impacts – such as paper and energy – are more akin to domestic activities.

Environmentalists, on the other hand, have criticized the certifiers' 'eco-logos' on the grounds that their attainment does not indicate good environmental performance. The logo merely indicates that the company is complying with a standard such as EMAS. The standard itself merely indicates a consistent approach to the environment, and is not a measure of excellence (though ISO 14001 requires the organization to commit itself to continuous improvement).

Whether or not the company opts for certification, an EMS makes it less likely to face an environmental problem or litigation. It also gives the company more information about, and more control over, its impacts and processes.

Table 5: Comparison of EMAS and ISO 14001

Issue	EMAS	ISO 14001
Develop an environmental policy; make it publicly available?	Yes	Yes
Carry out preliminary environmental review?	Yes	No
Set targets?	Yes	Yes
Develop an environmental programme?	Yes	Yes

Issue *(cont.)*	**EMAS** *(cont.)*	**ISO 14001** *(cont.)*
Environmental audits?	Yes. Assesses not only the EMS but also the company policy and site programme requirements, including legislation.	Yes. But ISO 14001 does not specify audit frequency, nor is the audit methodology set out in detail.
Publicly publish an environmental statement?	Yes	No
Make the programme publicly available?	Yes	No
Make the environmental management system publicly available?	Yes	No
Get independent validation?	Yes	Yes
Produce a register of effects?	Yes	No. But the firm must document activities that have an impact on the environment. This is tantamount to requiring a register of effects.
Produce a register of legislation?	Yes	No. But the firm must identify its legal requirements.
Must contractors and suppliers be controlled?	Yes	No – the firm merely communicates the required procedures.
What types of organization can get certified?	Only certain industries (and local government in the UK).	All kinds of organizations.
Who can get certified – sites or organizations?	Only sites.	Organizations or sites can participate.
Developed by:	European Committee for Standardisation (CEN)	International Standards Organization (ISO)
Recognized where?	Europe-wide.	World-wide.

Best Practice

- Evaluate the potential for controlling the organization's impacts by introducing an EMS.
- Draw up a plan for introducing an EMS.

See also: BS 7750; Documentation; EMAS; Human resources; ISO 14001; Objectives; Programme; Strategy; Targets.

Environmental Performance Reporting: *See EMAS*

Environmental Protection Act 1990 – UK

The act, known as EPA 90, (together with the *Water Act*) introduced the principle of 'the polluter pays' to the UK and required polluting processes to be registered. The act divided industrial processes into potentially highly polluting processes (Part A) and less polluting processes (Part B).

Part A processes are regulated by the *Environment Agency*, while Part B processes are controlled by the local authority (Local Authority Air Pollution Control – LAAPC). Manufacturers must obtain from the agency or local authority a licence to carry out the process, and they have to pay for each process. The company must apply BATNEEC (Best Available Techniques Not Entailing Excessive Cost). Process guidance notes show companies the BATNEEC for each process.

EPA 90 also introduced the 'duty of care' on anyone who produces or transports waste, and required the latter to become licensed. Penalties under the act include prison and unlimited fines.

Environmental Protection Agency (EPA) – USA

Pioneering US federal agency set up in 1970 by President Nixon to ensure compliance with environmental clean-up laws. The EPA has substantially reduced pollution in the US, due to the introduction of stringent federal laws. For example, the emission of *particulates* has fallen from nearly 25 million tonnes a year to under ten million.

Recently, the EPA has introduced the Common Sense Initiative (CSI). This is an attempt at consensus-based reform. The CSI focuses on the environmental performance of entire industries. It has chosen six sectors, representing 12 per cent of industry's total *toxic emissions* and 10 per cent of gross domestic product (GDP): automotive assembly, computers and electronics, iron and steel, metal finishing, petroleum refining, and printing.

The Environmental Defense Fund is concerned that CSI is really deregulation in disguise. Some see it as a reflection of Republican hostility to federal laws. But the EPA believes that CSI is an opportunity to find 'cleaner, cheaper, smarter' alternatives to a regulatory system that is inflexible, high-cost and diminishing in returns.

See also: Toxics Release Inventory.

Environmental Statement: *see Statement, Environmental*

Enzymes

Enzymes increase the rate of some chemical reactions by acting as a catalyst. They are used in laundry liquid and washing powder. They help remove protein stains (egg, chocolate, milk and blood). They enable washing to be done at lower temperatures, and thus save energy. Enzymes are not harmful to the environment.

EQO/EQS – EU

In the European Union, an Environmental Quality Objective relates to the quality of receiving water (for example, a lake) after being mixed with discharges. The water should be suitable for its designated use (such as bathing water). This is measured by pH or levels of arsenic or copper in the water.

In the UK, EQO stands for Environmental Quality Order. An EQO defines the use that is to be made of a particular river or lake (for example, suitable for drinking water). The EQS (Environmental Quality Standards) then define the concentrations of *chemicals* below which there will be no effect on the EQO.

See also: UES; WQO

Ethical Investment

Investing in socially responsible funds. This includes avoiding companies that damage the environment. There are two main types of investment. The first are ethical trusts which avoid investing in alcohol, tobacco, gambling, armaments, film producers, and those trading with unsavoury regimes. The second type are the green trusts which invest in companies that clean up or reduce pollution.

Despite interest from individual investors, corporate fund managers have been slow to adopt ethical policies. In 1995 a UK study showed that even among charities, which are likely to be more aware of ethics, only 7 per cent had imposed ethical restrictions on their investments. This is partly because of constraints imposed on trustees to invest for maximum returns and for the benefit of the members. Such constraints are, however, being progressively loosened to permit ethical investment.

Green and ethical unit trusts perform at least as well as the average unit trust. A survey by Micropal showed that over three years ethical and green funds returned UK£150 for every UK£100 invested, compared with UK£149 for trusts as a whole.

Sin Stocks Do Well

In spite of this, companies selling non-ethical products ('sin stocks'), such as alcohol, tobacco, gambling, fast food and armaments, also fare well according to a survey by the *Sunday Times*. They comprise 13 per cent of the UK's *Financial Times* All-Share index by value, and they tend to outperform the market. The survey showed that between 1985 and 1995 sin stocks easily beat the *Financial Times* All-Share Index, and massively outperformed the two longest running ethical funds run by Friends Provident and United Charities. Ethical investors may choose to accept a lower return as the cost of conscientious investment.

There are many shades of grey in terms of 'sin stocks', and advisers may offer the investor a choice of whether a company derives less than 10 or 20 per cent of its revenue from pollution. Moreover, a company which had a strongly positive environmental stance could outweigh a weak negative score on another criterion. No company is perfect, so fund managers like Friends Provident look for firms which are 'caring rather than harming', and those that are doing more good than harm.

Best Practice

- Companies should ensure that their products and services do not pollute, thus avoiding future rejection by investors.

Ethylene Dichloride

Dangerous substance on the UK *Red List* of dangerous substances.

Ethylene: *see Hydrocarbons*

Ethylene Oxide

Dangerous *chemical* whose import, export, marketing and use in the EC is controlled (Regulation EC 3135/94).

Best Practice

- Avoid its use.

Euro II

European emission standard for diesel engines.

Best Practice

- Assess whether the organization's vehicles conform to Euro II and plan the phasing-out of non-conforming vehicles.

European Environmental Agency – EU

Based in Copenhagen, the European Environmental Agency (EEA) was established by the European Union through a regulation passed in May 1990. The EEA reports not to the EU Commission but to its own management board and scientific committee. This is designed to help the agency be independent and credible, an important factor in the battle between European nations.

The EEA collects and analyses environmental data, to assist the EU in improving its decision-making on the environment, and to ensure that the public is fully informed about the state of the environment. However, it is not an enforcement agency. For instance, the EEA does not aim to expand into managing environmental issues, arbitrate on conflicts, or oversee the implementation of EU legislation. The agency's prime interest is in ground *water pollution* by *pesticides, heavy metals* and *nitrates*, which the agency is determined to arrest. Other concerns are:

- polluted and derelict industrial sites, which the agency believes are a time bomb that will eventually affect the water-table;
- urban pollution from *organic* compounds and micro-contaminants;
- the quantity of domestic and industrial waste – it wants to find ways to reduce the rubbish problem;
- nature conservation, which is in need of evaluation, according to the agency – it wants to see more conservation of forests and prevention of soil erosion.

The EEA also aims to improve the quality of information provided by European states, which is often inadequate and which prevents a proper analysis of the environmental position.

See also: Environment Agency; Environmental Protection Agency.

European Waste Catalogue – EU

Published in the *Official Journal* L 5/15, January 1994. It is a harmonized list of wastes intended to provide common terminology throughout the community. A separate list of hazardous wastes is drawn up under the Hazardous Waste Directive (91/689/EEC).

Eutrophication

Process whereby rivers become clogged with weeds and green algae. This depletes the oxygen in the water, leading to the death of fish. It also blocks out the sunlight, stopping photosynthesis. The solids also sink to the river bed and form a blanket which smothers other species.

Eutrophication (which means 'good food') is caused by nutrient-rich *fertilizer* and *sewage* or other *organic* matter leaching into the water. There its micro-organisms, together with the algae already in the river, consume large amounts of oxygen and increase in size, leading to 'algal bloom'.

See also: Agriculture; Nitrogen; Organic; Water pollution.

EVABAT

Economically Viable Application of Best Available Technology. The same principle as *BATNEEC*.

Evaluation and Control of Risks of Existing Substances – EU

Directive 793/93/EC. If a company makes or imports a quantity of dangerous substances (as listed by the EU in *EINECS*), it has to submit its data to the EU. Greater controls exist for bigger quantities.

Extinction

Different species have always flourished or become extinct, but today man's impact on the environment is causing 25,000 times the normal loss of species. The problem started back in 1681 when mankind made the dodo, a flightless bird that lived in Mauritius, extinct.

Britain has lost more than 100 species this century, including the horned dung beetle, last seen in 1955, and the mouse eared bat, last seen in 1990. In the USA, 500 plant and animals species have ceased to exist since the 1500s. Species become extinct when their food or habitat is destroyed. This is caused, for example, by logging and by development – the building of roads or buildings – which in turn is caused by population growth, the growing number of cars, society's affluence and mobility. The US Wilderness Society reckons that up to 20 per cent of the world's existing species could have become extinct by the year 2000.

Species are also being brought to extinction by hunting. For example, the Indochinese tiger is hunted in Cambodia, Burma, Vietnam and Laos so remorselessly that the entire subspecies could be extinct within ten years. Tigers are sometimes killed to protect livestock, but most are hunted because they are used in Chinese medicine and for the magical powers thought to be conferred by their teeth, skin, claws and whiskers. Similarly, rhinoceroses have been slaughtered for their horn, which is thought by some people in developing countries to have aphrodisiac powers. Gamekeepers now cut off rhinoceroses' horns, to make the beasts valueless to poachers.

It is important to prevent abnormal extinction because plants and animals provide raw materials for drugs, disease-resistant crops and other genetic material. Only 1 per cent of wild species have been analysed.

Best Practice

- Commission an *EIA* before undertaking any development.
- Avoid development in areas which are home to scarce or declining species.
- Do not buy products whose production has caused the loss of habitats (such as plywood made from rainforest timber).
- Farmers should aid biodiversity by adopting greener methods.

See also: Nature conservation; Wildlife trade.

Exxon Valdez

Exxon-owned oil tanker which spilt more than 200,000 bbl. of oil on Prince William Sound, Alaska, in March 1989. The accident is reputed to have cost the company US$5 billion by 1994, with a further US$5 billion threatened by the courts.

In 1991, Exxon agreed to pay US$1 billion to settle state and federal claims. The company pleaded guilty to four federal misdemeanour criminal charges. In 1994, Exxon was ordered to pay punitive damages of US$5 billion and US$287 million compensation for damage to fish stocks. The payment was to be divided among fishermen, property owners, native Alaskans and coastal authorities. The civil and criminal recoveries (damages) were thought to be the largest ever in an environmental case. Exxon was expected to appeal.

See also: Amoco Cadiz; Ceres Principles; Kuwait; Oil and gas industry; Shell.

Fertilizers

Used as a plant feed to increase the size of crops. Fertilizers tend to be *nitrogen-* or *phosphate-*based and their excessive use causes river pollution. This happens when too much nitrogen or phosphate seeps into the water course, where it promotes the growth of algae, which clog the river and take out oxygen from the water.

See also: Eutrophication; Phosphates.

Fetotoxic

Capable of damaging the foetus in the womb. Such substances include *dioxin*.

FGD

Flue Gas Desulphurization. A method of extracting sulphur from the flue gases in coal-fired power stations and industry, to reduce *acid rain*. For every 10 million tonnes of coal burned, FGD reduces *sulphur dioxide* emissions from 265,000 tonnes to 26,000 tonnes. The extra output is 700,000 tonnes of limestone which can be converted into one million tonnes of limestone and is sold to industry for making into plaster and plasterboard. However, FGD is expensive: fitting it in one power station alone, Drax in England, cost UK£685 million.

An FGD unit cost Holliday Pigments of Hull, England, UK£7.2 million, but cut sulphur dioxide emissions by 99.5 per cent, from 4000 tonnes to just 20. The company makes ultramarine pigment, used in plastics, cosmetics, paints and coatings. The raw materials for ultramarine are china clay, soda ash and sulphur which, when heated together, produce the distinctive blue colour. At Holliday Pigments, the FGD plant converts the sulphur dioxide into high-quality sulphuric acid, which is then sold.

See also: Energy; Electricity generating industry; Sulphur dioxide.

Filling Stations

Impacts include:

- Leaking underground storage tanks can contaminate the land.
- Emission of benzene, a *VOC* which is a carcinogen and a contributor to smog. This is released when storage tanks or vehicles are being filled.

Federal regulations in the US to protect ground water include compulsory liability insurance, leak detection systems and anti-corrosive tanks. When published in 1991, it was feared that the regulations would lead to the closure of half of all retail gasoline stations, especially those in small towns, due to the cost of compliance. It is thought that the European industry might face similar controls in the future.

Benzene vapours can be controlled by vapour-balancing and recovery equipment at filling stations. EU legislation requires all major filling stations to be equipped with vapour recovery.

See also: Garages; Resource Conservation and Recovery Act.

Financial Services: *see Banking and Finance Industry*

Fine Paper: *see Paper*

Fire Protection

In uncontrolled circumstances fire has major environmental consequences. It can release *toxins* and *particulates* and destroy people, other species and assets. A fire risk strategy starts with a fire survey, which should be carried out at regular intervals. This will identify the most likely causes of fire and indicate how to prevent them. The *audit* should cover all areas of the building, including production facilities, offices, storage areas, basements and roof spaces. Fires often start in unlikely places because these are the areas where fire safety has been overlooked.

In assessing the risks of fire, *auditors* should look at the main causes of fire: electrical hazards, hot work, smoking, flammable liquids, and the threat of arson. In recent years, the use of *halon* fire extinguishers has been criticised. Halon, while effective at putting out fires, is an *ozone-depleting substance*. Therefore, the organization should check whether its extinguishers are halon based; if they are, it should take advice on replacing them.

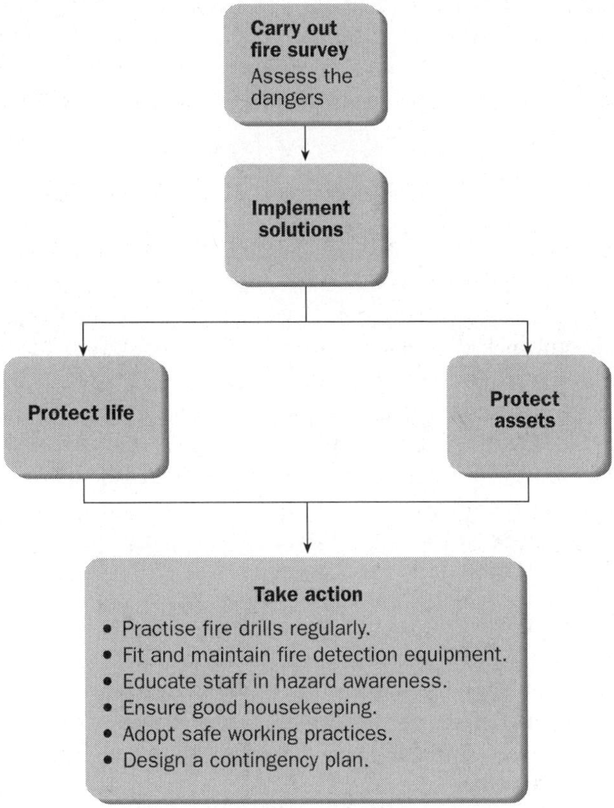

Figure 8: Fire Protection Starts with a Survey

Best Practice

- Carry out a fire audit and then take appropriate action to minimize the likelihood of fire.
- Consider replacing halon extinguishers.

Fishing Industry

The main impact of the fishing industry is the depletion of fish stocks in the oceans, caused by overfishing. Many species are now endangered as a result.

Overfishing

Overfishing in the North Sea during the 1960s and 1970s led to the collapse of sea mackerel and herring stocks. Mackerel has never recovered, but herring, which recovered after a ban, has sunk again to dangerously low levels. Part of the problem are industrial fisheries. Over half the weight of fish caught in the North Sea is for industrial processing whose catch will become pig food and oil for margarine, biscuits and cakes. Unilever, Sainsbury's and McVities have decided to stop using fish oil from industrial fisheries, and this decision has been seen as an example of *sustainable* corporate behaviour.

The EU and national governments are seeking to make the industry operate in a sustainable way by cutting the catches. This is being done by imposing quotas and by offering incentives to boat owners to take boats out of commission. These measures are causing frustration in communities which traditionally earned their living from fishing.

Fish Farming and Pollution

To reduce the uncertainty, cost, dangers and seasonality of sea fishing, the industry has increasingly turned to fish farming. While this has boosted the local economy, there are also fears about the environmental problems caused by 'intensive aquaculture', involving captive fish which are treated with growth hormones and chemical *pesticides* and fungicides. In Scotland, lochs have been polluted and wild fish genes affected by the escape of introduced farmed species.

In Thailand, India and Bangladesh, king prawns are now produced in land-based ponds filled with sea water, fish meal, chemicals and *fertilizers*. The salt water and contaminated waste have polluted coastal areas, depriving fishermen and rice growers of their livelihood. Large areas of mangrove swamp have been destroyed, depleting fish stocks, and agricultural land has been turned from paddy fields into prawn ponds.

Drift nets

Another impact is the 'wall of death' – the long nets that are set to catch tuna. These also catch anything that swims into them, and conservationists have been concerned about the drowning of *dolphins*. Many processors and supermarkets now deal only with suppliers who do not use these nets. The United Nations banned drift nets in 1989.

Best Practice

- Supermarkets, importers and processors should ensure that fish comes from sustainable sources which do not damage the environment or local economies.

See also: Aquariums; Dolphins.

Fleet Factors

A decision of the US Appeals Court (US versus Fleet Factors Corp, May 1990). It ruled that a secured creditor may incur *CERCLA* liability, without being an operator, by participating in the financial management of a company. A 1992 decision by the US *EPA* provided lenders with an exemption, but this was overturned in 1994. The sequence of events was as follows.

(1) Lenders Become Liable

Prior to the case, secured creditors were likely to escape liability for *Superfund* clean-up costs. Fleet Factors, a creditor of a bankrupt borrower, had approved shipment of goods, set prices for inventory, and approved decisions on redundancies. The court refused to limit liability to cases where the secured creditor participated in day-to-day operations. The court decided that the creditor would be liable if it could affect the disposal of *hazardous waste* but chose not to. Furthermore, the court said that potential creditors should investigate thoroughly the waste treatment systems and policies of potential debtors, and should assess their potential liability.

The Fleet Factors decision caused concern to banks and finance companies around the world, who now feel exposed when lending to industry, especially as the ruling may be matched by similar legislation in other countries. In the EC directive on civil liability for damage caused by waste, liability could fall similarly on a secured lender.

(2) EPA Frees Lenders from Liability

In 1992, the US Environmental Protection Agency exempted lenders from the threat of Superfund liability. It ruled that 'owners and operators who without participating in the management' hold ownership primarily to protect security interest would be exempt.

(3) Lenders Become Liable Again

However, in 1994, in the case Kelley versus EPA, a US court overturned the EPA's exemption of lenders from liability. The Chemical Manufacturers Association and the State of Michigan brought the case, not wanting to be prevented from suing lenders. The court agreed that the EPA did not have the right to define the scope for lender liability, and that CERCLA had designated the courts, not the EPA, as the adjudicator of the scope of CERCLA liability. However, the petitioners acceded that the EPA's rule could be sustained as a policy statement, which leaves the law in some uncertainty.

Best Practice

- Lenders should carry out an assessment of an organization's environmental risks before lending money.

See also: CERCLA; Liability; Superfund.

Flixborough: *see Cyclohexane*

Floor and Wall Tiles

The EU may launch an *eco-label*, following a study by Italy.

Flora and Fauna

Plants and animals, ie *wildlife*.

Flue Gas Desulphurization: *see FGD*

Flue Stack

Chimney, typically in a coal power station or incinerator. The control of flue gases (especially the acids that produce *acid rain*, and toxic gases such as *dioxins*) is important.

See also: Energy; FGD.

Fluidized Bed

A process used to absorb gases and reduce airborne pollution in power stations. It is also used as a heat treatment to harden steel, where it is safer and less environmentally damaging than the traditional salt bath technique.

Fluorine

A *halogen*. Fluorine is corrosive and poisonous.

Best Practice

- Do not use if possible.

Food Chain

Each member of a food chain feeds on the one below. If some species are destroyed (for example, through habitat loss), the food chain will be damaged and larger creatures may also disappear. A simple food chain is: Grass → Cow → Humans. Likewise, if poisons are absorbed by small creatures, they may be passed up the food chain. If mankind is at the top of the food chain, we will consume the poisons. Interconnecting food chains are known as a food web.

Food Processing Industry

The industry is largely controlled by the food retailers, and nowadays the consumer (a stern master) expects fresh food from around the globe irrespective of the season. Today's larger stores need larger suppliers capable of delivering vast quantities of identical food products to central warehouses. All this encourages major suppliers and long-distance distribution.

The impacts of the food processing industry include *solid waste* from food and *packaging*, *energy*, *water use*, and *water pollution*.

Best Practice

Food processors can reduce their impacts through the following measures:

- Recycle food waste for animal feed.
- Improve filtration and treatment of waste water.
- Reduce water use through *closed loop systems* and more process controls.
- Recycle cardboard packaging waste.
- Use returnable *transport* packaging (for example, ingredient drums).
- Process waste into by-products. For example, in the coconut industry, coconut water can be made into juice and the hair into matting.
- Adopt better process control and more training to reduce solid waste.
- Improve stock control to reduce waste.

See also: Agriculture.

Forests: *see Timber – Tropical; Timber Industry – Temperate; Trees*

Forest Stewardship Council (FSC)

Founded in 1993, the FSC is an alliance of environmentalists and industry which has defined world-wide guidelines for *sustainable* forestry. These are applied by certification companies in Britain, the US and other countries. The products from these forests could include paper (virgin paper, since it comes from forests), wooden kitchen utensils, furniture, and wooden-handled tools.

As well as supporting FSC, the supermarket chain Sainsbury's has set up its own 'Timbertracker' programme, which consists of a supplier's questionnaire to check the origin of all products that contain virgin wood or paper. The chain is committed not to buy from suppliers whose products do not come from well-managed forests, or whose origin is unknown. The supermarket is also encouraging its suppliers to become independently certified to FSC.

Best Practice

- Ensure that all wood and paper products that contain virgin fibre come from FSC-registered forests.

See also: Timber industry – temperate; Timber industry – tropical; Trees.

Formaldehyde

Colourless toxic gas. Made from methanol or petroleum gases, it is used to produce synthetic resins and is a disinfectant and a preservative. It is found in chipboard furniture and is sometimes called formalin. One of the *aldehydes*, formaldehyde irritates the mucous membranes of the eyes, nose and throat and is suspected of causing cancer.

Best Practice

- Avoid use where possible.

Fossil Fuels

Oil, coal and gas. They are called fossil fuels because they are the fossilized remains of dead plants and creatures. They produce *greenhouse gas* and *acid rain* when burnt in power stations. They are also finite and *non-renewable*, having been produced through the decay of plants and animals over a period of millions of years. It would take the same length of time to make more of these fuels. Fuel consumption costs money as well as depleting a non-renewable resource, so organizations benefit by reducing their fossil fuel use.

Reserves

At present rates of consumption, the world will have used up its proven supplies of oil in 30 years, and its proven natural gas in 40. Reserves of coal are much more abundant, with enough to last over 200 years. A mere 20 countries control 95 per cent of proven reserves, according to the *Atlas of the Environment*, and more than half of them are in the Middle East.

The industry will undoubtedly discover new reserves (for the world has been forecasting the end of fossil fuel supplies since the 1970s). But these will be less accessible, and all the easily available fuels are already accounted for. For example, the oil in Siberia is difficult to extract and distribute, while most of the discovered but unexploited oil is of relatively low quality.

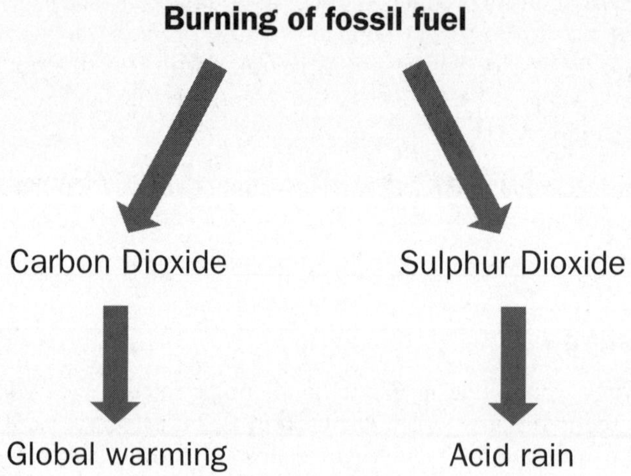

Figure 9: The Impacts of Burning Fossil Fuels

Best Practice

For organizations:

- Record the consumption of fuels.
- Develop a plan to reduce their use.

See also: Energy; Energy management; Renewable resources.

Freedom of Access to Information on the Environment Directive – EU

Directive 90/313 requires member states to ensure that public authorities make available environmental information to anyone on request. This might include matters of marine pollution, the offshore oil industry, *pesticides*, surveillance data on *chemicals* and radionuclides in food, and new chemicals. Exceptions include public confidentiality and security, and matters which are sub judice.

Freon

A Du Pont product used as an aerosol propellant, freon is made from *CFCs*, and damages the *ozone layer*. Banned in the US in 1996.

Best Practice

- Do not use.

Friendly, Environmentally: *see Environmentally Friendly*

Friends of the Earth: *see Chemical Release Inventory; Drinking Water Directive; Gas Industry*

Fuel: *see Energy; Fossil Fuels*

Fuel Cells

Produce energy without combustion and have virtually no environmental impact. They combine hydrogen and oxygen electrochemically to produce electricity, water and heat.

In the USA, the ONSI Corporation builds 200-kilowatt power plants, which provide enough energy to power a single building. Hospitals are major customers. Compared with a conventional diesel engine that would be needed to power a site of similar size, the fuel cells have one thousandth of the emissions. Fuel cells are also seen as a promising technology for motor cars.

Fur and Hide

Fur is a natural and renewable resource, as is the hide used in leather shoes or coats. They are usually good energy insulators and are rainproof, and their use means that society is not using non-renewables like oil-based plastic products. All things being equal, it is preferable to make and use fur and hides. However, there are three criticisms of fur production, all of which relate to cruelty:

(1) *Farming conditions:* Some animals such as mink are, it is said, farmed in cruel conditions. This can be overcome by providing more humane conditions, as also with battery hens. This issue relates more to animal welfare than environmental issues.
(2) *Leg-hold traps:* Some animals such as foxes are caught in *leg-hold traps*, which are said to be cruel.
(3) *Culling:* Animals like *seals* are reduced in number, generally by being clubbed, which opponents say is barbaric.

See also: Fishing industry; Seals.

Furans

Abbreviated name for polychlorinated dibenzofurans, of which there are 135 compounds. Similar to *dioxins*, they are highly *toxic* and are created in incineration.

Furniture

The two major issues relating to office furniture are:

- purchase of environmentally sound furniture;
- disposal or recycling of old furniture.

Purchase of Furniture

Instead of buying new items of furniture, it may be possible to refurbish existing ones. Metal office furniture can be refurbished and repainted. This considerably lengthens its life. When it comes to buying new goods, some office furniture, including desks, is made from recycled material, which makes it an environmentally sound purchase. Laminated desks, shelves and cupboards are often made from chipboard, which may use *formaldehyde*. Organizations should buy wood products that are formaldehyde-free. Desks, especially executive ones, are sometimes made from tropical timbers. These may have contributed to the destruction of the rainforest unless they come from sustainably managed sources. Upholstered furniture, furthermore, occasionally uses foams which produce toxic fumes when burnt. These should be avoided.

Disposal

Organizations can offer old furniture to charities. By donating its old furniture to charity, one bank reduced the number of items sent to landfill by 60 per cent, which reduced the costs by UK£200 per branch. In six months, the bank gave 20 charities 448 items, worth UK£28,000. In the UK, FRN (Furniture Recycling Network) represents 100 charitable furniture recycling projects.

See also: Office.

Furniture Care Products

The EC has prepared proposals for an *eco-label* for *aerosol* and pump-action furniture sprays. Aerosols account for 80 per cent of the European furniture polish market, and compressed air products are now available. These are significantly better in environmental terms, emitting 60 per cent fewer *VOCs*.

Best Practice

- Use eco-labelled products when available.

Garages and Vehicle Maintenance

Garages produce *solid waste* in the form of old vehicle parts, worn tyres, oily rags and so on. They may also fit and remove brakes containing asbestos. *Liquid wastes* include waste oils, degreasing and cleaning fluids, paint residues, and contaminated cleaning water. Emissions to air include the use of *solvents* and vehicle emissions (comprising smoke, *particulates, carbon dioxide, carbon monoxide* etc). Garages also use many *toxic* and *hazardous substances.*

Managing Impacts

Used engine oil, a suspected carcinogen, should be handled carefully. It should be taken to a recycling point where it can be recycled into lubricant or heating oil. Used oil should never be poured into drains or water courses because it is toxic. Used oil contains hydrocarbons, some of which are carcinogenic, as well as lead and other chemicals which could contaminate rivers and end up in the water supply.

The garage or transport department should keep all vehicles properly tuned and serviced: this means observing the manufacturer's service intervals and watching out for faults.

Testing Emissions

US plans to tighten emission standards were criticized by the owners of small garages who feared that they would be unable to afford the costly and sophisticated vehicle testing equipment, and would therefore lose their repair businesses. The plans were laid under the 1990 amendment to the US *Clean Air Act.*

Best Practice

- Fluids and materials should be recycled or reused wherever possible. They should be disposed of according to government regulations.
- Environmentally sound procedures should be laid down for the disposal of solid waste, such as tyres and vehicle parts.
- An *audit* should be undertaken, aimed at minimizing the garage's impacts and reducing the use of toxic materials and air pollutants.

See also: Filling stations.

Gases: *see Air Pollution*

Gas Industry

The industry's impacts include:

- damage done in exploration (loss of species, destruction of habitats);
- energy losses in conversion;
- *contaminated land:* sites of former coal gas (or 'Town' gas) works are often contaminated by the by-products of the process, including cyanide, phenols, lead, cadmium and mercury.

A survey by Friends of the Earth concluded that 68 sites in the UK, many of which are now developed, may be suffering unrecorded contamination. The gas works operated from the early nineteenth century until their replacement by natural gas in the 1970s. In 1994, British Gas was carrying a UK£133 million burden on its balance sheet for contaminated land liability. According to Friends of the Earth, British Gas has refused to release information it holds about levels of pollution at its sites.

See also: Energy.

Gasoline: *see Petrol*

Gas Stations: *see Filling Stations*

GEMI

Global Environmental Management Initiative: a tool to help management assess its environmental performance against the 16 principles of the *ICC Business Charter*. Its Environmental Self-Assessment Programme (ESAP) has four levels of performance: compliance, system development, integration and total quality. GEMI is an internal tool and does not involve a public report.

See also: Charters, environmental.

General Product Safety Directive: *see Product Liability*

Genetically Modified Organisms (GMOs)

The main purpose of genetically modified organisms is to provide crops which are resistant to disease or predators, or which provide more food. Mankind has always tried to improve the quality of livestock and arable crops, but genetic engineering allows us to make much greater changes within the environment.

Impacts

There are three problems:

(1) *The impact on other species:* For example, pollen from genetically engineered oilseed rape can travel much further than had been predicted. This means it has the potential for reseeding itself as a 'superweed'. The same problems have already been seen in the introduction of non-engineered but alien species, such as the cane toad in Australia and the grey squirrel in Britain.

(2) *Misuse of technology:* Critics says that most of the genetically engineered species released so far in the US have been developed by major agrochemical companies to develop farmers' loyalty to their own *herbicides*. For example, sugar beet could be engineered to tolerate regular applications of the herbicide Roundup. This contrasts with the original assertions of scientists that genetic engineering would reduce the need for *pesticides*. Likewise, the dream of feeding the world's hungry seems also to have been overlooked.

(3) Applications of herbicide may kill other plants and species and thereby reduce biodiversity locally.

Legislation

EC Directives 94/15/EC, 90/219/EC and 90/220/EEC, and Decision 94/730/EC control the use of genetically modified crops in the European Union. In the UK, GMOs are governed under the Environmental Protection Act 1990 and the Genetically Modified Organisms Regulations 1992 and 1993. The regulations introduce a system of consents for the release and marketing of GMOs and provide public registers.

Glass

The use of glass as a *packaging* material has declined proportionately to plastic, being heavier (and therefore adding to *transport* costs). It is also more hazardous when broken.

Impacts

Glass production requires high temperature furnaces. It therefore uses energy and produces oxides of *sulphur*, *nitrogen* and *carbon*. These contribute to *acid rain* and the *greenhouse effect*, so taking steps to minimize their emissions is important. Glass takes years to biodegrade.

Positive impacts include the fact that glass is made from abundant raw materials (such as sand, soda ash and limestone). Waste glass generated during manufacturing is recycled. It can also be easily recycled after use by the consumer.

Recycling

The amount of glass recycling has grown substantially. The average recovery rate in OECD countries rose from 22 per cent in 1980 to 32 per cent in the early 1990s. In some European countries, recycled glass makes up more than 50 per cent of all glass used.

Best Practice

- Ensure that the organization's glass is recycled.

See also: Recycling.

Global Warming

Gradual increase in average world temperatures. Caused by a build-up of *greenhouse gases* in the atmosphere from power stations and other sources (see Figure 10). According to the *Intergovernmental Panel on Climate Change* (*IPCC*), the average temperature of the earth's atmosphere will rise by one to 3.5 degrees C over the next century. The theory is now fact, according to the IPCC.

Insurance companies agree with the IPCC. In 1996, a group of 58 international insurance companies called on industrialized governments to achieve early and substantial reductions in greenhouse emissions. They believe that global warming is leading to more extreme weather patterns and higher insurance payouts. A single hurricane in the United States could cost the global insurance industry US$50 billion (UK£33 billion).

Alarmed by the scientists' predictions, 153 governments at the 1992 UN Earth Summit at Rio de Janeiro pledged (in the *Convention on Climate Change*) to stabilize their greenhouse gas emissions at 1990 levels by the end of the 1990s.

Effects of global warming

The warming, which is more than the total increase over the past 10,000 years, will melt ice caps. This may cause sea levels to rise by approximately 65 cm, resulting in the loss of low-lying land. Climate change could become much more extreme, with storms more common. Global warming could also create both drier and wetter weather patterns in different regions, disrupting food production. Higher temperatures and humidity could lead to an increase in tropical diseases, such as malaria and yellow fever.

Based on 80 years' data, the US government's national climatic centre in Asheville, North Carolina, has found that tropical-style cloud bursts are increasing in Europe. There has been a steady increase in sudden, violent downpours, with as much rain falling in a day as normally falls in months. The result will be much heavier rain in a shorter time.

According to supercomputer models run by the UK's Meteorological Office, the overall quantity of rain will rise. This has implications for water companies, agriculture and industry. Long periods of warm, dry weather broken by sudden downpours will make rain harder to collect as millions of gallons run off the hard baked land and are swept away by rivers to the sea. *Fertilizers* and *pesticides* will accumulate on land in dry periods and could be washed suddenly into rivers. The pollutants may be so concentrated that fish will be killed and other *wildlife* put at risk. The UK's National Rivers Authority has already had to investigate cases of fish dying after violent thunderstorms. Global warming would also increase death from cardio-respiratory disease. A rise of a few degrees would increase the number of New Yorkers dying from the summer heat from 320 to 880 on average.

Higher sea levels will cause widespread flooding and erosion. This will affect tens of millions of people in some of the world's most crowded areas, many of whom will be forced to migrate. A World Bank study projects that a sea level rise of 50 to 100 cm would flood 48 Chinese cities, displacing 67 million people. In India, seven million people would lose their homes. Greater hunger and thirst will afflict the health of poorer people, who are already plagued by famine and disease. Southern China, Bangladesh and Egypt will lose huge tracts of land, creating millions of environmental refugees.

Global warming only needs to increase average temperatures by a small amount for the weather to change dramatically. The Gulf Stream, which brings warm air to Britain and Western Europe, has stopped working recently, and it is thought that melting ice caps in the Arctic have interfered with the current that propels the Gulf Stream by upsetting the salinity of the Gulf of Mexico. The loss of the Gulf Stream could bring Siberian cold conditions to Britain.

Is Global Warming Real?

Some scientists (though increasingly fewer) say that because the earth's climate is so complex, changes are within the bounds of natural variability. Others point out that climate rises and falls naturally. Ice fairs on the frozen River Thames in the mini Ice Age of the seventeenth century, and evidence of flourishing civilizations in what is now African desert, demonstrate natural temperature fluctuations. Some scientists believe that there are naturally occurring 1000 to 3000 year cycles in which temperatures oscillate between cold and warm extremes. However, the *IPCC* believes that global warming is due to man, not nature. Research published in 1997 showed that the levels of warming in the period to 1996 were much less than predicted. This suggests that the effects of man's activity may be more complex than previously realized.

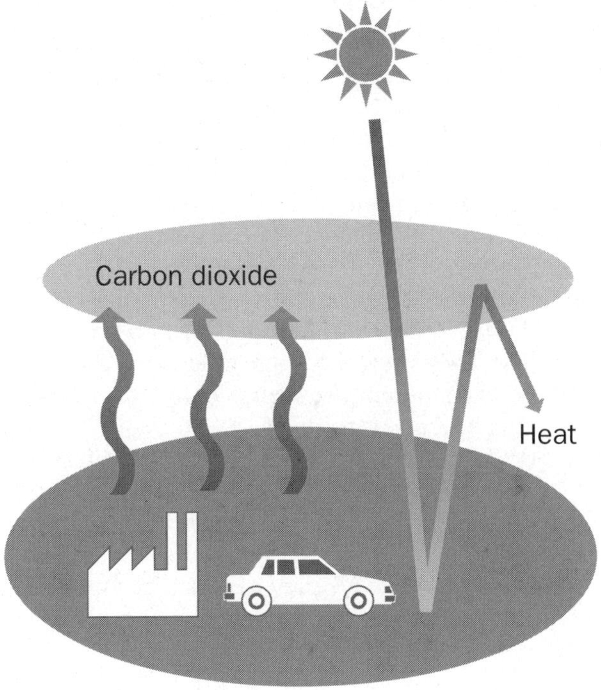

Figure 10: The Effect of Carbon Dioxide on Global Warming

Best Practice

- To reduce the effects of global warming, everyone should burn fewer combustible materials (which means using less electricity).
- Governments should invest in *renewable energy*.
- Companies can reduce their output of *carbon dioxide* by reducing their energy consumption through improved energy management.

See also: Energy; Managed retreat.

GMOs: *see Genetically Modified Organisms*

Good Neighbour Agreements

Introduced by Communities for a Better Environment in Minnesota. The agreements are negotiated with local companies on pollution reduction and prevention. Nevertheless, they are rejected by many companies because of their controversial aim of encouraging companies to reduce their use of *toxic* materials.

Government

Governments have three ways of reducing pollution:

(1) *Exhortation:* They can encourage companies to be environmentally sound. This produces an uneven response and sometimes allows the polluter to gain a cost advantage over the environmentally responsible company. The US's *Environmental Protection Agency* went back to this strategy with its voluntary targets (see: Toxics Release Inventory), and with its *Common Sense Initiative.* However, many companies respond only when required to by law, on the (probably mistaken) grounds that higher environmental standards make the company less competitive.

However, some forms of creative encouragement may work. In 1995 Indonesia placed 187 factories into one of five categories, based on their water discharge. Gold was for excellent, green for very good, blue for adequate, red for those violating environmental standards, and black for the worst polluters. In that year, no company earned a gold rating, and the government released the names of those businesses which fell into the green category. It also threatened to release the names of the firms in the red and black category. Many poor-ranking companies have since improved, and Indonesia plans to expand its programme to include *air pollution* and *hazardous waste.*

(2) *Legislation:* The second option is legislation, which requires companies to operate in specific ways. The European Union has produced some 200 environmental directives in the last 20 years.

(3) *Market instruments:* The third means is the use of financial (or market) instruments, such as environmental taxes and levies, and subsidies and grants. They include emission charges and *tradable permits.* For example, governments are likely to introduce landfill taxes as a way of reducing the volume of rubbish produced. An example of subsidy is the one provided by the UK for fuel generated from renewable sources. Differential taxes include the lower duty on city *diesel* in Sweden, which encourages drivers to use this less polluting fuel.

Subsidies and Taxes that Encourage Good Environmental Performance

Taxes that 'make the polluter pay' are politically popular because they attack the polluter and reward the clean firm. As an example of this, presorted waste material taken to treatment plants in Copenhagen, Denmark, is taxed 50 to 70 per cent less than material which is taken to *landfill* or to incineration. Another example is the UK tax on unleaded petrol, which is 9 per cent less than for leaded fuel. This encourages drivers to buy unleaded fuel and use *cars* that take it. The share of unleaded petrol in the UK rose from 0 to 50 per cent between 1987 and 1994, and is projected to rise to 90 per cent by 2012. However, the affected industry sometimes responds to market instruments by raising fears about job losses.

The Impact of Higher Controls and Taxes

Legislation and financial instruments affect companies' profits, and governments tread a tightrope between reducing pollution and impeding the market. Multinational organizations invest globally and are constantly in search of cheaper sites. Higher standards in advanced countries encourage the movement of capital from wealthy industrial nations to the developing countries, though the need of companies to be close to their customers is a restraining factor. Thus, environmental taxes and legislation represent a potential loss of jobs and investment that governments are prepared to make. As national wealth grows, legislators decide to trade added wealth for the sake of a cleaner environment. For many years, Scottish oil industry commentators worried that the British government's environmental legislation would encourage oil companies to cease exploring for oil in the North Sea off Scotland. At the same time, environmental legislation and tax can create innovation. Germany's introduction of stringent laws ahead of other EU countries is thought to be partially responsible for its lead in environmental control technology.

Moreover, the supra-national legislation of trading blocks such as the EU creates a level playing field for all companies within the economic area. This means that individual companies do not lose out, because all companies have to conform. Organizations outside the trading block sometimes see the legislation as an unfair barrier to entry. However, the growing pollution controls in South-East Asia mean that the differences between major trading blocks are likely to be slight.

See also: Environment agency; Technology.

Green Belt

A designated area, often surrounding a city, upon which most new building is prohibited. The green belt serves to discourage urban sprawl and ribbon development.

Developers routinely want to build on green belt land because it is, they say, where people prefer to live. Developing the green belt, however, becomes self-defeating, because the people who move to a green belt development soon find themselves living in a town.

Green Dot

Packaging recovery system, as used in Germany and France. Denotes reusable packaging, which will be collected under a national waste recovery scheme, such as Germany's *DSD*.

See also: DSD, Packaging; Packaging and Packaging Waste Directive.

Green Grid

A tool, developed by Kit Sadgrove, for assessing the organization's current environmental profile. It shows that there are only four positions a company can adopt: that of leader, conformer, laggard and punished. These positions reflect the organization's values. The company's location on the grid depends on its commitment to environmental management. The grid also shows whether the company is seen as green or grey (that is, environmentally responsible or irresponsible).

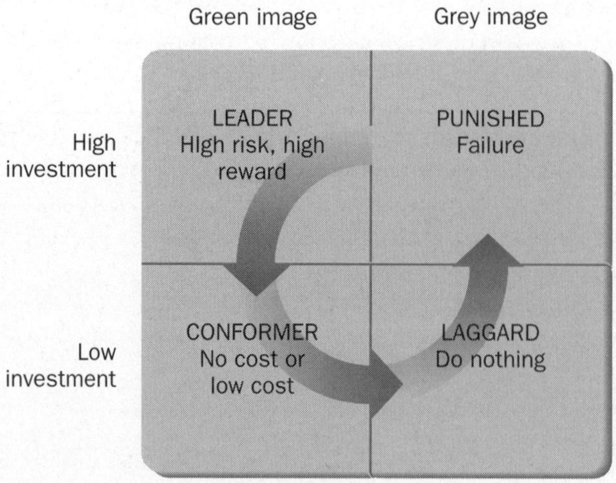

Figure 11: The Green Grid

As suggested in Figure 11, the Leader is a company which prides itself on its environmental advances. It publishes annual statistics about its declining output of waste, and its products use less energy than its competitors. The company has been working for many years to become green and is at last seeing some payback. A Leader is exposed to criticism from opponents, who may try to find some aspect in which it is grey, not green. Its opponents will then try to make the company seem hypocritical.

The Conformer manages the environment and does all that the law requires. But it does so with some reluctance. It asks stern questions about the financial benefits of any environmental investment, and will only commit money if there are good reasons for doing so. In doing so, the Conformer gets a green image without having to invest too heavily. This is a logical position to adopt, and one where the majority of companies place themselves. It gives them the advantages of a green image without the risk that is associated with being a leader. It knows that a company which puts its head over the parapet is likely to get it shot off.

The Laggard is a company which pays little attention to green issues. It has ignored many of the innovations which other companies have introduced (such as environmental committees). It produces a lot of waste material and has little understanding of environmental legislation. The Laggard is not hostile to green issues; it simply fails to discuss them. One of Britain's biggest housebuilders, a company whose environmental impacts range from quarried products to the use of rainforest timber, has privately admitted complete ignorance of green issues.

Leaders that stop innovating become Conformers. Similarly, Conformers that grow complacent become Laggards. And Laggards who refuse to take action become Punished. A company becomes punished in two ways: by the market and by the courts. Customers start to buy from a greener competitor, and so the company's revenue declines. Or the company may be taken to court for pollution offences. It ends up paying to expensively retro-fit pollution control technology; the court may even require it to cease production until it overcomes the pollution problem. Whatever form the punishment takes, the company faces high costs (or losses) and still retains its dirty image.

How to Apply the Grid

It is difficult for an organization to be objective about its own position; companies often believe they are more advanced than they are. Laggards usually reckon they are Conformers. The checklist in Box 4 helps to identify any organization's position on the grid. The list contains a series of statements about the company's environmental performance. Tick all the statements which apply to your organization. You will find that most of the ticks lie in one of the four quadrants. This is the company's true position.

Box 4: Green Grid Checklist

The Leader

- ❑ The organization is registered to *ISO 14001* or *EMAS*.
- ❑ Most staff have received formal environmental training.
- ❑ Environmental impact is formally considered in new product development.
- ❑ The CEO has talked publicly and favourably about green issues in the last six months.

The Conformer

- ❑ The organization has set a target for gaining ISO 14001 or EMAS.
- ❑ The company has introduced environmental improvements into its main products or processes.
- ❑ Selected managers have attended seminars or conferences on green issues.
- ❑ The company has a written environmental policy statement.
- ❑ An environmental audit has taken place within the last three years.

The Laggard

- ❑ The organization lacks a written environmental policy.
- ❑ Much of the company's revenue is in markets threatened by green legislation (for example, foundries).
- ❑ The company believes that green issues are not important to its customers.
- ❑ The environment appears on the board's agenda, but time usually prevents a discussion.

The Punished

- ❑ Sales have fallen due to competitors' innovations, which have included environmental improvements.
- ❑ The company has had several reportable pollution incidents within the last two years.
- ❑ The company has been taken to court in the last 12 months for an environmental offence.

A wide spread of ticks indicates a company in which different divisions are moving at different speeds, or a company in a dirty industry which is cleaning up its act.

Greenhouse Gas

The main greenhouse gas is *carbon dioxide* (CO_2). Others include *nitrous oxide* (N_2O), methane and some organochloride compounds used in *solvents*. They include perfluorocarbons (*PFCs*) and sulphuric fluoride-6, which have replaced *CFCs*.

Greenhouse gases come from power stations and other sources. They trap the sun's rays inside the earth's atmosphere, causing the temperature to rise (see Figure 10). This is the effect known as *global warming* or the 'greenhouse effect'.

Best Practice

- Governments are seeking to cut emissions of CO_2 and other greenhouse gases, by reducing their nation's energy consumption.
- Companies can reduce greenhouse gas emissions by saving energy.

See also: Energy management.

Greenpeace

An environmental pressure group that claims 4.5 million supporters world-wide. Best known for its campaigns to stop whaling and nuclear power, and its use of fast inflatable boats. One of its ships was sunk and a crew member drowned, apparently through sabotage by the French secret service.

In 1996, Greenpeace was ordered to pay UK£115,000 to British Nuclear Fuels by a French court for being in breach of a court injunction, when it tried to stop a shipment of nuclear waste.

See also: Liability; Litigation; Shell.

Greenwash

Environmental whitewash. The term refers to environmental policies, charters or activities which lack rigour or sincerity, and which are merely window dressing. The term applies also to spurious product claims (for example, washing-up liquids which state they are 'nitrate free'. This is irrelevant since no washing-up liquid contains *nitrates*).

Best Practice

- Ensure that all environmental claims and activities are relevant, honest and rigorous.

See also: Marketing.

Grey List

List of dangerous substances, originally defined in Directive 76/464/EEC. They are a lesser threat than the substances in the *Black List*, and are controlled by quality standards set by member states. Substances include:

(1) the following metalloids and metals and their compounds:
  - zinc, copper, nickel, chromium, lead;
  - selenium, arsenic, antimony, molybdenum, titanium;
  - tin, barium, beryllium, boron, uranium;
  - vanadium, cobalt, thallium, tellurium, silver;

(2) biocides and their derivatives appearing in the *Black List*.

(3) substances which have a deleterious effect on the taste and/or smell of products for human consumption, derived from the aquatic environment, and compounds (ie fish and shellfish);

(4) *toxic* or persistent organic compounds of silicon which may give rise to such compounds in water, excluding those which are biologically harmless or which rapidly biodegrade in water;

(5) inorganic compounds of phosphorus and elemental phosphorus;

(6) non-persistent mineral oils and hydrocarbons of petroleum origin;

(7) cyanides, fluorides;

(8) substances which have an adverse effect on the oxygen balance, particularly ammonia and nitrites.

Best Practice

- Avoid the use of Grey List substances if they can be avoided.

Grey Water

Waste water not contaminated with urine or faeces. Grey water need not be extensively purified if it has only been lightly used.

Grounds

Companies with land holdings should manage them in a way that does not harm nature. This will entail carrying out a *flora and fauna* survey to establish whether any rare or declining species inhabit nearby. The company should then draw up a grounds management policy and plan.

The policy should reject the use of routine *pesticides*. The plan should provide habitats for local and important species. This may entail stopping old drainage ditches, or building nesting boxes for birds or bats. The site should provide a corridor for wildlife to move through. This can be achieved by providing hedges. Part of the land holding should be left to grow wild, since many kinds of wildlife need undisturbed land. Grassed areas should not be overlooked for their wildlife value. The regime should tolerate *biodiversity* by permitting other kinds of plants. The grass should not be cut too short, since this reduces the number of species which can use it. Pesticides and *fertilizers* should not be used routinely.

Planting should encourage wildlife. This might involve the use of shrubs which attract butterflies, bees or birds. Sweet-smelling or attractive plants will visually improve the environment for staff and visitors. The planting strategy may also encourage traditional varieties of plants, which will boost biodiversity.

See also: Nature conservation.

Growing media

The EU has been preparing an *eco-label* for the growing media.

See also: Eco-label; Soil improvers.

Habitat

A place where a plant or animal lives. It may also be a place where groups of plants and animals live.

See also: Ecosystem; Environment.

Habitats Directive – EU

The Conservation of Natural Habitats and of Wild Flora and Fauna (92/43/EEC – the 'Habitats Directive'). Member states should select, register, manage and protect sites which are important habitats. These sites are known as Special Areas of Conservation (SAC) and Special Protection Areas (SPA). Governments should restrict planning permission and ensure that such sites are not developed in a way that would significantly affect them.

Best Practice

- Identify whether the organization has any sites within SPAs or SACs. If it has, identify the legal controls on planning and apply them. Then ensure that the organization adheres to those controls.

Hairsprays

The EU is preparing an *eco-label* for hairsprays. This follows concern over *VOC* air pollution and *solid waste* caused by *aerosols*. The eco-label will include the use of pump-action sprays.

Halogens

Generic name for the elements fluorine, *chlorine*, *bromine* and *iodine*. Halogenation is the introduction of a halogen atom into an organic (carbon) compound in place of a hydrogen atom. Thus the halogenation (or bromination) of benzene produces bromobenzene.

Halons

Halons are substances used in fire-fighting systems in locations where water cannot be used, such as computer rooms. While very effective in combating fire, halons damage the *ozone layer*, and their production was halted in 1994 under the *Montreal Protocol*. Some observers believe that the smoke and damage caused by fire will be worse than the effect caused by the halons in extinguishing the fire.

Some halons are long lived, as shown in Table 6, so the effect of reductions in their use will not be felt for some time:

Table 6: Life Time of Halogen in Years

Substance	Lifetime
Halon 1211	12
Halon 1301	101
Halon 2402	Unknown

Best Practice

- Cease buying halon extinguishers and sprinkler systems.
- Use halon extinguishers only on real fires.
- Establish a halon bank to supply short-term future needs if necessary.
- Replace halon-based fire extinguishers and sprinkler systems if a suitable alternative is available (eg HFC 227).

See also: Fire protection.

Hazardous Substances

Hazardous substances are those which pose a threat to humans or the environment. Some hazardous substances are obvious: they come in a tanker with a big HAZCHEM label on it. Others are more difficult to spot. Flour, cement and shampoos are three ordinary substances that can cause health hazards. Hazardous substances affect people in many different ways. They include the following.

Table 7: Hazardous Substances

Item	Examples of hazard posed
Dust	Can be breathed.
Chemicals	Irritate the skin.
Vapours	Cause breathing difficulties.
Poisonous plant material	Can be swallowed.
Micro-organisms	Can be swallowed.

Some hazards affect individual workers and are therefore health and safety (rather than environmental) matters. They include sharp objects that can be injected into the body, or high pressure equipment that can damage eyesight. Virtually anything in excess is toxic. For example, drinking four times the normal intake of water leads to death from uraemia.

The effects of hazardous substances can be instant or may build up slowly over several years. Some may affect only people with allergies. Others may be harmful only when mixed with another substance (a chemical cocktail).

The following checklist analyses whether hazardous substances are used in the organization, in which case it is likely to be subject to legislation.

- ❑ Do you use toxic substances?
- ❑ Do you use substances that cause asthma?
- ❑ Do you use substances that cause severe dermatitis?
- ❑ Do you use chrome solutions?

- ❑ Do you use substances that cause cancer?
- ❑ Do you use substances used for fumigation?
- ❑ Do your staff suffer similar related ailments?
- ❑ Is your industry known to cause certain ailments?
- ❑ Do suppliers provide raw materials which contain dangerous substances?

A 'yes' answer to any of these questions means that the organization should implement controls (in the UK, the *COSHH* regulations).

Taking Action to Control Hazardous Substances

The presence of hazardous substances may require some or all of the following practices:

- Identify any hazardous substances that are: brought in, made in production, produced as finished products.
- Assess what hazardous substances are used in maintenance, cleaning, research or testing.
- Assess the risks they pose.
- Consider how they are moved around the site. Could this be done more safely?
- In what way could accidents occur? Who would be affected, and to what extent?

Minimizing the Risk

- Introduce less harmful alternatives where possible.
- Keep proper records.
- Do not introduce new material on site until full documentation is available and understood.
- Store hazardous substances carefully in locked rooms with adequate ventilation, away from the workplace.
- Label all substances prominently.
- Ensure that all production processes are carried out in a safe manner. Ensure management supervision to maintain standards.
- Provide regular training – in handling and using substances, in reducing risk and in identifying symptoms. Provide first-aid training appropriate to the substances handled.
- Inform staff of the dangers of all chemicals they use.
- Reduce the number of people exposed to the hazards and the duration of their exposure.
- Provide exhaust ventilation to remove fumes or gas.
- Provide protective clothing.
- Use mechanical handling systems to reduce human contact.
- Appoint a suitable person to carry out regular health checks of all staff. Their skills and qualifications will depend on the nature of the substances.
- Collect regular data (by checking employees' health or skin). Analyse the information for ailments, report any found and take action to stop the ailments. Report any symptoms immediately to a doctor.
- Implement a safety plan for dealing with emergencies. Agree a spillage procedure and communicate it to staff.

UK Legislation

In the UK, hazardous substances are controlled by the *COSHH* (Control of Substances Hazardous to Health) Regulations. Under the *Planning (Hazardous Substances) Act 1990*, 71 substances (selected for their explosive or inflammable properties) now need consent if they are present on a site in certain quantities. The exception is for companies which have held such substances continuously from June 1991 to June 1992.

Best Practice

- Commission a legal compliance *audit* to ensure that the organization is working within the law.
- Undertake written risk assessments or *HAZOP* studies to check that risks are known and properly managed.
- Reduce the hazards by substituting safer substances.
- Introduce programmes to cut hazardous waste and emissions.
- Implement emergency planning.
- Introduce an *EMS*, another way of gaining greater control over dangerous substances.

See also: Chemical industry; Chemicals; COSHH; Dangerous substances; Emergencies; Pollution; Toxic.

Hazardous Waste

Waste which poses a threat to humans or the environment. It is a more general term than *toxic* waste; the latter being a special type of hazardous waste. There are legal controls on the disposal of hazardous waste, because careless disposal would be harmful.

Products in this category include anti-freeze, *asbestos* fire blankets, brake fluid, fluorescent lights, furniture polish, oven cleaners, *oil*, old medicines, paints and *solvents*, *pesticides* and *herbicides*, *PCBs*, *PCNs*, stain removers, and wood preservatives. The EC has published a list of wastes (as Decision 94/904/EC) while two Directives (94/31/EC and 91/689/EEC) control them.

The degree of hazard may be measured by the following characteristics:

- toxicity (how poisonous it is);
- persistence (how long it takes to decompose);
- bioaccumulation (the extent to which it builds up in the *food chain*).

There is particular concern about *toxic* waste – that which can cause injury or death to humans or other species (such as pesticides).

See also: Hazardous substances; Toxic; Waste management.

Hazardous Waste Incineration Directive – EU

This directive was passed in 1994. It sets licensing and operational requirements for hazardous waste incinerators and for industrial facilities using such waste as fuel. It sets limits on waste gas emissions and the quality of *waste water* which has been used to 'scrub' (or purify) *flue gases*.

See also: Incineration; Waste management.

HAZOP

A method for preempting catastrophes. It asks the question: 'What if?', but does so in a controlled and thorough manner. HAZOP is useful for preventing environmental incidents.

HAZOP, which stands for hazard and operability, takes each of the organization's processes in turn and assesses what would happen if a change took place. That change could be a rise in temperature, a fall in pressure or the introduction of a raw material. HAZOP examines the consequence of such a change; if it would cause pollution or an explosion, the HAZOP team decides how to prevent the change from taking place. Typical solutions include additional electronic monitoring, alarms and cut-off systems.

The methodology uses a set of 'property words', such as flow, temperature, pressure, level, time, mixing, contamination, and steam. It then applies 'guide words', such as 'more', 'less', 'none', 'reverse', 'part of', 'as well as' and 'other than'. For example, it asks what would happen if a process continued for too long (a combination of 'more' and 'time'). This might cause a chemical reaction to take place. If that reaction was hazardous, the team should decide how to prevent the process from continuing beyond its proper duration.

Supporters of HAZOP point out that processes work well until a change is introduced (such as a rise in temperature), which is when problems occur. They point out that many of the world's great industrial disasters could have been foreseen and prevented if a HAZOP study had been undertaken.

See also: Chemicals; Chemical industry; Emergencies; Hazardous substances.

HCFC

Hydro-chlorofluorocarbons. *CFC* substitutes which deplete the *ozone layer*, but not as badly as CFCs. HCFCs are also *greenhouse gases*, albeit not as potent as *carbon dioxide*. They will be phased out by the year 2030. HCFCs are more expensive than CFCs, which causes difficulties for poorer countries.

See also: Ozone-depleting substances.

Health Services: *see Hospitals*

Heating

Space and water heating represents a big proportion of a building's energy consumption, and most organizations spend more than they need. Draughts, lack of insulation, loss of steam and hot water in pipes, leaking taps and lack of localized heating controls all lead to wasted energy. The choice of fuel, equipment, controls, and maintenance will affect annual consumption and the amount of pollution caused. Heat recovery will minimize the loss of heat into the atmosphere.

Best Practice

- Meter energy used for heating.
- Carry out an energy audit.
- Identify ways of reducing heat.

See also: Building design; Energy management.

Heavy Metals

Metals with a high specific gravity (or density), normally defined as more than six grams per cubic centimetre (g/cm_3). They include chromium, mercury, iron, thallium, copper, lead, zinc, and cadmium. They also include gold and platinum. Some, such as cadmium, are highly poisonous.

Hedges

Hedges are of great environmental importance. They act as *wildlife* corridors, allowing wildlife to travel in safety. They also provide a source of food and shelter to a large number of species. Hedges need to be substantial enough to provide security. There has been a sustained destruction of hedges as farmers and landowners create bigger fields which can be more easily managed.

Best Practice

- Farmers and landowners should plant hedges at site boundaries and link them to other hedges, to create a wildlife corridor.

Helsinki Resolution on Forestry

A resolution adopted by the Ministerial Conference on the Protection of Forests in Europe. The resolution was adopted in Helsinki in June 1993. It defines environmentally sound forestry management as:

> The stewardship and use of forests and forest land in a way, and at a rate, that maintains their *biodiversity*, productivity, regeneration capacity, vitality and their potential to fulfil, now and in the future, relevant ecological, economic and social functions, at local, national and global levels, and that does not cause damage to their eco-systems.

See also: Timber; Rio de Janeiro forest management principles.

Herbicides: *see Pesticides*

Hexachlorobenzene

Used to treat seed grain. It is on the EC *Black List* of dangerous *substances.*

Best Practice

- Do not use.

Hexachlorobutadiene

Hazardous substance on the EC *Black List*.

Best Practice

- Do not use.

Hexachlorocyclohexane

On the EC *Black List* of dangerous substances and is the subject of EC Directive 84/491/EEC.

Best Practice

- Do not use.

Hexachloroethane

On the EU *Black List* of dangerous substances. In the EU its use is prohibited in the manufacture or processing of non-ferrous metals.

Best Practice

- Do not use.

Hexane

Gas thought to be responsible for an explosion in Mexico City in 1992, as a result of which 600 people were sent to hospital. A cooking oil company was said to have pumped hexane, which was used to extract edible oils from seeds, into the sewage system. Others blamed Pemex (Petroleos Mexicanos), which was involved in three explosions in the 1980s, alleging that the company accidentally dumped flammable gases into the river.

Hexavalent: *see Chromium*

HFC

Substitutes for *CFCs*, HFCs are *greenhouse gases*. HFC-134a is a well-known product which, however, requires special equipment.

HMSO – UK

A system for rating the environmental attractiveness of different brands of paper. The scheme has been developed by Her Majesty's Stationery Office (HMSO) in the UK.

See also: Paper labelling schemes.

Hospitals and Health Services

Though hospitals are rightly seen as places of health and healing, they also have major environmental impacts. The main ones include the following:

1 *Poor-quality incinerators:* Since *clinical waste* has to be incinerated, major hospitals have usually been built with their own incinerator. In the UK many of these have been found inadequate and have had to be scrapped or *retro-fitted* to reduce their emissions in line with clean air legislation.
2 *Solid waste:* Whether the waste goes to incineration or to landfill sites, hospitals produce huge quantities of *solid waste*. This has grown with the advent of disposable products and devices, their use fuelled by fears of cross-infection, AIDS, patient litigation and cheap plastics. Waste can be reduced by analysing over a continuous period the waste produced in each department, and planning for its reduction.
3 *Use of energy:* Hospitals use large amounts of *energy*, especially those which were built in earlier times when insulation was not a concern. Energy is wasted in many ways, such as a failure to insulate lengths of hot water piping.
4 *Water use:* Health service units consume large amounts of water, and while this is inevitable for an organization concerned with public health, water is wasted by leaking from old pipes and taps.

Best Practice

- *Audit* the unit for its environmental *impacts* and introduce a programme to reduce the main ones.

See also: Energy management; Packaging; Solid waste; Waste management.

Hotels: *see Catering and Hotel Industry*

Household Equipment

Household equipment can be divided into white goods (washing machines, dish-washers, fridges and freezers), and brown goods (such as televisions and hi-fis).

Impacts

Household equipment uses *energy* and, in some cases, water and detergents.

Improvements

1 *Energy:* Spurred on by the *eco-labels*, companies have reduced the amount of energy they use. For example, AEG has reduced the amount of energy used in its dishwashers from 2.6 kilowatts per hour (kWh) to 0.2 kWh.
2 *Water:* A 1950s AEG washing machine used 200 litres of water per wash. Today, its equipment uses just 75 litres.
3 *Detergent:* More precise dosing and drainage is helping companies to reduce the amount of detergent required or wasted.
4 *CFCs: CFCs* have been phased out of fridges and freezers, but have been replaced in some cases by substances which still deplete the *ozone layer*, albeit not so badly (see: ozone-depleting substances).

HSWA: *see Resource Conservation and Recovery Act*

Human Resources

The company should appoint a member of the board to take responsibility for environmental strategy. Responsibility for day-to-day environmental performance should rest with line managers. Environmental targets and responsibilities should be included in line managers' job specifications, and all staff whose work could have an environmental impact should receive training.

Line managers are often supported by an environmental manager who provides advice and information. The environmental manager may operate the *environmental management system* and act as a channel for environmental reports and complaints. The environmental manager may have other responsibilities, including health and safety, or quality, depending on the size of the organization and the scale of its impacts.

Ocassionally organizations set up an environmental committee, consisting of a representative from each department. The committee (sometimes called a Green Team) will ensure that important issues are discussed and brought to management's attention. The committee can act as a think tank, and can propose solutions for environmental problems. It can improve communications and help to spread good environmental practice throughout the business. However, the environmental committee does not usually have authority to take action. As noted, this is the responsibility of the board or line managers.

Department work teams, of the kind used in total quality management, are also useful for identifying how to minimize waste and improve processes. Companies with different divisions should build up a network of divisional environmental contacts, coordinated by a group environmental manager. Pilkington has a disk-based 'Green Directory' which lists over 200 environmental experts within the group and gives details of their expertise. The directory is regularly updated and made available to anyone who needs it.

Box 5: Human Resource Responsibilities

Task	Title
Develop environmental policy.	Chief executive; board member responsible for the environment
Produce objectives, targets and programmes.	Line managers
Manage the *environmental management system.*	Environmental manager
Ensure compliance with regulations.	Production manager
Comply with written procedures.	Staff

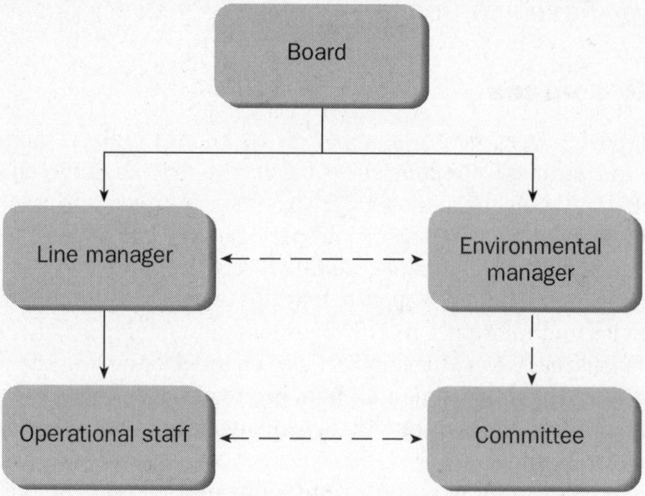

Figure 12: Responsibility for Environmental Issues

From Figure 12, it is clear that responsibility for environmental issues should rest with line managers, but environmental managers need to liaise extensively.

Best Practice

- Identify the roles and responsibilities necessary to manage the organization's impacts, and allocate these roles to specific members of staff.

See also: Continuous improvement; Training.

Hydrocarbons

Compounds of hydrogen and carbon. They are emitted from petrol evaporation, *solvent* evaporation, *car* exhausts and the burning of coal. They react with *nitrogen oxides* to form ground level *ozone*. Some hydrocarbons are toxic. Hydrocarbons are either aliphatic compounds or aromatic compounds. The aliphatic compounds are:

- alkanes (or paraffins), notably methane, ethane, propane, and butane; they are obtained from natural gas or oil, and have many uses;
- alkenes (or olefins), notably ethene or ethylene; they are obtained from petroleum, and are used as starting materials in industrial chemistry;
- alkynes (notably acetylene); they are extremely reactive and explosive.

The aromatic compounds include *benzene* and its derivatives such as *PAHs*. They are known as 'aromatic' from the distinctive smell of benzene.

See also: Black List; Red List.

Hydrology

The study of water, especially where it comes from and how it is distributed. The hydrological or water cycle is the cyclic movement of water from the sea to the atmosphere and back, via precipitation, evaporation, and the flow of rivers and streams. Hydrology is one of the issues to be covered in an *environmental impact assessment*.

IBM: *see Computers; PERI*

ICC

International Chamber of Commerce. Its Business Charter for Sustainable Development has been adopted by 1200 firms worldwide. To be accepted by the ICC, organizations must demonstrate commitment to good environmental practice, though the ICC carries out no monitoring of companies' compliance. Many, therefore, see the charter as a statement of good intentions. The charter is as follows.

1 *Corporate Priority:* To recognize environmental management as amongst the highest corporate priorities and as a key determinant to *sustainable development*; to establish policies, programmes and practices for conducting operations in an environmentally sound manner.
2 *Integrated Management:* To integrate these policies, programmes and practices fully into each business as an essential element of management in all its functions.
3 *Process Improvement:* To continue to improve policies, programmes and environmental performance, taking into account technical developments, scientific understanding, consumer needs and community expectations with legal regulations as a starting point; and to apply the same environmental criteria internationally.
4 *Employee Education:* To educate, train and motivate employees to conduct their activities in an environmentally responsible manner.
5 *Prior Assessment:* To assess environmental impacts before starting any new activity or project and before decommissioning a facility or leaving a site.
6 *Products and Services:* To develop and provide services that have no undue environmental impact and are safe in their intended use, that are efficient in their consumption of energy and natural resources, and can be recycled, reused or disposed of safely.
7 *Customer Advice:* To advise and, where relevant, educate customers, distributors and the public in the safe use, transport, storage and disposal of products provided; and to apply similar considerations to the provisions of services.
8 *Facilities and Operations:* To develop, design and operate facilities and conduct activities taking into consideration the efficient use of energy and materials, the sustainable use of *renewable resources*, the minimization of adverse environmental impact and waste generation, and the safe and responsible disposal of residual wastes.

9 *Research:* To conduct or support research on the environmental impacts of raw materials, products, processes, emissions and wastes associated with the enterprise and on the means of minimizing such adverse impacts.

10 *Precautionary Approach:* To modify the manufacture, marketing or use of products or services, or the conduct of activities, consistent with scientific and technical understanding, to prevent serious or irreversible environmental degradation.

11 *Contractors and Suppliers:* To promote the adoption of these principles by contractors acting on behalf of the enterprise, encouraging and, where appropriate, requiring improvements in their practices to make them consistent with those of the enterprise; and to encourage the wider adoption of these principles by suppliers.

12 *Emergency Preparedness:* To develop and maintain, where significant hazards exist, emergency preparedness plans in conjunction with the emergency services, relevant authorities and the local community, recognizing potential transboundary impacts.

13 *Transfer of Technology:* To contribute to the transfer of environmentally sound technology and management methods throughout the industrial and public sectors.

14 *Contributing to the Common Effect:* To contribute to the development of public policy and to business, governmental, and intergovernmental programmes and education initiatives that will enhance environmental awareness and protection.

15 *Openness to Concerns:* To foster openness and dialogue with employees and the public, anticipating and responding to the concerns about potential hazards and the impacts of operations, products, wastes or services, including those of transboundary or global significance.

16 *Compliance and Auditing:* To measure environmental performance; to conduct regular environmental *audits* and assessments of compliance with company requirements, legal requirements and these principles; and periodically provide appropriate information to the Board of Directors, shareholders, employees, the authorities and the public.

The charter can be implemented by adopting an environmental management system, such as *ISO 14001*. However, the clauses of the charter are written in a sufficiently general way so as to allow the company to avoid taking inconvenient action. None of the ICC clauses commit the organization to doing anything, since they use the infinitive form ('to measure...to conduct') rather than the future tense 'we will...'. As such, the charter is considerably less demanding than the *Ceres Principles*. However, under a committed chief executive the ICC Charter (as with any policy document) could be a tool for substantially reducing a company's impacts.

Best Practice

- The organization should sign up to the ICC Charter and implement it effectively.

See also: CERES Principles; Charters, environmental; GEMI; Policy, environmental.

IMO: *see SEA*

Impact, Environmental

Any change to the environment (whether good or bad) that results from the organization's activities, products or services (see Figure 13). Generally, impacts are adverse and are often (but not always) a euphemism for pollution. For example, smoke and oil spills cause pollution, while *CFCs* damage the *ozone layer*, the latter impact not being pollution in the sense of making something dirty. However, impacts can also be positive (for example, conservation measures that protect *wildlife*).

It is important to identify major impacts (such as *water pollution* from manufacturing), rather than minor ones (such as food waste in the canteen). This is discussed further under *Register of Effects*. Organizations should also consider their *potential* impacts, because they could cause the firm legal, financial or image problems.

There is increasing pressure to measure impacts on air or water in parts per billion or even per trillion. In other words, standards are continuing to rise.

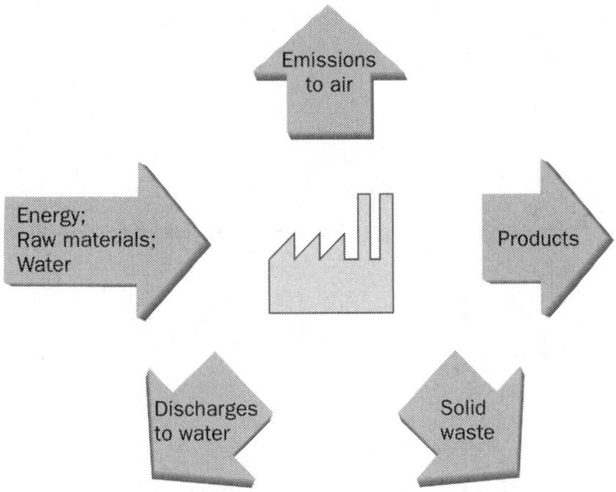

Figure 13: Environmental Impacts: Inputs, Outputs and the Effects of Processes.

Identifying Impacts

ISO 14001 recommends that organizations take the following steps:

1 *Select an activity or process:* The activity should be large enough for meaningful examination and small enough to be sufficiently understood.
2 *Identify its environmental aspects:* You should identify as many aspects as possible associated with the activity or process. Aspects include discharges, emissions, consumption or reuse of a material or noise.
3 *Identify environmental impacts:* Identify as many impacts as possible (both actual and potential, positive and negative) associated with each aspect. An example is shown in Table 8.

Table 8: Identifying Environmental Impacts

Activity	Aspect	Impact
Vehicle	Use of maintenance oils. Emissions to air. Use of cleaning cloths.	Disposal of lubricating oil. Use of *VOC*s. Solid waste.

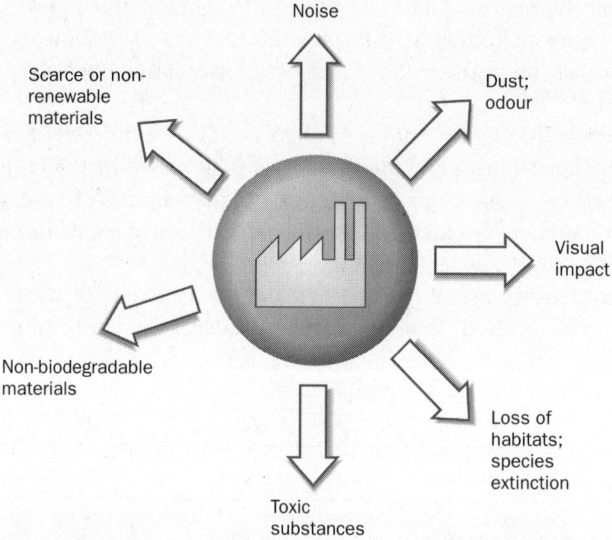

Figure 14: Detailed Environmental Impacts

See also: Aspects; Register of Effects.

Incineration

Disposal of *solid waste* through burning. In the old days, people got rid of much of their waste by throwing it on to the fires at home. People still throw material into the fire, except that the fire is now a large, enclosed and often distant incinerator.

Incineration is especially useful for breaking down *toxic* compounds, making them less harmful. When combined with *energy* recovery, incineration generates power. Many countries are turning to incineration. Japan, Switzerland and Luxembourg incinerate more than 65 per cent of their waste. The proportion of this waste that also generates energy in these countries is 27 per cent, 80 per cent and 100 per cent respectively. However, incineration is some four times as expensive as *landfill*.

Impacts

Incineration can release toxic substances (such as *dioxins* and *furans*) unless it is carried out at very high temperatures. Standards for incinerators have been growing, in recognition of the pollution and health risks caused by old plant. Local residents are often opposed to the siting of incinerators near their homes, fearing the release of toxic fumes (including carcinogenic dioxins) into the air.

Mitigation

The risks of releasing toxins can be reduced by ensuring good work practices. Residents' fears can be allayed by greater openness and better communication, including the holding of open days and the setting up of community liaison committees.

Legislation

An EC Directive on Incineration of Hazardous Waste was passed in 1994.

The future

Unless incineration is proven to be hazardous to health, it is likely that the practice will grow. Municipal waste authorities, such as the UK's Yorkshire Water, are now incinerating *sewage* sludge which, it is said, cannot be accommodated elsewhere. As many countries will ban the sea dumping of sewage before the end of the century, the problem of disposal will grow.

See also: Energy from waste; Landfill; Waste management; Waste management industry.

Indoor Pollution

Indoor *air pollution* is caused when pollutants are released and trapped inside buildings. Airborne 'respirable particles' in the range of 0.01 to 10 microns in diameter are the most potentially damaging to lungs. So small that they can bypass our natural filters, they lodge in the lungs and cause serious respiratory problems and cancer.

Some indoor pollution comes from industrial processes – the fumes, smoke and dust they produce – and from modern office buildings which lack windows that open. Office particles include *carbon monoxide* from cigarette smoke, bacteria from *air-conditioning* plants, and *hydrocarbons* or *solvents* from adhesives, cleaners, paints and timber. They are thought to cause headaches, nausea and even cancer. Other possible causes include formaldehyde from chipboard.

There are, however, few firm facts about office-type indoor pollution, and much of the evidence is confusing and contradictory. Many of the problems are generally not life threatening, but their long-term effects could have a greater economic impact than more visible and more directly life-threatening pollution. Little is known about the indoor effect of *chemicals* in everyday use, such as *hairsprays* and highlighters, nor the vapours exuded from synthetic materials used in modern buildings. Nevertheless, the problem is sufficiently severe for the US Environmental Protection Agency to cite indoor pollution as a leading cause of environmental cancer.

In sealed, modern air-conditioned offices, indoor pollution gives rise to *sick building syndrome*. The UK House of Commons Environment Committee has calculated the cost (in terms of absenteeism, reduced productivity and remedial measures) as between UK£330 and UK£650 million a year.

Capturing Indoor Air Pollutants

Pollutants can be captured either at source or as fugitive emissions. Source capture is suitable for industrial processes which produce specific particles. Fugitive capture is suitable for diffuse contaminants. The ways of trapping particles comprise:

- *Windows that open*, which merely disperse the air. This is suitable only for low-toxicity diffuse pollutants and is not well controlled.
- *Mechanical filters.* These capture the larger particles (five microns and larger). Such particles comprise only about 5 per cent of all airborne contaminants, and include cement dust, pollen, fly ash, and some bacteria. In industrial situations, a hood and extractor fan is used to capture the air.
- *Electrostatic air cleaner.* This traps up to 95 per cent of all particles, notably those down to 0.01 micron. These include oil smoke, carbon black, welding and brazing fumes and fine fly ash. It works by electrically charging the particles and then attracting them.

In cool or cold seasons, the cleaned air should be recirculated back into the building, to reduce *heating* costs and help *energy* conservation.

See also: Air pollution; Office; Sick Building Syndrome; Welding and brazing.

Industrial Alcohol

Various types of *hydrocarbons*, especially methyl alcohol (*methanol* or wood spirit), which is a good *solvent*. It is used in dyeing and making formaldehyde, varnishes and polishes. Isopropyl alcohol is used as a solvent, preservative and in making perfumes and cosmetics.

Information, Management

The organization needs information to make environmental decisions. These include decisions about investment, process methods and controls. It also needs information to monitor its progress in meeting environmental targets. Information to be collected can include:

- volumes of *solid waste*, split by type (for example, paper, plastic);
- volumes of emissions to air, by gas (for example, SO_2);
- discharges to water; pH levels; or *BOD*; presence of particular substances or pollutants;
- consumption of energy, by site or plant;
- consumption of key non-renewable or *toxic* materials;
- complaints, by type.

Information can be gathered by environmental *audits* and by capturing specific process data (such as volumes of solid waste taken by the waste contractor). The information should be gathered regularly and communicated to relevant staff and *interested parties*. It should be kept in an accessible manual. A procedure should be in place to regularly update the information. The following information can be communicated:

- internally (through notice boards, E-mail, meetings etc);
- externally (through reports, press information, advertising, industry association newsletters, direct mail, etc).

Some multi-site companies collate initiatives and solutions that have been adopted by one member of the group, and disseminate them to other units. The aim is to identify successful solutions to common problems. A summary sheet identifies the problem, the solution arrived at and the benefits it provided. The case history in *Cups* (page 89) derives from one such solution.

See also: Environmental management system; Preliminary review; Monitoring; Report; Statement.

Initial Review: *see Preliminary Review*

Insecticides *see Pesticides*

Insulation

Insulation is a low-cost way of reducing *energy* consumption in buildings, and at the same time reducing the amount of *greenhouse gas* and other pollutants produced by power stations.

Insulating heating pipes saved one company 80 per cent of its heating losses. Other strategies include double- or triple-glazed windows, low emissivity glass, and roof and wall insulation. These can substantially reduce energy loss, as well as providing a more comfortable environment for the inhabitants.

Insulation materials used to be made with *ozone-depleting CFCs* or *HCFCs*, though some are made from recycled newspapers and other environmentally sound materials. Man-made mineral fibres are also used in insulation (such as rockwool), and some are carcinogens.

EU Eco-Label

Denmark has prepared proposals for an EU *eco-label* for insulation products. This will cover thermal insulation materials used on internal, external, cavity wall and roof insulation.

Best Practice

- Make or use only eco-labelled products, when available.

See also: Building design; Energy management.

Insurance

Hit by major claims for *asbestos* and pollution, insurance companies are now more cautious about providing cover for pollution claims. Cover tends to be more restricted and more expensive. Insurance will increasingly depend on the corporation's ability to demonstrate a commitment to environmental management, and will be available only for sudden and accidental incidents.

These restrictions are also affecting the professions. Professional indemnity insurers are suspending environmental cover for all chartered surveyors. The insurers are concerned about the surveyors' lack of qualifications to give environmental advice. Surveyors who want insurance now have to demonstrate technical, legal and professional experience. This exemplifies the trend for insurers to exclude environmental liabilities from their coverage.

The biggest environmental problem for insurance companies and their clients is thought to be contaminated land. The past is coming back to haunt industry and its insurers in the form of *Superfund* and the not infrequent discovery that land has been polluted decades ago by a previous site owner.

Large companies should consider setting up self-insurance schemes. RTZ, a mining firm, contributes US$15,000,000 annually to a fund which gives the firm protection for a period of 30 years. In the US, over 30 industrial insurance pools have been set up.

Best Practice

- Assess the company's current and past processes, as well as its post-operational and waste handling practices.
- If potential problems are discovered, investigate the scale of the impacts by taking measurements and assessing the scale of the company's potential liabilities.
- Tackle the causes of existing pollution without delay and put in place a programme of remedial action to clean up problems caused by past processes.
- Seek novel ways (if necessary) of providing insurance against pollution, especially gradual pollution.

See also: Liability.

Integrated Pollution Control: *see IPC*

Integrated Pollution Prevention and Control (IPPC)

A European directive that requires member states to control all industrial waste (whether to air, water or land) by one regulatory authority. This prevents the transference of pollution from one medium to another. Each plant will have a single licence governing emissions to air, water and land, rather than separate ones for each type of pollution. The legislation applies to many industries, including energy, steel, *chemicals*, *food processing*, factory farming, and the *paper and pulp* industry.

Some states, notably France, Denmark, Ireland and the UK, already take a unified approach to licensing polluting plants. The legislation will bring the greatest changes in Southern member states, many of which have industrial licensing, are governed by several authorities and have laws for individual emissions. National authorities will set emission limits for each plant. Existing plant will have several years to comply with the legislation.

See also: IPC.

Intel: *see Computers*

Interested Party

An individual or group concerned with, or affected by, an organization's environmental *performance*. This can include employees, trade unions, local residents and elected representatives. Organizations should define who their interested parties are and communicate with them. The term 'interested party' comes from *ISO 14001*.

See also: Communication; Public relations.

Intergovernmental Panel on Climate Change (IPCC)

A body of more than 300 scientists set up by the United Nations to examine the threat of *global warming*. It has forecast a rise in temperature, resulting in higher sea levels, and the loss of low-lying land. Changed weather patterns will also occur.

See also: Global warming.

Internal Audit: *see Environmental Audit; Local Authority*

International Chamber of Commerce: *see ICC*

International Whaling Commission (IWC)

An association of 24 countries connected with whaling. The IWC has successfully gained agreement from its members to protect whales, some of which are nearing extinction. In an effort to maintain its pro-whaling stance, Norway has threatened to leave the IWC while Japan, another whaling nation, has also sought to avoid restrictions on the killing of whales. In 1994, the IWC named the Southern Ocean (around Antarctica) as a whale sanctuary.

See also: Whales.

Ion Exchange: *see Liquid Waste*

Ionizing Radiation

Radiation from nuclear power and X-rays produces electrically charged particles (ions) in the material it strikes. This causes changes in living tissue, including cancer. Radiation is also used in radiotherapy, for the treatment of cancers, and to check for cracks in oil pipelines. Exposure may also come from the testing of *nuclear* devices, and accidents in the handling of *nuclear* material, including nuclear weapons. (Marshalling yards used by trains carrying spent nuclear fuel have been found to be radioactive.)

Advocates of nuclear power point out that the majority of radiation comes from natural radioactivity in the air and the ground; but this is for the average person (and is arrived at by dividing the entire nuclear dose by the total population). It does not take into account the higher doses to which certain people (for example, those living downwind of a nuclear power plant) are exposed. In addition, releases to air from nuclear tests or the extraction of uranium soon become 'natural background radiation'.

Some food processors want to use irradiated fresh food, but this has met with some consumer resistance, since the treated food would not show signs of decay. Non-ionising radiation, such as radio or ultraviolet rays, does not have this effect (though UV rays can also cause skin cancer).

Best Practice

- Adopt stringent work practices when using ionizing radiation.

See also: Nuclear industry.

IPC – UK

Integrated Pollution Control. A system for controlling all industrial wastes – whether to air, land or water, by one regulatory authority. It involves polluters having to pay for a consent to emit their pollution. This approach has been adopted by the EC for all member states.

See also: Integrated pollution prevention and control.

IPPC: *see Integrated Pollution Prevention and Control*

IRBM – UK

Integrated River Basin Management. The basis on which the UK's Environment Agency operates, namely that its regions are based on the natural catchment areas of river basins. This reduces the risk that pollution from one region could flow into another, creating management problems for the agency.

Iron and Steel Industry: *see Steel*

ISO 9000

Quality management standard upon which *ISO 14001* is based.

ISO 14001

A standard created by the International Organization for Standardization (ISO) for managing a company's environmental *impacts*. During the late 1980s, it was apparent that some companies were using *greenwash* (claiming to be environmentally sound while ignoring major impacts). The claims of even the greenest of firms were not *audited* and therefore lacked objectivity and independence. In addition, many initiatives were failing because they lacked the rigour of a management system (with its planned audits checking whether procedures were being followed).

It became clear that an *environmental management system* was needed, and some ISO member states wanted to use *ISO 9000*, the quality standard. Meanwhile the UK rushed out its own British Standard, *BS 7750*, and other countries, notably Canada and Ireland, did the same. ISO decided to produce a separate standard for managing the environment, which became ISO 14001.

ISO 14001 is a clear descendant of ISO 9000, with its combination of policy document, written procedures, audits, and management reviews. ISO 14001 has a bigger scope than the quality standard, since environmental issues affect more departments, but the elements are recognizable to those familiar with ISO 9000. ISO 14001 is not a guarantee of environmental excellence, but rather an assurance that the organization has a management system that identifies and manages the major environmental impacts. This means that two companies in the same industry can adopt different levels of environmental excellence, and both be certified to ISO 14001. In practice, the differences are unlikely to be large.

While it represents a challenge to the organizations that implement it, ISO 14001 is not the pinnacle of environmental excellence. Some companies may choose to upgrade from ISO 14001 to *EMAS*, which requires a public report and a formal register of effects. More details about how to implement ISO 14001 can be found under the headings listed in '*See also*' (page 176).

Requirement of ISO 14001

To gain ISO 14001, a company must demonstrate to a *certifier* that it has the following elements in place:

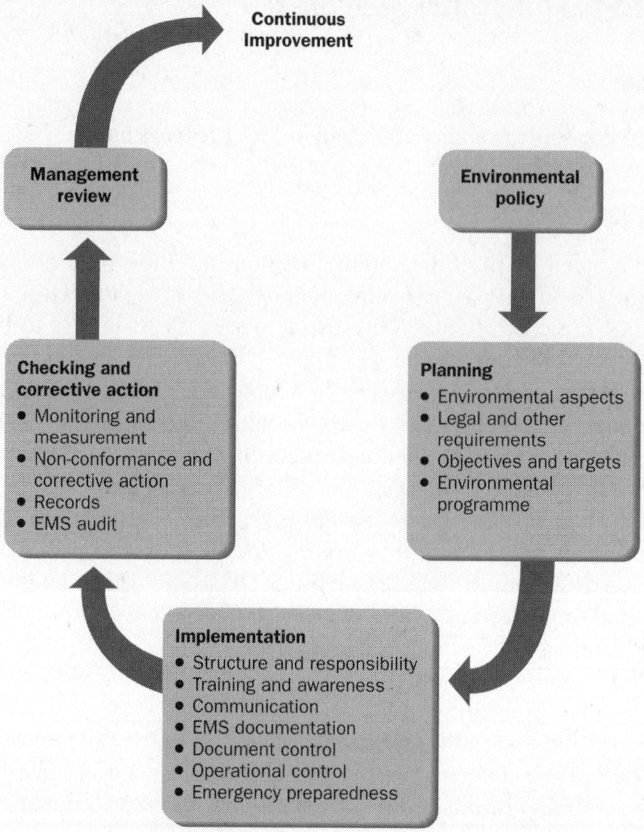

Figure 15: The Five Elements of ISO 14001

Requirement	Notes
Written environmental *policy*	The policy should include a commitment to continual improvement. It should be available to the public, and should commit the company to comply with legislation.
Procedure to identify environmental *aspects*	The organization should identify the ways in which it affects the environment (for example, through solid waste).
Procedure to identify legal requirements	The organization must know what environmental laws govern it. A subscription to an environmental newsletter would be one solution.

Requirement (*cont.*)	**Notes** (*cont.*)
Objectives and *targets*	Objectives and targets should exist at every relevant level in the organization. They must be consistent with the *policy* (above).
Programme	A programme will consist of the activities needed to achieve the objectives and targets (above). The organization should identify the person responsible for each element of the programme, and set a time frame.
Identified roles and responsibilities	The company should define who is responsible for carrying out different tasks that affect the environment. It should also nominate an executive to manage the *EMS*.
Effective *Training*	People whose jobs affect the environment must be properly trained. They should understand the impacts of their work, and the need to conform with the *EMS.*
Good *Communication*	The organization should communicate environmental issues well, both within the company and outside it.
Documentation	The organization must describe its *EMS* in writing. It should control its essential documents (especially procedures), keep them updated, and make sure that only current copies are in circulation.
Operational control	The organization must know how its *processes* affect the environment. It must control them in order to reduce their impact. That means having written *procedures* for them.
Emergency planning	The organization should have an emergency plan.
Monitoring and measurement of key processes	The organization should regularly measure the impact of its main processes.

Requirement	Notes
Control over *non-conformances*	The organization should investigate problems and resolve them. This includes complaints and incidents, and problems identified in audits.
Records	The organization should keep records that show how it manages its impacts. This might include emission or discharge records.
EMS Audits	Audits will show whether staff are adhering to the *EMS*. It will also highlight areas for improvement.
Management *Review*	Top management should regularly meet to assess the working of the *EMS*. The agenda could include the findings from recent audits, and an analysis of *records* (above).

Best Practice

- Implement ISO 14001, or a similar environmental standard, and have it certified.

See also: Environmental management system; EMS audit; Objectives; Operational control; Preliminary review; Procedures; Records; Register of Effects; Register of Legislation; Review; Targets.

ISO 14010

General guidelines for environmental auditing. The document defines auditing terms (such as 'client'). It requires auditors to use professional care, adopt systematic procedures and take into account the reliability of the data. ISO 14010 also sets out the information to be included in a report (objectives of the audit, the names of team members, and so on).

ISO 14011

This document gives guidelines for *audit* procedures. It gives typical audit objectives (such as determining whether the *EMS* has been properly implemented), and it defines the roles of the lead auditor, other team members and the client.

ISO 14011 encourages the team to review the client's documentation before starting the audit, and it outlines the factors to be taken into account when planning the audit (such as scheduling meetings). It explains the purpose of the opening and closing meetings, and indicates the contents of the audit report.

ISO 14012

This document sets out qualifications needs by environmental auditors.

ISO 14020

International standard for environmental labelling. It defines two types of labels:

- *Type 1:* This relates to 'multi-criteria' awards made by third parties (such as the EU's *eco-label*). This is covered in ISO 14024.
- *Type II:* This relates to 'self declaration' environmental claims made by manufacturers, distributors and retailers. This is found in ISO 14021.

At the time of writing, ISO 14020 and ISO 14023, which are normative references to 14021, had not been issued. A normative reference contains provisions which must be taken as part of the general standard (and contrasts with 'informative references' which are not obligatory).

ISO 14040

International standard for life-cycle analysis. It consists of the main standard (14040) and three other documents:

- *ISO 14040:* Life-cycle analysis: general principles and practices. This presents the general guidelines and key considerations, and is the main part of the standard.
- *ISO 14041:* Life-cycle inventory analysis.
- *ISO 14042:* Life-cycle impact assessment.
- *ISO 14043:* Life-cycle improvement assessment.

See also: ISO 14001; Life-cycle analysis.

IT Equipment: *see Computers*

IT Industry

The environmental impacts of the IT industry comprise:

- *solid waste* (including the waste of superseded products discarded by users);
- emissions to air (through the use of *solvents* and *ozone-depleting substances*, whose use the industry has substantially reduced);
- use of *fossil fuels* from the product's motors and fans;
- use of paper associated with the products;
- CFCs: formerly used in the computer industry to clean semiconductor housings and the chips themselves; today, other methods are used.

Some IT equipment is environmentally sound. For example, telephone equipment helps to reduce travel (and with it congestion, *air pollution* and the use of fossil fuels). Similarly, disks can be re-used many times. There is now a big industry in recycling printer cartridges.

Use of Energy

Some firms have introduced automated power management, where the PC switches into a reduced power 'standby' mode after a period of inactivity, and a further power-reduced 'sleep' state after another. This can reduce energy by 40 to 60 per cent. In Switzerland, PC power consumption must be reported to the government, and targets have been set for reducing PC and printer power consumption. Processor chips have been redesigned to use CMOS and other low-power technologies (such as the Intel SL chip). Drive manufacturers have also reduced their power requirements: disk drives now use only half the power they used to. Software companies are also providing power management tools.

See also: Computers; Energy Star.

IUCN

International Union for the Conservation of Nature and Natural Resources. IUCN compiles the Red Data book on endangered species. One of the biggest nature conservation bodies in the world, it holds the triennial World Conservation Congress.

Ivory

Material provided by the tusks of elephants, walruses and narwhals. Easy to carve and polish, ivory has been used for many decorative and household objects, such as knife handles and combs.

Trade in ivory was banned in 1990 under the *CITES* convention. This followed concern about the threatened extinction of the elephant. The African elephant declined from 1.3 million in the 1970s to 650,000 at the end of the 1980s. Between 1981 and 1989, Zambia lost 80 per cent of its elephants, Kenya lost 75 per cent, and Tanzania lost 70 per cent. However, the African elephant has made such a successful come-back that some countries are seeking to reintroduce the ivory trade.

Trade in antiques is legal, but any activity that promotes ivory also increases its demand and leads to more poaching. Poaching will only halt when demand falls, and this means that businesses should not trade in any form of ivory. Ivorine is an environmentally acceptable alternative for the replacement of piano keys.

Best Practice

- Do not deal in either fresh or carved ivory.

See also: Wildlife trade.

IWC: *see International Whaling Commission*

Kitchen Towels: *see Toilet Paper*

Kuwait

As it retreated from Kuwait in 1991, the Iraqi Army damaged nearly 800 Kuwaiti oil wells as well as oil tanks, poisoning 300 miles (483 km) of coast and 600 square miles (965 square km) of the Persian Gulf. Between 60 to 120 million barrels of oil were released, causing havoc among the fragile eco-systems that the Gulf nourishes.

In four weeks, from 16 May, the fires generated 86 billion watts of heat (equivalent to a 500-acre – 202 ha – forest fire), and 12,000 metric tonnes of particles fell each day. In addition, 1.9 million metric tonnes of *carbon dioxide* were created each day, along with 20,000 metric tonnes of *sulphur dioxide*. 600 wells became flaming columns, and it took six months to bring them under control, the last being capped on 6 November 1991. Despite the oil's devastation, the *wildlife* is expected to eventually recover.

However, the Gulf War is not the only source of oil pollution. An average of 250,000 barrels of oil spill into the Persian Gulf each year. Land reclamation is another cause of environmental damage. Along the coast, mangroves and coral reefs have been destroyed as development continues to grow.

LAAPC – UK

Local Authority Air Pollution Control. Under the Environmental Protection Act 1990, local authorities are responsible for controlling *air pollution* from the UK's moderately polluting industrial establishments, which comprise 25,000 plants. Bigger polluters are governed by the UK Environment Agency.

Labelling

The following environmental information may be shown on a label:

- *Source:* What is the product made from? What proportion is recycled and what proportion is biodegradable?
- *Usage instructions:* How can you avoid wasting the product? What dangers might the product pose – for example, toxicity?
- *Maintenance:* Can the product be mended? Can parts be obtained for it? Can it be upgraded?
- *Reuse:* Can the product be reused or refilled?
- *Disposal:* Can the product be recycled or taken back, and if so, how? If not, how should the product be safely disposed of? What problems might be caused by other forms of disposal – for example, incineration?

See also: Certification and labelling scheme; Design; Packaging.

LAC – UK

Local Advisory Committee, set up under the Environment Act 1995.

Landfill

The disposal of *solid waste* in rubbish dumps. Landfill is an inexpensive solution for waste; properly designed and managed sites serve as large bio-reactors which decompose the biodegradable material. Landfill also serves to fill up holes caused by quarrying. When full, sites can become nature reserves or forests. However, as seen below, landfill also has many drawbacks.

- Landfill sites are unpopular among local residents because of the lorry movements, odour, the danger of explosion, flies, scavengers, visual intrusion, the loss of views, and possibly toxic airborne gases.
- *Methane* is an explosive *greenhouse gas* which results from decomposing material in landfill sites, and which can seep into the air. Nowadays pipes are sunk into the site to draw off the gas. This then drives generators which produce electricity.
- In the past, housing developments have been built on old landfill sites where they later suffer from methane emissions.
- As rainwater percolates through the tip, and is joined by decomposing waste, a liquid, known as leachate, is produced. In old sites, this toxic material can escape into water courses. More modern sites are lined with impermeable clay and plastic sheeting to prevent this happening. The leachate can be drained and treated.
- If refuse is left open to the air, vermin will be attracted to the site and may spread disease.
- Due to the anaerobic (airless) conditions in some landfill sites, much of the rubbish does not biodegrade. Specialist archaeologists can exhume decades-old newspapers which are perfectly readable. Site operators are now increasing the rate at which waste degrades by increasing the water in them (because the wetter the waste, the faster it degrades).

Management of these problems depends on the skill, efficiency and commitment of the operator, as well as effective control by the regulatory authority.

Landfill Philosophies

At one time, sites allowed material to leach down into the water-table, on the grounds that the soil and rock it passed through, and the groundwater it mixed with, would 'dilute and attenuate' any toxins (a philosophy similar to '*dilute and disperse*'). However, this meant that pollutants started to turn up in rivers.

Today, sites tend to follow a 'concentrate and contain' strategy, in which the bottom of the site is lined with an impermeable barrier (often of clay), and the leachate is drawn off by pipes sunk into the site. This runs the risk that rainwater will saturate the site and cause leachate to spill overland. It also risks a build-up of *methane*.

Finding New Sites

It is becoming increasingly difficult to find new landfill sites because of the factors mentioned above, and because of the resulting opposition of *NIMBYs*. In addition, a decline in non-renewable resources (such as oil), and an awareness of our squandering nature is making the dumping of *solid waste* less acceptable.

The East Coast of the US is expected to run out of landfill sites by the end of the 1990s. The EPA estimates that 80 per cent of all landfills nation-wide will close and new sites must be found. There is more room in the Western states, but landfill sites and their toxic contents are unpopular. Old sites, many of them closed, are a particular hazard. Two of Britain's remaining areas of lowland heath, together with a coastal marsh used by large numbers of migratory birds, were found in 1991 to have been contaminated by leachate from closed landfill sites. The three sites, each of which is either a SSSI (Site of Special Scientific Interest) or a National Nature Reserve, have high levels of ammonia, which is affecting the local species. Liability is difficult to assess in such cases.

The costs of landfill are likely to grow as governments tax landfill waste. In 1995 the UK government announced such a tax, which would be collected by landfill site operators. The tax is expected to increase waste disposal costs by 30 per cent according to Jones Lang Wooton, international estate agents. This will have a direct effect on companies who pay to have their rubbish removed, and will therefore encourage them to minimize their waste.

Toxic Sites

Regulators are increasingly likely to insist that toxic waste is incinerated. But in the US, one in four people lives within four miles (6.5 km) of a toxic waste dump.

Best Practice

Companies which dispose of large quantities of waste to landfill should:
- Seek ways of reducing the amount of waste.
- Budget for rising landfill costs.

For site management:
- If the site is not based on impermeable strata, such as clay, its bottom should be lined with an impermeable layer of plastic or rubber to prevent leachate. Pipes should draw off the methane gas.
- To prevent odour, scavengers and wind-blown material, some sites place an inert cover, such as clay, over each day's waste. However, this reduces the amount of decomposition, so other sites now cover the day's work with hessian or a similar biodegradable material.

See also: Contaminated land; Incineration: Lekkerklerk; Methane, Recycling; Waste management industry.

Landfill of Waste Directive – EU

This directive harmonizes member states' legislation on landfill sites. It introduces a licensing scheme for operators and makes them liable for pollution. Operators must give financial guarantees to ensure that obligations even after the site is closed are met, via a landfill after-care fund. Co-disposal of waste can only take place in countries (namely the UK) where it has been practised and is likely to be banned completely. The directive defines three types of waste: inert, non-hazardous, and hazardous and member states must introduce criteria for assigning different kinds of waste to each category. The EU sees landfill as the method of last resort, and this directive seeks to minimize its impacts on the environment.

Land-mines

Approximately 100 million land-mines have been planted around the world and are being deployed at the rate of two million a year. They kill 10,000 civilians a year, while thousands more are maimed. At least 30 to 40 per cent of victims are children. Most land-mines are in poor countries, notably Cambodia, Angola, Mozambique, Somalia, Afghanistan and Iraq.

When detonated, a Valmara 69 land-mine (as used by Iraq in the Gulf War) springs half a metre into the air, blasting 1000 ball bearings in every direction at over 1000 miles an hour (1609 km per hour). Anyone within a 25-metre radius will be torn to pieces. These devices can be linked together to increase the kill radius. A Valmara land-mine costs just UK£30.

Land-mines are an important environmental issue because they take large areas of land out of use. Mined areas prevent people from feeding themselves by growing crops or rearing animals, and this leads to great hardship among already poor people. The United Nations is seeking support for the banning of land-mine production and the removal of as many existing land-mines as possible. At present, the UN removes 85,000 a year, at a cost of US$300 to US$1000 each.

See also: Defence industry.

Land Reclamation: *see Contaminated Land; Derelict Land*

Landscaping

Landscaping helps to soften harsh commercial outlines. It can screen visually unattractive parts of a site (such as *waste disposal*) and act as a sound barrier. Organizations should consult an ecological expert before starting work. For example, indigenous tree and plant species should be chosen because they are more useful to local *wildlife*. Landscaping can include ponds, which are invaluable for wildlife, and also a wilderness area, which is even more attractive to both *flora and fauna*. Some plants flourish on contaminated land and even help to remediate it.

When landscaping, thought should be given to pedestrian and bicycle routes, rather than treating them as secondary to vehicle routes.

See also: Grounds; Nature conservation.

Large Combustion Plants Directive – EU

EC Directives 94/66/EC and 88/609/EEC which require member states to introduce programmes to reduce total emissions from new and existing power stations. The directives set emission limits for SO_2, NO_x and dust.

Large Quantity Generator – US

An organization that generates more than 1000 kilograms of hazardous waste a month.

Laundry Detergents

Detergents use *nitrates* and *phosphates*, which cause *eutrophication*, as well as *chemicals* which are toxic to aquatic species. The EU has prepared proposals for an *eco-label* for household laundry detergents with the aim of reducing the *water pollution* they cause. Set by Germany, the criteria for winning an eco-label are:

- ingredients (total chemicals, critical dilution volume), phosphates, soluble and insoluble organics (aerobic and non-aerobic), non-biodegradable organics and *biological oxygen demand* (*BOD*);
- *packaging*;
- correct dosage (to prevent excess chemicals getting into water courses);
- information on the pack, including labelling of ingredients;
- fit for the purpose;
- validity of advertising claims.

A provisional criterion for phosphates has been included, to take account of eutrophication.

At the time of launch, some 15 per cent of detergents in Europe pass the criteria. This figure may increase as manufacturers bring their products into line. The UK's National Consumer Council criticized detergent companies, in a report commissioned by the government, for making spurious claims that their products are '*biodegradable*'. All British detergents, says the council, already met EU standards for biodegradability. Similar spurious claims were also found on shampoos and conditioners.

Best Practice

- Make or use only eco-labelled products when available.
- Use detergents made from natural vegetable oil.

See also: Cleaning agents; Eco-label.

LCA: *see Life-Cycle Analysis*

Lead

A useful industrial metal, lead is employed as a roof flashing in construction, in old plumbing, in paint, batteries, solder, as an anti-knock additive in petrol, and in gun cartridges. It can also be found in used engine oil.

Impacts

Lead is blamed for reducing IQ in children, especially where they have ingested lead from old paint. Lead is also thought to shorten people's life span, to produce kidney tumours and to increase susceptibility to infections. This has led to major international action to phase out its use. However, some studies have shown that children in areas of dense traffic have no more lead in their bodies than children in low traffic areas. Other studies have shown that children with lead in their bodies are no less intelligent than those without. Yet there is a degree of misinformation surrounding lead; and tetraethyl or tetramethyl lead (which is used as an anti-knock additive in petrol) is especially toxic.

Lead has been largely reduced or stopped in petrol, though other additives have been added. For instance, the US has banned lead from petrol since 1970, though other additives have replaced it, boosting the environmental burden. The EC has banned the use of leaded paints (lead carbamates and sulphates) for general artistic use, while permitting them for restoration or maintenance of works of art or historic buildings.

The US banned lead shot in gun cartridges in 1991. Alternatives made from steel and bismuth are now used instead. Canada has banned the use of lead shot in gun cartridges from 1997. According to a study quoted in the *Financial Times Environmental Liability Report*, hunters were putting two million kilograms of lead into the Canadian environment every year, and several hundred thousand geese and ducks were dying slow, agonizing deaths every year after swallowing lead pellets.

See also: Cars; Catalytic converter; Petrol; TEL.

Leg-Hold Traps

Many people now believe that leg-hold traps are cruel. They cause the animal undue pain and often break limbs. Animals have often chewed through their own leg in order to free themselves. An animal can be held in a trap for a long time because traps are set over a wide area and in such wild terrain that it takes days for the trapper to visit all of them. The steel leg-hold trap is now banned in more than 60 countries, and in eight US and three Australian states.

Because of the bans, and perhaps because of fur becoming less fashionable, the number of animals caught in Canada has slumped. The harvest of 'furbearers' has fallen from 3.2 million in 1986 to 815,000 in 1992. Nevertheless, despite spending more than Cdn$9.3 million on research between 1983 and 1997, Canada has failed to develop an acceptably 'humane' trap.

In 1991 the EU passed a resolution prohibiting the use of leg-hold traps within the union. It also banned the import of pelts from countries including Canada and the US which permit trapping methods that do not meet international humane trapping standards. Canada says that it is more humane to let an animal be free throughout its lifetime and kill it in its last 24 hours of life rather than keep it in a cage for years. Canada also says that the EU ban is simply designed to protect its own fur industry by shutting out the Canadians. However, more than half the fur produced in Canada is now farmed in ranches. Sales of ranched fur have also fallen. Canadian fur ranches produced 1.46 million pelts in 1986 compared with one million pelts in 1992.

Best Practice

- Alternative methods of killing are being developed, such as padded traps. The recommended 'quick-kill' traps have been found to be too expensive and heavy, but traps with rubber jaws may be a better solution.

See also: Fur.

Legionnaire's Disease

An illness caused by inadequate maintenance of an *air-conditioning* system. This exposes people to infection by inhaling the legionella bacterium.

See also: Indoor pollution; Sick building syndrome.

Legislation

Environmental legislation has grown all over the world since the 1970s. In some places, notably the US, politicians are seeking to undo what they see as excessive laws which impose an undue burden on firms and municipal authorities. In other countries, the amount of legislation is still growing.

The US Conference of Mayors says that complying with the Clean Air Act and nine other environmental laws costs the 1050 American cities with populations above 30,000 an estimated US$6.4 billion in 1993 – nearly 12 per cent of all local tax revenues. Supporters of the legislation say that people will get sick if looser controls permit bacteria in drinking water and the siting of toxic waste dumps next to housing estates. Opponents want more flexible legislation which will allow controls to reflect local conditions. However, advocates say that would create an 'uneven playing field'.

Among US citizens, only 18 per cent polled in 1994 thought that environmental regulations had gone too far while 41 per cent – the largest group – said they do not go far enough in protecting the environment. The European Union has had a major impact on legislation in member states. In the EU, environmental legislation often starts with a directive or regulation, which is then implemented locally by national parliaments. Many firms feel that the EU and other national governments are meddlesome, and actively lobby to reduce the scale of new and existing environmental laws. But there are advantages in replacing 15 or more different national laws (in the case of Europe) with a single one, and in introducing a level playing field for all players. It is clear that higher standards benefit the most efficient and cleanest companies, and penalize the dirty firms who have not moved with the times.

Many people see environmental legislation as a spur to innovation and best practice. The US lobby group Environmental Industries Commission says it is no coincidence that tightly regulated countries like Germany, the US and Japan have the biggest share of the US$250 billion global environment industry.

Best Practice

- The organization should be aware of all environmental legislation, including consents and permits and local controls.
- It should have a written procedure for all affected *processes*, and should carry out regular *audits* to check compliance.

See also: Government; Register of legislation.

Lekkerklerk, The Netherlands

An estimated 250 houses were built between 1972 and 1975 on top of an illegal dump of toxic chemicals from the dyestuffs industry, including toluene. After residents suffered various illnesses, the authorities found that the houses and drinking water were contaminated. The area was evacuated and the site cleared up in 1981, at a cost of UK£156 million.

Liability

Draconian US product liability laws have led to the American courts making huge awards. This has affected the American and UK insurance industry (especially Lloyds of London), and the ability of some companies to operate profitably and to innovate.

The first big product liability claims were against *asbestos*. Staff who contracted asbestosis initially got small sums from workers' compensation schemes. Then, in 1969, Thelma Borel, the widow of a dead asbestos worker, won US$79,000 in a court action against Fibreboard Paper Products, an asbestos firm. The award triggered claims from thousands of other sick asbestos workers in the US, and meant that other asbestos firms were liable for illness caused by their products. It also meant that people could sue firms directly.

When the asbestos companies were found to have hidden medical evidence, the courts were appalled; this led to larger and punitive damages, with James Cavett, a retired boiler maker, receiving US$2.3 million in 1982. Apart from asbestos, there have also been big awards against manufacturers of silicon breast implants, against accountants, and against firms which caused pollution incidents. These kinds of claims caused London United Investments to crash, owing US$10.8 billion. The firm underwrote high-risk liability insurance for North American companies and professionals against legal awards.

Environmental liability is reasonably easy to prove in the case of oil spills or similar kinds of pollution. Companies should be able to demonstrate 'due diligence' in that they took precautions to prevent an accident from happening. Installing an *environmental management system* is the best way to achieve this. Responding quickly to an environmental disaster, and preventing its spread, will also reduce the company's costs.

However, liability for illnesses caused by emissions to air is much less easily proven in law. A UK£6 million law suit in 1995 failed to demonstrate that toxic emissions from a Rechem incinerator were responsible for causing sickness in a herd of cows. The judge decided that overfeeding the herd had caused the problem.

Faced with the costs of mopping up pollution, authorities are likely to seek redress from banks which have lent money to the offending business. The bank is an obvious target because it has money. In the US, the *Fleet Factors* case sought to place liability with the banks, who (needless to say) strongly contend this principle.

Liability of Insurers

In California, the Supreme Court ruled in 1991 that property insurers are liable for costs when policy holders are ordered to clean up sites polluted with *toxic waste*. The case involved FMC, a chemical and weapons company, which was sued for polluting land at 79 sites in 22 states.

In another case in 1992, the US Ninth Circuit Court of Appeal decided that an insurance company had to pay Intel's clean-up costs, even though Intel had voluntarily decided to undertake the work. The court decided that Intel was entitled to cooperate with the Environmental Protection Agency, rather than wait to be coerced. It ruled that cooperation would be cheaper for the insured company, which would sooner or later be required to meet its obligations.

According to lawyers Simmons & Simmons, this ruling could affect other countries' policies, including the UK's CGL (Comprehensive General Liability) policies, in cases where a polluter undertakes voluntary clean-up as an alternative to being forced to do so under a regulator's statutory powers.

International Standards

Adopting lower standards in overseas operations than would be acceptable in the West also constitutes a liability. Thor Chemicals, a British chemical firm, was sued in the UK courts for negligence over mercury poisoning, which was alleged to have seriously injured two of its employees in Natal, South Africa, and to have killed a third.

Environmental Audits and Liability

Firms sometimes instigate an *audit* in order to assess their risk of environmental damage and hence the scale of their liability. Paradoxically, the audit can make the firm more liable if it reveals risks which need to be resolved, and which the firm may be unable to pay for in the short term. This is the 'smoking gun' principle. Likewise, an opponent may call for the audit to be produced in court, and this too could harm the firm. Some lawyers are seeking for audit information to be made 'privileged'. This would mean that the firm would not have to produce it as evidence.

Another solution would be for the company to commission two firms of consultants, one of which would carry out small-scale compliance audits, while the other would investigate wider issues. If only one firm is used, it should keep two separate sets of files. Information about an audit should be restricted in its circulation until a decision has been made about its legal implications.

See also: Exxon Valdez; Insurance; Litigation; Product Liability; Shell.

Life-Cycle Analysis (LCA)

LCA analyses a product's impact on the environment by examining all its effects, from 'the *cradle to the grave*'. This includes its raw materials, production method, impacts in use, and the effects of disposal. These impacts may be classified as follows:

- raw materials used (their scarcity, toxicity, impact on nature and whether they are renewable);

- energy and resources (such as water) used in manufacture;
- pollutants and wastes generated by the manufacturing process, and the extent of recycling;
- type of *packaging* used and its ease of reuse or recycling;
- *energy* used and *pollution* caused in distribution;
- pollutants, energy and resources involved when the product is in use;
- the effects of final disposal after it has served its purpose (including recycling and biodegradability).

It follows that anyone carrying out an LCA has to trace the product back to raw material suppliers. The company has to decide how far back it will go, since all products start as basic elements, such as oil, iron ore, or grains of wheat. Studies in the motor trade have shown that suppliers' products make up a large proportion of a *car's* total toxic release. They include primary metal processors, rubber and wire products, and industrial *chemical* sectors.

Conclusions are often open to dispute, especially when comparisons are made between different kinds of impact (deciding, for example, whether disposable nappies [diapers] are better than towelling nappies).

LCA is most effective when it is used to identify and reduce areas of high environmental impact. These include lessening the product's use of energy, increasing its flexibility, and lengthening its life. Thus, when preparing an *eco-label* for washing machines, it was found that the impacts involved in the product's use (namely the detergent, energy and water used for washing clothes) greatly outweighed the impacts used in making the machines. The eco-label that resulted from this LCA encourages manufacturers to develop machines that use less detergent, electricity and water.

LCA and the EU's Eco-Label

The European Union has issued guidelines on LCA. Drawn up by a group of 'sages', the guidelines use a methodology which aims to be scientifically sound and workable. The EU LCA does the following:

- It compares different products on the basis of their common function.
- It relates environmental impacts, at all stages from cradle to grave, to market changes and technology improvements.
- It helps to minimize data required for applications, by identifying well-founded environmental criteria.

Standards

An international standard, *ISO 14040*, has been prepared to give guidance.

	Product Life Cycle				
	Pre-production	Production	Distribution and packaging	Use	Disposal
Solid waste					
Soil pollution and degradation					
Water contamination					
Air contamination					
Noise					
Consumption of energy					
Consumption of non-renewable resources					
Effect on eco-systems					

Source: EU Eco-Labelling Board (adapted)

Figure 16: A Matrix for Assessing a Product's Lifetime Impact

See also: Cradle to grave; Eco-label; ISO 14040.

Lighting

Impacts

Unnecessary lighting causes pollution. It increases the amount of electricity required from power stations. These, in turn, emit *air pollution* and use non-renewable *fossil fuels*, such as coal and oil.

Eco-Labelling

A European *eco-label* exists for light bulbs. The criteria for single-ended bulbs are:

- *energy* efficiency (light output efficacy is related to lamp wattage);
- *mercury* (no more than 10 milligrams (mg) or 1.4 mg of mercury per mega-lumen hour of light output);
- *packaging* (no laminates or composite plastics; cardboard packaging must contain at least 65 per cent recycled material);
- product information (operation at low temperatures, dimmer switches, size and shape);
- Lifetime (must exceed 8000 hours).

Compact fluorescent lamps took just 3 per cent of the market in 1995, and the EU hopes to increase the penetration of these lamps because they use five times less electricity than ordinary filament bulbs and last eight times longer. High-pressure sodium lamps achieve the same results for industrial and road lighting.

At present, only compact fluorescents meet the *eco-label* criteria. If each of the 145 million households in Europe replaced just three of their bulbs with compact fluorescents, the total energy saving would equal the output of ten 600 megawatt power stations.

Disposal

Older fluorescent light tubes may use mercury ballasts and other toxic materials. They should be disposed of as hazardous waste.

Best Practice

- Reduce lighting where appropriate by using lower wattage lights, by having centrally controlled lighting (usually with manual overrides), and by replacing tungsten lights with fluorescent or compact fluorescent lights.
- Replace ordinary fluorescents with high-frequency ones which use 30 per cent less energy.
- Dispose of light bulbs in an appropriate manner.
- Use only eco-labelled bulbs when available.

See also: Electricity-generating industry; Energy management; Office.

Light Pollution

Astronomers are having increasing difficulty seeing the stars because of the amounts of artificial light thrown up by an increasingly urban and lighted society. While lights are useful in deterring theft, they can also be anti-social if they cause glare, prevent neighbours from sleeping, or make the neighbourhood look like Alcatraz. The darkest shadows are found beside the brightest lights, so lights are not always as effective as they might be.

Best Practice

- *Audit* the site for anti-social lighting.
- Assess whether more use of narrow spotlights and downlighters can prevent light from spilling outside the site.
- See whether crime prevention techniques, such as a clear area around the site perimeter, would serve to deter crime just as well as bright lights.

Limit Value

A fixed emission standard applied to hazardous *chemicals* (such as those on the *Black List*). This will be defined as a maximum concentration of a specific pollutant being discharged from a plant.

Lindane

A hazardous organophosphorus *insecticide* used in wood preservatives and on brassicas, root vegetables, seed treatments, and domestic pests. Being fat soluble, it does not break down and is sometimes found in milk and cheese. In 1996, unexpectedly high levels of lindane were found in UK supermarket milk. The Ministry of Agriculture said that an adult would need to drink ten litres of contaminated milk a day for the acceptable daily intake (ADI) of lindane to be exceeded.

Impacts

Lindane is suspected of causing breast cancer. Lincolnshire has the highest rate of breast cancer in the UK (40 per cent more than average) and is one of the biggest suppliers of vegetables. Some link this with the use of lindane in *pesticides*. Lindane is an *oestrogen mimic* and a possible cause of birth defects. It is now banned in 17 countries. However, in 1993 the UK's Health and Safety Executive said that lindane 'is a useful ingredient in medicines and wood preservatives, of long proven value.'

Best Practice

- Do not use.

Liquid Waste

The old policy of pouring liquid waste down the drain is no longer acceptable in advanced nations and an increasing number of developing countries. Apart from the poorest nations, most states now set pollution limits on each factory, and water companies charge polluters for disposing of their waste.

As with solid and airborne waste, it is good practice to identify the waste streams and separate them. Then the organization should see whether the waste can be made less hazardous or polluting, whether by changing the process *chemicals* or by redesigning the process. A less satisfactory solution is to treat the waste, either chemically or physically, as shown in Tables 9 and 10.

Plants in some industries, such as pulp mills and ethylene plants, are creating closed-water systems. Here, water is internally recycled and liquid discharge is eliminated.

Case Study 18: Saving Money by Reducing Liquid Waste

At ICI Paints in Stowmarket, England, the company disposed of 3000 tonnes of *waste water* a year, costing UK£100,000 a year plus a further UK£100,000 in material value. The company reduced water use by changing washing practices and reusing some washings, which together reduced the demand for water. Thus, with little capital investment, the waste water fell from 3000 tonnes to 1400 tonnes. Microfiltration then reduced the cost of waste paint further, so that costs were a mere 5 per cent of what they were in 1989.

Best Practice

When handling effluent:

- Quantify the effluent.
- Record any spills.
- Separate waste water streams, where cost effective.
- Reduce the impact of water pollution by filtration, chemical, or biological treatment.
- Alter the process to use less toxic compounds.
- Reduce water pollution by installing effluent treatment plants, by filtration and other techniques.
- Introduce a system which continuously measures and monitors the effluent. The system should close down the polluting process if target levels are exceeded, or if liquid is likely to overflow.
- Regularly calibrate water-monitoring equipment.
- Ensure that the location and purpose of all drains, pipelines and outfalls are known and mapped. Colour code foul and surface water drains.
- Ensure that tanks containing oil and other pollutants are bunded (surrounded by a leak-proof basin).
- Ensure that all interceptors are oil-escape proof.

To reduce effluent:

- Set targets for the disposal of liquid effluent into drains or water courses. Reduce the limit annually.
- Alter the production process.
- Improve housekeeping.
- Improve cleaning methods.
- Extend the life of process solutions by topping up, filtration, etc.
- Dry clean (by scraping) to remove solid pollutants.
- Check for leaks and spillages in company activities. Repair leaks and alter systems to stop spillages. Check, in particular, that fuelling points do not leak.
- Train staff to understand the nature of water pollution and how to prevent it.

Table 9: Physical Treatment of Waste Waters

Process	Aim	Examples
Screening	Remove coarse solids	Vegetable canneries, paper mills
Centrifuging	Concentrate solids	Sludge dewatering in chemical industry
Filtration	Concentrate fine solids	Final polishing and sludge dewatering in chemical and metal processing
Sedimentation	Remove settled solids	Separation of inorganic solids in ore extraction, coal and clay production
Flotation	Remove low-specific gravity solids and liquids	Separation of oil, grease and solids in chemical and food industry
Freezing	Concentrate liquids and sludges	Recovery of pickle liquor and non-ferrous metals
Solvent extraction	Recover valuable materials	Coal carbonizing and plastics manufacture
Ion exchange	Separate and concentrate	Metal processing
Reverse osmosis	Separate dissolved solids	Desalination of process and wash water
Adsorption	Concentrate and remove trace impurities	Pesticide manufacture, dyestuffs removal

Source: Harrison (ed), (1990) *Pollution: Causes, Effects and Control,* Royal Society of Chemistry

Table 10: Chemicals Used to Treat Industrial Waste Liquids

Chemical	Purpose
Calcium hydroxide	pH adjustment, precipitation of metals and assisting sedimentation
Sodium hydroxide	Used mainly for pH adjustment in place of lime
Sodium carbonate	pH adjustment and precipitation of metals with soluble hydroxide
Carbon dioxide	pH adjustment
Aluminium sulphate	Solids separation
Ferrous sulphate	Solids separation
Chlorine	Oxidation

Source: Harrison (ed), (1990) *Pollution: Causes, Effects and Control,* Royal Society of Chemistry

See also: Reed bed technology; Waste management; Water pollution.

Litigation

Regulators, pressure groups, consumers and employees have become increasingly litigious; and the development of 'no-win, no-fee' cases in the UK will encourage more litigation. On the other hand, claimants often fail to win their case. In law, it is difficult to prove in court that a specific *chemical* has caused ill health. Also, many companies prefer to make an out-of-court settlement, which the claimant may accept, knowing that he may become liable for the court costs if the case goes against him. Thus little is provided in law one way or another.

ADR

With the concern about delays and costs resulting from conventional litigation, some disputants are turning to alternative dispute resolution (ADR). According to Simmons and Simmons, the most common forms of ADR are mediation, executive tribunal (or 'mini-trial'), independent expert appraisal and non-binding adjudication. These techniques can be used instead of, or as well as, litigation or arbitration.

In the US, ADR has been used to resolve disputes concerning product liability, toxic torts, *hazardous* waste, *water pollution* and planning matters. In some cases, the ADR involved 100 parties.

The advantages are preservation of business relationships through negotiated settlement, faster resolution and protection of business confidentiality. The solutions are also likely to be more flexible.

In 1993 Southern California Edison Company used ADR to settle a suit from an environmental organization alleging that the firm's *nuclear* plant had damaged sea life. The parties agreed to a two-day mini-trial. At the end of the case, Edison agreed to spend money on restoring specified wetlands and contributed a significant sum towards a marine environment education centre in southern California. The outcome was thought to be more apposite and imaginative than what a court would have awarded.

Threats from Non-Governmental Organizations

Having a positive relationship with the regulatory authority does not preclude a company from prosecution. In 1991, Greenpeace successfully prosecuted Albright & Wilson, a chemical company, for discharging excessive amounts of copper, chromium, zinc and nickel into the Irish Sea. The company was fined UK£2000 and ordered to pay UK£20,000 in costs. The regulatory authority, the *National Rivers Authority* (*NRA*) had known about the company's discharges but had taken the view that prosecution was not the appropriate way to deal with it. Greenpeace warned that it would not hesitate to prosecute in cases where a regulatory authority exercises its discretion not to take legal action against 'environmental vandals'.

However, Greenpeace also makes mistakes. In 1994, Teesside Magistrates ordered the pressure group to pay UK£29,000 costs after it withdrew an action against ICI. Greenpeace claimed that samples it had taken from the company's Wilton works in Teesside contained four chemicals which the company had no consent to discharge. But further analysis of its samples revealed discrepancies against the original findings.

Litter

Litter is a form of pollution. Customers of fast food outlets, newsagents and other stores are particularly prone to create litter. Organizations in such markets can provide litter bins and ensure that they are regularly emptied.

Local Authorities

The local or municipal authority influences the environment in many ways:

- *As a large organization.* Local authorities are major organizations in their own right, often employing thousands of staff. Their policies on their own vehicles, stationery and building maintenance will have a major impact on the environment.
- *Departments with major environmental effects.* For example, grounds departments may have environmentally sound policies towards the use of *pesticides*, peat and wild flowers. A highways department can influence the local environment by its attitudes towards cyclists and pedestrians, and by the use of traffic calming methods.
- *Other departments.* A public housing department may choose to use environmentally sound building methods and materials. An education department can encourage environmental awareness in young people.
- *As a planning authority.* The local authority's power to grant or withhold building permits is one of its most potent and long-lasting environmental influences. For example, the habit of granting permission for distant out-of-town shopping centres has impoverished town and city centres.
- *By dispensing information, grants and advice.* Many local authorities can give grants for environmental improvements, and this can influence the local environment. For example, some authorities give grants to help companies undertake an environmental *audit* or introduce an *EMS*.

The Charter

Many local authorities have produced an environmental charter, their version of the corporate environmental policy. As with any policy, this can be followed or ignored, and often the most destructive of authorities have eloquent charters committing them to *sustainable* management.

Internal Audit

Local authorities often commission an audit on their environmental performance (usually called an internal audit). Since the first flush of enthusiasm for the environment has passed, any authority that was going to commission an audit will have done so; the more committed authorities may be considering follow-up audits. Since many local authorities are short of money and staff for the most basic of services (such as care for the elderly), recommendations that require money are unlikely to be implemented.

State of the Environment Report

Some local authorities have commissioned a *State of the Environment Report*, which outlines the levels of pollution, amenities and facilities within the authority's boundary. These often gather statistical data from various sources and are designed to guide future strategy. The reports vary greatly in size, and what really counts is the authority's financial resources and its commitment to good environmental management. For example, the local authority can, through its planning powers, have a major influence on planning (always providing there is a growing rather than declining demand for development). However, the local authority's ability to influence local businesses is weak, except by force of law. One authority found it virtually impossible to give away 50-per cent grants for environmental audits.

EMAS for Local Authorities

The UK has developed a version of *EMAS* for local authorities, created by the Local Government Management Board (LGMB). This considers two kinds of impacts: direct ones (caused by the authority's own waste and energy outputs), and the service (or indirect impacts) created by its regulatory and planning powers, such as land-use controls.

Implementing EMAS at the Planning, Transport and Economic Strategy Department of Warwickshire County Council in the UK has revealed savings of UK£70,000. Examples include:

- Street lamps were changed from 80 watt mercury bulbs to 70 watt high-pressure sodium lamps. The new bulbs produce better light and are cheaper and safer to dispose of. Savings are estimated at UK£28,000.
- The county council's fleet has been streamlined, which will save fuel and contribute to lower exhaust emissions. Estimated savings are UK£35,000.
- Installing an 'ice-alert' system has prevented a number of precautionary gritting runs being carried out. This has saved salt, wear and tear on gritting lorries, and will have helped to avoid unnecessary pollution. Savings are estimated at UK£4500.
- Using recycled laser printer cartridges would save UK£50,000 a year.

UK Legal Responsibilities

In the UK, local authorities are responsible for controlling the following:

- *air pollution* from the 25,000 lesser-polluting industrial sites;
- household and some commercial and industrial waste collection;
- promotion of waste prevention, reduction and recycling;
- the control of most contaminated land sites;
- food safety.

Case Study 19: Sheffield City Council

In arriving at its green purchasing policy, Sheffield City Council has had to face several problems. They include:

- *Availability:* Where demand exceeds supply in some products, the council has to ensure that it can maintain supplies. This can take priority over environmental considerations.
- *Devolved purchasing:* Schools, social services homes and other parts of the council make their own management decisions, including control of their spending. The solution to this problem lies in communicating the council's environmental policy. The council has issued a booklet called *Buying a Better Future*.
- *Increased prices:* There is often a premium to be paid for green products. In cases of budgetary constraint, this may prove unacceptable. The council keeps pressure on suppliers to reduce costs.
- *Hype:* Manufacturers are liable to put spurious green claims on their products. The council recognizes that it has to become knowledgeable: it cannot rely on manufacturers' claims.
- *Partnerships:* The council is trying to build better relationships between itself, environmentalists and suppliers to develop more environmentally friendly products. In particular, it is encouraging suppliers to produce better *packaging*, including the use of biodegradable or returnable packaging.
- *Final disposal: Waste disposal* brings many problems, particularly for products such as vehicle tyres and certain plastics which cannot be disposed of in an environmentally friendly way. The council emphasizes the need for products whose disposal does not cause difficulty.

Best Practice

Local authorities should:

- Commission an environmental audit if one has not been done in the last four to five years and implement its findings.
- Commission a *State of the Environment Report*, if one has not been done in the last four to five years, and adopt its recommendations.
- Consider getting registered to *EMAS*.

See also: Air quality; Composting; Contaminated land; EMAS; Environment Act; Environmental Protection Act; Recycling; Roads; Strategy, environmental.

Logging: see *Timber Industry – Temperate; Timber Industry – Tropical; Trees*

Logistics: see *Distribution*

London Dumping Convention (LDC)

The London Dumping Convention (LDC) has been accepted by countries responsible for 65 per cent of the world's fleet. Delegates to the convention agreed to phase out the dumping of industrial waste at sea by the end of 1995. The resolution is not legally binding but could have an impact in reducing waste disposal at sea.

The LDC divides substances into three categories. The first are substances that are completely banned. They include *organohalon* compounds, persistent plastics, crude oil, high-level *radioactive* waste, and materials produced for biological or chemical warfare. A second category of substance may only be dumped after a special permit has been issued. The third category can be dumped after a general permit has been issued.

The dumping of *sewage* sludge and other wastes has decreased since the London Dumping Convention came into force. However, sea-based dumping is likely to continue for some time, controlled by the LDC. In addition, disposal or treatment of wastes on land is not necessarily less damaging to the environment. However, dumping at sea puts human health at risk due to:

- pathogens;
- increased *eutrophication* from nutrients contained in wastes;
- the *toxic* effects of some substances on marine life;
- the damaging effect of dumping on fishing, recreation and other activities.

See also: Sea; Waste management; Water pollution.

Los Angeles

City with the worst smog in the US. Current proposals are to create a market for pollution permits. Industrial polluters would be assigned a number of shares, each representing a permitted amount of pollution. They could be bought and sold. The regulators could then gradually reduce the polluting value of each share. The scheme is thought to free businesses from present detailed restrictions on emissions. Environmental groups plan to buy some of the shares to prevent them from being used.

Love Canal, New York, US

Site of a *chemical* pollution disaster. The site, near Niagara City, USA, was an abandoned canal (built by William T Love in the nineteenth century). Between 1932 and 1950, the canal was used by the Hooker Chemicals and Plastics Corporation as a dump for its waste materials. Approximately 20,000 tonnes of hazardous waste were dumped in the canal before it was sold in 1953, and a housing estate and school were built on it.

In 1977, following ill health among residents, the air, water supplies and land were found to be polluted More than 240 families were evacuated, and in 1978 President Carter declared the site a Federal Disaster Area. This was the first executive order relating to hazardous waste. The cost of the clean-up was

US $100 million. As a result of publicity surrounding Love Canal, toxic waste became a political issue and led to *CERCLA* legislation in the US, making industrial nations around the world aware of the problems of contaminated land.

See also: Landfill.

Lubricants: *see Oil*

LULU

Locally Undesirable Land Uses. The things you would not want to find in your backyard, such as a toxic waste incinerator or a *landfill* site. LULUs tend to be sited in poor communities. This can look like discrimination against poor people, or reflect their weaker ability to fight development. But some believe that LULUs drive down land prices and thus attract poorer people.

Maintenance, Buildings: *see Building Design; Office*

Maintenance, Grounds: *see Grounds; Nature Conservation*

Maintenance, Vehicle: *see Garages*

Managed Retreat

Removing man-made sea defences or making gaps in them, thereby allowing the sea to wash further inshore. This policy has developed after governments realized that holding back the sea has sometimes unforeseen consequences, including flooding, coastal erosion and ever-more costly repairs. In some cases, managed retreat has taken place in response to increasingly stormy weather.

The construction of a weir at Porlock Bay in Somerset, England, reduced the action of long-shore drift. As a result, a natural shingle ridge, formerly replenished by the long-shore drift, declined in height. The sea increasingly breached the ridge during stormy weather, flooding the hinterland, so plans have been laid to allow the sea to inundate the area behind the ridge.

See also: Global warming.

Management: *see Strategy*

Man-Made Mineral Fibres (MMF)

These small fibres can cause irritation to the lung passages and are thought to cause cancer.

Marketing

The key environmental issues in marketing are: market research, new product development, and advertising and labelling claims.

Marketing Research

Companies should identify the level of interest in green issues on the part of their stakeholders – customers, shareholders, employees and local residents. If green matters are not important to them, it may not be worth spending too much money elaborating on the issues involved. On the other hand, it is easy to be complacent; if a new entrant to the market launches a green product, the consumer's attitudes may quickly change.

If green issues seem important, companies should identify – through market research – whether a particular organization is seen as environmentally responsible, and how it compares with its competitors. Having identified the important issues (such as *packaging*, ingredients, fuel consumption, etc), companies should then benchmark their product or service against the best in the market, and similar outside organizations, and seek to reduce their impacts.

Corporate research is also important for large companies which are in the public eye. Public utilities and large corporations need a good image – especially because the government has the option of regulating the market more closely if it believes that companies are failing to behave responsibly. Tracking research should be carried out continuously, to assess whether the company's image is improving and to see the impact of events. In this way companies can evaluate the effect of pollution incidents and green advertising claims.

New Product Development

All organizations need to rejuvenate their products and services, because today's standards are higher than those of the past, and this process is likely to continue. In the environmental arena, this means producing products and services which pollute less and use fewer resources. This may mean developing a R&D programme, or carrying out more marketing research.

Advertising and Labelling Claims

Telling the customer about the product's environmental benefits can give the organization a competitive advantage. Consumers want to know that their purchases are not causing undue environmental damage. This gives the green product an advantage over its rivals. Therefore, genuine environmental advantages should be highlighted. However, environmental benefit is only one aspect of the product's performance, and customers will only buy a green brand when it performs at least as well as competing products.

Sometimes, a green stance is useful where the product or service is identical in all other ways. A bank that is able to demonstrate environmental probity (such as the Co-op Bank in the UK) may win more new business. A green benefit is often a performance benefit, too. A *car* that uses less fuel reduces the customer's motoring cost and makes him feel that he is helping the world by cutting the use of non-renewable resources. However, claims should be as specific as possible. It is reasonable to say, 'Made from 100 per cent post-consumer waste' (a detailed and verifiable claim); but it is not right to say, 'Environmentally friendly' (a vague claim). Claims should be supportable (that is, companies should hold substantiation for all factual green claims). Claims should not be:

- Misleading or partial (such as advertisements claiming that *nuclear power* is environmentally sound because it does not emit CO_2, while omitting to mention that the waste must be stored for centuries and an explosion could make the land uninhabitable). Claims that chickens or their eggs are free range have often been found flawed. A properly free range hen should roam around a field, will not be debeaked, and will not be fed antibiotics.
- An infringement of green principles (for example, *car* ads that encourage people to drive fast).
- Vague (the words 'environmentally friendly' should not appear on *packaging*, because they are unspecific).
- Unfairly implied by the brand name or packaging (such as pictures showing a traditional farming scene when the product is intensively farmed).
- Debatable or unsubstantiated (such as claiming that air dryers are environmentally better than hand towels).
- Out of date (using statistics that are a decade old).
- Misleading (showing a three-arrow recycling mark on a plastic bin liner, with the words 'can be recycled' – everything can be recycled, given long enough. The three-arrow mark should only be used to denote 'made from recycled materials'. It should always be qualified with a caption, such as 'made from 100 per cent recycled materials'.)
- Cloaked in extravagant language.
- Absolute (claiming, for example, that 'our product does not harm the environment'), unless there is convincing evidence that the product will have no effect on the environment.

See also: Green grid; Packaging; Public relations; Strategy, environmental.

Markets for Environmental Technology

German companies lead the world in meeting the growing demand for environmental technology. They have more than 20 per cent of an international market worth more than UK£135 billion a year, and one which is expected to increase to more than UK£400 billion by the year 2000.

According to a report by Environmental Policy Consultancy, major new markets beckon suppliers whose products meet the demands of future environmental legislation. However, the demand is a zero-sum game: the new products will be at the expense of old ones. Markets likely to experience growth include:

- *air pollution* control;
- alternative *energy* (solar power, wind power, biofuels);
- bio-friendly chemicals (biotechnology, gentle chemistry);
- cleaning systems (including low- and high-tech solutions and systems for contaminated land);
- consultancy services (in *waste reduction*, emission control, recycling, and environmental protection;

- energy management;
- energy reduction (insulation, improved building materials, lighting, heating, cooking, etc.);
- environmental monitoring (measuring, control and analysis equipment and systems);
- information (such as publications or exhibitions);
- *landfill* management, landfill gas systems;
- marine pollution control;
- natural materials (such as cotton, wood, linen or linoleum);
- nature conservation or products that aid nature;
- noise abatement;
- odour control;
- pollution control (such as filtration equipment to improve water quality; gas filtration systems to reduce emissions of *sulphur dioxide* and *carbon dioxide*);
- process control (such as electronic controls for mixing, monitoring and warning);
- raw materials (products and systems that minimize the use of non-renewable or damaging raw materials);
- recycled products;
- recycling systems;
- soil remediation and site clean-up;
- *solid waste* (treatment and recycling of recoverable waste);
- test laboratories;
- *transport* (new fuels, leaner engines, public transport systems);
- *waste management* (treatment systems, including bio-treatment and incinerators);
- water and *sewage* treatment.

See also: Technology.

MARPOL

Protocol on the Prevention of Pollution from Ships. The Marpol 73/78 Convention set strict limits on operational discharges from ships of oil, noxious substances and garbage (ship-generated rubbish). This standard is enforced by the states which signed the Marpol Convention. Ships are increasingly fitted with sewage and garbage disposal equipment.

Mass Balance

Term used to describe the amount of raw materials and *energy* used in making products, the value of the products themselves, and the amount of waste produced.

Material Organizations (MO) – UK

Proposed organizations overseeing the interests of individual materials (for instance, aluminium, paper and plastic) for the UK *packaging recovery system*.

See also: Valpak.

Mattresses

The EU is proposing to launch an *eco-label* for mattresses. The Greek and French eco-labelling organizations have carried out a joint study which will lead to the creation of environmental criteria.

Best Practice

- Make or use only eco-labelled products, when available.

Measurement: *see Performance*

Mercury

A useful element with many roles: mercury is used to stop mildew and is a catalyst in many reactions. It is also a disinfectant. It is used in chemical manufacturing, measuring instruments, medicine, lighting, batteries, and explosives. Mercury is also potentially hazardous. It is on the EC *Black List* of dangerous substances, and is the subject of various EC directives and national and international legislation.

Yet, there is sparse evidence that mercury itself causes health hazards. The problem occurs when people eat food contaminated by industrially produced organo-mercury compounds, notably *methyl mercury*, which is much more toxic. In Iraq in 1971 to 1972, 3000 people died from eating seed grain treated with methyl mercury fungicide.

See also: Minimata Bay.

Mesothelioma

A cancer, linked to the inhalation of *asbestos*.

See also: Asbestos.

Metaldehyde

Pesticide, used as slug poison. Dangerous to domestic animals.

Best Practice

- Do not use.

Metal Industry

Includes smelters, foundries, iron and steel works, and metal working and finishing works. The main impacts are:

- the use of non-renewable raw materials (some of which are abundant);
- substantial use of *energy*, especially in refining;
- fumes, dust and toxic emissions from mining;
- *air pollution* from plating and welding operations;
- air pollution from the dusts and fumes found in metal working, which can give rise to workplace cancers (these emissions can be managed by the use of extraction fans linked to filters or electrostatic cleaners);
- *solid* and *liquid waste*, including metal particles from machining, including swarf (this can often be recycled or sold for recycling);
- *liquid effluent*, which includes degreasing and cleaning liquids, coolants and lubricants, used rinsing baths, and plating and anodizing solutions. Used cutting or coolant oil can be a problem. This should be disposed of in an environmentally sound manner. Care should also be to prevent or reduce the amount of oily floor cleaning water from entering the drains. Cleaning the cutting oil from the metal has tended to require the use of chlorinated *solvents*. Europe's metal degreasing industry alone produces 400 kilotonnes of *VOCs* a year. Using biodegradable cutting oils may allow an alkaline degreasing solution. Thorn Jarnkonst, a Swedish lighting manufacturer, saved US$25,000 a year from changing to an alkaline degrease.

Acids and alkalines need to be pH balanced before being discharged to drains, while liquids containing metals or chemicals should be treated to remove the pollutants from the water. Some liquid wastes can be precipitated to remove the solids. Settlement is also used to separate liquids and solids. Flotation may also be used; gas bubbles carry the solids to the top of the liquid, where they may be skimmed off. Filtration is also a possibility, as is ion exchange.

Metals such as copper or platinum are a finite resource and their value makes recycling worthwhile. However, some areas are likely to decline: advances in technology mean that optical-fibre cable has greater carrying capacity and uses less natural resources than copper.

See also: Air pollution; Antimony; Beryllium; Cadmium; Copper; Liquid waste; Steel; Volatile organic compounds; Zinc.

Methane

Greenhouse gas, produced by cows, sheep, termites and vegetarians, as well as *landfill* sites and rice fields. At least 300 million tonnes are released every year into the atmosphere. Methane is an explosive gas produced during the decay and fermentation of plant material, especially cellulose.

In landfill sites, methane and other gases can migrate over great distances. They can also build up and explode. For this reason methane should be vented to the air by the use of pipes sunk into waste tips. Some sites use flares to burn off the gas. A better solution is to use methane as a source of *energy*.

See also: Landfill.

Methanol

Methyl alcohol or wood alcohol. A colourless, poisonous, flammable liquid. Originally distilled from wood. Used as a *solvent*, antifreeze, and a raw material for other *chemicals*.

Methiocarb

A slug poison. Can be lethal to domestic animals.

Best Practice

- Do not use.

Methyl

When a metal is 'methylated', by combining with a 'methyl group' (such as methanol), it becomes much more toxic. The same applies to 'ethylated' products, such as tetraethyl lead or *TEL*.

Methyl Bromide

Toxic substance used in pest control and fumigation. Under the *Montreal Protocol*, the rate of production was to be frozen at 1991 levels by 1995.

Best Practice

- Avoid its use where possible.

Methyl Chloroform

Ozone depleting substance, phased out in 1996 under the *Montreal Protocol*.

Methyl Isocyanate

An ingredient in the production of *carbaryl*. It caused the disaster at *Bhopal*.

Best Practice

- Do not use.

Methyl Mercury

Used as a seed dressing to prevent mould and added to paint for the same purpose. Methyl mercury is 50 times more *toxic* than *mercury* and stays in the body 14 times as long. The same applies to ethyl mercury. These substances can cause permanent brain damage if ingested in quantities of 20 to 40 parts per million.

Best Practice

- Methyl mercury must be disposed of very carefully.

Microwaves

Microwave technology could be a partial solution for *waste disposal*. Microwaving a car tyre splits it into nine pounds (four kg) of *carbon* suitable for use in steel making, four pounds (1.8 kg) of steel, a gallon of oil (4.5 litres) and two ounces of *sulphur*.

Microwaving produces no hazardous airborne emissions or toxic ash. Apart from tyres, it can also split medical and household wastes into oil, carbon and other useful industrial materials. The process can also capture and use the heat generated. However, one manufacturer, Environmental Waste Management Corporation (EWMC) of Toronto, Canada, ran into difficulties when a customer went to court, claiming Cdn$25 million in lost profit and alleging that the system processed only a fraction of its claimed volume.

See also: Telecommunications supply industry.

Military

The military has become much more aware of environmental issues, and its attention is largely focused on its huge land holdings. Since this land has not suffered the kind of development seen elsewhere, and has often been barred to civilians for decades, it has often become a site for important habitats.

In the US, the Defense Department owns 25 million acres (10 million ha) of land, and in 1990 launched the Legacy Resource Management Programme to oversee its compliance with government environmental laws and to maintain the ecology of the sites.

See also: Defence industry.

Mill Broke

Paper produced in the paper-making process and which is only suitable for repulping. This includes wet paper taken from the paper machine and dry paper trimmings. Mill broke is used in recycled paper, but since it has not reached the consumer, it is considered to be less environmentally useful. If consumers used only virgin and mill-broke paper, there would be a big increase in waste paper going to *landfill*.

Best Practice

- Ensure that any recycled paper used by the organization contains post-consumer waste.

See also: Paper; Paper, board and pulp industry.

Milwaukee

In 1993 six people died and 400,000 became ill, after drinking contaminated municipal water. The bacterium cryptosporidium is thought to have entered the water system from agricultural run-off.

See also: Cars.

Minimata Bay

Site of *mercury* poisoning, Japan. Illness caused by *methyl mercury* was first noted here in 1953 when 700 villagers became bedridden and 40 per cent died; babies were born with cerebral palsy. The cause of the poisoning was mercury effluent being discharged into the bay by a vinyl chloride factory whose process involved the use of mercuric chloride.

See also: Mercury.

Mineral Oils

Persistent oils are on the EC *Black List* of dangerous substances.

Mining Industry

Mining produces many of the world's raw materials – iron, copper, bauxite, as well as precious minerals such as gold and diamonds.

Impacts

Mining consumes non-renewable resources. Creating spoil heaps can also damage habitats and create pollution. Transport movement around the site also creates noise and intrusion. Subsidence can also be a problem. Treatment of staff in developing countries is also difficult. For example, RTZ has been criticized for environmental degradation at Bougainville in the Pacific and for alleged human rights abuses in Indonesia.

Closed mines are notorious for causing *water pollution*. When the Wheal Jane tin mine was closed in 1992 and its equipment was sold, including the pumps that had kept the 1500-foot (457-metres) shafts dry, 12 million gallons (55 million litres) of water containing heavy metals polluted stretches of the River Fal and its estuary in Cornwall, England.

Best Practice

- Site operations should be managed in a way that minimizes the impact on local population, such as avoiding the damage caused by open-cast mining and banning vehicle movements at anti-social hours.
- A mine should be thoroughly exhausted before it is closed.
- Spoil heaps should be landscaped and planted. Lichens can be used to remove heavy metals from the metal ore, a method that is cheaper and less polluting than other techniques.
- A plan for after-care should be instituted.

See also: Contaminated land; Derelict land; Public relations; Quarrying industry.

Monitoring

Monitoring can involve the use of either physical devices (which sound an alarm if effluent levels rise), or management monitoring (such as record keeping and review meetings).

See also: Register of effects; EMS; Performance.

Monochloro-Difluromethane

Hazardous *chemical*, which causes breathing difficulties by removing oxygen from the air. It is a refrigerant that is found in commercial refrigerators and *air-conditioners*.

Monoculture

Growing only one species. There are two main disadvantages of this:

(1) Agriculture becomes over-reliant on one crop. A virus could subsequently wipe out the entire crop.

(2) *Wildlife* species use different plants for food and shelter. Growing only one crop, therefore, has the additional effect of reducing other species.

An estimated 91 per cent of field corn varieties planted in the US 100 years ago no longer exist, according to the United Nations Food and Agricultural Organization (FAO). In China alone, 9000 wheat varieties have been lost since the 1950s. The FAO warns that variety in the world's species is decreasing rapidly as commercial farming grows. This reduction means that if pests or environmental disasters kill those few varieties, there will be none to fall back on.

See also: Agriculture; Timber industry – temperate.

Montreal Protocol

In 1987, 98 nations signed the Montreal Protocol, committing themselves to phasing out the production and use of *ozone-depleting substances*. Chief among these are *CFCs*.

As later modified by the London Conference, the protocol aimed to discontinue the production of CFCs and halons by the year 2000. Controls on two other ozone-depleting substances, carbon tetrachloride and *methyl chloroform*, were also agreed. Du Pont subsequently announced the *HCFC* substitutes for CFCs.

Best Practice

- Ensure that the organization is aware of any ozone-depleting substances (ODS) used and government timetables to phase them out (in many cases these timetables have been brought forward).
- Develop a plan to meet the government requirements and get rid of all ODS.

Motor Industry

The *car* economy continues to grow. In 1994, output in Asia/Pacific rose by 18 per cent. China's production rocketed in 1994 by 28 per cent in one year. Many of the American, Japanese, French and German car makers have invested large sums to build cars in the fast-growing Asian economies.

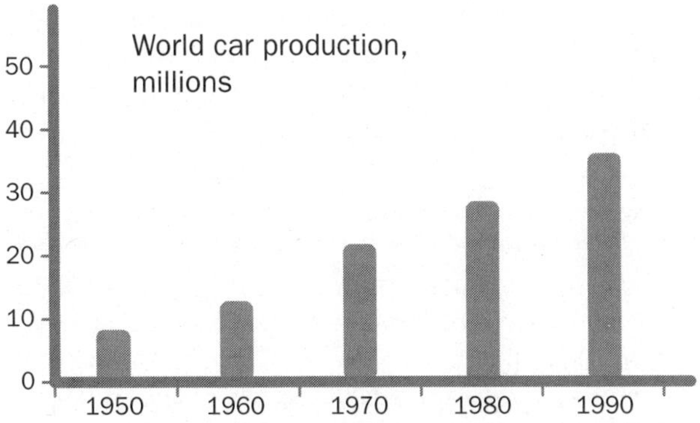

Figure 17: The Rise of the Car

The motor industry's major impacts come from two sources:

1 *Manufacturing impacts:* These include the use of non-renewable and hazardous materials, *energy*, emissions to air and water, and *solid waste*.

2 *In-use impacts:* the consumption of *fossil fuels* and the production of *greenhouse* and polluting gases from exhausts, the resulting production of smog, and the creation of congestion.

The industry has reduced its impacts by introducing *catalytic converters* and lean-burn engines. Manufacturers are also increasing the amount of recycled and recyclable material in their vehicles. They are also reducing and recycling more of their solid waste. Companies should reduce the amount of toxic materials used in vehicle manufacture, including the use of *lead* and *cadmium* in paint. A policy of not producing gas guzzlers is also essential for the committed company.

Other environmental improvements include reduced wind resistance, improved spray control, and improved control over used engine oil which is thought to produce a risk of cancer.

Alternatives to the Internal Combustion Engine

Since California introduced legislation to control *air pollution*, the industry has been trying to develop alternative vehicles. Success with electric cars has proved elusive, not least because the petrol car is highly versatile, being ideal for short and long journeys, and fast and slow driving. The battery car soon runs out of power, takes hours to recharge and moves slowly. Some observers believe the electric car will be used for shopping trips in the two-car family, while others believe the solution lies in a vehicle equipped to use either the battery or the internal combustion engine.

The Rocky Mountain Institute, run by Amory Lovins and based near Aspen, Colorado, believes that a 'hyper car' combining ultra-light, 'ultra slippery' carbon-fibre construction with hybrid-electric propulsion (including solar power) is likely to be in production soon. Meanwhile the US Advanced Battery Consortium (USABC), funded by government and industry, has committed US$262 million to battery development.

One of the most promising technologies is hydrogen. Daimler Benz has unveiled a vehicle powered by *fuel cells*. These use hydrogen and oxygen from the air to turn an electric motor. Their only emission is water vapour and, unlike battery cars, their range is limited only to the next filling station. General Motors and Mazda are also keen to exploit fuel cells.

Case Study 20: 470,000 Cadillacs Are Recalled

Nearly half a million Cadillacs were recalled in 1995 because they emitted three times the legal limit of *carbon monoxide*. General Motors agreed to modify the 4.9-litre engined *cars* at a cost of US$25 million. It also agreed to pay US$11 million in fines and to spend US$8.5 million on buying old cars for disposal and replacing smoky school buses with cleaner models.

Enforcing the Clean Air Act, the US Justice Department said the case was the first court-ordered pollution recall. It held that GM sold the cars knowing they produced too much carbon monoxide. The government said the problem started after GM modified the engines, following complaints that Cadillacs were stalling at low speeds when the air-conditioning was on.

See also: Automotive industry; Cars; Distribution, physical; Fuel cells; Metal industry; Tyres.

MRL

Maximum Residue Level. A measure used for *pesticide* levels in foods.

See also: ADI.

Municipal: *see Local Authorities*

Mutagenic

Causing inheritable genetic damage (that is, genetic damage which may be passed to descendants).

NACCB – UK

A government standards organization, now renamed *UKAS*.

NAPM: *see Paper Labelling Schemes*

Nappies, Sanitary Protection and Incontinence Products

Most nappies and adult incontinence (inco) products are now disposable and their sheer quantity has created many environmental impacts. The main ones are:

- A large increase in the production of pulp material and plastic for use in inco products.
- A large increase in solid waste.
- In hospitals, there is also an associated operational problem, namely that the liquid content of black bags filled with inco products is much higher than average. This causes problems with achieving a sufficient temperature in hospital incinerators. Insufficient temperature causes the production of toxic *dioxins* from plastics and other materials that are being burnt at the same time.
- Waste regulatory authorities are also expressing concern about the storage of used inco products and their disposal in the domestic waste stream to *landfill*.

Manufacturers of disposables say that their products save the impacts caused by washing and the use of detergent. Nevertheless, the use of disposables creates major waste streams. There are various ways of reducing these environmental impacts. The solutions include:

- separating the plastic and recycling it into useful plastic;
- cleaning the pulp and using it in other products;
- composting the pulp;
- in hospitals, using bed pans and commodes;
- employing reusable washable products.

The first three strategies are being piloted in the US, many of them sponsored by Proctor and Gamble, who make such products. An additional solution would be to make the plastic from vegetable-based products. This would then be biodegradable and would have a much lower environmental impact.

A UK hospital study showed that major savings would be produced by the reintroduction of reusable inco products; however, it also showed that staff did not like them, not least because they had to take incontinent users to the toilet throughout the night.

Napthylamine

Dangerous *chemical* whose import, export, marketing and use in the EC is controlled (Regulation EC 3135/94).

National Park

Many countries have developed national parks in areas which are environmentally important. National parks seek to conserve wild species and the unspoilt appearance of the area by restricting development. This sometimes leads to conflict between conservationists (who want unspoiled land) and business people (who offer jobs and prosperity).

National Power: *see Purchasing*

Nature Conservation

As land has been developed for roads, housing, industry, commerce and cities, and as mankind has polluted the rivers and land, many species have suffered *extinction* or are threatened. However, it is not all bad news. In some places, conservation measures have reversed the loss. Zimbabwe's Hwange National Park now has 10,000 too many elephants for the available food and water, and their excessive consumption of these resources is killing thousands of other animals.

Industry can reduce its damage by conducting an *EIA* for any new development, by practising good conservation techniques, and by assisting *wildlife* charities. As a good corporate citizen, companies should help to conserve wildlife, particularly in the case of landowners, who have a responsibility to protect and foster habitats for wildlife. In the US, James River Corporation has set aside 40,000 acres (16,188 ha) for nature conservation in Maine, and maintains habitats for black bear in Mississippi and Louisiana. Less dramatic examples of wildlife conservation by other firms are equally important.

In addition to farmers and agribusinesses, some surprising organizations own large areas of land. They include forestry businesses, local authorities, public utilities, educational establishments, builders, retailers, rail companies and docks. They also include large manufacturers (such as defence manufacturers, petro-chemical companies, and aircraft, ship or vehicle manufacturers).

An organization that owns land should undertake an ecological *audit* of its land holdings. This will include a review of how the land might be made more environmentally useful. The firm should then devise a plan for land management. This may include a programme of planting, clearing, landscaping and restocking. Creating a nature reserve (that is, land where wildlife is formally encouraged) will endear the firm to its stakeholders.

The plan should assess what kinds of wildlife are most at risk and which are most important to protect. Where the firm has tenant farmers or other occupiers, agreements should be reached as to *sustainable* and less-intensive methods of farming or construction. Brownfield sites (decayed inner-city areas) should not be ignored. There are many strategies which assist wildlife in maintaining a toe-hold for the future.

Nature conservation is particularly important where development takes place. This applies to planning authorities, developers and building owners. An *environmental impact assessment* should be carried out before work begins, to find out the existing *flora and fauna*, to ascertain possible threats, and to establish how they may be preserved.

Best Practice

- Carry out an ecological survey of all land holdings.
- Produce a plan for optimizing wildlife conservation.
- Take special care when developing a site: undertake an EIA.

See also: Biodiversity; CITES; Construction industry; Deforestation; Environmental impact assessment; Extinction; Grounds; Landscaping; Roads; Timber.

N-Hexane

Toxic substance used in printing.

Best Practice

- Avoid where possible.

Nickel

A hard silvery metal, similar to iron. It is used in alloys, such as stainless steel, armour plating and coinage. Nickel is slightly toxic and when fed to rats causes shortened longevity and heart attacks. It may also cause lung cancer in the workplace. Nickel carbonyl, a combination of nickel and *carbon monoxide*, is a carcinogen and is found in cigarette smoke.

Best Practice

- Nickel emissions in smoke stacks should be controlled.

Nigeria: *see Shell*

NIMBY

Not In My Backyard. A NIMBY is someone who will not accept controversial developments (such as a toxic waste incinerator) in his/her neighbourhood but might accept them in someone else's.

See also: Banana.

Nitrates

Nitrogen compounds that promote plant growth and are used in agricultural *fertilizers*. Where nitrates get into rivers in excessive quantities, they cause *eutrophication*. Nitrates may also be implicated in methaemoglobinemia, or blue baby syndrome, although the evidence for this is sparse.

Governments are seeking to reduce the amount of fertilizer applied to the land (see: *Nitrates Directive*).

Best Practice

- Agricultural businesses should avoid applying excessive amounts of fertilizer.

Nitrates Directive

EC Directive 91/676. Requires EC member states to designate as nitrate-vulnerable zones (NVZs) all areas of land which drain into waters affected or at risk of nitrate pollution. NVZs are areas of compulsory imposition and no compensation is payable.

The UK's Nitrate Sensitive Areas (NSA) will encourage even higher standards by making payments to farmers who voluntarily initiate changes to farming practices that will significantly reduce nitrate leaching.

Nitric Acid

Nitric acid is used to make *fertilizers* (such as ammonium nitrate), explosives (such as TNT), and man-made fibres (such as nylon and terylene). Nitric acid is also an air pollutant formed from oxidized *nitrogen dioxide*, largely from power stations. In this form, nitric acid becomes *acid rain*.

See also: Sulphuric acid.

Nitric Oxide (NO): *see Nitrogen Oxides*

Nitrobiphenyl

Dangerous *chemical* whose import, export, marketing and use in the EU is controlled (Regulation EC 3135/94).

Nitrogen, Nitrogen Cycle

Nitrogen is a colourless and odourless gas that makes up 78 per cent of the earth's atmosphere. It forms a range of compounds, including:

- *ammonia*;
- *nitrogen oxides*;
- *nitric acid*;
- *nitrates*.

Nitrogen gas in the atmosphere is converted to ammonia by lightning, cosmic radiation, certain soil bacteria, and *fertilizer* manufacturers. In the soil, ammonia is converted by other bacteria to nitrites and then nitrates. Some nitrates are converted back into nitrogen gas in the atmosphere. But most nitrates are used by plants to create amino acids and proteins. When animals eat those plants, they incorporate the material into their tissues and eventually excrete it, whereupon it turns to ammonia and the cycle continues.

Nitrogen Dioxide (NO_2)

A pollutant which irritates the bronchial tubes in the lungs, causing irritation to the throat and chest. Hot sunny weather increases the concentration of NO_2.

Nitrogen dioxide produces *smog* and it also leads to *acid rain*. It does this by reacting with water and oxygen to produce nitric acid which, when diluted in rain, turns the rain acidic, thereby producing acid rain. In the UK, 40 per cent of all nitrogen dioxide emissions come from power station gases, and a further 40 per cent from vehicle exhausts. Another 9 per cent comes from industry, while other sources are individually responsible for less than 3 per cent.

Table 11: Air Quality Standards and Guidelines for Nitrogen Dioxide

Organization	Limit, in parts per billion (ppb)	Sampling method
UK Department of the Environment		
very good	<50	peak hourly average concentration in a 24-hour period
good	50–99	
poor	100–299	
very poor	300+	
European Union	104.6	98 percentile of hourly means
	70.6	98 percentile of hourly means
	26.2	50 percentile of hourly means calendar year of data
World Health Organization	210	one-hour mean
	80	daily mean

Nitrogen Oxides (NO_x)

Nitrogen oxides comprise:

- *nitric oxide* (NO) – this is converted via oxidation in the atmosphere to NO_2;
- *nitrogen dioxide* (NO_2);
- *nitrous oxide* (N_2O).

Of the three, NO and NO_2 are the main pollutants.

Nitrous Oxide (N_2O)

Naturally formed by microbes in the soil, nitrous oxide is not normally polluting. It is used as an anaesthetic (namely, 'laughing gas').

Noise

Noise affecting employees is governed by health and safety regulations. Noise can also affect local residents, particularly where a factory operates through the night or starts early in the morning. Noise also comes from lorries moving through residential areas, especially in the area of the warehouse or factory. Noise is an important issue for aircraft manufacturers, airports, hauliers, manufacturers, depots and warehouses.

Best Practice

- Obtain noise readings as a benchmark.
- Set targets for noise reduction.

- Reduce the noise of the operation by prevention at source, followed by containment. Buy quieter machinery or fit it with silencers. Shield the workers by enclosing the equipment. Reduce the amount of noise leaving the plant by building sound-proof, automatically closing doors. Or build walls or earth screens around the site, if necessary, to stop noise leaving the site.
- Plan lorry movements so as to minimize noise at unsocial hours, and avoid unnecessary travel through residential areas.
- Have a procedure for handling noise complaints, if appropriate.

Non-Conformance: *see Conformance*

Non-Renewable Resources

Non-renewables can be divided into fuels and materials:

- Oil, coal and natural gas are three common non-renewable fuels.
- Other non-renewable resources include quarried materials (such as marble or limestone) which are used in construction or road building.

Best Practice

- Substitute non-renewables with *renewable resources* wherever possible.

Nonylphenol

An industrial detergent which is thought to mimic the action of the female hormone *oestrogen*, and reduce sperm count and quality in males. The *chemical* industry believes that the evidence for this is slim.

Nordic Swan

An environmental label applied in Scandinavian countries to paper. A mill's emissions and discharges must fall within stated boundaries in five areas. The Nordic Swan label permits a mill to use virgin paper.

See also: Paper; Labelling.

North-East Atlantic Convention

The International Convention to Protect the Environment of the North-East Atlantic was signed in Paris in 1992. It replaced the convention for the Prevention of Marine Pollution by Dumping from Ships and Aircraft, signed in Oslo in 1972.

The convention bans the dumping of all waste from the year 2005, with an earlier time scale for other materials such as *sewage* sludge. It also sets up a permit system for the dumping of disused off-shore installations and pipelines.

NO_x

Nitric oxide (*NO*) or *nitrogen dioxide* (NO_2). Created through combustion (burning), especially from power stations and *car* exhausts. It produces *acid rain.*

NTA

Nitrilo-Tri-Acetic Acid. Used as a substitute for *phosphate* in detergents. It is a complexing agent – it combines with heavy metals such as *cadmium*, *lead* and *mercury* and reintroduces them into the water supply. It is considered an environmental hazard.

Nuclear Power Industry

Nuclear power was heralded in the 1950s as a clean, modern power that promised virtually free *energy* through 'atoms for peace'. By the mid 1990s the industry was in decline as many Western countries had turned their back on nuclear power. Britain's decision in 1995 to scrap two power stations which would have cost UK£5 billion was a sign of a failure of confidence in the industry.

Harnessing atomic fission proved more difficult than imagined, and the costs of higher safety standards were also a problem. Decommissioning costs were a high and sometimes unknown cost. The economies of scale promised by nuclear power stations have been found wanting. Cost-over-runs, a glut of natural gas, costly de-commissioning and the arrival of local *combined heat and power* (*CHP*) plants helped to make nuclear power expensive. It was the economics, therefore, that killed off nuclear power, not the green protesters nor even the threat of a nuclear disaster.

The exception may be France, the world's leading nuclear power, which in 1986 generated 65 per cent of its energy from nuclear power (compared with West Germany at 31 per cent, Great Britain at 19 per cent and the US at 16 per cent). France's self-image, coupled with a major and long-term education programme, has meant that nuclear power is accepted in France with less fuss than elsewhere.

Environmental Issues

The industry emits no *greenhouse gases* and so claims that nuclear power is more environmentally sound than *fossil fuels*. It also points out that nuclear energy is safer when compared with the many people who die in coal mining or oil drilling tragedies. The industry is also more controlled than before. Discharges from Sellafield, the UK's largest source of man-made nuclear emissions, are now 3 per cent of what they were in 1979 (though the reader might wonder about the scale of those previous, fairly recent emissions).

Impacts

Opponents say that power stations need to reprocess their spent fuel, a procedure that involves producing plutonium, which is used by the nuclear arms industry. The spent fuel then needs to be stored for thousands of years.

A nuclear explosion (as at *Chernobyl*) would cause unparalleled destruction. However, the industry points out that Chernobyl was designed and maintained in ways that would have been unacceptable in the West. In the UK, there were 13 'level 2' incidents between 1989 and 1992. A level 2 incident is one which 'has the potential for safety consequences'. By comparison, the 1979 incident at *Three Mile Island*, which damaged a reactor core, was level 5.

At the Wylfa power station in Wales in 1995, part of a crane snapped off and fell 40 feet (12 metres) into the reactor. This caused a blockage that could have caused overheating in one of the 6000 fuel channels, and a serious radiation leak could have resulted. It was nine hours before the company shut down the plant. Protesters said that the company put profit before safety, because shutting down the plant would have cost the firm revenue. The prosecutor said Nuclear Electric had been lucky, and that in theory 'there should have been a melt-down'. The firm was fined UK£250,000 plus costs of UK£138,000.

Nuclear power remains controversial. Germany has had to deploy 15,000 police on occasions to protect reprocessed nuclear fuel being transported to its burial site in Gorleben, south of Hamburg. Approximately 110 train loads are due to be transported there between 1996 and 2004. Protesters have ripped up rails, set fire to signal boxes and thrown petrol bombs in scenes resembling partisan warfare.

One of the biggest difficulties facing nuclear operators is the disposal of waste. Britain has been seeking for many years to store its waste in an underground repository at the Sellafield nuclear complex in Cumbria. A British proposal in 1996 to build an underground laboratory to gauge the site's geological suitability for storage so incensed the Irish government that it sent a minister to protest at the public hearing. The Irish have consistently opposed what they call 'an underground nuclear dump being built virtually on the edge of the Irish Sea'.

Therefore, storage of spent fuel is a major problem for the industry. Radioactivity from plutonium waste at Dounreay in Scotland will be dangerous for thousands of years, according to the UK government's Radioactive Waste Advisory Committee. In 1996, the committee reported that the dump, located in a 65-metre deep shaft which is close to the Dounreay beach, was in danger of being breached by the sea within the next 40 years, and would cost up to UK£200 million to make safe. So great was the danger that the 'cheap' option (at UK£100 million) of sealing the shaft was not acceptable.

An international moratorium has halted the dumping of nuclear waste in the North Atlantic. As the waste is produced by many industries other than nuclear power, countries are now trying to find disposal sites on land.

Nuclear Power in Poorer Countries

Possibly the greatest danger lies in the nuclear stations of developing and former communist countries. In 1995, Armenia switched back on its outmoded Metsamor reactor in order to bring power to a country whose capital was rationed to less than one hour of electricity a day.

Located in the Caucasus, a geologically unstable area, the reactor was closed in 1989 after an earthquake, whose epicentre was just 60 miles (97 km) away, killed 25,000 people. The reactor, which was built in 1979 to a 1958 design, is top of the American energy department's 'most dangerous reactors' list. The department has reported numerous shortcomings, including a grossly undersized emergency cooling system. Valves in the cooling system pop open every few seconds, according to one US report, spraying steam into the hall. At the plant's exit, radiation detectors have been switched off.

See also: Ionizing radiation.

Nuclear Weapons: *see Defence Industry*

Objectives, Environmental

Environmental objectives state the organization's goals. They stem from the company's environmental *policy*, though some companies amalgamate their policy and objectives. Objectives tend to be stated in general terms (for example, 'to reduce energy consumption'), while targets are detailed and quantified (for example, 'to reduce energy consumption to 15 gigajoules per tonne (Gj/t) within the next five years').

Equally, the organization could set a policy of complying with all relevant environmental legislation, and the objectives may be: 'to comply with [the specific piece of legislation]'.

Best Practice

- Set corporate or site objectives.
- Ensure they conform to a recognized standard, such as *EMAS* or *ISO 14000*.

See also: Policy.

Odour

Companies should treat odour as an environmental *impact* and seek to prevent it. Odours are especially common in *agriculture*, *food processing* and *chemical* plants.

Certain types of smell, such as sulphur, are distasteful and may make local residents hostile towards the plant. Additionally, research shows that local residents believe that a malodorous plant is more hazardous. For these two reasons, the organization should ensure that smells are minimized or stopped altogether.

In past times, people accepted smells and air pollution as an inevitable part of industry and jobs. More recently, society has shown its unwillingness to put up with *air pollution*, and the same is likely to happen to odour.

Case Study 21: Allied Colloids

Allied Colloids, a chemical manufacturer in Bradford, England, was the subject of many complaints from local residents over odour. It also suffered other problems. A blaze at the site in 1992 left eight employees in hospital, and the firm was fined UK£100,000. In 1994, 28 tonnes of ferric sulphate leaked from a tank and entered outside drains. In 1995, eight employees were taken to hospital after a vessel overheated, an audible alarm was cancelled, and toxic fumes were released. By contrast, the oil giant Texaco, whose plant also released odours, offered to buy houses in the vicinity of its Pembroke refinery at prices above the market value, as a 'good neighbour' gesture. It spent UK£2.5 million buying and then demolishing the houses.

See also: Audit, environmental; Impact, environmental.

Oestrogen Mimics

Some chemicals, such as *2,4-D, aldicarb, benomyl, lindane, nonlyphenol, organochlorines, organophosphates, permethrin,* and *phthalates* are now thought to mimic the action of oestrogen. This reduces the quality and quantity of male sperm.

Best Practice

- Do not use.

Office

Impacts

Impacts include: consumption of resources during construction, visual impact, use of energy for lights and heating, use of water, consumption of resources (such as paper), production of *solid waste* (waste paper), commuting by staff, and harmful substances. Responsibility is often divided and therefore elusive. Some impacts (such as *air-conditioning*) may be the responsibility of the building owner. Some (such as toxic materials) may involve the office cleaning company. Others, such as paper use, are under the control of the tenants. Managing all the impacts often requires joint action.

Atmosphere

Badly positioned VDUs and copiers, noisy equipment and wrong lighting can make employees ill.

See: Sick building syndrome.

Cartridges

Use remanufactured cartridges for copiers and printers. Return used cartridges for remanufacture.

See: Cartridges, copier and printer.

Energy

Offices use large amounts of energy. Reduce this by using low-energy lights, by training staff to be environmentally aware, by buying energy efficient equipment, and by switching off computers when not needed.

See: Energy management.

Furniture

It may be more environmentally sound to refurbish office desks and filing cabinets rather than buy new ones. Companies can even buy desks made from old milk and fruit juice cartons.

Paper

Companies should use recycled letterheads, envelopes, note pads, fax rolls and filing products. They use much less energy than their virgin equivalents.

Solvents

Solvents are found in correction fluid, marker pens and adhesives, and photocopiers. Use solvent-free brands.

Solid waste

Paper, glass, aluminium cans and plastic can be collected in separate bins for recycling. Consider giving the proceeds to charity.

When refurbishing the office, the organization can lengthen the life of old furniture by selling it to a second-hand furniture dealer, sending it to a local auction house, or giving it to a non-profit organization. You can offer old carpets to a local school or play group. Avoid throwing away worn chairs: see if the seats can be recovered.

Best Practice

- Conduct an environmental *audit* of the office, and take action to reduce the significant impacts.

See also: Commuting; Energy management; Furniture; Office equipment; Paper; Sick building syndrome; Teleworking.

Office Equipment

Impacts

Office equipment, such as photocopiers, laser and inkjet printers, consume energy. According to the US Environmental Protection Agency (EPA), office equipment consumes 5 per cent of all US power requirements, a percentage that will double by the year 2000. In Europe, PC products consume 7 per cent of all power and, at current growth rates, Europe will require an extra two power stations each year just to keep pace.

A lot of energy is wasted: between 30 and 40 per cent of PCs are left switched on overnight and at weekends. Even during the day, much use is wasted. The EPA reckons that computers are used for only one third of the time that they are switched on and only looked at 20 per cent of the time they are displaying. It may be noted that screensaver programmes use 20 per cent more power, typically, than a blank screen. Many users fear that switching a computer on and off will harm it. This may have been true for early computers but is now unfounded.

Best Practice

The important environmental factors in buying office equipment are:

- *Energy efficiency* – ask the supplier for precise energy information. Use equipment awarded an *Energy Star*. Buy equipment which has 'standby' and 'sleep' modes.
- Energy use – encourage staff to switch off equipment when it is not needed.
- Night time and weekends – ensure that all machines are switched off, except for those which need to be left on (such as fax machines).
- Monitors – make sure the monitor can tilt easily to prevent glare and is well-shielded against radiation.
- Keyboards – ensure that the keyboard is ergonomically designed so as to minimize upper limb disorders.
- All equipment with motors – make sure that the *noise* is not irritating or disruptive. This includes fans, computers and printers. Keep noisy equipment away from staff.

See also: Computers; IT industry; Office.

Oil; Oil and Gas Industry

Oil is the basis of an endless list of products in modern life, including plastics, fuel, clothing, furniture and vehicles. The role of natural gas tends to be more limited to its use as a fuel, but the two industries are similar when it comes to exploration and extraction.

The first process is exploration, which may involve digging test wells. This is followed by extraction, which requires drilling, removing the crude oil or gas, and distributing it by pipe line and ship to a processing refinery, where the oil is separated into its different grades. It will then travel, often by road tanker, to filling stations or other destinations. Each of these stages has the potential for environmental *impact*.

In the North Sea alone, there are 150 oil and gas production platforms producing 123 million tonnes of oil and 48,000 million cubic metres of gas a year. This scale of operation could lead to major spills, were it not for the emphasis on safety and environmental protection.

The industry's impacts comprise:

- depletion of a *non-renewable resource* (though oil companies are adept at finding new sources);
- loss of habitats through development;
- pollution of land and water through oil spills (The most notorious of these was *Exxon Valdez*, though oil spills reportedly occur on a big scale in Russia, the world's largest oil producer. In 1994, 100,000 tonnes of oil leaked from a pipeline in Usinsk, Russia, damaging the fragile tundra.);
- the discharge of oil-based drilling mud cuttings from rigs;

- sludge from the refining process;
- industrial *solid waste* from refining;
- *Flue gases*: emissions of CO_2, SO_2 and other gases from combustion, through vehicle exhausts and power stations;
- emissions of *VOCs/VAHs* when petrol tankers fill underground tanks at garages;
- addition of polluting substances in petrol, such as substitutes for lead;
- ground contamination from spills of lubricant and other oils by trade and end users.

Oil Spills

The costs of litigation over oil spills, already high in the US, are likely to increase around the world. In 1991, British Steel was fined UK£200,000 for spilling 16 tonnes of fuel oil into the Severn Estuary, as a result of a cracked pipe seal at one of its works. This shows that all businesses, not just oil companies, need to control their use of oil.

Oil spills affect mammals with watery habitats (such as otters) and aquatic birds because oil coats their feathers, reducing buoyancy and insulation. Ingestion of the oil, as they try to clean themselves, can then poison the bird. Fish and other marine species can be either killed or tainted, causing problems for the fishing industry.

It is not just oil spills, but also the use of engine oil and motor boat exhausts, as well as the flow from factories and from port operations, and the additives (such as surfactants), that cause environmental damage. The industry seeks to confine oil spills by the use of booms. Where this is not possible, oil spills are dispersed by:

- drift (caused by the currents and tides);
- evaporation (which can take up to 50 per cent of an oil slick's volume loss);
- the break-up of the oil film into droplets;
- the use of chemical dispersants. (It is now known that the use of dispersants can cause as much of an environmental problem as the oil itself. Sometimes the best solution is to let nature and the tides take their course.)

The Offshore Industry

The UK's Offshore Installations (Safety Case) Regulations 1992 require offshore operators to submit a safety case to the Health and Safety Executive for assessment and acceptance. It is unlawful to operate an installation without an accepted safety case. The law follows the *Piper Alpha* disaster in the North Sea. The safety case is a manual setting out procedures for ensuring safety on board the oil rig.

Recycling

Used oil should be collected and passed to a recycling point (often at garages or municipal refuse centres). In California, a tenth of all lubricating oil sold has been used before as engine oil. Heathrow Airport, London, recycles 1500 gallons (6819 litres) of waste oil a year.

Best Practice

Oil companies should:

- Carry out an *EIA* before beginning exploration or development.
- Invest in the development of *renewable* energies.
- Promote the development of less-polluting vehicles.
- Implement an *EMS* at all sites.
- Ensure that the high standards of environmental performance and monitoring are maintained.

Oil users should:

- Supervise oil deliveries. Even a small escape can spread over a wide area, harming birds, fish and other aquatic species.
- Make sure that oil storage tanks are enclosed by a secure bund (or basin) from which oil cannot escape.
- Check regularly for potential leaks.
- Not pour used oil down the drain. This causes pollution and in many places is illegal: take used oil to a recycling bank.

See also: Alexander Keilland; Amoco Cadiz ; Chemical industry; Exxon Valdez; Indoor pollution; Piper Alpha; Shell.

Operational Control

Operational control involves the use of written *procedures* for *processes* that have an environmental *impact*. These procedures represent Best Practice, or the correct way to undertake an activity. They are useful for new staff and ensure that all staff operate in the same way. This reduces variation in the organization's products or services, and reduces the risk of an environmental incident.

Procedures are often accompanied by related documents (such as scale drawings, or illustrations of the finished product, or jigs etc). *EMS* audits are needed to check that the procedures are being followed.

In ISO 9000, operational control is mainly confined to production, but environmental impacts and incidents can occur in many other departments, so an *environmental management system* (EMS) has a wider scope.

Areas suitable for operational control:
R&D; laboratories
Design
Engineering
Purchasing
Raw materials handling; goods in
Production; operations
Warehousing
Distribution
Contractors
Marketing and advertising
Customer service
Property management, acquisition and divestment and construction

See also: Documentation; Environmental management system; Procedures.

Optical Brighteners

Substances added to washing powders to give the illusion of brightness. They have no cleaning properties and are said to cause allergic reactions and irritation to sensitive skin. The UK's Soap and Detergent Industry Association says that there is no evidence to support this claim. Consumers are concerned about the whiteness of their wash, and even some powder marketed as 'environmentally sound' includes a small amount of optical brighteners.

Organic

Chemistry

In chemistry, organic refers to the huge number of carbon compounds. Of the five million known compounds, four and a half million contain carbon. They are called 'organic' because all living things (organisms) are made from carbon compounds. By contrast, inorganic refers to non-carbon elements and their compounds.

Many industries, including dyeing, explosives, plastics and pharmaceuticals, rely heavily on organic chemistry. Organic compounds include the numerous *hydrocarbons*, which contribute substantially to the environmental burden.

Solid Waste

In the context of *waste management*, organic refers to material from living things. Organic waste contains micro-organisms and is best treated and made inert (rather than being put into *landfill*). Organic waste includes leaves, grass, vegetable peel, wood and animal remains. It comprises proteins, carbohydrates and fats.

Organic waste comes from many sources, including *food processors*, breweries, dairies, *sewage*, and *agriculture*. If it gets into a water course it can cause problems of *eutrophication*, where it stimulates the growth of tiny green plants called algae, which then rob the water of oxygen. This kills fish and other creatures.

Organic waste can be turned into useful by-products, notably soil conditioner or *fertilizer*. For example, paper makers end up with a potentially useful organic paper sludge. The same applies to *sewage* sludge and the waste from fruit processors. Using this waste reduces the need for costly waste disposal.

Providing there is not too much organic material for the receiving medium (land or water), the waste will decompose into harmless elements of its own accord in a process of natural self-purification. A problem arises when waste exceeds the ability of the soil or water to biodegrade, and it gives off methane or hydrogen sulphide. The pathogens in the waste (such as E. Coli) may also infect humans or other species.

Case Study 22: Disposing of Organic Wastes

Organic Waste Processing Ltd (OWP), based in Northamptonshire, UK, converts almost any organic slurry into dry inert products which are harmless to the environment if dumped, and much of which can be sold as high-quality animal feed supplements, soil conditioners, or slow-release *fertilizers*. The company treats wastes from bakeries, food processors (which use fruit, vegetable or meat), supermarkets, breweries and wineries, as well as *agricultural* waste. OWP treats the waste with bacteria in digesting tanks. The material is then dried and the water is reused in the system.

See also: Agriculture; Composting; Hydrocarbons.

Organochlorines

Compounds which contain *chlorine, carbon* and hydrogen. They include *PCBs, CFCs, pesticides* such as *DDT, dioxins* and *furans*, and *PVC*. Organochlorines are toxic, *bioaccumulative*, and *persistent*. Efforts are being made to find alternatives.

Best Practice

- Avoid their use wherever possible.

See also: Chlorine.

Organohalon

Hazardous chemical on the EC *Black List*.

Organolead: *see Lead*

Organomercury: *see Mercury*

Organophosphates

Pesticide used since the 1960s to protect crops and livestock, notably in sheep dip. It is used in cat flea collars, wood worm treatment, flame retardant treatments, and to treat children's head lice. It is also used in Sarin, the nerve gas, originally employed in warfare. Organophosphates (OPs) occur in the natural environment, in snake and spider venom. The ancient Vikings used to eat a nut containing an OP which made them frenzied, thus enabling them to kill more efficiently. Organophosphates are both inexpensive and highly effective, but there is growing criticism over their effects.

Impact

The products are toxic, though toxicity varies among the different compounds. There is some evidence to link OP with nervous disorders and suicidal depression. Suicide is common among farming communities and it was once attributed to financial pressure and loneliness. Today, it is sometimes ascribed to the use of organophosphorus.

OP and OC (organochlorines) are now recognized as capable of mimicking the action of *oestrogen*. This serves to reduce the quality and quantity of male sperm.

Best Practice

- Avoid their use wherever possible.

Organophosphorus: *see Phosphorus*

Organotin

Hazardous substance used as a biocide and as a stabilizer for *PVC*. Its compounds are used in anti-fouling paints, wood preservatives, fungicides and *insecticides*. Some compounds are extremely toxic, especially to aquatic species, and organotin is on the EC *Black List* of dangerous substances. TBT anti-fouling paint is now banned in France, Ireland, the US and Scandinavia.

Best Practice

- Avoid use where possible

See also: TBTO.

Outfall

Point where waste water drains into a river or the sea. Typically refers to *sewage* or industrial effluent.

Oxides of Nitrogen: *see Nitrogen Oxides*

Ozone

Ozone performs two separate functions:

(1) Ozone in the stratosphere shields the earth from the sun's harmful ultraviolet rays. Without this ozone layer, we would suffer excessive exposure to ultraviolet, causing burning of the skin and melanomas (skin cancer).

Following the *Montreal Protocol*, governments are phasing out the use of ozone-depleting products.

(2) Ground-level ozone is produced when hydrocarbons and oxides of *nitrogen* combine in sunlight. It is most common in summer. Ozone irritates the lungs, causing coughing. It also stings the eyes, nose and throat. Asthmatics and joggers are particularly at risk. Thus, stratospheric ozone is a good thing, while ground-level ozone is undesirable.

See also: CFCs; Ozone-depleting substances; Ozone layer.

Ozone-Depleting Substances (ODS)

Substances that deplete the ozone layer include:

- *CFCs* (CFC-11, CFC-12, CFC-113, CFC-114, CFC-115);
- *HCFCs*;
- *halons* (halon 1211, halon 1301, and halon 2402);
- *carbon tetrachloride*;
- *trichloroethane*;
- *methyl bromide*;
- hydrobromofluorocarbons.

ODS are controlled by the *Montreal Protocol*. In Europe, the protocol has been implemented by EU Regulations 3093/94, which control the production and use of ODS. Since the Montreal Protocol, companies have aimed to introduce substances which are less harmful than CFCs, such as HFC-134a which has eleven times less effect on the ozone layer than CFC-12.

Best Practice

- Check whether the organization is using any ozone depleting substances, and if so take steps to stop their use.

See also: Methyl chloroform; Ozone; Ozone layer.

Ozone Layer

A layer 15 to 20 km above the earth's surface, which absorbs some of the sun's harmful *ultraviolet (UV)* radiation. The layer has been eroded by the use of *CFCs*, leading to the creation of a hole over the South Pole. Exposure to UV light can increase the risk of skin cancer and eye cataracts, depress the human immune system and harm aquatic systems and crops.

According to the World Meteorological Organization (WMO), the hole in the ozone layer doubled in size in 1994. It stretches over an area of 3.9 million square miles (6.3 million square km) – equivalent to the size of Europe. Since the hole is centred over the unpopulated South Pole, it does not have a major effect. However, when a small hole passed over the Falkland Islands in October 1994, a girl suffered third degree burns after being exposed to the sun for only 30 minutes.

In 1956, the ozone layer was 8 miles (13 km) thick over the Antarctic. Today parts of it are less than 3 miles (5 km) thick. WMO says that levels of protective ozone will decline by 6 per cent over the next decade. Each 1 per cent increase in the amount of ultraviolet radiation reaching human beings increases the chances of getting skin cancer by 2 per cent, according to the UN. However, some scientists says that the size and importance of the hole have been greatly exaggerated. According to the European Ozone Research Co-ordinating Group at Cambridge University, the hole is roughly the same size as in recent years.

Scientists blame *CFCs* for the destruction of the ozone layer. Their production has now been phased out, though many fridges and air-conditioning units still contain CFCs.

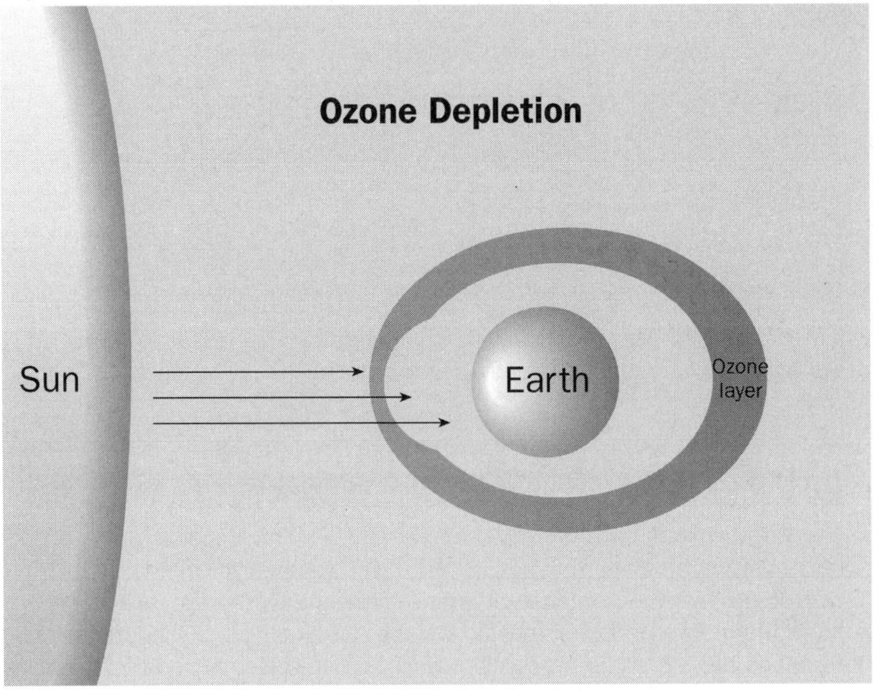

Figure 18: The Impact of Ozone Depletion

Best Practice

- Phase out or convert all equipment that uses CFCs.
- Ensure that CFCs are not lost when equipment is being disposed of.

Packaging

Packaging ensures that the consumer receives the product in good condition. It also communicates the contents and encourages the consumer to buy. No company willingly spends more on packaging than is absolutely necessary. However, layers of protective or brightly coloured packaging materials are a source of concern to many consumers, most of whom are now environmentally aware. Older consumers are also conscious of the 'old days' when packaging was either non-existent or made of paper and card. As a result, excessive packaging has come to be seen as wrong.

Many companies have made efforts to reduce their packaging. Plastic bags and bottles have become thinner, and toothpaste tubes have lost their cardboard cover. But the customer's concerns about packaging remain, and as governments increasingly demand a reduction in packaging, it makes financial and marketing sense to minimize the packaging while still protecting and branding the product.

Good environmental practice demands that packaging should be the minimum required to protect the product from damage or contamination. Companies can improve their packaging through three principles: reduce, recycle and reuse.

Reduce

This involves removing unnecessary packaging. For example:

- Frozen burgers can be packed in cartons without the polythene flow wrap previously used.
- Pump-action toothpaste and roll-on deodorants are now sold without cardboard boxes.
- Varta, the battery company, uses a card pack rather than a plastic bubble pack.
- Many plastic refuse sacks now include a proportion of recycled material.

Other examples of reduction include lightweighting (using, for example, ultra lightweight plastic milk bottles). Providing concentrate packs (such as washing powder) is another solution.

Case Study 23: Hospital Packaging

The Royal Hallamshire Hospital in Sheffield, England, found that surgeons were having to discard up to 30 packages for every operation. This was because all sterile products were kept in individual packs on the shelves. Now the hospital gets a manufacturer to assemble the same products in one pack in a clean room, with the result that only one outer package is used. The packs are still customized for each operation but there has been a big drop in packaging materials.

Recycle

It is environmentally better to use recycled rather than virgin materials in packaging, where possible, because this cuts the amount of packaging going to *landfill* or *incineration*. Many plastic bags are now made from recycled plastic. The packaging type (the type of plastic used) should be clearly marked, to facilitate recycling.

Figure 19: The Three Arrow Mark

The 'three arrow' mark should only be used to denote 'made from recycled materials'. It should not be used to mean 'can be recycled'.

Re-use

Ideally, transport or outer packaging should be returned to the supplier wherever possible (such as reusable plastic trays or roll cages). This is discussed further under *Refillables*.

Packaging to Avoid

Packaging which is hazardous and difficult to recycle or biodegrade includes:

- packaging that gives off poisonous fumes, such as *PVC* or polystyrene;
- packaging that does not biodegrade, such as bubble wrap plastic; products can be protected with loose biodegradable material, such as shredded paper, or in cartons made from recycled pulp;
- aerosols: they are heavily packaged, difficult to dispose of, and many are powered by dangerous propane or butane;
- laminated packaging, which uses two types of packaging (for example card and aluminium); it is hard to recycle and should therefore be avoided.

Legislation

Made anxious by rising levels of packaging waste, different countries have introduced packaging laws. Germany's packaging law introduced the idea of '*producer responsibility*'. Manufacturers pay a levy to have their packaging recycled.

The EU has introduced a *Packaging and Packaging Waste Directive*, which aims to reduce the amount of material going to *landfill* and to increase the amount of packaging that is recycled. All EU member states are obliged to implement the directive, which means that packaging waste will increasingly be more costly.

Eco-Label

The EU has considered the introduction of an *eco-label* for packaging materials. An Italian study concluded that the criteria should reflect four key areas: reduction of material, reuse, recycling and disposal. The study had difficulty distinguishing between types of packaging materials. As a result, packaging in its own right will not be eco-labelled. It is thought that the results of the study would be used in eco-labels for other products.

Best Practice

- Assess how much packaging adds to the cost of your product. See whether simpler packaging could reduce the cost.
- Evaluate whether the packaging could be made biodegradable, recyclable, reusable or safer. Use recycled materials where possible.
- Make packaging lighter in weight (to reduce *energy* use in manufacture and distribution).
- Provide refillable packaging.
- Produce returnable packaging (such as roll cages).
- Improve dosing or dispensing (to reduce amount of product wasted).
- Work with suppliers to improve packaging.
- Reduce the warehouse-to-retailer packaging.
- Make or use only eco-labelled products, when available.

See also: Aerosols; Labelling; Packaging and Packaging Waste Directive; Packaging Recovery System; Waste management.

Packaging and Packaging Waste Directive – EU

A European Union directive which requires member states to reduce the amount of *packaging* being dumped in *landfill* sites. The directive requires countries to recover between 50 and 65 per cent by weight of all packaging. Recovery includes reuse, recycling and incineration with energy recovery. In addition, the EU requires member states to recycle between 25 per cent and 45 per cent of all packaging, and not less than 15 per cent of each individual material (glass, plastic, paper and metals). Packaging must be marked to indicate the type of material(s) used, and whether it can be recycled.

See also: Packaging; Packaging recovery system.

Packaging Recovery System

Several European countries have introduced packaging recovery schemes. The best known is Germany's *DSD* green dot scheme. France has its *eco emballage* green dot scheme for consumer products.

The European Union has introduced a *Packaging and Packaging Waste Directive*, which requires countries to reduce their waste, and a packaging recovery system is a major element in this.

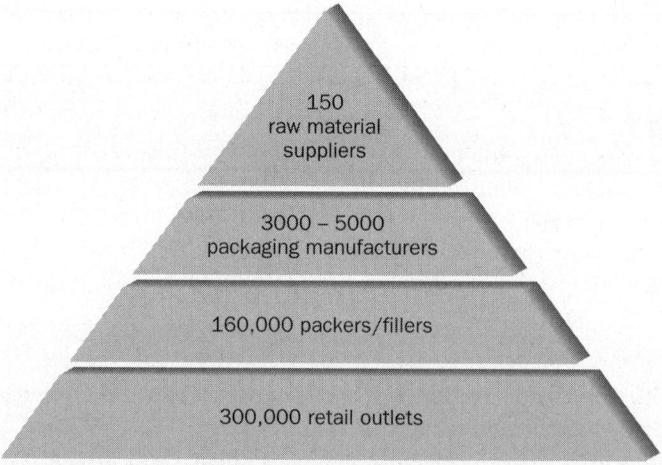

Figure 20: The UK Packaging Chain: The higher up the chain a packaging levy is placed, the fewer participants and the less administration is required.

PAHs

Poylnuclear (or polycyclic) aromatic hydrocarbons, such as anthracene, biphenyl and naphthalene. Eight PAHs are carcinogens, with benzo(a)pyrene the most carcinogenic. They are produced in nature by forest fires and volcanic eruptions, while anthropogenic (man-made) sources are diesel engines, cooking ovens, asphalt manufacture, *fossil-fuelled* furnaces, cigarettes and barbecues. PAHs are PICs (the *products of incomplete combustion*).

Paint and Pigments

Solvents are one of paint's biggest impacts. Paint has traditionally contained solvents to carry the pigment to the surface being painted. Paint manufacturers have been moving to water-based, solvent-free paint. In industrial processes, electrostatic spraying is used to attract the paint particles to an earthed object which is to be painted. This substantially reduces the amount of solvents needed and the waste produced.

Other toxic materials used in paint include *cadmium* (which is used in orange and yellow colours, and which is a dangerous heavy metal). *Lead* is no longer used in paints, except in a few specialist applications. Paint can also contain *mercury* and *antimony*.

Paint also involves waste. A quantity of paint is often left over at the end of each painting job and has to be disposed of. Paint mixing systems obviate this waste, though they are more suitable for larger jobs or continuous painting activities. Heden MacLellan Holdings has a technique for tackling paint residues; the process drives off solvents and water vapour, and then cures the residual resins, thus encapsulating any heavy metals.

Case Study 24: Reducing Paint Wastes

Holden Hydroman of Tewkesbury, England, upgraded its spray booths to increase capacity, improve the quality of the components, improve working conditions, and reduce waste. The company, which supplies plastic components to the automotive industry, invested in new spray guns and a sludge handling system. Holden also matched paint tank sizes to order size, which reduced wastage. As a result, paint waste was reduced by UK£20,000 and disposal costs by UK£4000. The investment cost UK£20,000, and payback was ten months.

Recycling

Paint can now be recycled. Daimler Benz strips paint from old bumpers, and in addition to recycling the plastic from the bumper, also processes the paint into secondary polyol, a high-grade base material.

Eco-Labelling

The EU has been preparing an *eco-label* for paints. The main concern is to reduce the level of *VOCs* (or solvents) which cause *air pollution*. The eco-label assesses two classes of paint: matt and gloss, with provision for semi-sheen paints, and encourages the newer high-solids gloss paints. The criteria are:

- fitness for use;
- white pigments (paints);
- VOC content;

- *volatile aromatic hydrocarbon* content;
- *water pollution* when tools are cleaned (the packaging should state how tools should be cleaned in order to limit pollution);
- *solid waste:* residues and the container (packaging should recommend storage conditions after opening);
- pigments and other substances (ingredients must not contain substances using or based on cadmium, lead, chromium VI, mercury, arsenic, dibutyl, dioctyl, or phthalates).

Best Practice

- Use solvent-free paint where possible.
- Make or use only eco-labelled products, when available.

Paper

Despite (or perhaps because of) the computer, we use as much paper as ever. The average office worker uses 20,000 sheets of paper a year, costing about UK£60, according to the UK's Building Research Establishment.

Designing a major building, such as London's Royal Opera House, uses 1.6 million sheets of paper, according to software company Cimage. Even more paper is needed to maintain working drawings. An oil rig requires seven copies of 1.2 million documents, with over 400 copies for the safety case (the health and safety manual). In such cases, electronic document handling saves paper, space and money.

The Huge Range of Paper Uses

This includes: photocopy paper; envelopes; brochures and leaflets; price lists; computer paper; invoices and statements; forms; note pads; fax paper; pay slips; annual report and accounts; letterheads; memos; compliments slips; business cards; and diaries.

Source

Paper is made from wood which is grown as a *sustainable* crop in temperate forests in Scandinavia, the UK, Canada and many other countries. Claims such as: 'not made from tropical forests' and 'produced from sustainable forests' are a misnomer, since tropical trees are not used for paper making. Paper has always been produced from managed forests, and paper-making rarely causes tree loss. Paper is also being made from new raw materials, including bagasse – the fibrous residue from sugar cane.

Impacts

Paper makes up a large proportion of *landfill* waste. In addition, paper-making imposes an environmental burden (for which, see: *Paper and Pulp Industry*). It is a mistake to assume that paper 'produced from sustainably managed forests' is necessarily environmentally sound. Paper production has been a highly polluting process, though the industry has taken steps to reduce its impacts. To convert trees into paper requires a lot of *energy*, water and *bleach*. Recycled paper is much less demanding on the environment, because it uses less energy and bleach.

Recycling

Paper is easily recyclable, and a tree which takes years to grow should not be discarded after 20 minutes' existence as a newspaper. (Much recycled paper is used in tissues and paper towels, which are destined, after their brief life, for landfill.) The most valuable paper for recycling is office white paper. Lower grades which are less attractive include thermal fax paper, sticky notes, any paper with glue on it, card, laminates, newspapers and magazines. Most of this can, however, be recycled. The plastic should be removed from window envelopes before putting into a recycling bin.

Buying recycled paper can be good for the economy. Over 60 per cent of the UK's paper and board is imported. Recycling would reduce this by two million tonnes or more. It is also good business practice since waste disposal costs money. Smith and Nephew collected all its waste paper over a period of three months. The company then reused the paper for photocopying or scrap pads and found it had reduced its waste paper generation by 70 per cent.

Paper can be recycled three to four times without significant loss of fibre strength. After six or seven times the fibre becomes weak and is unsuitable for some kinds of paper. (Incineration can then recover the energy through heat.) Paper makers cannot, therefore, rely entirely on recycled old paper. They need a certain amount of virgin fibre.

Quality

Whereas recycled paper was once of inferior shade and regularity, today most products are indistinguishable from virgin paper apart from being a shade less bright. This demonstrates the paper's authenticity and is part of its character. Some firms use mottled recycled paper in its environmental communications in order to emphasize their green credentials.

Disposal

The UK recycles 35 per cent of all paper and board, about the same as the US (37 per cent). The rest is disposed of in *landfill* and incineration. Paper biodegrades much more rapidly than other *packaging* materials, such as plastic. On the other hand, the anaerobic (airless) conditions of many landfill sites has meant that paper does not decay in them.

Apart from recycling, waste paper can serve other uses. In eight months in 1993, 1050 tonnes of UK surplus phone books and Yellow Pages directories were shredded and used for animal bedding, while a further 600 tonnes were used for insulation.

EU Eco-Label

Following a Danish study, the EU has issued proposals for an eco-label for fine paper (covering writing, photocopy and computer paper). The eco-label will be similar to that for *toilet paper*. The criteria relate to the use of *renewable resources* (recycled paper), *water pollution* and *solid waste*.

Best Practice

Companies can minimize the volume of paper used through the following measures:

- Discourage the memo-sending culture.
- Do not send out multiple copies of minutes of meetings.
- Put company notices on notice boards rather than sending a copy to every member of staff.
- Consider abandoning the use of envelopes for some internal mail.
- Coordinate mailings to customers. One bank saved 17.5 million envelopes a year, and saving of UK£200,000 in envelopes and UK£3 million in postage, by combining multiple statements for customers with more than one account.
- Encourage one-page reports.
- Reuse scrap paper for notes.
- Photocopy on both sides of the paper.
- Be selective about producing computer print-outs.
- Use E-mail or groupware for internal communications.
- Develop workflow document systems that are screen-based rather than paper-based.
- Send and receive invoices and orders by EDI (electronic data interchange), a paperless system which sends information by modem.
- Do not use separate fax header sheets – use 'Post-it' notes instead, or better still, use the word processor's facilities to paste a small fax header at the top of the first page.
- Send and receive faxes on a computer rather than on paper.
- Charge each department for the stationery it uses. Alternatively, set each department an annual target for reducing paper use; then charge a premium for usage over that amount.

Companies can reduce their paper impacts by the following measures:

- Use recycled paper products as the norm. See: *Paper Labelling Schemes.*
- Collect office paper for recycling.
- For major paper contracts, seek information from the supplier on the following factors: any accreditation of the paper by independent bodies; the proportion of pre- and post-consumer waste in the paper; the de-inking process used in the recycling process; the type and amount of emissions to air and water; energy consumed during paper manufacture; the management of the forests supplying the pulp.

See also: Paper, board and pulp industry; Paper labelling schemes; Toilet paper.

Paper, Board and Pulp Industry

The impacts of the paper industry comprise:

- *Water use:* The paper industry is a big user of water. This can be reduced by reusing the process water. This allowed the PT IKPP plant in Indonesia to reduce its water consumption by 23 per cent.

- *Water pollution,* especially from chlorine bleach (which is used for whitening the paper): In place of chlorine, the industry is increasingly using oxygen. This lowers the effluent's *COD* and *BOD*, thereby causing less water pollution. Mills can also use the enzyme xylanase which breaks up the dark fibres, and which can cut chlorine use by a third.
- *Discharges from pulp mills of phenyl mercury,* This converts to methyl mercury, which is toxic.
- *Emissions to air of sulphur dioxide.* This comes from the chemical pulping process which uses sulphur to free lignin from the cellulose fibres. The dissolved lignin can be burnt to recover the chemicals, and the *energy* can be used to power the plant.
- *Energy:* Paper-making uses large amounts of energy, because the pulp has to be cooked. The heat can be recovered from the digesters and used to heat the wash water. Recycled paper uses up to 50 per cent less energy than its virgin equivalent.
- *Planting in the wrong places, and the use of inappropriate trees:* With a growing demand for paper, plantation forests often replace natural ancient woodland or are planted on ecologically important sites. Thirsty trees, such as eucalyptus, are planted in parts of the world where they would not grow naturally, thus putting a burden on limited water supplies. In the UK, the blanket planting of pine trees, a species that many British types of *wildlife* cannot use, also hinders nature conservation. Dense forests into which the sunlight cannot penetrate also prevent photosynthesis by plant species.
- *Harm to wildlife:* The trees are grown and cut rapidly and are not allowed to die and rot. As a result, wildlife species never get established. In Sweden, 1000 forest species are on the endangered list.

Nevertheless, the industry is much less polluting than before. In 1995, some mills discharged only 0.4 kilograms of chlorine effluent per tonne of bleached pulp, compared with 4.6 kilograms in 1986. This has resulted from longer pulp cooking (which removes more of the discolouring resin, lignin) thus reducing the need for bleaching. Some plants have changed the bleaching method from chlorine gas to chlorine dioxide or to hydrogen peroxide and enzymes. In addition, *sulphur dioxide* emissions have greatly fallen. Paper plants are also recycling much of their water, to reduce their demand for water and reduce potential pollution.

The Impact of Recycled Paper

The production of recycled paper is considerably reducing the environmental burden – notably by:

- the absence of chlorine bleach;
- the reduced energy required to produce recycled paper;
- the reduction of waste paper going to *landfill.*

Critics sometimes point to the impact from the sludge formed during the de-inking process, when the ink is detached from waste paper by flotation or washing. The sludge, which can contain heavy metals, is sent to landfill. However, the volume of sludge is considerably less than the disposal of printed paper that is sent to landfill. Moreover, the ink that forms the sludge would have been present anyway if the paper had been landfilled.

Case Study 25: Problems for a Polluting Paper Mill

Society is unwilling to accept the previously high levels of pollution. At Humboldt Bay, California, surfers took legal action against two paper mills owned by the Louisiana-Pacific Corporation and Simpson Paper Company. Annually, the two mills pumped nearly 40 million gallons of water containing toxic waste into the ocean. The companies agreed to pay US$5.8 million in fines and to spend up to US$100 million in cleaning up their effluent.

See also: Timber, paper.

Paper Labelling Schemes

Many papers carry a 'recycled' label, and this claim should be treated with caution. Some 'recycled' paper has never left the manufacturer's mill. This is '*mill broke*', paper which has not met the mill's specification when tested at the end of the production line, and has been repulped. However, although it claims to be recycled, it has never gone out into the world, nor been used.

This kind of claim has led to the creation of various labelling schemes, each of which have their own merits. The major ones are discussed below.

ABCD

The ABCD scheme is the basis of many labelling schemes. It divides the content of a paper into four sources:

(A) mill off-cuts/mill broke (waste from the paper mill, which has not got into circulation);

(B) white pre-consumer waste (this could be waste from an envelope manufacturer);

(C) post-consumer waste from end users, including white office paper and coloured paper;

(D) post-consumer mechanical waste, made from low-grade paper, such as newspaper.

This system clarifies the meaning of the word 'recycled'. It prevents a paper mill from misleading the public by calling paper made from its own waste 'recycled'. Thus, a paper labelled 75C/25D comprises 75 per cent high-quality post-consumer waste and 25 per cent post-consumer mechanical waste. This is an environmentally sound paper.

Blue Angel

A German standard which states that papers must be made from 100 per cent recycled waste paper, 51 per cent of which must be post-consumer. Its refusal to allow a proportion of virgin material has led to low-grade paper.

NAPM

UK National Association of Paper Merchants. Signifies that the paper contains at least 75 per cent post-consumer recycled paper. The recycled content must not include the paper maker's grade paper, such as newspaper. However, it can include any paper that has left the mill, such as off-cuts from converters or printers. The remaining 25 per cent can be of virgin pulp or pre-consumer waste, and this gives manufacturers the scope to make fair- to good-quality paper. NAPM is a good all-purpose standard, though less rigorous than Blue Angel.

Nordic Swan

An award based on emissions to air and land. The label applies to both virgin and recycled paper.

HMSO

A 0 to 100 ranking developed by Her Majesty's Stationery Office (HMSO) in the UK. It is based on the proportion of virgin fibres and pre- and post-consumer waste. The higher the score (the nearer to 100), the more environmentally beneficial the paper is. The scoring system multiplies the percentage of fibre content by its relevant value. For example, a 100-per cent recycled paper might contain the following:

15 per cent virgin fibre or broke	=	15×0.0	=	0.0
65 per cent pre-consumer waste	=	65×0.5	=	32.5
20 per cent post-consumer waste	=	20×1.0	=	20.0
Total score:	=			52.5

A paper that scores 52.5 has made a slight effort to look environmentally sound, but its comparatively low score indicates that it is environmentally not as attractive as it could be, and few of its fibres have been really recycled.

Eco-Label

The EU has prepared proposals for an eco-label (see *Paper*). Some people have criticized the eco-label for its 'pass or fail' strategy. They claim that some papers which are environmentally sound will not succeed in gaining an eco-label. Eco-label supporters point out that the eco-label will encourage manufacturers to improve the environmental attractiveness of their paper.

Best Practice

- Determine which paper-labelling scheme suits the organization, and then adopt a policy of purchasing only paper that carries the label.

Paraquat

An extremely toxic weed killer which has no antidote, and kills more people than any other *pesticide*. Banned in Denmark and not approved in Finland, Austria and Luxembourg.

Best Practice

- Do not use.

Particulates

Minute carbon particles in soot, fumes and dust which are emitted from combustion (burning) processes, especially from *diesel* engines. These particles can cause breathing difficulties and worsen asthma if breathed in at high concentrations. They are potentially carcinogenic.

Best Practice

- Maintain diesel vehicles properly.
- Monitor news on particulates and use it to maintain and revise corporate strategy.

See also: Cars; Diesel; PM10s.

PBBs (Polybrominated Biphenyls)

Used as fire retardant in plastics, textiles and foam furnishings. When, in 1973, it accidentally got into animal feed in Michigan, it resulted in the death of 25,000 cows and 1.6 million chickens, to keep PBBs out of the food chain. It does not seem to have caused serious illness in humans. Brominated flame retards (of which PBB is one and PBDE another) are *persistent, toxic,* and *bioaccumulative.* The industry says that different PBBs have different levels of toxicity.

Best Practice

- Avoid their use.

PCBs (Polychlorinated Biphenyls)

PCBs are an inflammable and carcinogenic oil, made from chlorinated hydrocarbons. They were developed to insulate transformers, telephone exchanges and other equipment. They are no longer used but are found in old equipment. In 1994 there were an estimated 8000 tonnes of PCBs remaining in the UK.

Impacts

If PCBs get into water courses, they accumulate in the bodies of water-based creatures and enter the food chain. They can cause *chloracne,* vomiting, abdominal pain and other symptoms. Due to voluntary controls, followed by legislation, PCB levels are declining in many waters.

Legislation

Countries participating in the International North Sea Conference have agreed to phase out and destroy PCBs by the end of 1999, and in the UK this was implemented in the 1993 *UK Action Plan for the Phasing out ...of PCBs.* The EU has placed restrictions on the supply or use of preparations or waste with a PCB content higher than 50 parts per million. They were banned in the UK under the Control of Pollution Regulations 1986.

Substitutes

PCBs have been substituted with PCNs (polychlorinated naphthalenes), which are also hazardous.

Disposal

The oil must be disposed of properly, usually through high temperature incineration by licensed contractors. Inadequate incineration can create *dioxins* and *furans*.

Best Practice

- *Audit* to see whether the company has any equipment containing PCBs or PCNs.
- Phase out all such equipment in a planned way, disposing of it in a legally approved manner.

See also: Hazardous waste; Yusho disease.

PCNs: *see PCBs*

PCP: *see Pentachlorophenol*

Peat

Peat is an excellent growing medium for young plants because it holds water extremely well. This makes it sought after by horticulturists, garden centres and gardeners. On average, everyone in the UK uses the equivalent of a 40-litre bag each year.

However, the bogs, from which peat is extracted, are environmentally important because they are home to many rare species, especially wading birds. Peat is made from the decomposition of plants and animals, in the same way as oil and coal, though it is younger. It takes thousands of years to develop, which makes it a *non-renewable resource*.

Impacts

Farmers drain wetlands to make them suitable for arable crops and pasture. They also spray *herbicides* which kill the wild flowers and other food plants. Otters lose their homes during the periodic river bank clearances. As a result, various *wildlife* species disappear.

Best Practice

- For landscape planting, use a peat substitute, such as coconut fibre.

See also: Wetlands.

Pentachlorophenol (PCP)

A fungicide, used in wood preservatives and to prevent mildew from rotting cloth. Being toxic and non-degradable, it is banned in 17 countries (including Germany), and is on the list of hazardous substances published by the EU and the UK governments. Subject to EC Directives 91/7341/EEC, 86/280/EEC, and 76/769/EEC. Its import into and export from the EC is restricted.

Best Practice

- Avoid its use.

See also: Red List; Black List.

Perchloroethylene

A solvent used in *dry cleaning*. In the US, it is seen as an air pollutant and a probable human carcinogen. It is known as 'Perc' and in California dry cleaners must put the word in big letters in their windows. One alternative is Aquatex, a water-based cleaning system which is said to clean and protect garments.

See also: Trichloroethylene.

Performance, Environmental

The measurable results of an organization's environmental *impacts*. The measures include emissions to air, waste and land; the use of energy, etc. These are *performance indicators*. As standards are rising, organizations should seek to continually improve their performance.

Why Monitor?

Organizations need to monitor environmental performance for several reasons, some internal, some external.

Internal Reasons:

- To monitor the organization's progress and improvement over time and against others.
- To make a business case for environmental policy and actions.
- To demonstrate that financial resources are being used well.
- To set priorities for action.

External reasons

- Regulators may demand the information.
- Standards such as *EMAS* and *ISO 14001* require measurements of performance.
- Customers increasingly want evidence of an organization's probity.
- Shareholders may be influenced by the company's environmental commitment.

What Should Be Measured?

The organization might measure its performance in the following areas:

- legislation: regulatory compliance;
- management system: compliance to the stated management system;
- staff: employees – roles and responsibilities, awareness and training;
- raw materials and energy: raw materials use; resource conservation; hazardous materials; use of energy;
- assets: property management (to what extent are impacts, such as energy use, being cut?);
- supplies management: suppliers, contractors and other partners (what proportion could be described as environmentally aware?);
- marketing and communications: product development (to what extent do new products offer more environmental benefits than before?); environmental communications;

- emergencies: emergency preparedness;
- process control: process management, and risk reduction; process change; prevention of pollution;
- ecology: nature conservation;
- development: acquisition and divestment; capital projects;
- waste: scale of waste, reduction in wastes; water management (waste, storm, ground); air quality management; energy management;
- transportation: delivery of raw materials to the plant; delivery of finished products to customers.

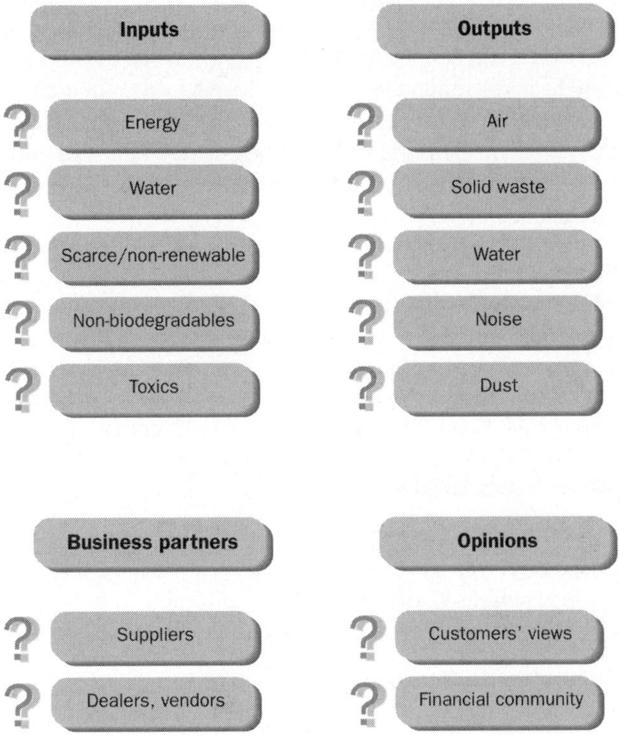

Figure 21: Measuring Performance Factors

Success in Measuring Performance

ISO is preparing a standard for evaluating environmental performance, terms and definitions. As defined in Croners Environmental Management, several factors determine whether the measures chosen will be a success. They include the following:

- *Comparison:* Companies should measure impacts over time and against other organizations, or with legal limits. This puts the results into perspective and provides benchmarks.
- *Controllable:* There must be a relationship between the measure and the actions needed to improve it.

- *Comprehensive:* Since no single measure covers all the company's impacts, there must be enough measurements to provide a satisfactory picture.
- *Costs:* There must be money and people to produce the measurements. If the measurements are too expensive, they will cease to be made.
- *Credible:* The measures must be credible to the various audiences. Include bad news, such as environmental incidents or prosecutions. There must be no '*greenwash*', for example glossing over uncomfortable details. The use of external *certifiers* makes a report more credible.
- *Customers:* Every measure must have a clearly defined audience whose needs should be considered in determining what and how to measure.
- *Continuous improvement:* Companies should compare their measures with *best practice* companies (by benchmarking). Targets which do not stretch performance rarely impress audiences. But the targets must be achievable if they are to motivate staff.
- *Positive factors:* The measures should not be entirely negative and solely about adverse impacts. The company should also measure the good news – notably, the company's successes.

Best Practice

- Determine the measures which identify the organization's major impacts.
- Set targets for the reduction of these impacts.

See also: Envirometrics; Objectives; Performance, environmental; Report; Targets.

Performance Indicators

Performance indicators demonstrate the scale of the company's environmental impacts and (viewed over time) its progress in reducing them. Performance indicators may be used in setting targets – for example – to reduce the amount of CO_2 released into the atmosphere by 100 tonnes a year, a drop of 6 per cent.

Sample Performance Indicators

These include:

- amount of raw materials used (per unit of output);
- amount of *energy* used (per unit of output);
- output of specific pollutants (CO_2, CO, NO_x, SO_2, etc);
- waste produced (per unit of output);
- percentage waste recycled;
- number of environmental incidents;
- number of prosecutions;
- number of vehicle kilometres (per unit of output);
- investment in environmental protection.

Choice of Units

Units can be in the form of:

- volume;
- concentration (*BOD*, etc);
- cost;
- HR units (for example, training hours);
- risk.

Units can also be:

- Standardized (or normalized), for example, Mj of energy per 1000 tonnes of output;
- tracked over time.

Case Study 26: Measuring Performance in a Multi-Site Organization

Companies can set standardized performance goals for their divisions and then review progress. In 1996, Coats Viyella reported that 88 per cent of its sites had an environmental policy and 62 per cent of them had achieved best practice in implementing it. A further 98 per cent had established an environmental forum, and 53 per cent had attained best practice in its use.

See also: Objectives; Performance; Report; Targets.

Perfume

Environmentalists say that the perfumes found in washing powders, shampoos and other cleaning agents are cosmetic and therefore a waste of resources. They can contain chemical impurities which are harmful to aquatic environments. Companies say that they send a message of cleanliness to the consumer and prevent overdosing or mixing of cleaning products. Perfumes made from natural substances are available and conform to IFRA standards.

Permethrin

A toxic *pesticide*, used against head lice, in timber treatment, to control insects in the home, and in all areas of *agriculture*. It is an *oestrogen mimic* and skin irritant. In 1995, the German government announced that permethrin may cause brain cancer.

Best Practice

- Do not use.

Persistent

Substances, especially toxins, which are extremely stable or which do not biodegrade are said to be persistent. While stable compounds (such as *DDT*) were once favoured for their effectiveness, scientists later realized that their persistence enables them to stay in the environment for a long time, possibly building up in the bodies of fish or animals and being passed up the *food chain*.

Pesticides

The generic name for fungicides, herbicides and insecticides (which kill fungi, plants and insects respectively), also known as biocides. They are designed to kill things which harm crops, livestock or humans. Pesticide use has grown substantially. In 1945, only eight million tonnes of pesticide were manufactured in the US. By 1985, that figure had grown to 107 million tonnes. Yet, no toxic data are available, according to the US regulatory authorities, for 66 per cent of pesticides.

In the UK, 97 per cent of arable crops in 1988 were treated with pesticides. In 1989, 29 million tonnes of pesticide were applied, equating to half a kilo of neat poison for every man, woman and child.

Pesticides have helped to eradicate malaria and greatly increase food production, but some have also brought unforeseen side-effects (for example, *DDT*). Pesticides are accused of creating a range of problems, from breast cancer and brain tumours to a decline in fertility. Environmentalists argue that since pesticides are designed to kill things, they are therefore dangerous. If they can kill insects and fungal infections, they may be able to harm human beings, especially over a long time. However, while pesticide residues may be detected in the aquatic environment and in foods, there is little scientific evidence to show that, if used properly, they cause harm. Nevertheless, while the links between pesticides and health problems are difficult to prove, some environmentalists and some scientists believe that pesticide use should be restricted on a precautionary basis. Some believe that by the time the links are proved, it will be too late.

Many pesticides are now banned. For example, Denmark has proposed restrictions on a group of herbicides known as *phenoxy acid* herbicides. They include *2,4-D*, mecoprop and diclorprop. The ban is linked to the threat they pose to the environment or human health.

Impacts

Spray drift can cause illness to walkers, animals and crops in neighbouring fields, as well as to the farm workers who apply it. Pesticide *residues* also end up in vegetables and fruit, though the permitted limits are now small. Pesticides have also helped to destroy wild flowers and reduce *biodiversity*.

Various illnesses and conditions are ascribed to pesticides, including asthma, eczema, irritable bowel syndrome, degenerative diseases such as Alzheimer's Disease and Parkinson's, and a reduction in human sperm count. Legal restrictions on pesticides are increasingly being introduced. In 1988, Sweden doubled its environmental levy on pesticides, aiming to cut pesticide use by 50 per cent from the average used in 1981 to 1985. By the end of the 1980s, pesticide use was down by 35 per cent.

Using good agricultural practice, farmers now cease spraying many weeks or months before harvesting. In addition, fewer, more highly targeted applications are used, rather than routine spraying.

Alternatives

Less toxic pesticides, such as glyphosate (which has been used since the 1970s), are being developed. A still better solution is the use of biological solutions, such as the introduction of predators or other deterrents, which obviate the use of chemicals. Organic farming (or farming with reduced inputs) is a solution being adopted by some farmers. The industry is also turning to *genetically modified organisms*, notably crops which are either resistant to certain types of fungicide, or which are resistant to certain pesticides. The latter use could lead to increased applications of pesticide.

Best Practice

Farmers should:

- Rotate crops effectively.
- Monitor pest infestations more closely.
- Avoid the routine application of pesticides unless essential. It is better to target specific pests when they occur.
- Decrease application rates.
- Avoid the problems of overspray and spray drift.
- Avoid pesticides which are persistent and broad spectrum.
- Use biological control agents (predators).

See also: Agriculture; Biodiversity; Nature Conservation.

PET

Plastic used to make drinks bottles. Because of their bulk and low value they are unsuitable for recycling. Incineration with *energy* recovery is seen as a good solution.

Petrochemicals

A collective name for companies that make products which rely on raw materials produced by 'cracking' (or splitting) oil into petrol and ethene. The resulting products, most of which are made from ethene, include plastics, paints, detergents, washing powders, drugs and cosmetics.

Petrol

The main impacts of petrol are:

- *Non-renewable resources*, such as *oil*, are consumed.
- Air pollutants are caused by the combustion of petrol. The main ones are *carbon monoxide*, *nitrous oxides* and *hydrocarbons*.
- *Lead* in leaded petrol: all new cars are now designed to run on lead-free petrol. In fact, cars manufactured by General Motors in the UK but destined for the US market could run on unleaded petrol since 1971.

- To compensate for the loss of lead, oil companies have added *benzene, toluene* and xylene. This has added to detrimental environmental impacts.

See also: Cars; Catalytic converter; Filling stations; Lead.

pH

A measure of a substance's acidity or alkalinity. Acids have a pH less than 7. The lower the number, the greater the acidity. Alkalines have a pH greater than 7.

Phenol

An *organic* compound known as carbolic acid. A white solid in appearance, it is used as a disinfectant and in the production of drugs, weedkillers, and synthetic resins. Many phenol compounds are in use.

See also: Chlorinated phenols.

Phenoxy Acid

Toxic *herbicides*, notably 2,4,5-T and 2,4-D. Both of these were mixed with *dioxin* to create the toxic defoliant *Agent Orange*, which was used in the Vietnam War.

Best Practice

- Do not use.

See also: 2,4-D; Black List; Pesticides.

Phosgene

Poisonous gas used in World War I and now used to make the insecticide *carbaryl*. It is produced by the reaction of *chlorine* and *carbon monoxide*.

Best Practice

- Avoid its use.

See also: Bhopal; Chlorine.

Phosphates

Used as *fertilizers* and water softeners. When they leach into water courses, they can overfertilize plants in water, leading to *eutrophication*. This can kill aquatic species, including fish. Detergent companies (which use phosphates in some detergents) point out that only 15 to 25 per cent of phosphates in water come from detergents (most come from fertilizers). Phosphates are banned in Norway and Switzerland, and other countries have imposed controls.

Zeolites and polycarboxylates (PCAs) are sometimes used as 'green' water softeners. However, they are less effective, so the consumer may use more non-phosphate detergent to achieve the same cleanliness. This results in the pouring of bleach and brighteners down the drain, causing more pollution.

Best Practice

- Do not overuse as a fertilizer.
- In detergents, make, specify or use only products bearing an *eco-label.*

See also: Eutrophication; Laundry detergents; Phosphorus.

Phosphorus

Phosphorus and organophosphorus compounds are toxic substances used in chemical manufacture, sheep dip and crop spraying. They are on the EC *Black List* of dangerous substances. When phosphorus gets into water courses, usually from *sewage* works, it causes *eutrophication.*

Best Practice

- Avoid wherever possible

Photochemical Smog: *see Smog*

Photocopiers

Photocopiers are found in even the smallest of offices and their speed and ease of use encourages paper consumption. For this reason, they have a big environmental *impact*; special attention should be paid to the choice of machine and the way it is used.

Best Practice

When leasing or buying new copiers:
- Make sure that the copier can easily produce double-sided copies: this will substantially reduce the amount of paper used.
- Ensure that the photocopier will readily accept different types of recycled paper.
- Ensure that the copier automatically changes to standby mode to reduce *energy use.*
- Make sure that the copier does not involve throwing away large disposable items (such as sealed cartridges) unless recycled replacements are available.

Best Practice

For photocopying practice:
- Brief staff to produce double-sided copies unless there is a reason not to.

See also: Furniture; Office; Office Equipment; Printers.

Photodegradable

Material that decomposes in sunlight. Photodegradable plastic bottles have not met with much commercial success, possibly due to manufacturers' fears that bottles will biodegrade before being sold or used.

Photographic Industry

Impacts include the use of large quantities of water, the use of hazardous chemicals and the creation of polluted waste water. This can be reduced by the use of a *closed-loop* process and by adopting various techniques to purify the water (such as water sterilization and *reverse osmosis*). The silver should be recovered from the waste and sold for recycling. A vacuum distillation may be used to recover the water from the waste concentrate.

See also: Printing.

Photovoltaics: *see Solar Energy*

Phthalates

Alleged *oestrogen mimic* which reduces male fertility. Used in *PVC* and other plastics.

Best Practice

- Do not use.

PICs: *see Products of Incomplete Combustion*

Pirimiphos-Methyl

Hazardous *pesticide* used against domestic pests, such as ants. Suspected of causing birth defects.

Best Practice

- Do not use.

Piper Alpha

A North Sea oil rig that exploded and caught fire on 6 July 1986, killing 167 men out of the 230 on board. The tragedy started when the gas processing system became faulty and a large flare developed. A gas leak began to build up and this eventually exploded. Diesel began to leak out and fuelled the flames, and there was a series of further explosions. The rig's communications system was put out of order, so no one could give or receive orders.

A gas jet then blew in the centre of the rig, and began to release hydrocarbon gas at 1800 pounds per square inch. A fireball enveloped the rig, and flames rose 700 feet (213 metres) into the sky. Those who could jumped into the water, while others were trapped inside the rig. The intense heat kept the rescue ships at bay. Finally, the remaining pipelines blew, burning hundreds of cubic feet of gas. The fire continued for four days.

The tragedy led to a government enquiry and the requirement for oil rigs to adopt an approved safety case (a safety plan).

See also: Exxon Valdez; Oil and gas industry.

Plan, Environmental: *see Programme*

Planning (Hazardous Substances) Act 1990 (UK): *see Hazardous Substances*

Plastic Cups: *see Cups*

Plastics

Made from oil, plastic resists decay so it can take centuries to break down naturally. Where the following plastics (or polymeric materials) occur in quantities greater than 50 grams, they should bear a permanent mark identifying the material:

- polypropylene;
- polystyrene;
- *PVC*;
- *HDPE*;
- *LDPE*;
- *ABS*;
- polyamide.

The mark should adopt the symbols or abbreviated terms given in ISO 1043.

Disposal

Incineration with heat recovery is seen as the *best practical* disposal solution. Plastics manufacturers recycle a high proportion of their waste but, once into the consumer waste stream, plastic is hard to recycle. Factors against recycling include the many varieties of plastic, the bulky size of many plastic bottles (though collapsible bottles would reduce the problem of bulk), and the low cost of virgin materials. In the US, only 2 per cent is recycled.

PET bottles have been melted and spun into fibres for carpets or insulation material in clothing and cars. In general, plastic is not recycled into food containers because of fears of contamination and food poisoning. Recycled plastics are also routinely made into plastic bags. It is possible to buy recycled plastic fence posts and bollards. In the UK, Cooper Clarke's interlocking plastic blocks are made from 96 per cent post-consumer recycled polyethylene and are used for emergency access lanes across grass and temporary parking areas. Anaplast makes cheerfully coloured pallets from old milk and beer crates.

Eco-Composites

Natural fibre-reinforced plastics (known as *eco-composites*) are being developed. Plastic can be made from vegetable oils, while the fibre comes from renewable raw material.

Biodegradable Plastic

Attempts to introduce biodegradable plastic were not very successful because the anaerobic conditions of landfill sites discourage decomposition. Some manufacturers were also unwilling to risk the bottles biodegrading while still on the supermarket shelf.

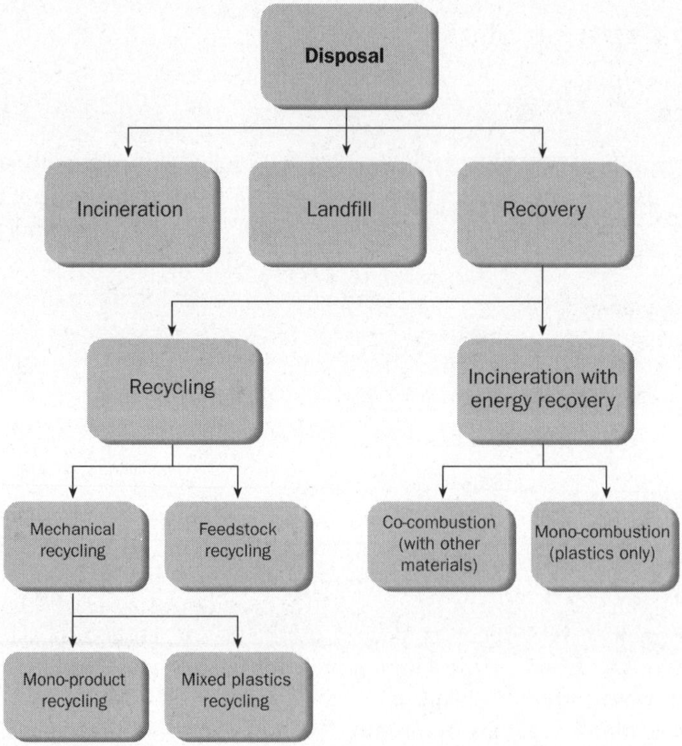

Figure 22: Waste Management System for Plastics

See also: Recycling.

Plating

Plating is used to protect steel or other metal components, or to coat printed circuit boards. Plating involves toxic heavy metals such as *zinc*, *nickel*, *copper* and chromium, which produce fumes and polluted *waste water*.

Companies can either subcontract plating operations to a specialist firm, or else reduce the hazard through computerizing and enclosing the operation, which provides more controlled temperature and raw material use. Alternatively, less toxic substances can be used (for example, copper pyrophosphate in place of copper cyanide). The use of ion exchange as a final rinse sometimes allows raw materials to be recovered and the water to be recycled.

See also: Cadmium.

Plume

Trail of smoke or other emissions from a chimney. The size and direction of the plume depends on:

- the material being burnt (for example, how sulphurous it is);
- the scrubbers (filters) installed in the chimney;
- the prevailing winds;
- the geography of the area.

These factors will dictate how high the chimney should be. For example, the plume from a plant sited in a valley might 'ground' on the hillside. Regulatory authorities may require a new process or chimney to be modelled, to ensure that it does not come to ground among the local population.

See also: Air pollution; Dilute and disperse.

PM_{10}s

Particles less than ten microns in diameter that are produced by combustion, especially from vehicles. They can stick in the lungs and cause breathing difficulties or cancer. PM_{10}s should not exceed 50 micrograms per cubic metre, measured over a 24-hour average.

Table 12: Air Quality Standards for PM_{10}s

Organization	Limit, in micrograms per cubic metre ($\mu g/m^3$)	Sampling method
EPAQS Recommended UK standard	50	24-hour running average
USA EPA (National Ambient Air Quality Standard – NAAQS)	150	Daily average

See also: Particulates.

Point Source

Pollution that comes from a single identifiable source, such as a factory. It contrasts with 'non-point' or diffuse sources, such as *acid rain* and run-off from agricultural land. Diffuse sources are more difficult to deal with because no single polluter can be identified.

Polaroid: *see CERES*

Policy, Environmental

A written statement that defines the company's attitude towards the environment. The policy provides a framework for the company's actions, and is used to set objectives and targets.

Topics To Be Considered

- the organization's mission, vision, or core values;
- compliance with the law and other criteria to which the organization subscribes;
- prevention of pollution;
- continual improvement (a requirement in some *EMSs*);
- requirements of *interested parties*;
- coordination with other policies (notably health and safety, and quality).

Sample Policy

A typical policy might contain these goals:

In all our activities, we aim to do the following:

- Comply with or exceed environmental laws.
- Reduce and stop pollution at source, by design and operational management.
- Minimise energy use.
- Reduce emissions to air, discharges to water, *solid waste* and the use of toxic materials.
- Provide products and services which facilitate *sustainable development*.
- Ensure, through education and training, that each employee is aware of our environmental objectives and can fulfil them.
- Develop environmental *performance indicators* which help us to evaluate our impacts.
- Use suppliers and other business partners who take a responsible attitude to the environment.
- Make good environmental practice an intrinsic part of corporate thinking and activity.
- Continually improve our environmental performance.
- Use best available techniques not entailing excessive cost.
- Maintain effective communications with interested parties.

The policy must be endorsed (and should be signed) by top management, without whose support the document will be worthless. Too many policies, once written, are ignored. The policy should not be too specific, since future plans and activities need room for manoeuvre. More detailed goals should be included in the company's environmental *objectives* or *targets*. The policy must also be communicated to employees, and a *certifier* may check that they understand it. It should be made available to all *interested parties* (who can include shareholders, local residents or the general public). The organization should review the policy periodically, to ensure it is still relevant.

Under *EMAS* and *ISO 14001*, the objectives must include a commitment to *continuous improvement*. The Institute of Directors (IOD) found that 37 per cent of its members had never discussed environmental issues at board level, and only 26 per cent had a written environmental policy. According to a survey by CCEM (Centre for Corporate Environmental Management), the following ten issues were the most commonly found in companies' environmental policies:

(1) waste minimization;
(2) legislative compliance;
(3) assessment of environmental performance;
(4) energy efficiency;
(5) shared responsibility (encouraging suppliers to go green);
(6) minimize impacts on the environment;
(7) environmental training;
(8) set targets and objectives;
(9) liaise with the local community;
(10) public disclosure.

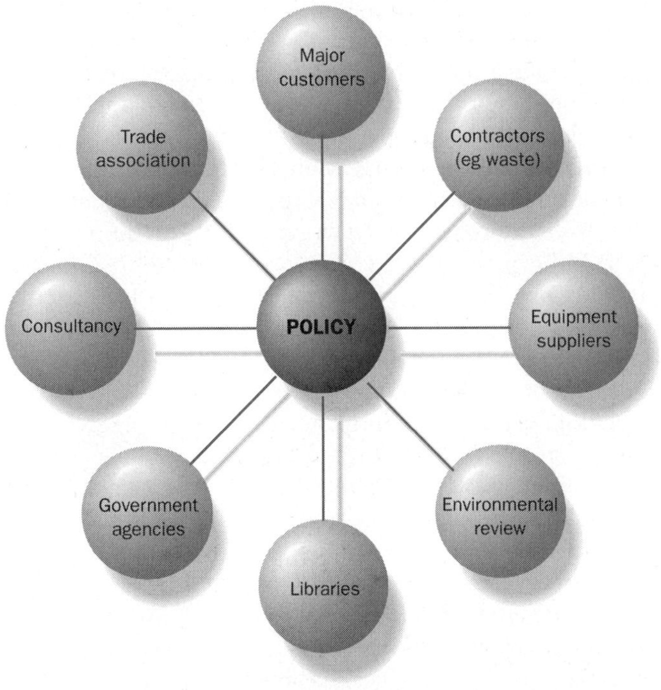

Figure 23: Preparing an Environmental Policy

Organizations and sources of information which may be consulted and taken into account when preparing an environmental policy.

Best Practice

- Produce an environmental policy.
- Ensure it conforms to a recognized standard, such as EMAS or ISO 14000.
- Assess regularly whether the policy is being effectively implemented (ie through an *audit*).

See also: Continuous improvement; EMAS; Environmental management system; ISO 14001; Objectives; Strategy; Targets.

'Polluter Pays' Principle

The principle that a company should pay for its pollution, whether by taxation, consents or litigation. The principle is designed to reduce pollution by making it expensive. It aims to move the cost of pollution from society to the polluter.

See also: Integrated Pollution Prevention and Control; IPC.

Pollution

Described as: 'Too high a concentration of a resource in the wrong place at the wrong time.' This definition indicates that pollution involves a misuse of resources. For example, a *nitrate fertilizer* will increase plant growth (which is probably a good thing), but if it is allowed into the water supply it leads to algal blooms and *eutrophication* (a bad thing).

Nature itself causes pollution when volcanoes spew out smoke, *particulates* and toxic gases. The eruption of Tambora in Sumatra in 1815 put 220 tonnes of particulates into the stratosphere, and it was so dense that the following two years were the coldest in history, causing crop shortages. Many polluting substances are found in nature (for example, the *heavy metals*), but it is their concentration by mankind that creates pollution. In addition, industry has synthesized many new chemical compounds that are not found in nature; it is the *toxic, persistent,* and *bioaccumulative* ones that cause the greatest danger.

However, pollution can also be caused by seemingly harmless substances. For example, ordinary *organic* food waste from a cake factory can kill the fish in a river, by depriving them of oxygen. Pollution can also be a sign of waste, or poor quality, signifying faulty products or processes. The most important issue in pollution is not the shock headlines but the long-term modifications to ecosystems that can occur if potentially toxic chemicals build up.

Pollution is often defined according to its 'receiving medium', that is: air, land or water. Pollution typically consists of a substance that will harm living organisms. It is likely to be unduly acid or alkaline, or highly reactive (whether corrosive, violent or simply a substance that creates changes – such as the algal blooms mentioned above). Sometimes pollution is a function of particle size: particulates, *asbestos* fibres, and man-made mineral fibres fall into this category. As Table 13 shows, it is better to prevent pollution from occurring in the first place, rather than trying to clean it up once it has been caused.

Table 13: Strategies for Dealing with the Threat of Pollution

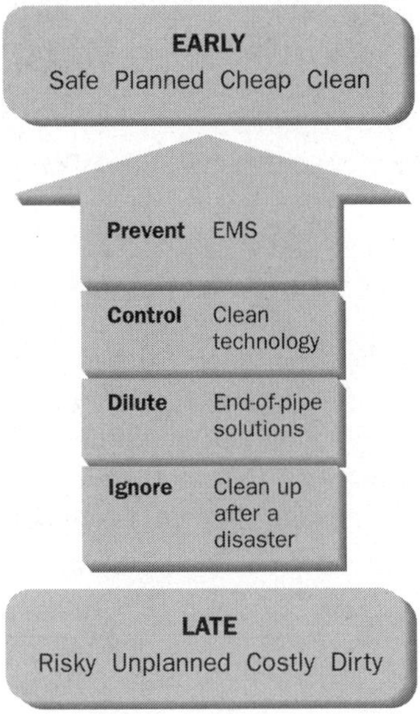

Most organizations move from a state of ignoring pollution to preventing it, this being the most trouble-free solution. To achieve this, they generally go from less successful strategies of diluting the pollution (see: *dilute and disperse*) and controlling it (for example, through better housekeeping) to preventing its occurrence.

See also: Air pollution; Cleaner production; Hazardous substances; Process; Liquid waste; Water pollution.

Pollution Prevention Act – USA

The 1990 act seeks to prevent pollution through reduced generation of pollutants at their source. It requires manufacturers to report annually on their efforts to reduce pollution and recycle their waste.

The act marked a turning point in US environmental protection policy. Hitherto, Congress had sought to control pollutants at the point where they are released into the environment (such as *end-of-pipe*). With the act, attention focused on the prevention of pollution at its point of origin.

Polymers; *see Plastics*

Polycyclic (or Polynuclear) Aromatic Hydrocarbons: *see PAHs*

Population Growth

From four billion people in the 1990s to possibly ten billion by the year 2100, the world's population is spiralling upwards. It is like a new Los Angeles forming every two weeks, and all these people need feeding. As more people inhabit the world, they consume more natural resources, such as wood, water and coal, and create more pollution. Therefore overpopulation is a threat to the environment.

Much of the industrialized West has achieved *zero population growth* (most are growing at less than 1 per cent while in countries such as Sweden and Austria the population is declining). As Figure 24 shows, the growth is coming from the less-developed nations, with India and China experiencing the greatest increases. This is due not to increased birth rates but to reduced mortality – people are living longer and fewer babies are dying, thanks to clean water, sanitation and disease eradication. Nor is the actual population growth rate the problem. India, which gained an extra 14 million people during 1985 to 1990, has a growth rate of only 2.1 per cent. Likewise, China, which grew by 12 million during the same period, grew at only 1.4 per cent. It is the size of the existing population that counts most.

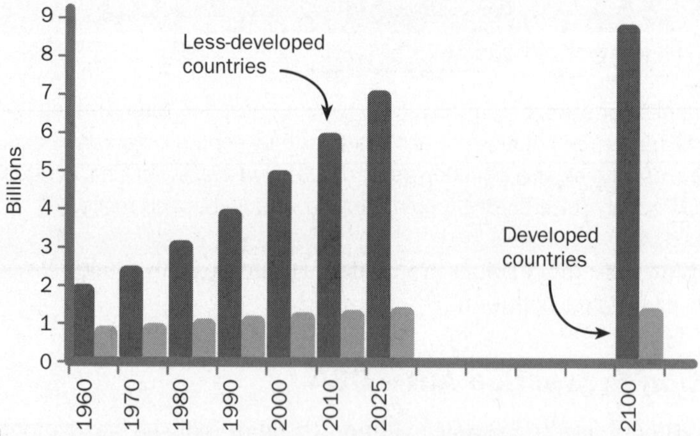

Figure 24: Global Population (Billions)

However, the picture is not overly bleak. Many of the world's largest cities, including those in the developing countries, have stopped growing; and while the world's population will continue to increase it is unlikely to attain catastrophic proportions – similar previous growths in the West have not caused the devastation that was predicted.

Best Practice

To prevent overpopulation:

- The education of women is strongly linked with reductions in childbirth. In Thailand, high female literacy has been accompanied by a halving of the birth rate.
- Access to family planning by those women who want to control the number of their children is also important.

Post-Consumer

Paper or material that has been used for its final and intended purpose. Likewise, 'pre-consumer' means that the material has not undergone its intended use.

Power Stations: *see Energy*

Precautionary Principle

The concept that the government should ban a material or pollutant if it caused significant damage to the environment, even if scientific knowledge was not conclusive. The principle was introduced in Article 130r of the EC Treaty. It was introduced into the UK in a 1990 UK White Paper. A chemical, therefore, could be banned if it were thought to be carcinogenic. Similarly, action might be taken to prevent *global warming*, even if irrefutable proof had not been established.

However, the principle is applied sparingly and only where 'the balance of likely costs and benefits justifies it'. Its full implementation would require governments to ban large numbers of products; which they are unlikely to do.

See also: Vorsorgeprinzip.

Preliminary Review

The organization's first environmental *audit*, also called a preparatory, scoping or initial review. This is a requirement for *EMAS*, but not for *ISO 14001* (though it is difficult to develop ISO 14001 without first carrying out some kind of preliminary audit). Even if the company does not intend to register to one of the standards, the preliminary review is an essential first step to understanding the nature and scale of the company's impacts.

The EMAS Review

The EMAS Review requires the following activities:

- Establish the issues that are making an impact on the environment (such as raw materials, *solid waste*, *energy* and so on).
- Determine which of these impacts needs to be improved.
- Assess how well the site conforms to current legislation.
- Measure consumption, emissions, etc (where possible).
- Determine where improvements can be made.
- Decide what needs to be done and which are the priorities.
- Make any policy changes indicated by the findings.
- Set specific objectives for company activities.

List of Topics To Be Covered

- legislative and regulatory requirements;
- *environmental impacts* of activities, products or services;
- corporate performance compared with internal criteria, external standards, regulations, and codes of practice;

- existing policies and procedures for purchasing;
- previous incidents of non-compliance;
- opportunities for competitive advantage;
- views of interested parties;
- organizational systems (such as *ISO 9000*) that enable environmental performance or impede it.

In carrying out a preliminary review, the site can be divided into departments or areas of environmental impact; a *questionnaire* should be issued to departmental heads. The results can then be collated.

The Outcome of the Review

The preliminary review provides the organization with its first information about the nature and scale of its impacts. It may also provide base-line data against which future audits may be compared. The preliminary review should also result in a list of the organization's impacts (this becomes the *register of effects*). They include pollution, waste, the use of inappropriate materials, and even the future effects of products or processes that are not in themselves harmful.

Documentation To Be Produced

The review should produce the following documents:

- a management report containing facts and figures and recommendations for action;
- an inventory of raw materials;
- an assessment of *energy* and water used;
- an inventory of waste produced (including emissions to air, scrap, and effluents);
- a register of all environmental regulations that are relevant to the site;
- an assessment of the management systems.

The initial review usually reveals a lack of environmental information (other than processes governed by legislation). This shows that the organization is not collecting figures on environmental impacts, which makes it difficult for the auditor to know the scale of the impacts. One recommendation of the review might be to collect data in a more systematic and thorough manner.

If the organization has recently conducted an environmental *audit*, it will not need to carry out a review. The audit will serve as the preliminary review, though it must be thorough enough to satisfy the *verifier* if the organization is seeking registration to *EMAS*. The results of the review should be produced as a written report, and the results communicated to relevant managers for action.

Sources of Information

In addition to the audit, many sources of advice may be used in preparing a preliminary review:

- government agencies – in relation to laws and permits;
- local libraries;
- similar organizations for exchange of information;

- industry associations;
- major corporate customers;
- manufacturers of equipment used by the organization;
- contractors (haulage companies, waste contractors);
- professional firms (lawyers, management consultants).

Best Practice

- Undertake or commission an initial review if this has not already happened.
- Use the results of the review to reduce the organization's impacts.

See also: Audit, environmental; EMS audit; Review, environmental.

Preparatory Review: *see Preliminary Review*

Preservation of Natural Habitats Directive: *see Habitats Directive*

Pressure Groups

Green pressure groups now gain support from all sections of society: they are no longer a minority. The actions of pressure groups can severely harm the company's plant or corporate image. Eco-guerrillas such as Earth First have buried metal fragments in trees, which can injure a logger. Activists fire-bombed Shell garages when they were angered by the firm's decision to dispose of the Brent Spar oil rig in the North Sea.

Companies which emit large amounts of pollutants and those in environmentally controversial industries should maintain a dialogue with any pressure group that targets them. The alternative – to ignore the group – is to invite more protest. The company should communicate its environmental targets, programme and achievements, and invite protesters into the plant.

Pressure groups sometimes unfairly target one company. Moreover, as Shell also found over the Brent Spar issue, scientific arguments do not always convince environmentalists (especially when the research data have been generated by company scientists). Moreover, dealing with hostile critics can take a lot of management time; and it is sometimes simpler to adopt higher standards and accept the costs that accompany them.

Tarmac, which built a much criticized road through Britain's Twyford Down, decided to pull out of the bidding for the equally controversial Newbury Bypass, after having its offices attacked and its shareholder meetings disrupted, and after the cost of clearing protesters from the site of the road rose to UK£20 million. Now the company wants to develop a more harmonious relationship with the environment and is reluctant to build low-cost roads that lack environmental measures.

People are likely to expect higher environmental standards in the coming years. Therefore companies should set themselves high standards today, in order to meet future expectations. As the movement matures, some groups are developing a partnership approach. The Environmental Careers Organization of Boston places retired engineers and scientists with community groups. The experts help them understand data supplied under the *Toxic Release Inventory*, and help to develop a new partnership between community and industry.

Best Practice

- Identify the impacts which might make the organization vulnerable to attack by pressure groups.
- Introduce a plan to reduce those impacts.
- Ensure that the organization has relevant information or a spokesperson for communicating with pressure groups.
- Introduce, if appropriate, a PR programme to improve the company's image or rectify misconceptions.

See also: Communications; Public relations; Report.

Printers, Computer

When buying a computer printer, choose one which accepts recycled paper, which powers down when idle (if it has a motor or fan), and which has low ozone emissions. Also check out whether recycled toner cartridges are readily available.

See also: Cartridges; Photocopiers.

Printing

Printing often uses virgin paper, whose production causes environmental problems (see: *Paper, board and pulp industry*). In addition, metallic inks come from a *non-renewable resource*, may be toxic and do not biodegrade after use.

Best Practice

- Use recycled paper, or at least paper which has been not bleached with chlorine.
- Use vegetable-based inks which come from a *renewable resource* and will *biodegrade* after disposal. Do not use inks which use *VOCs*.
- Do not use laminating or non-aqueous varnishes. This can make the paper non-recyclable.
- If you produce bound books or magazines, check if the printer can use glues which do not hinder the recycling process.

See also: ECF; Paper; Paper, board and pulp industry; Office paper; TCF.

Priority Pollutants – US

A list of dangerous substances drawn up by the *US Environmental Protection Agency* (*EPA*).

Procedures

A procedure is a written explanation of how to carry out a *process*. Originally used in quality programmes (to prevent scrap or faulty goods), they have now been adopted to prevent pollution. Procedures might cover:

- the correct operation of a boiler to prevent *air pollution*;
- controlling an effluent plant to prevent *water pollution*;
- the storage of used *packaging* for recycling;
- new product reviews to ensure that the product will not harm the environment;
- a checklist for new suppliers to ensure that their products do not carry environmental risks.

Once procedures are in place, the company should carry out *audits* to ensure that they are being adhered to. Written procedures ensure that new staff know what is expected of them and reduce uncertainty. Procedures should be kept to a minimum. They should be written in simple language and should be personally explained to all relevant staff.

Purpose of Procedures

In an *EMS*, procedures have the following aims:

- to prevent pollution;
- to conserve resources (such as raw materials, or *energy*);
- to provide information (for example, record keeping);
- to anticipate and respond to changing environmental requirements (in the law, emergencies, etc).

See also: Environmental management system; Operational control; Process.

Process

A process is one of the organization's activities. For example, in a ketchup factory, processes would include:

- mixing the ingredients;
- cooking the ingredients;
- filling the bottles;
- labelling them;
- boxing the bottles;
- distributing them to customers.

The ketchup factory also has countless other processes, such as order processing and new product development. Sweeping the floor is also a process.

Therefore a process is any work activity. Analysing a process (sometimes called 'process mapping') is a valuable way of examining environmental impacts. A process has three elements: inputs, the process itself, and outputs.

Inputs

Inputs include *energy* (especially electricity use), water and *raw materials*. They often include ready-made components. The organization may also have to look at how its raw materials were produced. This may mean auditing a supplier. For example, a company that assembles hi-fi equipment will need to see how the components it buys were made.

The less input, the less environmental damage will be caused. For example, plastic bottles nowadays use much less plastic than before. This means a saving on the amount of oil required to make the plastic.

The Process

As we have seen above, the process can be anything from sticking a label on a bottle to entering information into a computer. Where possible, the process should be improved so that it uses fewer inputs and produces less waste.

Outputs

The main output is the product. In some organizations the product is tangible – such as nuts and bolts. In others it is a service, such as package holidays or an arm of government. There are also unintended outputs, such as *solid waste* (rubbish), emissions to air, and discharges to water.

One important output is faulty goods or scrap. These not only add to the pile of waste, but they also cost the company money. Reducing scrap is therefore a profitable goal.

Management has always wanted to analyse processes, because doing them more efficiently allows the company to make a better product and save money. For the environmental manager, improving a process usually involves reducing the raw materials, the energy and the waste.

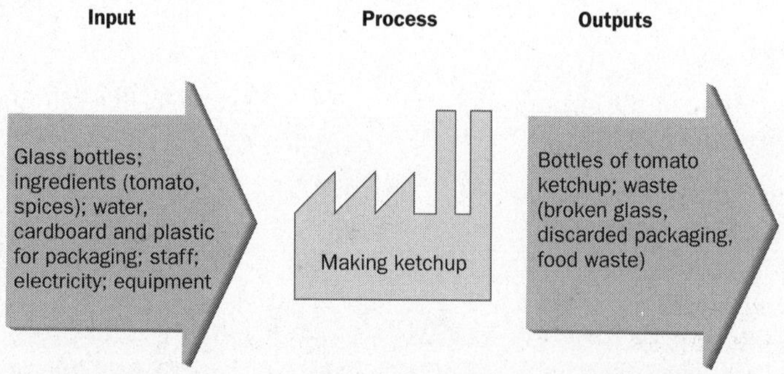

Figure 25: Inputs and Outputs for a Ketchup Factory

A Register of Effects

Once the organization has analysed its processes, it can draw up a *register of effects*.

See also: Impact, environmental; Pollution; Procedure; Review.

Procurement: *see Purchasing*

Producer Responsibility

The principle that those who produce *solid waste* (especially *packaging*) should be responsible for recycling it. This is in keeping with *'the polluter pays' principle. DSD* and *Eco-emballage*, the 'green dot' schemes, are examples of producer responsibility systems.

In the UK, the concept of producer responsibility was introduced in the UK Environment Act 1995 to meet the requirements of the EU's *Packaging and Packaging Waste Directive*. The UK law allows the Secretary of State to introduce regulations which increase the proportion of waste being reused, recovered or recycled. The UK law sets a framework where businesses will join an 'exemption scheme' (such as *VALPAK*), which will manage the recovery of waste.

See also: Packaging recovery system.

Production

See: Air pollution; Audit; Cleaner production; Emergencies; Hazardous substances; Liquid waste; Operational control; Solid waste; Waste management; Zero discharge. *See also* the entries for specific industries, such as Banking; Defence; Engineering; Gas; etc.

Product Liability

Product liability law is now standard throughout the European Union as a result of the Directive on General Product Safety. Introduced in the UK as the General Product Safety Regulations 1994, the directive benefits companies by preventing them from being undercut by rogue competitors. The legislation applies only to consumer goods, not capital goods, production equipment or products used exclusively in a business.

The main points of the directive have already been implemented by national governments, so in many countries its impact is less than might have been feared. Many products are exempted by being subject to existing EU safety legislation. They include medicines, toys and tobacco. Products which conform to existing health and safety requirements are assumed to be safe, until proved to the contrary. So no additional certificates need to be obtained.

Under the European legislation, companies have to make and sell only 'safe' products. This is realistically defined as: safe under normal conditions of use, and reflects the use to which a product is put. For example, a kitchen knife only becomes unsafe when misused. Higher standards are required for products used by vulnerable groups such as children. Companies may need to provide more obvious safety notices. In restaurants, for example, information sheets are now attached to children's high chairs, telling parents how to use the chair safely.

The law requires the risks to be identified on the packaging. Compaq Computer and Microsoft, two of the largest companies in the computer industry, have put warning labels on computer keyboards urging users to avoid possible injuries from their use. This follows concern about repetitive strain injury (RSI) caused by using computers. In the US, RSI is the leading form of job-related injury. Some believe that it affects five million US workers. The American Academy of Orthopaedic Surgeons estimates that such injuries cost US$27 billion (UK£17.4 billion) a year in medical costs and lost income.

Risk Assessment and Control

A producer should be aware of the risks that his products might present, be able to identify unsafe products, and be able to withdraw them from the market if necessary. This can mean:

- carrying out supplier assessment;
- doing inspections during manufacture;
- investigating complaints;
- using batch numbers so that faulty products can be identified;
- keeping distributors informed of the results of monitoring.

Best Practice

- Assess the safety implications of the organization's products and services.
- Ensure that the products and services do not pose undue risks to the consumer.
- Provide relevant safety information to customers, and identify the risks on the *packaging* if necessary.

See also: Liability.

Products of Incomplete Combustion (PICS)

Products such as *carbon monoxide*, which are created during inadequate incineration, and which can combine to produce dangerous compounds such as *dioxins* and *furans*. They are produced when a furnace, incinerator or power station fails to fully burn its fuel.

Programme, Environmental

A set of activities aimed at reducing the organization's impacts. The programme should be integrated into the organization's strategic plan and should focus on the most important and substantial issues. It should be reviewed periodically (probably annually). A programme should be supported by adequate resources (people and money) to make it work, and it should be developed from the company's environmental objectives. All activities should have target completion dates, and progress should be regularly monitored.

Sample Programme Activities

- Invest in new equipment (such as waste-monitoring devices).
- Set up a team to improve a *process*.
- Determine how to measure and monitor a certain type of pollution.
- Introduce a programme to reduce waste.
- Carry out research into new, less-polluting products.
- Review *policy* and operations in order to identify new objectives and targets.
- Attain greater awareness of suppliers' impacts and develop programmes to reduce them.
- Publish an annual *report* containing the company's policy and performance.
- Provide environmental training for staff.

Table 14: Sample Environmental Programme

Objective	Means of Achievement	Responsibility	Target date
Develop and install a system to monitor pH, flow rates and temperature of waste water	*(1)* Produce feasibility report.	AEJ/IBN	28/7
	(2) Discuss choice.	AEJ/RE	21/8
	(3) Order equipment.	RNL	3/10
	(4) Install and use.	IBN	15/12

Best Practice

- Establish a programme to reduce environmental effects.

See also: Environmental management system; Policy; Targets.

Publicly Owned Treatment Works (POTW) – US

Plant which is owned by a state or municipality and used to treat or recycle municipal *sewage* or liquid industrial waste.

Public Relations

Companies need to publicize their environmental advances because green issues are a source of concern to many of their stakeholders, notably staff, shareholders and the local population. It is wise not to make excessive claims about the company's excellent environmental performance, lest this be followed by an environmental disaster.

Companies should have their corporate claims verified by an independent organization. Companies can be certified to *EMAS* or *ISO 14001*. For example, timber growers can have their forestry practices accredited to the Forest Stewardship Council. For companies operating in high-profile activities such as resource extraction (oil, mining, etc), or those which deal with hazardous materials (such as waste incinerators), public relations is even more important. Companies should adopt the highest standards, reduce impacts and change controversial practices rather than seek to gloss over them. Critics are rarely mollified by attractive brochures and are only silenced when the contentious issue is resolved. The alternative strategy is to brazen it out with critics, a policy that most companies find difficult to sustain for more than a few years.

Sample Items That Can Be Communicated

- summary of the organization's activities;
- corporate policy;
- key *performance indicators*, indicating corporate progress achieved in reducing impacts;
- environmental achievements, including case history material;
- investment in the environment.

Case Study 27: Criticism of Corporate Behaviour

International flag bearer of Australian enterprise, BHP, has come under intense criticism for its involvement in Ok Teki mines in Papua New Guinea. Its story is relevant to any company that might invest in a developing nation.

With interests in steel, mining and petroleum, BHP grew rapidly during the 1990s and achieved a record profit in 1994 of Aus$1.6 billion (UK£770 million). But the 1995 annual general meeting lasted four hours, with critics dropping dead fish in front of Brian Lotton, the company's chairman.

A group of conservationists, landholders and church goers have alleged that 80,000 tonnes of waste is flowing from the BHP mines into the Papua New Guinea rivers, polluting the water, killing the fish and destroying the traditional lifestyle of 30,000 people. They have instituted a Aus$4 billion writ against the company. Recently, the Victoria Supreme Court found the company in contempt over its part in helping the Papua New Guinea government prepare legislation that would block compensation claims.

BHP says that it has brought much needed development in the form of roads, schools and hospitals. It says that a landslide in 1984 prevented it from building a *dam* that would catch the outflow from the mines. A safe alternative, it claims, has proved impossible to find. But many Australians believe that big companies should take care when getting involved in the traditional lifestyles of other nations.

This case study demonstrates that a corporate image cannot merely be massaged. The company's practices must conform to international standards if the firm is to avoid criticism.

Best Practice

- Identify the *interested parties* who might want to know about the organization.
- Identify the main issues that interested parties would want to know about.
- Prepare written materials that address the main issues.
- Implement a system for responding to complaints, enquiries and direct action.

See also: Marketing; Pressure groups; Report.

Public Transport

Public transport is desirable because one bus can carry 40 people in a space the size of two *cars*. Converting people from using cars to public transport rids the roads of many vehicles and engines, and reduces congestion and pollution.

Organizations generally assume that public transport is irrelevant to the needs of their staff, but this is not always the case. Some managers drive long distances, suffering stress as they do. By contrast, a city-to-city journey made by train or plane allows the executive to relax and to think.

Many metropolitan councils are seeking to invest in public transport, especially trams, after decades in which the car ruled supreme. However, finance is usually a problem. A tram system in Birmingham got UK£40 million from the Department of Transport, a UK£31 million grant from the European Commission, UK£17 million from sale of assets, UK£4 million for bridge repairs, and the UK£40 million balance from borrowing. It is expected to carry 50,000 people each day, eliminating 15,000 car journeys.

Public transport can also be profitable. Manchester's Metrolink, a tram system, is now making UK£4 million profit a year. Of course, trams take up room on the road system, but they are cheaper than underground systems. Cheaper still are guided bus ways, which run under their own *diesel power* outside city centres, but pick up an electric current as they move into towns. Edinburgh's system linking the city centre and the airport, uses 6 miles (9.6 km) of track and 2 miles (3.2 km) of road, and costs UK£30 million compared with hundreds of millions of pounds for a tram system.

Impacts

Aged and badly tuned buses are the major causes of pollution. The main issue has been the internal combustion engine which emits *air pollution* and *greenhouse gases*. Battery technology has restricted the speed and distance that can be travelled. Hybrid vehicles, where the combustion engine cuts in when going uphill or when the electric battery runs down, are thought to be promising. CNG (see below) is another solution.

Case Study 28: Compressed Natural Gas

In Southampton, England, Citybus is running 16 buses powered by compressed natural gas (CNG). CNG is seen as one of the cleanest *fossil fuels*. *Particulate* matter is reduced by 75 per cent, and NO_x levels reduced by 79 per cent. *Lead*, soot and *sulphur* are virtually eliminated, while *hydrocarbons* and *benzene* are substantially reduced. The buses are also quieter than petrol or diesel engines. They look similar to a normal bus, but have a roof pod which houses the gas tanks. Natural gas has a high ignition temperature, which makes it safer, and the purpose-built pressure vessels are stronger than conventional fuel tanks.

Public transport is especially important for companies visited by large numbers of the public (such as retailers, hoteliers and theme parks) and those with a big workforce. There are advantages in getting people to switch to public transport, especially less congestion and queuing at peak times, with an increase in productivity or throughput. Companies can help people to use public transport by:

- providing free transport to bus or rail stations;
- undertaking marketing initiatives with rail, bus and coach authorities, and adopting joint problem-solving approaches.

The following table shows the proportion of passengers using public transport:

Table 15: Percentage of Passengers Using Public Transport to Major Airports

	Percentage
Gatwick	36
Charles de Gaulle	33
Heathrow	33
Schiphol	30
Frankfurt	27
Manchester	16
JFK	8

Source: BAA, (1995) *Environmental Report*, BAA

Best Practice

For companies visited by large numbers of people:

- Regularly assess, through research, the modes of transport used.
- Develop a plan to increase the percentage of travellers who use public transport or car sharing.

For public transport operators:

- Ensure proper vehicle maintenance to minimize emissions and noise.
- Introduce a programme to replace ageing vehicles.
- Adopt more environmentally sound vehicles.
- Monitor developments for new types of vehicles.
- Adopt satellite tracking to minimize bunching and congestion.

See also: Airports; Cars; Motor industry.

Purchasing

Purchasing is an important part of any company's environmental strategy. Over 60 per cent of a product's value can consist of suppliers' components, and there is a trend to outsource even more of the company's activities. Buying products from environmentally aware suppliers makes good business sense. A supplier which damages the environment could create problems for your own company. Also, environmental probity is an indication of an ethical firm.

Most major companies have well-established methods of checking a supplier's quality. This can easily be extended to include the supplier's environmental probity. Many companies start by issuing a questionnaire, seeking environmental information from suppliers. This is only a partial solution, and wily suppliers are adept at circumventing tricky questions. Physical *audits* of a supplier are a more costly and difficult step, but for large contracts they may be essential.

Some companies start by assessing the environmental *impacts* of their biggest suppliers or for contracts over a certain value. The best solution is to develop a detailed understanding of major suppliers' businesses and their products. The company should also adopt a generic environmental procurement standard. This might include a ban on certain types of *packaging*. Individual contracts should also contain environmental clauses. For example, a contract for photocopy *paper* might require it to be made from 100 per cent recycled fibres.

Assessing a supplier's environmental impact is only one of many factors to be taken into account when awarding contracts and may not be an overriding one. Nevertheless, the ultimate aim should be to replace suppliers who are ignorant or wilfully negligent with those who demonstrate concern and who can demonstrate good environmental performance. This should form part of the company's risk management policy.

The purchasing department should set improvement targets. For example, it might aim within the next three years to increase water-based paint from 20 to 50 per cent of all paint purchased.

Extract from a Sample Questionnaire for Suppliers

☐ Do you have an environmental policy? If so, please enclose it.

☐ Have you undertaken a programme to reduce the company's environmental impacts? If so, please specify.

☐ Please define the contents of products supplied and state their main environmental impacts.

☐ Are any recycled materials used? If so, please specify.

☐ Please state how the product should be disposed of and whether recycling is possible.

☐ Please define the packaging materials.

☐ Do any of the products have environmental advantages (for example, made from biodegradable material)? If so, please specify.

Case Study 29: Environmental Bonds for Suppliers

Thorpe Marsh power station in the UK, which is owned by National Power, has introduced an environmental bond into contracts, particularly for on-site works. Contractors have to make available an 'on-demand' bond from a bank to cover immediate clean-up costs of any environmental accident or incident they cause. The bond is for UK£10,000 and National Power can call on it up to 25 times, making a total liability of UK£250,000. The contract makes it clear that the bond does not limit the contractor's legal liabilities.

Best Practice

- Evaluate major suppliers and their products and services.
- Set up an environmental accreditation programme for suppliers, dove-tailing it (if appropriate) into an existing quality accreditation programme.

See also: Environmental management system; Questionnaires; Raw materials.

Putrescible

A material that will rot. Includes fruit, vegetables and other *organic* matter. Putrescibles are best disposed of by composting, where they rot down to produce *fertilizer*.

PVC

Polyvinyl Chloride. One of the oldest plastics, first discovered in 1912, PVC is second only to polyethylene in its consumption. Worldwide use in 1994 was around 20 million tonnes, and European sales were worth UK£30 billion in 1994. The PVC industry employs 50,000 people in Europe, while a further one million are in related industries. The packaging symbol for PVC is a triangle with a '3' in it.

Uses

Approximately 53 per cent is used in building (such as pipes), 16 per cent in *packaging* (for example, plastic bottles), and 9 per cent in wire and cable, with other uses accounting for 22 per cent. PVC can be flexible or rigid, transparent or opaque, depending on additives used. It is difficult to ignite.

Impacts

PVC is made from *vinyl chloride*, a toxic chemical. To make PVC flexible, manufacturers add *phthalates*, which are thought to reduce human fertility. *Chlorine* also produces *dioxins*, which are toxic. When burnt, PVC gives off toxic hydrogen chloride fumes.

The EU has banned certain PVC products, while Sydney, Australia, won its bid to stage the Olympic Games in the year 2000 partly as a result of its commitment to environmental protection. This included no use of PVC in the stadium plumbing, drainage pipes, flooring or in electrical cabling.

Best Practice

- Use a substitute wherever possible.

See also: Chlorine; Minimata Bay.

Quarrying Industry

Quarries produce stone, slate, marble and minerals for road building and other construction. In the UK, every person 'uses' 6 tonnes of minerals a year, in products from tennis courts to toothpaste. The industry's impacts include dust, lorry movements, visual intrusion, destruction of *wildlife* habitats, loss of *non-renewable resources*, and *noise* from explosives.

The hostility of environmentalists and local people to quarrying is increasing the cost of extraction and is leading some operators to create super-quarries in remote areas, famed for their wilderness (such as the UK's Hebrides). Companies say this saves them opening many smaller sites to meet the demand for aggregates.

In the UK, 20 million tonnes of material are taken from the ten national parks. This is especially controversial, but quarry companies point to their inability to stop immediately or unilaterally, since this would penalize the responsible companies and would affect employment. Environmentalists say that dormant quarries should not be reopened, nor should new quarries be permitted. Extensions to existing quarries should also be refused. Quarry products should be taxed, they say, to reflect the full environmental cost, and to encourage recycling.

Case Study 30: The Price of Planning Permission

Planning permission is increasingly difficult to get. It took six years for ARC to get approval to extend Whatley Quarry in Somerset, England. The quarry extracts 3.5 million tonnes of aggregate a year, and the extension opens up a further 85 million tonnes of reserves.

At one point the quarry was invaded by 5000 protesters organised by Earth First, the green pressure group. They claimed that the countryside was being damaged for the sake of the government's road building programme. They also pointed out that the quarry was lowering the water-table that serves the historic city of Bath and other towns in the area. ARC says that the extension will protect local jobs, and the company is paying to replenish local rivers to offset the impact on the water-table.

The company is also paying dearly for its planning approval. It cost ARC over UK£2 million, most of which seems to have gone on a huge *environmental impact assessment*. The conditions imposed on the quarry's planning permission will cost ARC a further UK£1 million. This includes monitoring the hot springs in Bath to give early warning of any impact of the quarrying, and pumping groundwater into local rivers. The company is also giving UK£500,000 to two neighbouring villages which will be affected. The company has furthermore lost some of its pre-war extraction rights to extract as much material as it wanted. It is thought that these deals and restrictions will push up operators' costs for future planning requests.

Tarmac's EMS

Tarmac's UK quarries produce 30 million tonnes of sand and rock from 91 quarries. The company's *environmental management system* (*EMS*) has policies for the following impacts: community relations; planning permissions; restoration and after-care; land tenure; *ecology*; archaeology; *waste disposal*; *air emissions*; *noise*; water resources; lighting; *energy*; security and safety; blasting and vibration; good housekeeping; transport; and visual impact.

The company has procedures for each issue, and its performance has been assessed by independent auditors.

Best Practice

- Introduce an EMS to reduce the organization's impacts.
- Consider adopting 'internal quarrying' which allows the extraction of minerals while hardly altering the landscape.
- Using recycled road building material reduces the amount of virgin material required.
- Cutting back on the construction of new roads also reduces the need for quarrying.

See also: Mining.

Questionnaires

A questionnaire is a useful starting point for an environmental *audit*, especially for an outside auditor, because it:

- checks that all the relevant material is present before a physical audit is carried out, and therefore avoids wasted time during the audit;
- highlights key issues for investigation.

Questionnaires should be completed and analysed before a site audit begins. A full questionnaire can be given to the site environmental manager, while summary questionnaires, asking about departmental impacts, can be given to line managers. A full questionnaire might include the following elements:

- description of the company's main processes;
- nature of the company's impacts, especially emissions to air, discharges to water or *solid waste*;
- list of the company's raw materials and products stored on site, especially hazardous substances;
- information about the company's *environmental management system*, if one exists;
- transport of raw materials, fuel and finished products to and from the site;
- *emergency* plans and preparedness;
- plan of the site, showing the location of drains, storage tanks etc., neighbouring rivers, etc;
- history of the site, including former uses which might have contaminated the land;
- any consents or permits required by law for waste disposal or to operate certain processes;
- any contraventions of environmental legislation, and any current or past legal action taken against the company, any legal action taken by the company against a third party (for example, a supplier).

See also: Audit, environmental.

Radiation: *see Ionising Radiation*

Radon

An invisible, odourless gas that occurs naturally in the ground. It can seep into buildings, depending on the quantity of radium in the rocks. In the UK, radon is thought to be responsible for 900 deaths from lung cancer a year, making it the biggest cause of death after smoking.

Best Practice

- Carry out a radon survey on corporate property; if radon is found, take professional advice on suitable remedies.

Railroad: *see Railways*

Railways

Railways are environmentally sound in that they use less *energy* and physical space than roads to move large numbers of people. Without their ability to bring huge numbers of commuters in and out, large cities could not function.

Railways are particularly useful for medium-length journeys of 150 to 300 miles (240 to 480 km); beyond that, consumers prefer air travel. However, since the arrival of the motor *car*, railways have been in decline in many countries. Rail lacks the freedom, privacy and convenience that cars bring; and as railway use has fallen, the service has often declined in equal measure. Yet decline is not inevitable: in Ireland, passenger figures have doubled since 1972; and around the world light rail, trams and guided buses are increasingly successful in cities. Nevertheless, railways are not without their environmental problems. Sidings and depots are often the location of contaminated land, and marshalling yards used by trains carrying spent *nuclear* fuel for reprocessing have been found to be radioactive.

Helping Staff to Go by Rail

The organization should encourage staff to use the train for medium-distance routes. *Public transport* is safer, uses less land, causes less pollution, and costs less money than moving the same number of people by road. City-centre firms should encourage their employees to visit other city centres by rail. Rail is less stressful, and staff can work on the train – so it is doubly efficient. Buses and other mass-transit overground and underground systems are also a consideration. 'Park and ride' schemes now operate in many cities.

The company should offer season ticket loans, and consider offering a subsidy on these loans. It can provide company transport to the nearest rail station; and it can display bus and train maps on notice boards, making railway timetables readily accessible.

Sending Goods by Rail

If goods can travel by rail, they should do so. The rail system causes considerably less environmental damage than roads. Articulated lorries clog up the roads of many towns and cities. They cause noise and their size threatens pedestrians and other road users.

Best Practice

- Where appropriate, get senior staff to travel by rail as an example to other staff.
- Provide season ticket loans. Subsidize the loans.
- Assess whether the company's goods could be trunked by rail.

See also: Distribution; Roads.

Rainforest

Originally called jungles, rainforests grow in the middle of the globe between the tropics of Cancer and Capricorn. Rainforests are important because:

- They are rich in important and rare species whose extinction would be a sign of mankind's greed and thoughtlessness.
- Rainforest plants could yield important drugs and genetic material, as yet undiscovered.
- Rainforests are home to indigenous peoples whose way of life can be swept away by aggressive logging.

Rainforests are rapidly being cleared for logging, cattle ranching, housing and roads. For example, two-thirds of Madagascar's rainforest has been destroyed. South-East Asia is now the source of three-quarters of exported tropical timber. Yet, with deforestation taking place, by early next century it could have dropped to as little as 10 per cent. In 1987 the major importers of Asia/Pacific tropical hardwood were Japan and Singapore:

- Japan imported 1.2 million cubic metres of sawnwood and 900,000 cubic metres of plywood. Japan receives 53 per cent of the world's tropical hardwood. It is the country's biggest import after oil.

- Singapore imported one million cubic metres of sawnwood and 400,000 cubic metres of plywood.

Rainforests are surprisingly vulnerable, another reason for managing them properly. When an area has been cleared, new growth may not occur because the thin soil, which has been held together by the trees' roots, is washed away by erosion, leaving desert. Conservationists say that, in place of logging, companies should use the rainforest to produce renewable crops. These include fruit, nuts (whose annual crop in Amazonia is worth US$50 million), as well as manufactured timber products (such as garden furniture),

See also: Timber industry – tropical.

Ramsar Site

A place designated as a wetland of international importance. The 1971 Ramsar Convention on Wetlands of International Importance aims to stop the draining of *wetlands* for agricultural and development purposes. It is named after the town in Iran where the convention was adopted.

See also: Wetlands.

Raw Materials

The starting point for many environmental analyses. Raw materials can represent 60 per cent of a company's total costs and therefore play a significant role in the company's total impacts. An assessment of raw materials will include the following points:

- Raw materials should be made from *renewable resources* wherever possible and should not use scarce resources.
- Raw materials should be made from recycled material, wherever possible.
- They should use minimum *energy* in manufacture.
- They should cause minimum emissions to air and water during manufacture.
- Their *packaging* should be the minimum required to protect the contents.
- They should not be toxic, wherever possible.

Best Practice

- *Audit* the organization's raw materials, and where possible change those that have environmental *impacts*.

See also: Impact; Purchasing.

RCRA: *see Resource Conservation and Recovery Act*

Records

When an organization first starts to think about environmental management, it often finds that it lacks environmental records because the company has not kept such information. But as the company becomes more sophisticated, its green records become more mature, and the company begins to use them more effectively.

The method for determining which records to keep are as follows:

- Identify environmentally significant *processes* and issues in the organization.
- Define measurement method (frequency, responsibility, etc).
- Set up a system to record the information (for example, by introducing a new form and by training staff in recording and analysing the data).

Then the organization should use the records to their fullest, to:

- set targets;
- review progress;
- monitor for pollution;
- set 'close-down' values.

The Records to Keep

In *ISO 14001*, the kind of records that might be kept are as follows:

- legislative and regulatory requirements;
- permits;
- environmental *impacts*;
- training records;
- calibration and maintenance activity;
- details of non-conformances and incidents;
- complaints and follow-ups;
- product identification, composition;
- supplier and contractor information;
- *audits* and review records.

Best Practice

- Identify the organization's major impacts, and define what records should be kept to monitor and control them.

See also: Environmental management system.

Recycling

Recycling counteracts the trend towards disposable products and reflects society's concern about the rise in *solid waste*. Recycling has developed from being a minority practice adopted only by committed greens into a mainstream activity adopted by most corporations. Among businesses, the growth of recycling has been fuelled by several factors:

- The growing cost of waste disposal, caused by increasingly costly government controls over rubbish; reduced availability of *landfill* sites, due to existing sites being filled and consumers' dislike of having new sites in their neighbourhood.
- The realization that some solid waste could be sold or reused, thereby reducing costs.
- The growth of legislation that promotes recycling, such as a requirement for a certain level of recycled material in a product. For example, Toronto, Canada, requires daily newspapers to contain 50 per cent recycled fibre. Newspapers which do not comply are banned from city vending boxes. Other examples would be a tax on products which do not contain a specified proportion of recycled material, and a tax on disposing of waste. The UK's landfill tax is an example of the latter.

Benefits

For the company, the main benefit of recycling lies in cutting the costs of waste disposal. For society, recycling has three major benefits:

(1) It reduces the amount of *non-renewable resources* we consume (such as *oil* and *plastics*).
(2) It also reduces the demand for *energy* (because recycling is usually less energy intensive).
(3) It minimizes the build-up of *solid* and *liquid waste*, whose disposal is often polluting.

Recycling material is especially effective in cases where:

- The product is valuable (such as the silver in photographic process).
- Recycling involves less energy than making the virgin product. There is a 90 per cent reduction in energy use when recycling *aluminium*, compared with converting virgin aluminium from bauxite.
- Rising costs of disposal are another factor that makes recycling more profitable, such as when governments tax waste disposal, energy or specific raw materials (such as oil).
- Recycling has reached a critical mass. As the processing of recycled material grows, its cost falls. This means that much recycled material is now as cheap as its virgin equivalent, or even cheaper. Companies have begun to talk about 'green for free'.

Failures

Recycling initiatives sometimes fail when the material is bulky and inexpensive (such as *PET* bottles). Often the cost of making the product from virgin materials is lower than the transport, wages and equipment costs of reprocessing used material. Recycling often faces an initial difficulty because of the imbalance between supply and demand. For example, newspaper collection first foundered because there were insufficient mills which could recycle the paper. 'Closing the loop' is an often-heard term which involves materials continuing to be reused, rather than being sent to an incinerator or *landfill site*.

Germany's *DSD* scheme ran into difficulties when the amount of *packaging* waste began to accumulate mountains of waste for which there was no demand. Eventually, Germany started to ship the waste abroad, which destabilized fragile local recycling schemes. Later, more recycling plants were built.

Recycling Developments

Among major purchasers of *IT* products, 85 per cent recycle their paper, ink and toner *cartridges*, according to research by Conservation Communications. In the US, Seattle recovers the most waste: 45 per cent compared with a national average of 17 per cent. Recyclable material is collected free of charge, and residents pay according to the quantity of their non-recyclable rubbish.

Even the most surprising materials can be recycled. BT sells its old but wearable uniforms, once the corporate logo has been removed, and donates the income to charity. Where the logo cannot be removed, the uniform is shredded and used in various products, including furniture stuffing.

The Recycling Industry

Recycling is changing from being a small-scale activity carried out by boy scouts and volunteer conservationists to a professional and large-scale industry. For example, the Milton Keynes' scheme centres on a UK£6 million factory the size of four football pitches. It accommodates waste from local authorities around the UK as well as waste from Milton Keynes householders. Likewise, the Aylesford paper recycling plant produces newspaper used by national daily newspapers.

In the US, reverse vending machines (RVMs) are popular and are seen as efficient ways to operate deposit/refund systems that can substantially boost collection rates.

Best Practice

- List the organization's waste streams.
- Set up teams to investigate how each might be recycled.
- Set targets for waste recycling.
- Ensure that the company's purchasing contracts specify the use of recycled materials.

See also: Glass; Liquid waste; Metal; Oil; Paper; Printer cartridges; Solid waste; Tyres; Waste management.

Red List

List produced by the UK Department of the Environment on the 23 toxic substances which are harmful in water-borne environments. The list includes some heavy metals, *pesticides*, industrial chemicals and *solvents*. It comprises the following:

- *mercury* and its compounds;
- *cadmium* and its compounds;
- gamma-hexachlorocyclohexane;
- *DDT*;
- *pentachlorophenol* and its compounds;
- hexachlorobenzine;
- hexachlorobutadiene;
- *aldrin*, *dieldrin* and endrin;
- polychlorinated biphenyls;
- *dichlorvos*;
- 1,2-dichloroethane;
- trichlorobenzene;
- *atrazine* and *simazine*;
- *tributyltin* compounds;
- triphenyltin compounds;

- trifuralin;
- fenitrothion;
- azinphos-menthyl;
- malathion;
- *endosulfan*;
- *nonylphenol*.

The discharge of these substances is controlled, and polluters have to apply *BATNEEC*.

Best Practice

- Check whether the organization uses any of these substances and set targets for their reduction.

See also: Black List.

Reed Bed Technology

Reeds are a surprisingly good way to treat *liquid waste*, including *sewage* and the outflow from chemical plants. Their roots and micro-organisms remove solids and organic material as they pass through the reed bed, and add oxygen to the water at the same time.

A trial reed-bed works has been established at a reservoir at Heathrow Airport, London. The trial bed could treat all the sewage from a village of 200 to 300 inhabitants. British Steel Strip Products at Llanwern, South Wales, feeds its liquid effluents into a bed of phragmites reeds, where contaminants are broken down into simple non-toxic compounds by micro-organisms that inhabit the root system. The company expects that the 18-acre (seven hectare) reed bed will replace the existing treatment plant, with big savings in *energy* and reduced effluent-disposal costs.

Refillable, Returnable

Refillable containers used to be important in the soft drinks market, and when Schweppes started selling non-returnable bottles it caused an outcry. Likewise, the UK milk bottle, which was reused up to 12 times, is under pressure as families buy their milk in plastic containers from supermarkets. In future, more containers will be refillable. This is already happening in the grocery trade where stock is delivered in returnable roll cages. Similarly, detergent companies offer robust tin or plastic boxes into which their refill packs can be decanted. On-site refilling, as happens in the Body Shop, is less likely, though the Dutch government has been encouraging suppliers to offer bulk products to supermarkets for the consumer to refill his or her own package.

While retailers show little sign of adopting on-site refilling, they and the makers of branded goods are increasingly providing refill packs (for example, for detergents and for pump action household cleaners and shampoos). These use considerably less packaging.

Best Practice

- Assess whether the organization could provide or use refillable or returnable containers.

Refrigerants

As *CFCs* are phased out, the options available for refrigerants are:

- *HCFCs*, which deplete the *ozone layer*, albeit not as badly as CFCs. They will be phased out by the year 2030. They are more expensive than CFCs, which causes difficulties for poorer countries.
- *HFCs*, which are *greenhouse gases*. HFC-134a is a well-known product which, however, requires special equipment.
- *Hydrocarbons*, which were used before CFCs took over. They are inflammable.
- *Ammonia*, which is inflammable and toxic.

Best Practice

- Assess what refrigerants, if any, the organization uses. Ensure that they conform to legislation and have the least possible environmental *impact*.

Refrigerators

The EU has drafted proposals for an *eco-label* for refrigerators.

See also: Washing machines.

Register of Effects

A company seeking *ISO 14001* or *EMAS* needs a list of its main environmental *impacts* and risks. The register should concentrate on significant effects. The use of office paper in a chemical factory is unlikely to be significant, compared with its discharge of effluent or emissions to the atmosphere. The process of developing a register is as follows:

- Generate an 'exhaustive list' of all effects. This can be prepared using a ready-made checklist (such as the ones found in *audit*, environmental; *preliminary review*; or *report, environmental*).
- Assess the significance of the effects.
- Produce a register of significant effects.

The purpose of this somewhat laborious method is to ensure that the company does not overlook any important impacts.

How to Determine Significance

The company should concentrate on minimizing its significant effects. But how do you measure significance? The best way is to assess:

- the probability that it will happen;
- the severity of the impact.

Probability can be measured on a 1 to 4 scale, showing the likelihood of its occurrence:

Table 16: Probability of Environmental Effects

Level	Description
(1)	Very unlikely to happen.
(2)	Unlikely to happen, or happens rarely.
(3)	Likely to happen, or happens occasionally.
(4)	Very likely to happen, or happens regularly.

Severity can be measured in a similar way. Each impact can be given a number indicating the scale of its severity:

Table 17: Severity of Environmental Effects

Level	Description
(1)	Insignificant
(2)	Minor
(3)	Substantial
(4)	Catastrophic

Each potential event now has two ratings (for probability and severity). When the two numbers are multiplied, the result is the risk factor. Thus, the risk of a factory polluting the local river might be 'unlikely' *(2)* and its effect would be 'substantial' *(3)*. This would produce a risk factor of 6 *(2 × 3)*.

The company can now see which effects have the greatest risk, and which should therefore be prioritized. This results in the Register of Significant Effects. The company, furthermore, may decide a cut-off point where every impact carrying a factor of 9 or more is rated as 'significant'.

Other Factors to Consider

Apart from probability and severity, you can also consider the following factors:

- the duration of the impact (is it brief or for a long time?);
- number of people affected (some would include this under Severity);
- the legal impact (could the company lose its permit to operate?);
- the financial effect (could the company be fined; what would the clean-up measures cost?);
- the effect of the impact on other processes or activities (could it halt the plant?);
- the cost of changing the impact (what investment would be needed?);
- the concerns of interested parties (do pressure groups want to make an issue out of it; is it worth fighting over?);
- impact on the organization's public image (how would the public react if it happened; what would be the long-term effect on the corporate image?).

Case Study 31: National Power's Effects

After setting criteria for determining its significant effects, National Power, which runs power stations, found that the following were significant:

1 *Acidic gases:* The company is aiming to reduce its emissions of *sulphur dioxide* and oxides of *nitrogen*.
2 *Carbon dioxide:* This is a *greenhouse gas* produced by power stations. National Power produces one fifth of the UK's CO_2.
3 *Local air quality:* The combustion process releases dust, metallic and *volatile organic compounds*.
4 *Water quality:* The power stations use water for cooling. This is taken from rivers and returned a few degrees warmer. The company is monitoring the quality of this effluent.
5 *Wastes and ash:* In 1994–1995 the coal-fired stations produced 5.4 million tonnes of coal ash, of which it sold 2.6 million tonnes, mainly to the construction industry, the rest being *landfilled*. The oil-fired stations produced 176 tonnes of ash which was landfilled.

Interestingly, while tackling these effects in a thorough manner, the company also applied to burn Orimulsion, a cheap and dirty mix of bitumen and water, at its Pembroke power station. In the company's words, this plan caused 'public concern'.

Table 18 provides an example of how to record environmental effects.

Table 18: Recording the Register of Effects

	Current activities			**Future planned activities**
	Normal operating conditions	Abnormal conditions*	Incidents, accidents and emergencies	
Emissions to air				
Discharges to water				
Solid waste				
Toxic materials				
Energy use				
Scarce or non-renewable material				
Damage to nature (including contaminated land)				
Noise				
Odour				
Dust				
Visual impact				
Other impacts (list)				

* Especially start-up and shut-down activities.

Best Practice

- Draw up a register of effects if the organization does not already have one.

See also: Impact, environmental.

Register of Legislation

EMAS requires the organization to keep a register of legislation, while *ISO 14001* does not. But ISO 14001 requires the organization to know about the legislation that affects it, which makes a register essential.

The register is a list of all the environmental legislation that applies to the organization. Without such a register, the company will not know whether its activities are within the law. The register should include national laws, local laws, stipulations by regulatory authorities, and EC or other international laws (including conventions). Therefore, it should include authorizations, licences and permits. It may also include codes of practice (for example, those developed by the trade association) to which it conforms.

The register should explain in clear language what the organization must do to conform to each piece of legislation. For example, it may define the maximum emissions that a specific process may emit. It may refer the reader to a written procedure that controls the process and explains what to do if the process exceeds the permitted levels. The register should also include proposed laws where relevant.

For their register, many companies subscribe to a publication (such as the *Barbour Index*) which provides a regularly updated list of legislation. The *certifier* may want to know how the information in the register is communicated to employees, and how the information contained in it is updated.

Best Practice

- Draw up a register of legislation if the organization does not already have one.

See also: EMS; Government; Legislation; Review.

Regulatory Authority

An organization appointed by the government to oversee a specific industry (such as electricity) or an issue (such as an environment agency to supervise corporate pollution).

Remediation

Cleaning up *contaminated land.*

See also: Landfill.

Renewable Energy: *see Energy*

Renewable Resources

Renewable resources are those which can be regularly reproduced. Renewable fuels comprise mainly wind, water and solar power. Other renewable resources include material from plants and trees (such as wood and paper) or material from animals (food, skin and clothing). Nowadays, even fuel and plastics can be made from vegetable material. Renewables contrast with *non-renewable resources*, which cannot be made again.

Mercedes has replaced oil-based plastics in its E-class cars wherever possible. The seat backs are made from coconut fibres and pig hair, moulded on a latex base. This allows water vapour to escape, unlike the traditional foam, and reduces the discomfort of sweat. The interior door panels are made from flax and sisal. Mercedes reckons that these materials are more rigid in a crash than the previous epoxy resin.

See also: Fossil fuels.

REPAC – UK

Regional Environmental Protection Advisory Committee. The *Environment Act 1995* set up a REPAC for each region in England and Wales. It is established and maintained by the *Environment Agency*, which consults it on matters affecting the region. Thus the REPACs are channels for the flow of information from local communities to the UK's Environment Agency.

Report, Environmental

A report on how the company is managing the environment, sometimes linked to the shareholders' Annual Report. A survey by Company Reporting, the UK accounts monitor, found that 25 per cent of firms made some sort of environmental disclosure. However, there was also thought to be a drop in the quality of the information. There was a 50 per cent fall in the companies quantifying targets and a 23 per cent fall in quantifying achievements.

According to one assessment, only 200 out of 36,000 multinational businesses have publicly reported their environmental *performance* to stakeholders. This is due to the cost, fear of potential prosecution for admitted shortcomings, and lack of management information. Tracking performance from year to year is also made difficult by operational changes. Until investors see environmental issues as important, there is unlikely to be a major growth in reporting. When asked by NOP in 1994 about their main concerns when evaluating a company, 87 per cent of UK City analysts mentioned 'quality of management', 76 per cent mentioned profits, and only 4 per cent mentioned 'company environmental policy'.

It is not surprising, therefore, that research for the UK's National Rivers Authority (now the Environment Agency) found that of the first 74 prospectuses for company flotations in 1994, 70 per cent made no reference to environmental issues.

Contents of the Report

The report should cover the company's main impacts and explain how they are being managed. In the past, environmental data was a corporate secret, but companies are increasingly adopting an open information policy on the environment by providing annual figures. However, there is a residual fear that reporting environmental pollution could expose the company to litigation (by, for example, local residents).

The report should inform the reader of the position and progress on important environmental issues. These may include the following impacts:

- emissions to air;
- discharges to water;
- *solid waste* and *recycling*;
- *energy* and *fuel consumption* (electricity, oil, gas, coal);
- use of scarce resources;
- use of major *raw materials*;
- use of water;
- toxic materials;
- *noise*;
- *visual impacts*;
- number of *complaints*.

The company might also include the following aspects:

- *purchasing* (quantity of materials consumed, percentage of key raw materials that are environmentally responsible – such as made from recycled material).

The organization can also include health and safety indicators, such as:

- number of lost time accidents.

The report might also mention corporate environmental achievements, such as:

- awards won;
- the value of new investment in pollution-control equipment;
- amount of *recycling*;
- amount of material reclaimed (eg silver recovery in printing processes).

It should also mention legal measures:

- the number of complaints;
- prosecutions for breaches of environmental legislation (and indicate what steps have been taken to prevent a recurrence).

The environmental report sometimes accompanies the annual report, and it should be communicated to staff, shareholders, local residents, key suppliers and customers. The report should outline the company's environmental *targets* and reveal what progress is being made. This may be done through graphs showing quantities of *solid* and *liquid waste* produced and emissions to air. To permit a comparison with previous years, the information might be expressed as a constant (such as cubic metres of waste per 1000 tonnes of output). The graphs are expected to show a continuous improvement.

Report Criteria

Touche Ross identifies the following criteria for a report:

- Does it cover the appropriate subject areas (for example, *energy* consumption)?
- Are the measurements of the *impacts* relevant, sufficiently accurate and comprehensive?

- Does the report present the information in a way that allows a fair interpretation of the company's environmental *performance*?

Environmental reporting is still a qualitative and evolving process, with few authoritative guidelines or standards. As a result, *verification* is subject to the same limitations.

Case Study 32: BT Environmental Report Objectives

- To publish a balanced, open and honest view of BT's environmental performance.
- To record progress towards BT's environmental *policy* commitments.
- To demonstrate continuous improvement in environmental *performance* through the publication of specific targets.
- To contribute to the global debate on environmental management and *sustainable development.*
- To contribute to the development of recognized methods and standards of environmental reporting.

Best Practice

- Draw up a plan to communicate the organization's environmental profile through an environmental report, if one does not already exist.

See also: ACCA; CEFIC; EMAS; GEMI; Public relations; Statement; UNEP.

Research and Development: *see Markets for Environmental Technology; Marketing Research; Technology*

Residues

Small traces of chemicals, such as *pesticides*, which may be found in food. International standards for residues in food have been rising to levels which are now difficult to detect. However, environmentalists say that there may be no 'safe' limit for some toxic chemicals (such as *lindane*) and that they should not be used at all.

Resource Conservation and Recovery Act (RCRA)

US federal law of 1976 which regulates the creation, transport, treatment and disposal of solid and hazardous waste. It established a permit program regulating such waste. Violations are punishable by up to 15 years' imprisonment for knowingly endangering human life.

The Hazardous and Solid Waste Amendments (HSWA) of 1984 introduced many technical requirements. It and the later *SARA* brought in a nation-wide program to stop leaking underground storage tanks. Most underground tanks have to be registered.

See also: Filling stations.

Responsibilities: *see Staffing*

Responsible Care

A voluntary programme originated by the Canadian *chemical* industry as a means of improving performance in quality, health and safety, and more recently the environment. Though less onerous than *ISO 14001*, it involves mandatory third-party verification of risk assessment procedures. In the UK, it is run by the Chemical Industries Association (CIA).

Retail Industry

In retailing, stores have grown larger and a smaller number of companies have gained a greater share of the market. This has meant that retailers are better able to control the market and gain power over the packaged goods manufacturers who jostle for space on the retailers' shelves. This increased power has been used to good effect by some environmentally aware retailers, such as B&Q, a UK DIY chain which encourages its suppliers to reduce their impacts. Other stores still lack awareness.

There are two sets of retailing impacts:

1 *Store impacts:* Impacts similar to any other organization which owns or leases buildings (for example, loss of habitats when new buildings are built, *visual impact*, cleaning materials, and the energy used in heating and lighting).
2 *Product impacts:* The impacts of the products stocked by the store (including their packaging).

Store Impacts

Store impacts have been heightened by retailers' move to out-of-town shopping malls. Here they have the room to build large stores, the sort appreciated by consumers. However, they also encourage *car* use, cause an associated growth in *air pollution*, and contribute to the decline of *city* centres.

Product Impacts

As we have seen, retailers are in a powerful position to reduce the nation's environmental *impacts* by requiring their suppliers to adopt green practices. The retailer can also materially affect the situation by giving the consumer environmental information and by stocking environmentally sound products. Own-label products also allow the retailer to demonstrate its commitment to environmentally ethical trading.

In grocery retailing, recycled products have become available, such as kitchen towels and toilet tissue. Recycled *packaging* has become widespread for many items, including cartons for foods and washing powder. Recyclable and biodegradable alternatives to some types of plastic containers are also available. For example, *PET* soft drink bottles (which can be recycled) have replaced *PVC* ones (which cannot). Lightweight containers and refill packs are another example, though the manufacturers contribute more to these advances than the retailers.

Supermarkets have flirted with organic produce, though the cost has driven down consumer demand. Some commentators believe that retailers are taking too big a margin on these goods, and research shows that organic goods need not be significantly more expensive. Moreover, there are many mid-way steps between intensive farming and organic farming, such as reducing the toxicity and frequency of routine chemicals used.

Case Study 33: Tesco's Recycling Initiatives

The supermarket chain Tesco created 700 jobs in a recycling scheme which will pay for itself and save the firm UK£12 million a year. Nine plants will recycle the 160,000 tonnes of cardboard packaging and 10,000 tonnes of plastic used annually in the company's 527 stores. The company also plans to save 50,000 tonnes of cardboard a year by using plastic trays with a lifetime of 20 years. Savings are made by reducing the amount of material used and by cutting waste-dumping charges.

Best Practice

Retailers should:

- Carry out an environmental *audit*
- Minimize *energy* use by draught-proofing, low-energy lights and other methods.
- Recycle packaging.
- Encourage returnable transport packaging (eg roller cages).
- Sell environmentally sound merchandise.
- Carry out a supplier audit (see: *Purchasing*).
- Undertake an *environmental impact assessment* for all new sites.

See also: Agriculture; Building design; Construction industry.

Retrofit

To modify equipment after it has been installed. Usually refers to the fitting of pollution-control devices. Generally more expensive than incorporating them into the original design.

Reverse Osmosis

A method of separating dissolved and *suspended solids* from water, using a membrane made of *organic material*. It is used to clean industrial *waste water* before it is discharged to a river or drain. The water is forced through the membrane under pressure, while the solids are held back. The process produces clean water and concentrated solids. The solids can sometimes be used as by-products: for example, the protein residue from potato starch processing can be used in cattle feed. The clean liquid can also be reused as process water.

See also: Liquid waste.

Reverse Vending Machine (RVM)

A machine that pays money when recyclable material is put into it.

Review, Environmental

An environmental review is the first *audit* undertaken by an organization. Its aim is to understand the organization's impacts. The review is mandatory under *EMAS*, and while not essential under *ISO 14001* is strongly recommended. The ISO guidance notes, in Annex A of the standard, say:

> An organization with no existing environmental management system should, as a first step, establish its current position with regard to the environment by means of a review. The aim should be to consider all environmental aspects of the organization as a basis for establishing the EMS.

The environmental review is discussed at greater length under *Preliminary Review*.

Note that the environmental review is different from the *Management Review*, which is a meeting, and which is discussed below.

Review, Management

In *ISO 14001* (as in *ISO 9000*) a 'review' is simply a meeting at which management assesses the effectiveness of the *environmental management system*. It should involve the executive with board level responsibility, because the meeting must have the power to create change.

The company's commitment to continual improvement (see ISO 14001) must operate in the review meeting. This could include identifying areas for improvement, or comparing progress against targets. All conclusions should be minuted and they should result in action. The review can be dove-tailed within the ISO 9000 review if the organization has implemented that standard.

Box 6: Topics for an Environmental Review

- Recent audit findings.
- The company's objectives, targets, etc. Are they still sufficient?
- The possible need for changes in the light of: changing legislation; changing requirements of interested parties (for example, higher consumer expectations); changes in the company's products; advances in science and technology.

See also: Review, environmental.

RID

Regulations on the international carriage of dangerous goods by rail.

RIDDOR – UK

The Reporting of Injuries, Diseases and Dangerous Occurrences Regulations 1985. Imposes duties on 'responsible persons' to report a range of occurrences to the authorities.

Rio: *see Earth Summit*

Risk Assessment and Management

Many pollution incidents and disasters could have been foreseen and prevented. This is the art of risk management. A risk assessment should ask two questions, 'What are the worst things that might happen?' and 'How do we prevent them happening?' As Figure 26 shows, the organization should identify and prioritize risks, set policies, implement policies, and monitor the risks. A contingency plan is also essential.

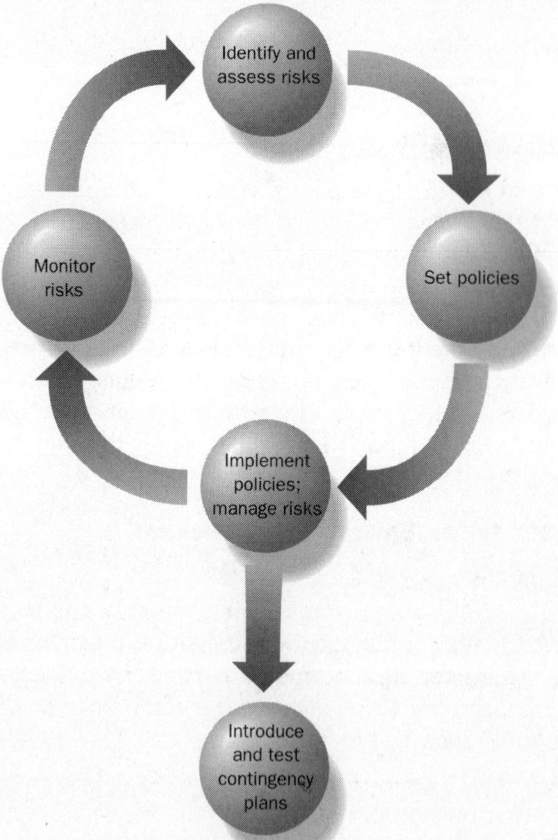

Figure 26: A Structure for Managing Risks

Risk assessment should examine the areas covered in an environmental *audit*, as shown in Figure 27, (for example, emissions to air and *solid waste*); but it should consider them from the point of view of potential impacts. Therefore, a chemical plant will have a mixture of impacts (such as odour or solid waste) and risks (such as explosion or fire).

Managing the identified risks may involve introducing policies, setting objectives and targets, and then creating a plan or programme. This is put into operation by setting up a system (an *EMS*) and managing people (which means either a TQM-type approach, or simply creating awareness through training).

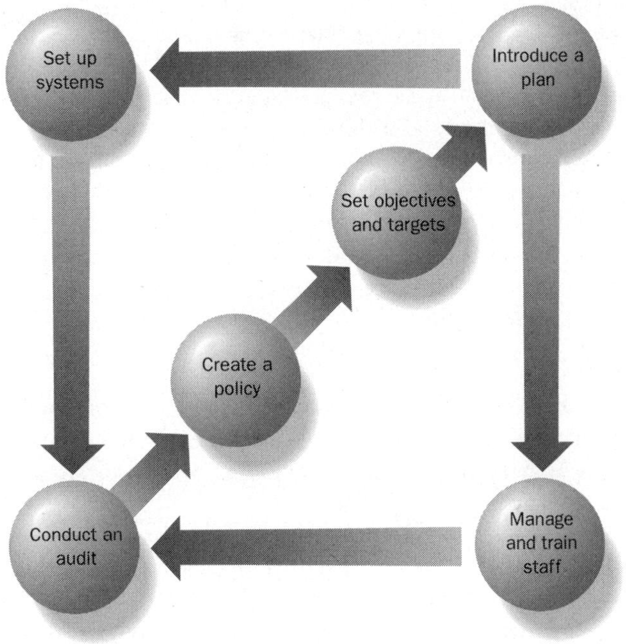

Figure 27: Action to Prevent Environmental Risk

Computer programs can now be used to model the risk of individual sites. Such programmes include WAZAN, the World Bank Hazard Analysis programme; and PHAST, the Process Hazards Assessments Screening Tools programme.

Best Practice

- Undertake a formal risk assessment for all new and existing processes.
- Adopt scenario planning to identify risks that are outside managers' normal expectations.
- Identify the key risks and create a plan to manage them.
- Introduce a management system to ensure the plan is adopted and adhered to. Undertake routine auditing.
- Undertake regular emergency drills for all major risks.

See also: Audit; Chemical industry; Impacts; EMS; HAZOP.

RME (Rapeseed Methyl Ester)

A 'biofuel', produced from rape. It is a *renewable* fuel, with economic fuel consumption, though it produces more *particulates, nitrous oxides* and *carbon monoxide* than conventional diesel.

See also: Cars; Diesel; Distribution.

Road Building

Roads are an essential part of modern life and their construction is driven by the ever-increasing levels of *car* ownership. Often the construction of new roads is brought about by the lack of inexpensive and comprehensive *public transport*, which in turn increases car usage. Impacts include the *noise* and dust from construction, the use of *non-renewable* aggregates, the loss of natural habitats and green space, and the increase in traffic (with all its impacts).

The worst impacts sometimes arise because the road is built in the cheapest possible way, cutting neighbourhoods in half or destroying important habitats. Insensitive construction can turn pedestrians and other road users into second-class citizens. On the other hand, some roads are clearly essential. By-passes can relieve traffic congestion and noise in towns and villages, and turn them into peaceful havens for the inhabitants.

Best Practice

- Undertake an *environmental impact assessment* before the road is designed.
- Build the road in an environmentally sensitive way. This means avoiding the destruction of important habitats or buildings. Sometimes a more circuitous route or a tunnel avoids these problems.
- Use recycled aggregates to minimize the impacts from *quarrying*.
- Incorporate different-coloured cycle paths, separated from the vehicle lanes.
- Incorporate pavements for pedestrians.
- Build *wildlife* runways to allow badgers and toads, etc to use their normal routes.
- Incorporate traffic calming measures.
- Link new roads to the public transport network (for example, rail).
- Cut the amount of noise and visual pollution by building banks.
- Allow verges to provide wildlife habitats.

See also: Cars; Construction industry; Quarrying; Roads.

Roads

Like people, most organizations are heavily dependent on roads to distribute their goods and to carry their executives and sales people. Yet, though once seen as the engine of progress, roads are facing increasing criticism around the world.

In the UK, the Royal Commission on Environmental Pollution (RCEP) reported in 1994 that large-scale road building is not the answer to transportation in the future. It concluded that roads lead to more cars and are in the end self-defeating. It said that large-scale changes in transport policy are needed to avoid further serious damage to the environment. It recommended a doubling of petrol prices in real terms by 2005, a halving of investment in trunk roads, and increased support for public transport.

The UK government scaled back its expensive road building programme as a result of its need to cut costs and in response to the continuing hostility to new roads all over the country – such as the extension of the M3 through Twyford Down and the M11 link road in the Lea Valley. Yet it also cut back on rail investment at the same time. If there is strong continued growth of car use in Britain, one third of the country's motorways and trunk roads will be constantly congested by 2005, says the government's Department of Transport. However, growth may be lower than this. Britain already has among the most densely used main roads in Europe, with 67 vehicles per mile (108 per kilometre) against an average of 44. Congestion currently costs Britain's economy UK£19 billion a year. This makes the case for an integrated transport policy in which rail and other forms of public transport take a larger share of passenger and goods traffic.

Many countries are wedded to the argument that roads are needed to support the forecast increase in vehicle use. However, traffic forecasting is a somewhat circular and often devious argument, since the increase in cars will only materialize if:

- The extra roads are built.
- Good public transport is not provided.
- There is no planning policy to reduce the need to travel (such as curtailing the growth of out-of-town shopping centres).

Case Study 34: Planning for Cars

In the small and historic city of Wells, in Somerset, England, planners decided to spend UK£14 million on a new road that cut through the local school's playing fields. Children who had formerly walked across sports fields to school now have to cross the new road, where noisy and polluting vehicles also pass within 100 metres of a primary school's windows. The decision to carve up the playing fields was made in 1996 despite 55 per cent of local inhabitants voting in an official poll to reject the plan.

Road Verges

As intensive farming has dislocated *wildlife* from the fields, roadside verges have become a lifeline for many species, especially wild flowers. Since 1945, 97 per cent of Britain's traditional meadows have disappeared, making verges the last hope for some species. Birds of prey have made a come-back in many places, thanks to the growth of small mammals which now live in the verges. An estimated 700 of the 1500 wild flower species growing in Britain occur on verges. There are 214,000 miles (344,000 km) of road in Britain, and double this length of verge, which in total covers 524,000 acres (820 square miles) – 212,000 ha.

Verges are far from homogeneous, matching the surrounding land. This can include *wetland*, moorland and upland. Verges must be managed sensitively, for the frequency and timing of their cutting affects their ability to hold *wildlife*. Flowering species should be allowed to set seed before being cut. Frequent cutting will favour lower-growing grasses and reduce wild flowers. On the other hand, infrequent or a cessation of cutting will favour brambles and nettles, which are favoured by butterflies and other species.

Some councils carry out a late-season full-width cut once every three years, with a partial cut in particular areas each autumn. Verges which hold important species should be identified with timber posts at each end, to which is attached a reference number. This will relate to the records and maintenance requirements of that site.

Case Study 35: Saving Money on Traffic Lights

If all the red traffic lights in the US were fitted with LEDs (light emitting diodes) rather than traditional bulbs, the nation could close one *nuclear power* station, according to California's Department of Transportation. Although the LEDs are more expensive, each LED lasts ten times as long, uses one seventh of the energy, and requires less maintenance.

The pay-back is three and a half years, and the LEDs are also easier to see in fog, which causes many accidents. The department reckons that if the LEDs were installed state-wide, they would save California US$74 million a year in electricity costs. That amounts to one tenth of the capacity of a nuclear power plant. If the scheme were adopted across the country, an entire nuclear plant's worth of electricity would be saved.

Best Practice

- Consider whether products could be trunked by rail.
- Consider whether company executives could use rail for city-to-city travel.
- Encourage staff to make maximum use of telephone, fax and teleconference rather than making unnecessary trips.

See also: Distribution; Local authorities, Road building.

Roles and Responsibilities: *see Staffing*

RSI

Repetitive Strain Injury. Includes upper limb pain in a keyboard user. Strictly speaking, this is a health and safety issue, but one which is sometimes incorporated under environmental issues because:

- It is a comparatively new topic of concern.
- It is associated with computer screens and the possible harmful effects of their rays.

Rubber

Natural rubber is a *renewable* natural resource, while synthetic rubber contains many additives, such as antimony and cadmium, both of which are toxic.

Russia

Russia has many important and rare species, a fifth of all the world's forests, the world's longest unspoilt coastline, and the oldest and deepest lake – Lake Baikal – home to hundreds of unique species. The Armur and Sakhalin regions in the far east of Russia are home to tigers and brown bears and the last 27 wild Amur leopards. While its environment is rich in resources, it also faces many threats. They include:

- the opening up of its tundra to oil exploration, and the destruction of important *wildlife's* habitats;
- the legacy of pollution caused by years of industrial damage;
- the similar legacy of poorly maintained nuclear submarines and spent fuel which has been dumped at sea or left in mouldering containers at the docks;
- the number of *nuclear power* stations which could, like Chernobyl, explode.

See also: Aral Sea; Nuclear power industry; Oil and gas industry.

Rylands versus Fletcher – UK

A long-standing case in UK law which states that anyone who brings on to his land for his own use anything which, should it escape, is likely to cause damage will be liable for the consequences. The rule is mitigated by the subsequently imposed requirement that the use must be unnatural. Thus, in a case where a tannery (Eastern Counties Leather) allowed *chemicals* to pollute a water course, the company was able to show that the chemicals were standard practice in the industry and were therefore not 'unnatural'.

Safe Drinking Water Act – US

The 1974 Act lets the Environmental Protection Agency set standards for contaminants in tap water. The law was amended in 1985 to upgrade many substandard municipal water systems. The law now covers 80 contaminants, including *pesticides* and *lead*. It also requires states to monitor their groundwater supplies, which are being depleted faster than they are being replenished. The law has been under threat from critics who believe that the US is hindered by excess legislation.

SAGE

Strategic Advisory Group on the Environment. A joint *ISO* and *IEC* group composed of experts in the field. This group led to the creation of an ISO technical committee (TC207) which aimed to standardize management systems and tools.

Sanitary Protection: *see Nappies*

SARA (Superfund Amendments and Reauthorization Act) – US

1986 Act which enlarged and reauthorized *CERCLA*, the initial Superfund law.

SCEEMAS – UK

The Small Company Environmental and Energy Management Assistance Scheme. Provides 40 to 50 per cent grants towards the cost of using a consultancy to carry out various green management tasks, specifically:

- undertaking an environmental *review*;
- developing an *environmental management system*;
- producing an environmental *statement*.

The scheme is open to manufacturers employing fewer than 250 staff. SCEEMAS is funded by the Department of the Environment, UK.

See also: EMAS; Environmental management system; ISO 14001.

Scientific Certification Services

SCS will certify any environmental claim made for a product. This is a simpler (but less comprehensive) system than examining the *cradle-to-grave* impacts. The certified products tend to be those where environmental issues are important or relevant – such as recycled notepaper.

See also: Certification and labelling schemes.

Scrap

Most companies produce scrap material. Where this can be reused, the only cost is that of lost time. However, where it has to be discarded, there is an environmental cost as well as the cost of the material. Scrap can be minimized by better training, by increasing employee motivation, and by making staff aware of the environmental problems caused by waste.

Sometimes, scrap is an inherent part of the process. In metalworking industries, manufacturers often find they dispose of large quantities of metal blanks. This kind of scrap can occasionally earn revenue when sent for recycling.

Best Practice

- *Audit* the organization's processes to identify the major waste streams.
- Set up teams to investigate how to reduce scrap (for example, by improving electronic controls or monitoring, and by reusing or recycling the scrap).
- Provide additional staff training to help them control the process better.
- Increase employee motivation to improve the quality of output.
- Make staff aware of the environmental problems caused by waste.

See also: Solid waste; Waste management.

Scrap Yards

The original recycling industry, little-changed despite society's new-found enthusiasm for conserving resources. A possible source of contaminated land, since scrap yards are likely to handle waste oils, old electrical equipment containing *PCBs*, and unmarked containers holding unknown chemicals.

Scrub

To purify waste gases (from a power station, incinerator or industrial combustion) using chemical treatment. It is better to adopt cleaner technology or fuels so that the waste gases are not produced in the first place.

See also: Fluidized bed.

Seals

Some pressure groups have called for protests against the culling of Canadian seals, mostly through clubbing, which they say is barbaric. They have called for a consumer boycott of Canadian salmon as a way of demonstrating opposition to seal culling. Most of the world's seal fur comes from Canada, 75 per cent of whose overseas markets lie in Europe. Although on first sight this is an animal welfare issue, it has implications for the environment.

Canadian seals are not an endangered species. Their numbers have doubled in the North-West Atlantic in the past ten years from 2.5 million to nearly five million. The Canadian seal population is thought to be growing by 5 per cent a year (about 250,000 seals). Since a seal eats or damages 40 pounds (18 kilograms) of fish per day, an extra 400,000 tonnes of fish are being killed. This is one of the causes that have put 30,000 fishermen out of work along the Canadian eastern seaboard.

Impact of the Seals on Fish Stocks

In 1994, the 4.8 million Canadian seals ate 6.9 million tonnes of fish from Atlantic waters, where restocking is needed. Canada permits the culling of up to 186,000 seals a year, with 60,000 being killed in 1994. Animal campaigners say these figures do not include the many seals which are maimed, injured or crawl away to die. However, the numbers are small compared with the millions of cows, pigs and chickens eaten each year, many of which are kept in battery cages for the whole of their lives.

Seal meat is a mainstay in the diet of many residents in Newfoundland; hides are used for manufacturing fur and leather goods. Canada also bans the sale of seals for individual body parts, such as penises, to countries such as China where they are used as aphrodisiacs. Protesters say that the authorities turn a blind eye, and much smuggling goes on.

An Emotional Issue

The big eyes and cuddly appearance of the seal play a part in Europe's outrage at the culling of this animal. It is significant that spiders and beetles have few charities dedicated to helping them survive. Hardly anyone noticed the extinction of the horned dung beetle in the UK in 1955.

Canada says that native Canadians have always killed seals, and that it is their way of life. Native Canadians do not have the same sentimental and contradictory attitude towards animals as Europeans. To them, all nature is cruel, and the *food chain* consists of prey and predators. Native Canadians kill only for subsistence and have never caused an animal to become extinct (unlike the Europeans and their compatriots elsewhere). Native Canadians, say their apologists, exist in an equilibrium with *wildlife*, and it is their only means of survival. Depriving them of seal hunting would lead to the same conditions of disease and despair found in American Indians when deprived of their land in the nineteenth century. The alternative is likely to be the exploitation of the land by oil companies, bringing the same kind of development and damage found in Alaska and Siberia.

See also: Fishing industry; Fur; Leg-hold traps.

Sea

Originally thought capable of dispersing any pollutants, the sea has long been the dumping ground for:

- river-borne waste (such as farm slurry and industrial waste);
- *sewage*;
- waste put directly into the sea itself from: ships' garbage; obsolete toxic armaments; oil discharges from the holds of tankers, and accidental oil spills.

The sea has the capacity to dilute *toxins* such as heavy metals to a level where they are no longer toxic, but the sheer quantity of waste has, in some cases, exceeded even the ocean's vast capacity to absorb mankind's waste. Today, around the world, sea dumping is being reduced and controlled, and the discharge of raw sewage is being halted, notably through the *London Dumping Convention*. In addition, IMO (the International Maritime Organization) has an International Maritime Dangerous Goods Code (sea) (IMDG).

Discharges of toxic waste into rivers is also more tightly controlled and, as a result, sea quality is improving in many areas. The annual amount of *mercury* entering the North Sea from the UK fell from ten to seven tonnes between 1985 and 1988, while *cadmium* fell from 39 to 31 tonnes, and *lindane* from 0.56 to 0.48 tonnes. Sea dumping of dredged material (for example, from harbour maintenance) is seen as acceptable, though controlled by licence, and its effect on the environment is monitored. However, wastes continue to flow into the sea from human activities. A study showed that pollution from the Rhine accounted for 40 to 50 per cent of all substances entering the North Sea.

See also: Amoco Cadiz; Defence industry; Dilute and disperse; London Dumping Convention; Marpol; North-East Atlantic Convention; Oil and gas industry; Russia; Sea transport; Sewage; Technology; Water use; Whales.

SEA (Strategic Environmental Assessment):

see Environmental Impact Assessment

Sea Transport

Since 71 per cent of the world's surface is covered with water, the international transport of bulk goods is usually moved by sea. This means that the sea will always be liable to pollution from dumping and accidents, especially as it is difficult to monitor ships at sea. In particular, the world's heavily used shipping lanes will always be at risk from collisions or accidents.

Oil Shipping

A lot of oil is spilled from sea transport. US studies show that 1.5 million tonnes of oil get into the sea each year as a result of shipping operations. At least 700,000 tonnes are from routine tanker operations, such as tank cleaning. A further 400,000 tonnes are from tanker accidents, 300,000 tonnes from the dumping of fuel and bilge oil, and the remainder is from other causes.

In 1989, three tankers in every 100 were involved in a serious casualty. The number of serious oil spills (more than 5000 barrels) has gone up to 36 a year. Norwegian government research shows that human error is responsible for 80 per cent of all marine accidents. Accidental spills are also related to the age of the tanker. Older ships lack the safety standards built into newer ones. Modern tankers have two hulls, which means that if the ship is holed, the oil is less likely to be discharged. The UN believes that legislation has prevented as much as ten million tonnes of oil being disposed of into the sea each year from pumping out oil-contaminated tank cleaning and ballast water.

The amount of oil entering the sea due to maritime accidents has also fallen in recent years, due to improved standards, navigational aids, training and watch-keeping, and traffic separation schemes. Shell has an accreditation system which ensures that it only charters ships that meet high standards and operate a monitoring system.

Best Practice

Shipping companies should:

- Train crews to be aware of the dangers of pollution and how to respond.
- Introduce newer, double-hulled and better-designed ships.
- Dispose of waste oils at port facilities.
- Never discharge in prohibited zones.
- Dispose of oil from tank cleaning into a slop tank.
- Ensure that ships carry a fast-response pollution plan.

See also: Oil and gas industry; London Dumping Convention; Sea.

SEFRA

Self-Financing Regulatory Agency (UK) – a government organization responsible for policing an area of activity (such as pollution control). A SEFRA is funded by charging those it polices.

Semi-Natural Forest or Community

Habitats or communities that have been only slightly modified by man. Thus few European forests have been untouched by man, but some closely resemble what nature intended and may include centuries-old plants or trees.

SEPA – UK

Scottish Environmental Protection Agency. Performs for Scotland the same functions as the *Environment Agency* does for England and Wales.

Set-Aside

EU grant paid to farmers for leaving arable land fallow, or using it as woodland or for recreation. The aim is to reduce the overproduction of food in the European Community. Critics say that farmers should be encouraged to farm organically (and thereby produce less) rather than be paid not to work the land.

Seveso

Town in northern Italy where, on 10 July 1976, an explosion at the Icsema *herbicides* plant owned by Hoffman La Roche released toxic gas into the air. The explosion created a dioxin called TCDD (tetrachlorodibenzo-p-dioxin). Its effect was similar to *Agent Orange*, the defoliant used in Vietnam. Unlike the disaster at *Bhopal*, there was no immediate panic or pain. But within 24 hours, trees and plants died, followed by birds and pets. Then children began to get rashes. Some days later, the inhabitants started getting *chloracne*, with boils erupting all over their body.

The ultimate death toll is unknown, because 10,000 fled the town. At least 40,000 pets and farm animals were dead from poisoning or had to be destroyed. Hoffman La Roche paid out UK£57 million and claimed that the disaster was a freak chance. Being stable, dioxin does not die, and the centre of Seveso has been sealed off forever.

See also: Chlorine.

Sewage

Sewage is the inevitable end result of eating. In the past, much sewage was untreated and simply dumped in the sea or rivers through outflow pipes. Providing the quantity was limited, bacteria would return the material to stable inorganic matter through the natural process of decomposition.

As human populations grow, the quantity of sewage also rises, and rivers and seas are unable to convert such an amount of waste. As a result, water becomes malodorous and anyone drinking it is likely to become ill. Hence the need to treat sewage so that it decomposes into natural elements.

Sewage companies that pump untreated or partially treated sewage into rivers and seas are contributing in a big way to pollution. However, over time, the amount of untreated sewage effluent is likely to decline as legislation becomes more stringent and treatment facilities improve. Initial sewage treatment involves screening, using a grate to remove large objects which might cause blockages. The sewage is then moved at a set speed which causes grit (which could damage pumps) to fall to the bottom. This is followed by sedimentation in a tank fitted with scrapers. This concentrates the solids, which are removed daily. The final treatment is biological, whereby bacteria consume the organic matter.

Sewage sludge is the residue left behind at a sewage works. It is often contaminated with heavy metals, since the sewers mix industrial and household waste. Some of the resulting sludge is used as agricultural *fertilizer*, as a result of its high *phosphorus* and *nitrogen* content. Half the UK's sewage sludge and one third of Germany's is used in this way. It is also put into *landfill* sites and disposed of by *incineration* (to recover the *energy* value). There is also the possibility of recovering the valuable heavy metals from sewage.

Best Practice

While nothing can be done to reduce the flow of sewage, sewage treatment companies should aim to:

- Reduce and extract the amount of pollutants entering the sewage stream. This reduces environmental pollution and allows more sewage to be used as *fertilizer*.
- Fully treat the sewage before discharging it into rivers and seas.

Shampoos

The EU is proposing to introduce an *eco-label* for shampoo. A study by the French eco-labelling organization has identified five different types of shampoo: family, baby, cosmetic and embellishing, cosmetic and conditioning, and special-use shampoo (eg dandruff).

Shell

Oil company which has faced controversy over the disposal of its Brent Spar oil rig, its operations in Nigeria and other issues.

Brent Spar

In 1995, Shell was forced to halt the dumping of its Brent Spar oil rig in the North Sea after accusations by Greenpeace that such action would cause environmental damage. Later Greenpeace admitted to errors in its methods of assessing the oil rig's waste, but not before protesters had fire bombed the company's petrol stations in Germany and boycotted them elsewhere.

Nigeria

In 1995, Shell was also in the news over the death of the Nigerian writer and activist Ken Saro-Wiwa, who had campaigned against the environmental damage he said the company had done to the Ogoni lands. The Nigerian military government tried him for incitement to murder and executed him despite a world outcry. Shell pointed out that it did not meddle in the internal affairs of nation states, though it did intercede at the last moment. Conservationists said that Shell could have exerted extra humanitarian pressure on the government if it had chosen to.

Since striking oil in 1958, Shell has extracted and sold an estimated US$30 billion worth of oil. Yet, according to a *Wall Street Journal* writer, the 500,000 Ogoni people still live in medieval squalor, surrounded by oil pollution, and in the shadow of an oil operation whose standards are lower than those applied in the West.

Peru

Shell was thrown out of Peru in 1988 after the company spent five years and US$200 million exploring for oil and gas. It had been accused of introducing diseases to the indigenous native peoples. However, in 1996 it signed an agreement with the government to develop the Camisea fields, a project costing US$2.5 billion. An *EIA* by Shell presented to the Ministry of Energy and Mines included the following geophysical impacts: risk of land slippage; accelerated soil erosion; alteration of soil quality by loss of top soil and overburden; contamination from spillage and contaminated discharges; and increased rate of river bank erosion due to *quarrying*. Most of the sites lie in virgin rainforest inhabited by native groups, many of whom have little contact with the outside world.

Shell's operating plan will contain many mitigating factors, including run-on and run-off drains to lessen erosion and the protection of bare soil surfaces. On completion of drilling, potentially contaminating materials will be removed from the site. The company will minimize the use of soluble salts in the drilling mud and monitor water quality. No access will be allowed at drill sites other than by helicopter.

Mersey Pollution

The company was fined a UK record UK£1 million for polluting the Mersey Estuary in England on 24 February 1990. The spill occurred when a pipeline carrying Venezuelan crude oil to Shell's Stanlow oil refinery split as a result of corrosion caused by sea water. At least 30,000 gallons (136,400 litres) of oil escaped, and the company failed to spot the leak for an hour. Once it was discovered, Shell, contrary to the advice of police and a pollution control officer, flushed out the corroded pipeline in an attempt to clear the blockage. This led to further discharge of oil. It was two hours before the National Rivers Authority was informed, and the information came from the local fire brigade, not the company.

In court, the company pleaded guilty. It argued, in mitigation, that the actions taken were decisions taken on the spot. They were based on the available information and were intended to minimize damage to the environment. However, the judge found that the company was negligent. He imposed a UK£1 million fine, the highest in a UK water pollution case. Controversially, the judge praised Shell for its 'outstanding record in the field of conservation and a generous supporter of the arts and other worthwhile causes'. Were it not for these matters, he said, the fine would have been much greater.

Shell is also estimated to have lost UK£1.4 million in operational losses and clean-up costs. A later report by the Department of Energy, UK, found that Shell's operation of the pipeline and its emergency procedures were inadequate. For example, the procedures manual did not tell staff what action to take in the event of a leak. Emergency equipment was also inadequate and not readily available.

This case history emphasizes the importance of sound procedures and of ensuring that both plant and equipment, and pollution control systems, are effective. It also demonstrates the need for close and swift cooperation with the authorities when an incident occurs.

See also: Liability; Oil and gas industry; Pressure groups; Sea transport.

Shoes

The EU is proposing to launch an *eco-label* for shoes. The Dutch eco-labelling board has issued proposals for environmental criteria.

Sick Building Syndrome (SBS)

The tendency of some modern buildings to cause illness among staff who work in them – an important part of indoor pollution. Symptoms of SBS include headaches, lethargy, itchy and watery eyes, dry skin, dry throats and chest complaints.

Causes

SBS can be caused by the *chemicals* in synthetic carpets and upholstery, *solvents*, adhesives, varnishes or by vehicle fumes getting into the *air-conditioning*. Bacterial infections from poorly maintained air-conditioning may also be to blame. SBS is prevalent in buildings whose windows cannot be opened, or which do not have an adequate flow of air. Sometimes the cause is not environmental: stress at work or a bad boss can trigger its symptoms.

Best Practice

- If SBS is suspected, commission an environmental *audit* to trace the cause of the problem. Specialist devices for measuring air quality will be needed.
- Solutions may include better design, improved ventilation, more control over the office environment by staff (for example, local heating controls), alterations to air-conditioning, and changing office fixtures and equipment.

See also: Indoor pollution; Office; Legionnaire's Disease.

Significance: *see Register of Effects*

Simazine

A toxic *pesticide*, most of whose uses are banned in the UK and other countries.

Best Practice

- Do not use.

Smog

An abbreviation of 'smoke fog'. The combination of smoke, fog and chemical vapours reacting in sunlight produce a toxic fog, of which the most famous example was the London smog of 5 to 8 December 1952, which killed 4000 people. It was found that smoke levels were 4000 $\mu g\ m^{-3}$, and it is known that increases in *sulphur dioxide* and smoke lead to an increase in sudden deaths and hospital admissions for respiratory problems. The reduction in severe smogs has been brought about by:

- clean air legislation;
- fuel substitution: a change from coal to electricity and gas – in other words, there has been a reduction in the number of coal fires, and an increase in gas and electrical central heating;
- improved controls in power stations;
- the centralization of electricity generation, leading to fewer, cleaner power stations with taller chimneys.

As a result, smog – while still common – is less of a killer. With the decline in solid fuel fires, it now comes from power station emissions, fuel vapours and vehicle exhausts. In some developing countries, smog results from the burning of low-grade petrol. Mexico City has suffered in this way in recent years.

A study showed that smog kills 350 Parisians a year, while air-pollution as a whole kills 60,000 people annually in the US.

See also: Benzene; Filling stations; Los Angeles; Nitrogen dioxide.

Smoking

Smoking is widely believed to cause lung cancer, heart disease, bronchitis and other cardio-vascular illnesses. In addition, passive smoking (or second-hand smoking) kills 60,000 non-smokers in the US, according to some researchers, a view contested by cigarette firms. Most large companies have introduced smoking bans.

A study carried out by the Organization for Economic Cooperation and Development (OECD) reports that buildings designed to allow occupants to smoke anywhere can cost up to 7 per cent more than buildings where smoking is banned. Many firms dedicate a smokers' room to discourage smokers from lounging outside the main doors. The smoking room should not be a place used by others, such as a canteen.

See also: Office.

Sodium Perborate

Sodium perborate and sodium percarbonate are two *bleaches* used in detergents. Both cause environmental problems. Perborate releases boron as it biodegrades, which can damage agricultural and aquatic plants. Percarbonate reacts with other chemicals unless a stabilizer is added, but *EDTA*, the most common one, is a chelator. This means that once it gets into the waterways it combines with toxic metals which can be carried into the drinking water and the *food chain*.

See also: Laundry detergents.

Soil Improvers

The EC *eco-label* on soil improvers is an attempt to reduce the demand for *peat*. The drainage of peat lands for *agriculture* and for the digging of peat has devastated species-rich *wetlands* around the globe.

To get an EU eco-label, soil improvers have to be made from waste materials such as composted *organic* material from domestic waste, *sewage* sludge or waste from agricultural or food processing. Waste peat products containing *peat* (such as mushroom compost) will be allowed but not unused virgin peat. The criteria are:

- conservation: the product must reuse materials which would otherwise go into the waste stream;
- information to users on the pack;
- water pollution: maximum level of nutrients such as *nitrogen*, to prevent *eutrophication*;
- soil pollution: maximum content of heavy metals;
- health and safety: maximum level of pathogens (namely salmonella and E. coli).
- nuisance: no persistent smell, fragments of glass, wire, or weed seeds.

Best Practice

- Use only soil improvers which carry an *eco-label* (when available).

See also: Eco-label; Growing media.

Soil: *see Contaminated Land*

Solar Energy

The conversion of sunlight to electricity. Solar energy can be used to heat buildings (through the use of atriums or trombe walls, with air transferring the heat through the building). It is also used to preheat water. Solar energy is found in pocket calculators and has been adopted in the Third World for lighting.

Regarded by many in business as a marginal *energy* source, solar power has been beset by high capital costs and low demand. However, solar power is set to grow substantially. If this happens, it will reduce the need for power stations that use polluting *fossil fuels* or potentially catastrophic *nuclear* energy.

From 1980 to the early 1990s, the cost of photovoltaics (PV) fell from US$20 per watt to US$5. The cost could fall a further 80 per cent within ten years according to researchers at the University of New South Wales, Australia. The breakthrough has been achieved by using lower-quality silicon as a semiconductor within the photovoltaic cell. In addition, there are likely to be efficiency gains in solar energy, with more power being produced from less light. It is, anyway, a misconception that the sun needs to be shining for solar energy units to work.

Case Study 36: Shingles

One new development is PV shingles. They look like asphalt roof tiles and are 100 times thinner and half the price of conventional PV panels. They are nailed on to roofs alongside ordinary roof tiles, and an electrician then wires the tiles to the electricity supply. United Solar Systems of Troy, Michigan, mass produces them in half-mile lengths which are cut to the finished size. The company reckons that at two to 30 cents a kilowatt hour, the price is similar to US utilities' peak rates. But the application is not limited to roofs. Canon, the camera and electronics company which is a partner in the product, is also applying the principle to *photocopiers* and other equipment.

Already, photovoltaics are providing buildings with a substantial proportion of their power. At the University of Northumbria, one third of the power required by its offices is provided by the PV cells which cover the building's south facing wall. In Oxfordshire, architect Susan Roafe's house is powered by solar power. Energy costs are expected to be 58 pence a year. Capital and running costs are said to be the same as conventional houses.

Governments and utilities are beginning to take solar power seriously. The Japanese government gives subsidies to people who buy solar power, while in Germany, 4000 people pledged to buy rooftop solar panels, a market reckoned to be worth DM100 million.

Best Practice

- Design new buildings to use the power of the sun for heating.
- Install solar collectors on roofs as an energy source if practical and cost effective.
- Use solar powered equipment where practical.

See also: Building design; Building services.

Solid Waste

The US *Environmental Protection Agency* (EPA) has a preferred hierarchy for treating solid waste, as shown in Figure 28.

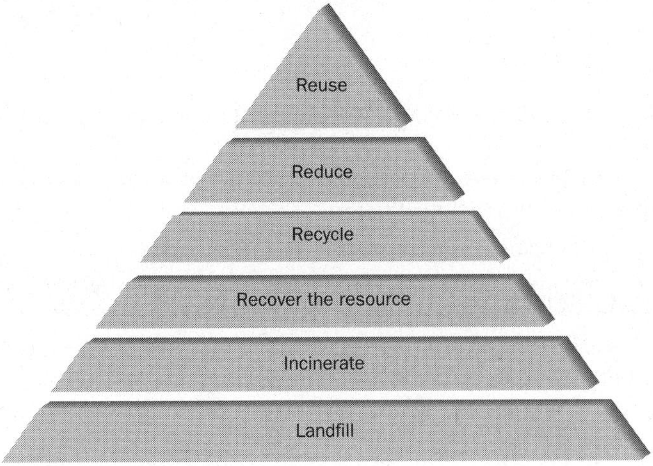

Figure 28: EPA's Hierarchy of Waste Treatment

After reducing use and recycling, the main methods of waste disposal are *landfill* and *incineration*. Of the 24 million tonnes of *hazardous waste* produced in *OECD* countries, 70 per cent is deposited in landfill. Incineration is expensive, and if the waste is not burnt at a sufficiently high temperature, *dioxins* can be created.

Dumping at sea, once common, has greatly reduced, due to international maritime agreements, though dredged material is dumped at sea. *Organic* waste can be reused in other products or as a *fertilizer* or soil conditioner. This includes manure from chickens, the residue from cider-making, and the waste from paper-making.

Crown Wood, a US manufacturer of television cabinets, went from being the largest industrial depositor in its local *landfill* site to the fourth largest. It did this by recycling corrugated boards, paper and *aluminium* cans, as well as reusing off-cuts of wood, and reducing the number of panels scrapped through faulty gluing. In the UK, IBM reuses or recycles 80 per cent by weight of its 'retired assets' (that is, old computers).

Best Practice

- Quantify the amount of solid waste by type (eg paper, glass, etc).
- Set targets for reducing the amount of *solid waste.*
- Produce plans to meet the target (for example, by increasing yields, or setting up teams to devise ways of reusing or recycling the remaining waste).

See also: Recycling; Landfill; Waste management; Waste transportation.

Solvents

Substances that dissolve other materials. They are used to carry fine particles (of paint or some other material) to a surface which is to be treated. There the solvent quickly evaporates. Solvents are used in adhesives, paint, degreasing and cleaning products.

Impacts

Solvents can cause dizziness and sleepiness. Long-term exposure can cause kidney problems.

Solvent recovery systems can involve using vacuum or extraction methods, followed by refrigeration and distillation.

Case Study 37: Avoiding Hazardous Waste from Solvents

At Collingwood, Ontario, Canada, Lof Glass has switched from a hydrocarbon-based degreaser to a citrus-based solvent designed for cleaning the small parts of mechanical and electrical equipment. The Voltz solvent does not contain chlorinated compounds, *ozone-depleting substances* or any known carcinogens. It is produced with natural citrus solvents and does not leave a reside upon drying.

When the chemical is contaminated, a flocculating chemical is added to allow contaminants and solids to drop to the bottom of the drum overnight, forming a sludge. The sludge is removed, *dewatered*, and disposed of in *landfill* as a non-hazardous waste. The Voltz product, depending on how extensively it is used, is reusable indefinitely. As a result of the change, all hazardous waste-disposal costs were eliminated.

Best Practice

- Avoid using solvents wherever possible. Switch to a water-based cleaning process, a dry clean method (such as scraping), or a non-hydrocarbon-based solvent.

See also: Hydrocarbons; Volatile organic compounds.

Southern Ocean Sanctuary

Area of water above *Antarctica* in which *whales* may not be killed.

South West Water: *see Aluminium*

Special Waste

Waste which is especially dangerous or difficult to dispose of, or waste which is 'intractable' (untreatable). It covers *acids*, industrial *solvents*, fly ash, *pesticides*, *batteries*, prescription drugs, pharmaceutical compounds, wood preservatives, waste oils, and photographic chemicals. Disposing of special wastes (such as solvents) is expensive and can become a fire or health risk.

In the UK, special waste is governed by the Special Waste Regulations 1996. It includes a UK£15 disposal charge, in line with '*the polluter pays*' principle.

Best Practice

- Avoid making or buying products which will constitute a special waste when disposed of.

Spoil

Waste material from *mining*. Spoil can be highly polluting (for example, some mining waste is *acidic* and harms aquatic life if it enters a water course). Spoil tips may need to be treated as *contaminated land*; the soil may require remediation. Spoil tips can also be unstable and liable to slip (as in the case of the Aberfan tragedy when a tip fell upon a Welsh school). In some cases, however, old spoil tips are found to be growing orchids and other important species.

See also: Contaminated land.

Sponsorship

Organizations, especially those with a high profile, often want to demonstrate that they are good corporate citizens by sponsoring environmental organizations or activities. Companies get a pay-off through an improved image, and the environment is improved at the same time.

Companies can sponsor environmental causes and groups in a variety of ways. Sponsorship can be in the form of money – as a grant for environmental *improvements* in the area. This is often urban renewal (such as dredging canals or clearing waste sites). In rural areas, companies can help to improve habitats for *wildlife*. Companies can also provide educational materials for adults or children; or they can sponsor academic research. Firms can also lend equipment (such as bulldozers or computers) or managers to environmental causes. Many companies provide sponsorship in the area in which they provide employment. They also sponsor activities which relate to their work. For example, a mining firm may sponsor research into remedying spoil heaps. It is also helpful to provide the green organization with some continuity. To have an impact, and to be able to plan, charitable groups need to be able to see ahead for three years. Investing in environmental sponsorship can give the company advantages. For example, it might pay a PhD student to investigate some issue of concern to the company, such as its liquid discharges.

Steps to Take in Sponsorship

(1) Establish your goals – why do you want to sponsor something?. This involves establishing a policy. Ensure that environmental sponsorship is not a substitute for improving the company's environmental *performance*.
(2) Create a guidance document outlining a budget and the kind of activity or grounds which might be sponsored.
(3) Then promote the organization's interest in sponsorship, being aware that this might result in a flood of applications.
(4) Choose a charity. Ensure in writing that each side knows what it will get out of the deal.

See also: Public relations.

SSSI (Site of Special Scientific Interest) – UK

An area of land notified under the Wildlife and Countryside Act of 1981 as being of special nature conservation interest. Designation gives the land only limited protection against development, and SSSIs are regularly built on in the interests of commercialism or *car* drivers.

Best Practice

- Companies with land holdings or which engage in construction should identify whether they own property on or near any SSSIs.
- They should ensure that new SSSIs are communicated to relevant staff.
- They should avoid developing SSSIs or permitting *pesticide* spray top drift on to it.

See also: EIA.

Stack: *see Flue Stack*

Staffing: *see Human Resources*

Stakeholders

People who have an interest in the organization. They include shareholders, employees, customers, suppliers and the community. Most are likely to be concerned about the company's attitude towards the environment.

Shareholders

These days shareholders are more likely to take the environment into account when choosing their investments. A polluting company is one which is liable to litigation or clean-up costs, and is therefore less likely to be profitable.

Employees

Research shows that graduates and younger managers do not want to work for a polluting company. This means that an organization with a poor image is unlikely to attract the best candidates. Moreover, employees who work for a polluting firm will consider that they also work for an equally sloppy manager.

Customers

Customers may become liable for a supplier's pollution. For example, if a pressure group accuses a car manufacturer of using *PVC* in its fascias, it may decide to change the fascia supplier.

The Community

The community suffers from any *noise*, fumes or water pollution caused by a local company. Their hostility can be expressed in many ways.

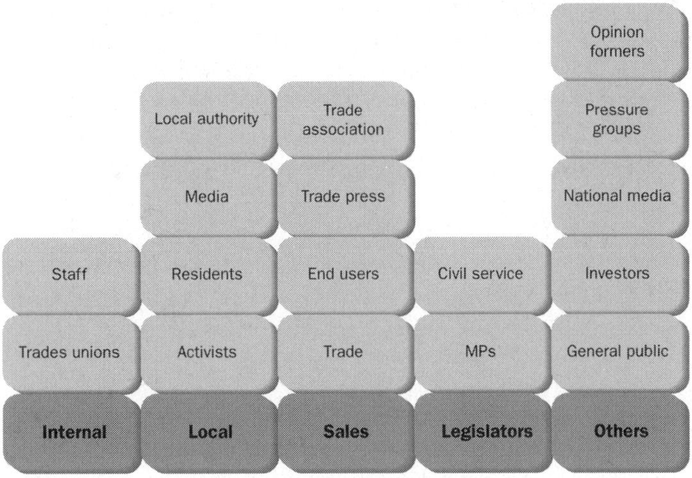

Figure 29: Stakeholders

See also: Human resources.

Statement, Environmental

(1) A Publicly Available Annual Report, Required by EMAS

The *EMAS* statement sets out the company's environmental *performance* in clear and concise terms. To gain EMAS registration, the statement must be approved by an accredited *verifier*. An EMAS statement must be written in a way that can be understood by the public, and this often means spelling out abbreviations and explaining technical terms.

EMAS specifies a maximum interval of three years, and also requires a simplified annual statement which is unverified (small and medium organizations may be excused this requirement).

The EMAS statement must contain the following elements:

- site activities;
- key issues;
- key data – pollutants, emissions, waste;
- other relevant factors;
- policy, systems, programme;
- changes since last statement;
- deadline for next statement;
- identity of the accredited verifier.

(2) A Report on a Company's Environmental Issues

The statement is sometimes no more than a few paragraphs, often contained in an annual report. A more detailed statement is called an environmental *report*.

(3) The Written Statement of an *EIA*

A statement tells planners and other interested parties about a project's environmental impacts. The UK's Department of the Environment has issued a guide on preparing an environmental statement (ES). It examines how to predict impacts and formulate mitigating measures. The guide suggests that the ES should be around 50-pages long, and no more than 150. It has ten appendices dealing with the key issues: such as human beings and noise and vibration.

See also: EMAS; Report.

Stationery: *see Paper*

Steel

One of the 'smoke stack' industries, steel-making is a big user of *energy* and a polluting process, given the air emissions created during smelting and the amount of *solid waste* produced. However, best practice can reduce this substantially. Advanced economies have put major environmental curbs on steel makers, and the investment in pollution control that this requires adds substantially to the costs. For this reason, steel-making favours developing countries.

Steel is easy to recycle and can be reprocessed almost indefinitely. Because steel is valuable, recycling makes economic sense.

See also: Metal industry.

Storage Tanks

Used for keeping fuel and other liquids, especially (but not exclusively) at petrol stations. The contents of storage tanks can leak into the ground, causing long-term pollution of water courses. Underground storage tanks are particularly difficult to inspect, and because their leaks are less likely to be noticed, they are particularly prone to leak. An estimated 2 per cent of underground petrol storage tanks leak which, in the UK, is like 64 oil tankers being discharged into the ground every three months. Underground storage tanks have been closely regulated in the US by the *Resource Conservation and Recovery Act*. Some companies, especially North American ones, now have stopped using them.

Particular care should be taken to avoid spillages when tanks are being filled or their contents drawn off. Frequent small spillages can create a big problem in the longer term. Fuel tanks also pose the risk of fire and explosion.

Best Practice

- Produce a list of all storage tanks, denoting their contents and identifying which are underground.
- Replace all underground storage tanks, with above or on-ground tanks, where possible.
- Ensure that a manager is responsible for storage tanks.
- Ensure that all tanks are bunded (that is, surrounded by a leak-proof reservoir, usually concrete).
- Regularly check the soundness of all tanks.

Strategic Environmental Assessment (SEA):

see Environmental Impact Assessment

Strategy, Environmental

The environment should be an inherent part of corporate strategy. This means taking environmental factors into account in areas such as new product development, capital investment, and total quality programmes. It means ensuring that good environmental practice becomes part of the culture.

The corporate strategy should take environmental matters seriously, because attempts at lip service create a dishonest atmosphere. Failure to take the environment seriously means that environmental problems are stored up for the future. Conversely, good environmental practice improves corporate performance, because it helps the company to solve its problems. Many companies have also found that they can save money by adopting environmentally sound methods (such as recycling).

However, many firms improve their environmental performance only when required to do so by law. According to *The Financial Times*, businesses are not convinced that being green will make them richer. This is despite years of exhortations from politicians and pressure groups that environmental improvements can be financially worthwhile.

What Does the Future Hold?

In the future, environmental issues will be still more challenging. Some of the potential changes are listed below:

- *Waste disposal* will be substantially more expensive. After waste minimization, incineration with heat recovery will be the preferred solution, despite technical problems and its heavy cost. Techniques such as microwaving will also grow in popularity.

- *Landfill* will be increasingly restricted. This will result from the imposition of taxes on *waste disposal*. Some local authorities will ban the tipping of certain types of waste, especially pollutants.
- *Pressure to get ISO 14001:* Large companies will increasingly demand that their suppliers have ISO 14001. They will do so in order to minimize their liability and because the standard will encourage them to choose environmentally responsible suppliers.
- *The CE mark* will be required for more products which are sold within the EU. The CE mark may contain extra environmental requirements.
- *Energy and fuel* from oil and gas will be more expensive. This will stem from many factors. The EU will want to reduce energy use for environmental reasons and will therefore apply targets for energy reduction. As North Sea oil runs out, the UK government will seek to reduce fuel imports, using tax as a weapon.
- *Distribution* will become more complex and more restricted. As traffic congestion grows in cities and motorways around the world, countries and municipalities will start to restrict traffic, including lorries. Deliveries will take longer and be more costly, and rail use will grow.
- *Legal action* for pollution will grow in frequency and fines will be heavier. Directors will be jailed more frequently. Communities and customers will be more ready to take action against firms.
- *Some raw materials* now in common use will be banned, due to their toxicity.
- *Eco-labels* will be common on all kinds of products. Customers will be disinclined to buy brands which do not carry the label.
- *Environmental performance* will be more visible. Companies will be expected to reveal environmental risk and pollution in their annual reports. Publication of environmental data will be the norm in many markets.

These forecasts may seem pessimistic, but there will also be good news:

- *New markets* will develop. They will include process control (such as monitoring devices), pollution control (such as filters), and waste management systems. Other growth markets, and the R&D strategies needed to create them, are documented in the author's book *The Green Manager's Handbook*.
- *Alternative fuels* will be more common. *Solar* and other technologies will be more effective, as will *battery* storage. This will create new marketing opportunities.
- *Environmentally responsible companies* will flourish. Because of all the changes mentioned above, firms which take the environment seriously will succeed. They will have lower costs and more attractive products. They will produce less waste and spend less time fire-fighting. In a pilot scheme, suppliers to the Rover *car* company each saved up to UK£100,000 in one year – through reduced waste and water, and through improved *energy* and process efficiency.

Eco-Centric Versus Techno-Centric

Conflicts arise when the organization's need for profit or cost control conflict with people's desire to protect the environment. Even where both parties agree that change is necessary, there is a conflict between eco-centric and techno-centric views. In car pollution, for example, a techno-centric view would involve fitting *catalytic converters*, while an eco-centric view would prefer to develop alternative vehicles or non-polluting modes of transport. This could also be described as the difference between light green and dark green thinking.

Often the information needed to reach a decision is clouded by emotion, because staff have vested interests to protect, such as a long-established but polluting process. Moreover, the company is often unable to take into account the full costs to society of any particular action. Thus, it is easy to judge the company's chemical waste disposal costs from a contractor's invoice. But it is less easy to see the impact of the same chemicals leaching from a *landfill* site into a river.

Best Practice

- Companies should incorporate environmental issues into their business plans.
- Adopting an *EMS* (*environmental management system*) will ensure that green issues become an integral part of company thinking.
- Environmental issues should be periodically reviewed by the board.

See also: Benefits; Marketing.

Sulphides

Sulphur combined with a metal, notably sodium or zinc. Sulphides are malodorous, corrosive and highly polluting in water. Sodium sulphide is used in sulphur dyes; hydrol may be used as a less-polluting substitute. It is also used in the tanning industry.

Best Practice

- Avoid where possible.

Sulphur Dioxide (SO_2)

Sulphur dioxide is produced when sulphur is burnt in air (for example, when sulphur-containing coal is burnt in a power station). It is a corrosive gas that is a major cause of *acid rain*. At least 70 per cent of the UK's sulphur dioxide emissions come from the burning of *fossil fuels* in power stations. Of this, 75 per cent of all sulphur dioxide emissions come from coal, with a further 15 per cent coming from fuel oil (notably petrol).

In 1986, UK urban sulphur dioxide emissions were only half of what they were in 1975, due to a decline in domestic coal fires. Nationally they fell by only 25 per cent, due to continuing emissions by power stations.

Sulphur dioxide is also an irritant which constricts people's air passages, making breathing difficult. Sulphur dioxide can be removed from emissions by installing *FGD* units.

See also: Diesel; Electricity-generating industry; Energy; FGD.

Sulphuric Acid

When a power station emits sulphur dioxide as a waste gas, it can be oxidized as sulphuric acid and then deposited on buildings, forests and lakes. This is known as *acid rain*. Apart from its role in acid rain, sulphuric acid is a widely used chemical. It is made from sulphur, water and air. It is used in *fertilizers* (ammonium sulphate), car *battery* acid, paint, rayon, explosives, oil refining, and soapless detergents.

Superfund: *see CERCLA*

Suppliers: *see Purchasing*

Surfactants

Abbreviation of 'surface active agents'. Surfactants act as water softeners and allow the detergent (the cleaning agent) to work. Today's surfactants are mostly made from petro-chemicals. They do not biodegrade as quickly as vegetable-based surfactants, and use up quantities of a *non-renewable resource*. They also release chemical impurities which may be harmful.

Detergent companies say that surfactants use only 1 per cent of the world demand for oil; but environmentalists say that reducing the amount of oil would prevent disasters such as the *Exxon Valdez*.

Best Practice

- Use vegetable surfactants.

See also: Cleaning agents; Laundry detergents.

Suspended Solids

The amount of solid material contained in water. This measure is sometimes used to define the level of polluting effluent from a plant. It is usually stated as TSS (total suspended solids). Suspended solids are measured by filtering a known volume of water through a standard glass fibre-filter paper; the results are expressed in miligrams per litre (mg/l_{-1}). Regulatory authorities may set a consent level (at, say, 50 mg/l_{-1}) which the plant may not exceed.

Best Practice

Suspended solids can be reduced by separating waste water streams, by filtration, biological treatment, and other water treatment processes.

See also: BOD; COD; Liquid waste; Water pollution.

Sustainable Development

Growth that meets the needs of the present without preventing future generations from achieving theirs. In other words, today's activities should not harm the future. It reflects the idea that 'we are borrowing the world from our children'. Acting sustainably involves:

- Avoiding the use of scarce or *non-renewable* raw materials.
- Preventing pollution.
- Maintaining *biodiversity*.

For example, *rainforests* can be managed in a sustainable way by leaving enough trees of each species so that the forest can regenerate itself, and by avoiding the destruction of native peoples' culture.

Organizations that are not managing sustainably are those which consume large quantities of *energy* or non-renewable resources, which produce or use toxic materials, or which generate large amounts of waste. As Heathrow Airport stated in an environmental report, 'Few organizations can hope to achieve sustainability in isolation from the rest of the economy and society which they serve'. It then identified areas where it can contribute towards to the principle of sustainability, such as *public transport* to the airport, and cutting energy consumption, emissions and waste.

Case Study 38: British Telecom

BT sees sustainable development as leading towards a telephone network powered by *renewable energy*, with hardware produced from non-oil derived *plastics*, and polymeric conductors in place of metal. It envisages the growing use of light as the transmission medium, leading to all-optical communication networks.

Sustainable development is a convenient and comforting philosophy because it lets society carry on consuming while believing itself to be green. It contrasts with the views of the more extreme environmentalists who believe that we should stop using *fossil fuels* and other non-renewable materials. Critics scornfully describe this as a 'back to the dark ages' philosophy. Nonetheless, some ideas now widely accepted, such as recycling, were once seen as idealistic, impractical and unnecessary. Today, some companies use a closed-water system, which means they do not need to extract water from the mains. Other firms' process water is returned to the river in a purer state than when it was extracted.

However, governments tend to define sustainable development as whatever they are currently doing. This lessens the significance of the words, so that they come to mean simply: paying lip service to conservation.

Table 19: The Requirements for Operating in a Sustainable Manner

Schedule for Sustainable Industry	
Raw materials	Raw materials are renewable and (where possible) have been recycled. No toxics are used.
Emissions to air	Preferably none. Any gases are scrubbed.
Solid waste	Any solid waste is reused or recycled
Discharge to water	Closed-loop system means that the firm needs little or no water.
Energy	Only renewable energy sources are used.
Products	Products produce no waste, or are readily recyclable. Packaging is returned for reuse or sent for recycling.

Best Practice

Managing sustainably is a goal to which few organizations conform, though an increasing number are achieving at least some of the criteria:

- Use only renewable energy.
- Do not use non-renewable resources such as oil or plastics.
- Ensure that all waste is recycled or is biodegradable.
- Do not use any toxic substances.
- Do not emit acidic, toxic or *greenhouse gas* emissions.
- Do not discharge polluted water.
- Ensure that all products and their *packaging* are biodegradable or recyclable.
- Ensure that all developments return the land to an ecologically sound state. Permanent developments can only be considered sustainable when they use 'brown' land (land which has already been used).

See also: Zero discharge; Cradle to grave.

SWQOs – UK: *see WQOs*

Take-back

The principle that companies should take back their products or *packaging*, once they have been used by the consumer. This is designed to reduce the amount of waste, especially material going to *landfill*. Companies which take back their old products are in the best position to refurbish or *recycle* them.

Take-back may become a requirement among more large corporate customers and may even become law in some countries. Companies offering to take back their products or packaging may gain a competitive advantage. For example, Cow & Gate gets its suppliers to provide vegetables in returnable bulk containers. Rank Xerox will take back all it produces, reusing parts and assemblies in new products.

Best Practice

- Establish whether the organization could take back its products and how they could be reused or recycled.

See also: Computers; Waste management.

Tanning Industry

Tanneries convert putrescible hides and skins into a stable leather, and different processes produce different types of leather. Tanneries use trivalent chromium, which produces a light thin leather suitable for shoes, clothing and upholstery. Tanneries should recover the chromium, especially since governments set limits on the quantity that may be discharged to outside drains. Recovery is achieved by adjusting pH, followed by precipitation, and then the addition of sulphuric acid.

Other tannery wastes include soil, blood, dung, sodium sulphide (from the dehairing process), calcium hydroxide (from liming), and ammonium chloride and sodium bisulphite from deliming. Before the wastes can be discharged to water, they are usually treated to balance the pH and reduce the *BOD* and *COD*.

See also: Chromium.

Targets, Environmental

Targets are the way in which companies put environmental *objectives* into practice. They help the company decide which impacts it needs to reduce and by how much. Targets are a useful tool for senior management. They encourage them to make policy and to delegate action, and they allow senior managers to periodically review progress made in achieving targets.

Targets should be achievable and should have a completion date. Some targets are completed when achieved (such as achieving legal consents for air quality), whereas others may be revised annually (such as improving fuel consumption by 15 per cent).

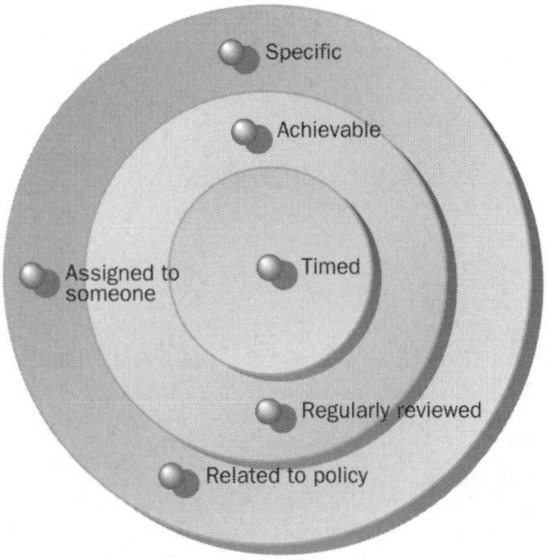

Figure 30: Requirements for an Environmental Target

Targets usually relate to the reduction of emissions to air, discharges to water or *solid waste*, or other environmental *impacts*. For water discharges, typical targets might be to:

- Review by 1 May 19XX the organization's use of *Red List* chemicals and investigate how to reduce or eliminate them.
- Ensure that all interceptors are maintained to an oil-escape proof standard by 31 Dec 19XX.
- Develop an awareness programme for staff of correct discharge procedures by 1 April 19XX.

To achieve its targets, the company needs an environmental *programme*.

Best Practice

- Identify the greatest environmental impacts and set targets for reducing or eliminating them.
- Adapt the 'best practice' points in this encyclopaedia as targets by adding appropriate figures and dates.

See also: Environmental management system; Objectives; Performance indicators.

TBT: *see Tributyl Tin Oxide*

TCDD: *see Seveso*

TCF

Totally Chlorine-Free. A term used to describe virgin paper which has not been *bleached* with *chlorine* gas or chlorine compound. Such papers are usually bleached with hydrogen peroxide. While TCF is an advance on old-style chlorine bleached papers, it is less sound than recycled paper.

Best Practice

- Use recycled rather than TCF paper.

See also: Paper; Paper, board and pulp industry; ECF.

TDS

Total Dissolved Solids. A measure of water purity and pollution.

See also: Suspended solids.

Technology

A 1995 report by the UK's Department of the Environment concluded that the environmental technology market had grown three times faster than the average of all manufacturing industry between 1985 and 1992. It put the 1992 UK market for environmental goods at UK£5.1 billion, close to an Ecotec estimate of UK£6.0 billion for environmental goods and services. The DoE report indicates that environmental technology employs 110,000 people in the UK.

The Organization for Economic Cooperation and Development (OECD) forecasts that the demand for *waste management* products and *air-pollution* control equipment will grow by over 50 per cent in the last years of the century, with water and effluent treatment products growing by a third. The US Environmental Protection Agency believes these predictions underestimate demand. The OECD also estimates the worldwide market for environmental goods and services at UK£130 billion in 1992. This is expected to reach UK£213 billion by the year 2000 and treble by 2010.

A survey of 116 UK firms in 1994 showed that 87 per cent planned to increase their use of environmental technology in the next five years. Three-quarters expected to spend up to 50 per cent more in that time, despite having already increased expenditure in the previous five years. At least 90 per cent said their driving force was legislation, while 62 per cent thought that company policy lay behind their investment decisions. Just 40 per cent said they were inspired by cost savings. Few were acting as a result of pressure from consumers or environmental groups.

In 1994, 62 per cent of the companies surveyed bought air monitors, while 41 per cent bought water monitors. This follows tighter controls on air pollution and trade effluent discharges in the UK's Environmental Protection Act. In contrast, only 5 per cent of firms bought any land remediation equipment after the government dropped its commitment to a register of contaminated land, though this has since been reversed.

The market is characterised by small suppliers and large customers, according to *The Financial Times*, with public utilities and multinational companies being the biggest customers. There also seems to be room for development. For example, 27 per cent of companies surveyed cannot find a solution for their particular environmental problem.

Best Practice

- Ensure the organization is using best available techniques not entailing excessive costs (*BATNEEC*).
- Monitor developments in the technological field.
- Evaluate whether the company should be selling its expertise or technology.

See also: Markets for environmental technology.

Telecommunications Supply Industry; Telephones

The telephone and telecommunications service is environmentally sound in that it reduces the need for travel and meetings and uses little *energy*. In particular, electronic mail and fax use fewer resources and energy than paper-based systems. The industry uses comparatively few disposable materials: most of its materials (cabling and capital equipment, etc) have a reasonably long life. However, mobile phones are accused of causing ill-health from microwave radiation. Possible problems include skin cancer, brain tumours, asthma and Alzheimer's disease. It is said that holding a mobile phone to your ear is like being inside a microwave oven – it cooks your brain. Nevertheless, the findings are inconclusive. The digging up of streets by cable companies produces noise and congestion, and kills trees.
See also: Trees; Utilities.

Teleworking

Working from home, while connected to the office by computer and telephone. Teleworking suits many groups. It pleases environmentalists because it reduces the pollution and congestion caused by *commuting*. It suits employers because it reduces the amount of expensive *office* space needed. And it suits many employees because it saves them the stressful and time-consuming journey into the city.

In the UK, over two million people are teleworkers and the numbers are set to grow with the advance of compact and inexpensive video telephones and *videoconferencing*. If 10 per cent of British workers stayed away from the office, peak road traffic would be reduced by 500,000 vehicles, with the associated saving in energy and pollution.

Teleworking is more appropriate for some staff than others. Heavy users of computers, such as programmers and data processors, are ideal, as are people who use regional offices (such as consultants and salespeople). Teleworking also allows employers to use freelance rather than permanent staff. Some companies experience difficulties with teleworking. They lose a degree of control over their staff, while employees miss the camaraderie. Decision-making and communication are also more problematic.

Best Practice

- Evaluate the use of teleworking in your organization.

TEL

Tetra-Ethyl Lead: an anti-knock agent used in leaded *petrol*. Highly toxic.

Best Practice

- Do not use.

See also: Lead; Methyl.

Teratogenic

Substance that causes malformations of the foetus, literally 'monster producing'. *Dioxins* are in this category.

Best Practice

- Avoid such substances.

Tetrachloroethane

A hazardous *organochlorine* solvent.

Best Practice

- Do not use.

Tetrachloroethylene

Solvent used to treat garments. Water pollutant. It is on the EU *Black List* of hazardous chemicals.

Best Practice

- Do not use.

Tetrachloromethane

One of the first dry cleaning solvents. Its fumes can cause cancer. It has since been substituted by *trichloroethane*.

Best Practice

- Do not use.

Textiles, Textile Industry

The industry's impacts include *liquid waste*, water use and *solid waste*. Liquid effluent can include *bleaches*, *acids*, dyes and grease. Impacts also include the use of *pesticides* and other chemicals in growing cotton (strictly an agricultural industry impact) and, in the case of synthetics, the use of a *non-renewable resource* (based on oil). Wool companies can also emit *organophosphate* and *organochlorine* sheep dip residues.

Companies can reduce scrap by using computerized spectrophotometers to assess dyeing colour accuracy. Some firms use a vacuum suction system to recover and reuse finishing chemicals. In addition, reusing the process water, after ultra filtration, serves to reduce the liquid effluent. Evaporation can reduce the waste to a concentrated sludge which can be *landfilled*. Some cotton dyeing firms use a cold pad batch-dyeing process which removes salt from the effluent, uses less chemicals, water and *energy*, and reduces the amount of effluent.

Eco-Labelling

The EU has prepared proposals for an *eco-label* for use on textiles, specifically T-shirts and bed linen. The eco-label will allow for 100 per cent cotton and polyester/cotton blends, and aims to reduce the impacts of polyester manufacturer, cotton treatment, and the garment manufacturing process. The criteria may include:

- fibre production;
- weaving;
- wet processing (washing, softening and bleaching);
- dyeing;
- finishing;
- waste water from wet treatments;
- fitness for use (physical properties and colour fastness).

See also: Cotton.

Thallium

Toxic heavy metal. Thallium sulphate is used as a rat poison.

Best Practice

- Do not use.

Three Mile Island

Nuclear power plant at Harrisburg, Pennsylvania, US which came close to exploding on 29 March 1979. If it had happened, the disaster could have destroyed Washington, DC. The reactor, which is normally submerged beneath cooling waters, became accidentally exposed to air. The rods started to melt and large quantities of radioactive gas were released. For three days there was a risk that the bubble of radioactive hydrogen would explode, causing a nuclear inferno. Residents within a five-mile (eight-km) radius were evacuated, but engineers managed to reduce and finally contain the gas bubble. Three Mile Island shattered the safe, clean image of nuclear power in the US.

See also: Chernobyl, Nuclear power.

Timber

Timber is the main product of the forestry industry. It comes from temperate forests (generally in the northern hemisphere), and from tropical forests (in equatorial forests in South America, the Philippines, etc). The two sectors of industry have both aroused environmental concern and for different reasons. These are discussed in the following entries under their respective headings.

Best Practice

- Use only timber which is verified as coming from a sustainably managed source.
- Avoid waste. Timber off-cuts can be used in wood chip wallpaper, as a filler in plastic moulding, in animal bedding, or as fuel.

See also: Forestry Stewardship Council; Timber industry – temperate; Timber industry – tropical; Trees.

Timber Industry – Temperate

World trade in forestry products is estimated to be worth US$100 billion a year, making it the third most valuable commodity trade internationally, after oil and gas. However, 85 per cent of all timber is used in its country of origin. In the EU, 25 per cent of land is under forest, while in Britain the figure is only 10 per cent. Britain currently imports 85 per cent of its timber requirements, making it the country's fourth biggest import (after vehicles, food and fuel). The industry provides a home for *wildlife* and offers an attractive amenity (there are 200 million day visits a year to UK's forests and woodlands).

The industry's products – timber and paper – are renewable and *biodegradable* and constantly replanted. Trees also absorb *CO_2*, the *greenhouse gas*, and the industry wastes very little. Small roundwood thinnings (branches) are pulped to make paper or chipped to make furniture. Bark is sold to horticulture as a substitute for *peat*, and the residues from sawmills go into paper and panelboard mills.

Impacts

Forestry companies have been criticized on the following grounds:

- They have planted quick-growing (and therefore profitable) pine trees in *environmentally sensitive areas* – ESAs – (such as the Flow Country in Scotland). This reduces the habitats of rare species.
- The tough bark of pine trees is home to far fewer species. An oak tree is home to six times as many insects as a spruce.
- Afforestation of pine trees creates a dark blanket of trees through which the sun cannot penetrate and which is unattractive to *wildlife*. Now forestry companies are leaving rides and other spaces which attract wildlife.
- Clear felling (chopping down all the trees in an area) deprives many species of their habitats (including birds, insects, animals, fungi and lichen). It is also visually intrusive. Clear felling is the inevitable consequence of the large equipment now used in tree harvesting and the introduction of 'efficient' management methods.
- Monoculture (planting only one species) reduces *biodiversity*.

With growing industry awareness, these problems seem to be reducing in scale, though there have been international protests about forestry practices at Clayoquot Sound, British Columbia, Canada, and at Europe's last fragment of primeval forest – the Bialowieza Forest in Poland. In the US, Earth First activists have planted spikes in trees which can maim or kill loggers if the chain saw comes into contact with them.

Mitigation

The *Forest Stewardship Council* has produced guidelines for eco-certification of logging. However, a US–Canadian proposal for an environmental forestry standard based on *ISO 14001* has met with criticism. Canada, says WWF, wants to apply its vague national standards to the rest of the world. This would lead, it says, to environmental certification of large-scale clear cutting and other environmentally damaging practices. Canada denies this. But 56 Canadian environmental and citizens' organizations have condemned Canada's national forestry standard. They say it will lead to eco-certificates being granted to destructive forestry methods.

Best Practice

Logging companies should:

- Reduce the size of clear-cuts to no more than 4 hectares, and leave some trees standing in those areas.
- Reduce or cease felling around important habitats such as lakes and rivers.
- Allow dead wood and thinnings to stay on the ground. It is a valuable habitat for many species and fertilizes the ground.
- Carry out ecological surveys and adopt the appropriate measures to maintain biological diversity.
- Plant a range of tree species, especially indigenous ones, and ensure that new tree plantings at least match the rate of felling.
- Avoid unnecessary *pesticides* and herbicides. Use biological means to control predators.
- Adopt independent certification on the source and eco-management of timber.

See also: Timber industry – tropical; Paper and pulp industry; Wood mark.

Timber Industry – Tropical

Industrialized countries such as Britain destroyed their forests over the past few hundred years for firewood, housing and warships. Now the tropical forests of Asia, Africa and South America are going the same way (though this time the timber is going into hotel foyers or plywood). The timber fetches high prices, so developing countries are keen to sell this raw material. The trouble is that the industry is depleting the forests at an unsustainable rate. The Côte d'Ivoire's forests are being cleared at the rate of 500,000 hectares a year, so that all exploitable areas will be exhausted by the end of the century.

In cutting down the trees, logging companies destroy the habitats of rare species and displace indigenous peoples. For every two or three trees felled per hectare, one third to two-thirds of the other trees are injured. The rainforest, furthermore, is surprisingly fragile. If an area has been cleared, the top soil is no longer held together by roots and the land quickly becomes barren. The timber trade tends to plant quick-growing and thirsty trees, such as eucalyptus, because they grow quickly and therefore provide a faster return. In areas of water shortage, such trees can take excessive amounts of valuable water.

Developing countries such as Brazil point out that it is hypocritical for the West to have consumed its own forests over the last 500 years, in the cause of economic development, and now criticize poor countries for doing the same. Countries such as Brazil expect the West to shoulder some of the costs of protecting the rainforest.

As customers become environmentally aware, some merchants now claim that their tropical timber is sustainably managed; but these claims are sometimes false. Identifying the provenance of sawn timber is very difficult.

Best Practice

- Only buy timber which has been managed sustainably. Since this is well nigh impossible to verify, some companies now buy only timber produced from temperate forests.

See also: Rainforest.

Timber Treatment

Often involves the use of toxic *pesticides*, which can harm many species (including humans) and give rise to contaminated land.

Best Practice

- Where the organization buys or uses timber, it should assess the substances that are used to protect it and weigh up the environmental advantages and drawbacks.

Titanium Dioxide

Used mainly as a white pigment for colourings in paint, textiles, building materials and inks. Its process produces two main by-products, sulphuric acid and iron salts (ferrous sulphate). If dumped in *landfill* or the ocean, these have adverse impacts.

In the EC, legislation now requires these waste products to be neutralized, which in turn creates saleable products. Neutralizing the sulphuric acid with limestone creates gypsum, which can be sold for use in plasterboard and cement.

TOCP

Triorthocresyl Phosphate. Has been used in the past to adulterate food and drink. In Morocco in 1959, 10,000 people were affected by consuming edible oil that was later found to have been a mixture of olive oil, TOCP and lubricating oil. The perpetrators were executed.

Toilet Paper

Led by Denmark, the EU has prepared criteria for an *eco-label* for toilet paper and kitchen towels. The eco-label aims to encourage the used of recycled material, as well as the reduction of water pollution. The criteria are as follows:

- use of *renewable resources*, mainly wood;
- *non-renewable resources* (coal, oil, gas) – those consumed for production of electricity and for on-site heat generation;
- *global warming* – emissions of CO_2;
- *acid rain* – emissions of SO_2 into the air;
- water pollution – *COD* (organic material to water) and AOX chlorinated organics to water (as a result of bleaching);
- volume of waste – where credit points are given for the use of recycled fibre, as this is considered removal of waste.

Some consumers refuse to buy toilet tissue made from recycled paper because they think it is made from used lavatory paper.

See also: Paper; Paper, board and pulp industry.

Toiletries, Cosmetics and Pharmaceutical Industry (TCP)

The industry's impacts include the use of petro-chemical substances, such as *solvents*, *detergents*, artificial colouring, preservatives, dyes and perfumes, which can cause air and water pollution. The *packaging*, often *aerosols* and often elaborate, also produces an environmental burden. The manufacturing process, too, can produce polluting discharges to water. The industry has also been accused of causing unnecessary animal suffering, and many companies have stopped *animal testing*.

Some companies have launched brands which convey images of environmental purity but whose green credentials are no more than skin deep. Of all the companies in the market, the Body Shop is best known for its commitment to environmental and fair trade policies. However, some of its methods came under attack in the US, despite its having set the pace in ethical trading. One criticism was the company's use of the term 'against animal testing', a weaker phrase than 'not tested on animals', and one that allows the company a way out.

Case Study 39: Weleda

In business for over 70 years, Weleda uses no chemical additives. Instead it uses natural essential oils to provide both the perfume and the shelf life, while any colouring comes from the natural ingredients themselves. Developed from the ideas of Dr Rudolf Steiner, and founded in Switzerland in 1923, the company adopts a holistic approach to health care. It grows over 300 species of plants and uses only organic methods of cultivation, free from artificial *fertilizers* or *pesticides*. The product ingredients are fully listed on the pack, and the company does not use aerosols. Now, with 26 companies around the world, Weleda does not test its products on animals, nor do its suppliers.

Toluene

A volatile, flammable, aromatic hydrocarbon liquid. It is released into the atmosphere following its use as an octane improver in petrol and as a solvent. It is also used to produce phenol and *TNT*. It is rapidly biodegraded and is most susceptible to breakdown by photo-oxidation in the atmosphere. Because of this rate of removal, it is only moderately toxic to aquatic organisms and is unlikely to cause problems in aquatic or terrestrial environments unless major spills occur. It is uncertain whether prolonged chronic exposure (through industrial pollution) could cause disease.

Toner Cartridges: *see Cartridges*

Tourism Industry

Tourism brings welcome income to places which might otherwise be poor, and around the world employs one person in fifty. It is possibly the world's biggest industry, with annual sales of US$2 trillion. At least 400 million people travel abroad every year, and 1.5 billion holiday in their own country.

Impacts

The tourist industry causes congestion, *noise* and fumes from *cars*, litter, the wearing away of paths, destruction of traditional ways of life, and loss of the peace and charm that often attracted tourists in the first place. Some of the worst effects were seen on the Spanish coasts in the 1970s when quiet fishing villages became huge, concreted and eventually unpopular resorts. For as tourism grows, so does the amount of *sewage*, *roads*, modern hotels and other development. There are also impacts on the local population who suffer alienation and the loss of their culture. Even the brochures cause damage. The UK industry produces 120 million of them, of which 38 million are thrown away. They cannot be recycled (it is claimed) because of the inks used in the printing process. The scrapped brochures cost 400,000 trees and UK£35 million.

Eco-Label

The EU is proposing to launch an *eco-label* for tourist services. The Greek eco-labelling organization has carried out a study, leading to proposals for environmental criteria.

Best Practice

Tourism companies can reduce the impact of their operations through the following measures:

- Produce and implement an environmental policy.
- Encourage green tourism, such as photo safaris.
- Educate customers to understand and respect local traditions and values.
- Use environmentally aware hotels and services. Choose small, privately owned hotels and shops, use *public transport* and employ local people as guides.
- Provide or use only eco-labelled services, when available.
- Hotels can make many changes, such as not changing room towels every day and encouraging guests to switch off lights when leaving rooms.

See also: Catering and hotel industry.

TEQ

Toxic Equivalent Value. A way of comparing the toxicity of different pollutants or emissions. By assessing the quantity and toxicity of each pollutant, TEQ allows the comparison of emissions from different sources. It also permits an assessment of the total environmental load from a particular source.

Toxic

Poisonous. Causing death or injury to living things. The word is more specific than 'hazardous' which describes all substances that pose a threat, whether in the short or long term.

See also: Hazardous substances.

Toxics Release Inventory (TRI) – US

A database created by the *Emergency Planning and Community Right-to-Know Act* of 1986. TRI is a computerized annual database of companies manufacturing and processing more than 300 chemicals. It tells local residents what chemicals they may be exposed to. It is also used to measure the success of the *Environmental Protection Agency's* goal of reducing pollution at source. TRI is available to the public.

In 1990 the EPA challenged industry to voluntarily reduce 17 high-priority chemicals by 33 per cent by 1991 and 50 per cent by 1995. By the end of 1992, 977 companies had committed themselves to the programme, and promised to reduce their emissions by nearly 250 million pounds (113 million kg).

Toxic Substances Control Act – US

This 1976 Act and its amendments authorizes the US *Environmental Protection Agency* to screen existing and new chemicals. It can regulate these chemicals, including banning them. Specific sections refer to *PCBs*, *asbestos*, *radon* and *lead*.

Toxic Waste: *see Hazardous Waste; Toxic.*

Toxin

A poison produced by a living organism, such as bacteria and fungi.

Tradeable Permits

Tradeable permits give a firm the right to produce a specific amount of pollution and allow polluters to buy and sell the permits. Companies which have invested in effective pollution controls do not need permits and can make money by selling them to companies which operate 'dirty' processes. Some environmental pressure groups buy permits to reduce the amount of air pollution.

California's South Coast Air Quality Management District uses tradeable permits to lower *sulphur dioxide* and *nitrous oxide* emissions from large producers by a targeted 7 per cent a year. In 1994, permits were trading for US$5000 per tonne of NO_x.

See also: Government.

Trade Effluent Regulations 1989 – UK

Controls the discharge to sewers of 24 dangerous substances listed by the EC.

See also: Water Industry Act.

Traffic Lights: *see Roads*

Training, Environmental

All employees should be aware of:

- the company's environmental *objectives*;
- the potential environmental *impacts* of their work and how to manage them.

This requires training, while managers or supervisors in key roles (especially the environmental manager) should receive more advanced training.

The Role of Training

Environmental training has several functions:

- To gain awareness of, and commitment to, the company's policy and objectives.
- To improve performance in specific areas (such as production or operations).
- To ensure regulatory compliance.

Employees can be trained in a range of topics, including global issues such as the causes and effects of pollution, legislation, industry issues, department problems, and especially how the person being trained can help the organization to reduce its impacts.

If the company has an *environmental management system*, the employee will need to know how it works and his role in it. Both management and workforce, furthermore, should be trained. Sometimes additional environmental training is given to departmental representatives to allow them to *audit* their area. Training can take many forms, apart from classroom learning. It might include a newsletter, an 'environment awareness week', a booklet showing staff how to reduce their impacts, or a video. Being on a project team provides valuable learning experiences.

The Institute of Environmental Managers (IEM) has reported that environmental managers lack an understanding of what *sustainable development* means for their business. This implies a need for further training.

Training Topics

The following topics may be considered for training. Virtually all of them contribute to profitability.

- corporate environmental *policy* (either to assist in its creation or to communicate its contents);
- *raw materials* (their use and impacts; the benefits of avoiding waste, the opportunities for changing raw materials);
- product *design* and process engineering (to ensure that designers and engineers take the environment into account when designing or revising products and processes);
- *process* operation and maintenance (to ensure that operators understand how to minimize the impacts of their process – this should include emissions to air, discharges to water, *solid waste* and the use of toxic and *non-renewable resources*;
- *energy* (to help staff reduce energy use);
- *waste minimization* (including reuse and recycling, as well as the need to get it 'right first time');
- *marketing* (to make marketing staff aware of the concerns of consumers and trade customers; to help them develop more environmentally sound products and processes);

- *purchasing* (to show purchasing staff how to incorporate environmental issues into their purchasing strategy);
- *distribution* and transport (to help logistics staff select the transport modes which offer the *best practical environmental option*);
- accidents and emergencies (to educate staff in how to handle *emergencies* and minimize their impact);
- *environmental management system* (to help staff understand how the EMS works, and to explain their role in it);
- auditor training (to show staff how to carry out an environmental audit).

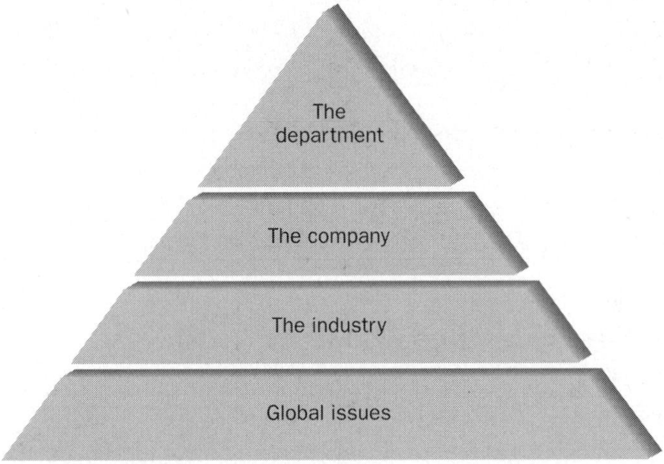

Figure 31: An Environmental Training Course Should Relate Each Department's Impacts to its Wider Context

Best Practice

- Identify training needs.
- Develop a training plan to meet these needs.
- Provide training for different groups of staff, including: employees whose work has a significant environmental impact; managers responsible for production; senior management; the environmental manager; all other members of staff.
- Keep records of training.
- Introduce other kinds of information which would support training (such as newsletters).
- Evaluate the success of the training.

See also: Awareness, environmental.

Trains: *see Railways*

Transfrontier Shipment of Waste Regulations – EU

The regulations provide red, amber and green lists of wastes whose shipment across European national boundaries is controlled. There is also Directive 84/631/EEC on the supervision and control of trans-frontier movements of *hazardous waste*.

In 1987, the Belgian region of Wallonia banned all imports of waste after it felt that it had been subject to a 'massive and abnormal' influx of waste from the Netherlands and Germany, which posed a real danger to the environment. The European Court of Justice found in 1992 that Wallonia had breached the directive mentioned above, but accepted Belgium's defence.

In 1992, the French Environment Ministry banned imports of domestic waste after it was discovered that German hospital waste was being illegally dumped in a French quarry.

See also: Basel convention; Waste management.

Transport: *see Cars; Distribution, Physical; Motor Industry; Public Transport; Roads; Waste transportation*

Transport of Dangerous Goods by Road – EU

Directive 94/55/EC which requires vocational training for certain drivers. The directive prohibits road transport of certain dangerous substances and subjects others to conditions regarding *packaging*, labelling and vehicle construction and operation. The goods are defined in the Annexes to the European Agreement on the Carriage of Dangerous Goods by Road (*ADR*).

Travel, Business

Business travel consumes *non-renewable fuels* and through combustion adds to pollution. Business travel can also consume large amounts of time and money. Reducing unnecessary business travel is good environmental practice and makes good business sense.

Best Practice

Companies can reduce business travel by the following measures:

- Ask employees to check whether their journey is really necessary.
- Set targets for a reduction in business miles travelled.
- Encourage the use of fax, telephone and videoconferencing.

Companies can reduce the impact of their business travel by:

- Encouraging employees to use rail rather than their cars.

See also: Distribution, physical; Cars.

Trees

Trees provide many crops, including timber, paper, firewood, nuts, and fruit. They are the habitat of many kinds of *wildlife*: an English oak can be home to 400 species of insects and mites. Tree roots can bind sandy soil and prevent the land from becoming desertified. Trees also filter and lock up noxious gases such as *carbon monoxide* and the *greenhouse gas carbon dioxide*. A tree-lined street may have only 15 per cent of the dust of a similar tree-less street. Trees emit the oxygen that humans require for breathing.

However, trees are not always a good thing. Farmers and landowners may plant them on ecologically valuable land (perhaps to take advantage of grants), with the result that important species which depend on meadows or *wetlands* lose their habitat. Companies should therefore avoid planting trees on valuable habitats such as unimproved grassland, heath land, wetlands and ancient woodlands. The best places for trees are next to existing woodland, agriculturally marginal land, on sloping land or land prone to erosion, and in corners or patches of land which are difficult to access by machinery.

Trees vary greatly in their value to *wildlife*. Local trees (and closely related non-native trees) are of greater value than non-native species, as the chart shows. New planting should be of species found in the area. Growing trees from the seed of neighbourhood trees will preserve the local genes.

Urban trees are both important and under threat. They act as sound barriers in cities and on motorways and soften the urban environment. But development endangers them. Cable companies are expected to dig trenches past every street tree in the UK over the next five years, and where they slice through the roots the tree is likely to die.

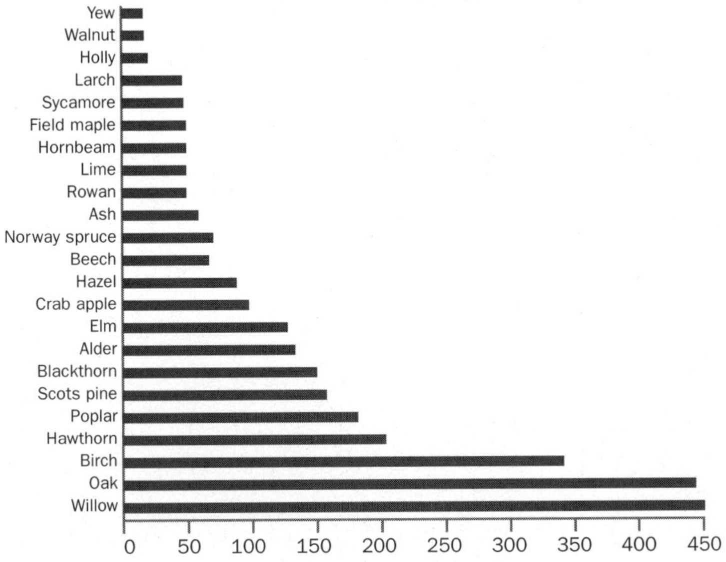

Figure 32: The Numbers of Insects and Mites Supported on Various English Trees

Best Practice

- Encourage the planting of native trees where appropriate.
- Avoid damaging trees when carrying out development

See also: Timber industry – temperate; Timber industry – tropical.

Tributyl Tin Oxide (TBTO)

Like other tributyltin (*TBT*) compounds which are from the *organotin* family, TBTO is a fungicide used in wood preservative and is used an as anti-fouling paint on boats. Banned in 17 countries.

Best Practice

- Do not use if possible.

Trichlorobenzene

A hazardous prescribed substance on the EU *Black List* and UK *Red List*.

Best Practice

- Do not use.

Trichloroethane (TCE)

An organochlorine solvent known as 'trike'. It can cause water pollution.

Best Practice

- Avoid where possible. Use water-based cleaning techniques instead.

Trichloroethylene

A *VOC* and air pollutant, used as a degreaser. Like perchloroethylene, its discharge to drains is controlled in many countries.

Trichlorophenol

The poisonous chemical which was released at *Seveso*, Italy, with catastrophic results.

Best Practice

- Do not use

Trietazine

A *herbicide* used on potatoes, peas and beans. Frequently found to exceed the permitted limit in UK drinking water.

Trike: *see Trichloroethane*

Trivalent: *see Chromium*

Tropical Timber – *see Timber*

TSS

Total Suspended Solids: measured in milligrams per litre (mg/l_{-1}) or kilograms per day (kg/day). A measure of pollution.

See also: Suspended solids.

Tyres

Over 110 million car tyres and 12 million truck tyres become waste each year in the EU. In the UK alone, 250,000 tonnes of tyres are annually scrapped. In the UK, 70 per cent by weight of used tyres are sent to *landfill*, and only 15 per cent for retread, even though this represents some 600,000 tyres a week being retreaded. EU proposals aim to double the amount of retread tyres by the year 2000.

Used tyres can be recycled for retreading, depending on their condition, and there is a growing network of 'tyre safes' – collection bins which operate like bottle banks. Tyres can also be used as fuel in energy-from-waste incinerators, which generate electricity, though the problem of toxic gases has to be carefully managed. The UK Elm Energy and Recycling Plant burns used tyres to produce electrical power, and has a capacity of 90,000 tonnes. It is equipped with state-of-the-art emission controls.

Case Study 40: Continental Tyres

In Germany, Continental Tyres formed a tyre disposal company which, in 1994, aimed to dispose of 120,000 tonnes of worn rubber, representing one fifth of the total amount discarded in that country. The company demonstrates how an interest in environmental issues can produce profit: it now makes filling station hoses which return the fuel vapours to the underground tank. Its impermeable hoses for vehicle air-conditioning systems almost completely prevent the loss of coolants; and it uses environmentally responsible materials for dashboards, door linings, centre consoles and seat backrests. It also markets a range of tyres which are said to have environmental benefits.

See also: Cars; Microwaves.

UES

Uniform Emission Standard. Sets limits for the concentration of a dangerous substance in water, usually expressed as monthly effluent concentrations.

See also: EQO/EQS; Limit value.

Ugilec

Dangerous chemical whose import, export, marketing and use in the EC is controlled (Regulation EC 3135/94).

Best Practice

- Do not use.

UKAS – UK

United Kingdom Accreditation Service. Formerly known as NACCB, this organization accredits (gives an official seal of approval to) the bodies who award *EMAS* and *ISO 14001* certificates.

Umwelthaftungsgesetz – Germany

German Environmental Liability Act (ELA) which came into effect in 1991. Improves the injured party's rights to compensation for damages caused by effects on the environment. This includes substances, vibrations, *noise*, pressure, radiation, gases, fumes or heat. Unlike normal law, the ELA puts the burden of proof on the operator of the installation. The injured party only has to prove that the installation is likely to have caused the damage.

Underground Storage Tank (UST): *see Storage tanks*

UNEP

United Nations Environment Programme, which is concerned with securing international agreement on environmental protection. It has produced a *Company Environmental Reporting* booklet, which has 50 items that can be covered, and recommends a minimum of 20 core requirements. They are as follows:

Management Systems

- environmental *policy*;
- *environmental management system*;
- management responsibility;
- legal compliance.

Input/Output Inventory

- material use;
- *energy* consumption;
- water consumption;
- health and safety;
- accidents and *emergency* response;
- wastes;
- *air emissions*;
- water effluents;
- product impacts.

Finance

- environmental spending;
- liabilities.

Stakeholder Relations

- employees;
- legislator and regulators;
- local communities;
- investors;
- industry Associations.

See also: Report, environmental.

Unilever: *see Fishing Industry*

Unimproved

Land that has not been drained, sprayed with pesticide or otherwise 'improved'. It is usually rich in species.

Urban Growth: *see Cities*

Utilities

Utilities comprise *gas*, *electricity*, *telephone* and telecommunication services, water and *sewage* companies. A typical impact for most utilities is the digging of trenches for new pipes and cables. This causes congestion and can kill trees. The congestion can be reduced by trenchless tunnelling. Coordination of digging programmes between utilities also reduces duplication (where the same road is repeatedly dug up by successive utilities).

VAHs: *see Volatile Aromatic Hydrocarbons*

Valdez Principles: *see Ceres Principles*

Validation: *see Verifier*

Valorplast

French plastics *packaging recovery system* for chemical producers, plastic treatment plants and mineral water producers.

Valpak

A proposed UK organization for overseeing a *packaging recovery system*.

See also: Packaging recovery system; Material Organizations.

Varta: *see Batteries*

Vehicles: *see Cars; Distribution, physical*

Verges: *see Roads*

Verification: *see Verifier*

Verifier

An approved independent organization that checks the accuracy of a company's *environmental statement*. This process is called validation, and is a component of the *EMAS* scheme. Submitting an environmental statement or report to independent verifiers adds to its credibility. Validation will also tell the company whether its systems are adequate, and whether it is managing its main environmental impacts. It also reduces the risk that the company's report contains errors or omissions.

The verifier will evaluate the company's management system, verify the data, and review the text of the report. It will then produce a verification statement which resembles the *auditor's* report in an annual financial report. EMAS verifiers can only operate within the industries specified by the accreditation body (*UKAS* in the UK), so not all verifiers can validate every industry.

Some companies want to produce a document for public consumption without necessarily conforming to EMAS criteria. This document would be called a *report*.

See also: Certifier; EMAS; Report; Statement.

Videoconferencing

The use of video cameras and telephone technology to let people see and talk to each other in a 'meeting', despite being in different locations. Videoconferencing reduces the need for people to travel to meetings and thus reduces pollution and costs.

Best Practice

- Evaluate the use of videoconferencing.

Vinyl Chloride

A carcinogen derived from *chlorine*. Used to make *PVC*. PVC products, such as food wrapping film, coat hangers, shower curtains, and margarine tubs, can give off vinyl chloride gas.

Visual Impact and Pollution

Ugly buildings, overhead wires, new roads and advertising hoardings in beauty spots are all examples of visual pollution. It is caused by buildings, *roads* and other human constructions, especially new ones, which do not fit into their surroundings. Rubbish and mess made by human activities, such as dumps and storage yards, are especially polluting. These can be screened from view by the use of fencing, hedges or trees.

Best Practice

- *Audit* for visual pollution. Take special consideration for sights that can be seen by the public.
- Produce a plan to reduce visual pollution. This can entail more landscaping, better *building design*, and better *waste management* and disposal.

See also: Impact, environmental.

VOCs: *see Volatile Organic Compounds*

Volatile Aromatic Hydrocarbons (VAHs)

Products such as *benzene*, *xylene* and *toluene*. Compounds include benzene derivatives such as *PAHs*. They are known as 'aromatic' from the distinctive smell of benzene.

Volatile Organic Compounds (VOCs)

Substances such as benzene and many solvents, which contain carbon and which evaporate easily. They react with *car* exhaust fumes in sunny weather to form *smog*. VOCs are used as a cleaning solvent, for example in the *metal* working industry, and are found in *wood preservatives*, *rubber*, printing ink, and *paints*. They are also used as a propellant in *aerosols*. VOCs are emitted through the evaporation of vehicle fuel and through particles being ejected from a storage tank which is filled by a petrol tanker.

In the UK, 60 per cent of emissions come from industrial processes, while road transport accounts for 34 per cent. In Germany, there was a reduction of 40,000 tonnes of waste solvents after ICI introduced gloss paints containing fewer than 10 per cent VOCs in place of an average 40 per cent level. The printing industry is seeking to replace VOCs with vegetable cleaning agents.

It is possible to incinerate VOC fumes but this is expensive. Another solution is to bombard the vapours with ultraviolet light and pass them through a fibrous compost. Bacteria break down the smog-forming vapours into *carbon dioxide* and water.

Legislation

A proposed EU directive will control the emission of VOCs from the storage of petrol, the distribution of petrol to terminals and service stations, and the refuelling of cars at service stations. The directive aims to cut emissions from this source by 90 per cent, equivalent to 500,000 tonnes a year. The commission's solutions included recovery or incineration and it is believed that the available technologies included the following:

- a balanced system to recover displacement losses;
- reduction of breathing losses from above-ground storage tanks by improving seals or attaching vapour recovery units;
- use of bottom-loading systems.

The UK government's VOC strategy aims to reduce VOCs by 30 per cent by 1999. This is designed to meet the UK's obligations under a protocol signed in 1991 under the UN's Economic Commission for Europe.

Best Practice

- Establish where VOCs are being used in the organization.
- Set a target for the reduction of VOC emissions. Create a plan to achieve the target.
- Major users (for example, vehicle workshops) should be equipped with solvent recovery systems.

See also: Cars; Paint and pigments; Solvents.

Vorsorgeprinzip

German *precautionary principle* concerned with 'the avoidance or reduction of risks to the environment before specific environmental hazards are encountered'. It involves the prevention and step-by-step reduction of pollution.

Waldsterben

'Forest death'. Affects 45 million hectares of temperate forests worldwide. Caused by *acid rain*.

Washing Machines

Washing machines use large amounts of *energy* and water. They also pump spent *detergents* into outside drains from where they can pollute water courses. As a result, the EU has sought to identify the energy use of each machine by introducing an energy label system. It has also set up an *eco-label* for washing machines that meet specified environmental criteria.

A study by the UK Eco-Labelling Board found that a washing machine's biggest impacts lay not in its manufacture but in its use of energy, water and detergent during its lifetime. The resulting eco-label takes this into account. A similar label exists for dishwashers. The EU criteria are as follows:

- maximum energy consumption;
- maximum water consumption;
- maximum detergent consumption;
- the machine must have clear markings identifying the right settings for fabric type and laundry code as well as energy and water-saving options;
- the manufacturers must supply advice to the customer on eight specific ways to reduce the environmental burden;
- components must be marked for recycling;
- the machine must remove specified amounts of stain in standard tests;
- the machine must have a specified rinse efficiency.

Hoover claimed it had trebled its market share in Germany as a result of winning an eco-label for its New Wave models. Many washing machine manufacturers have sought to reduce the amount of water used in their equipment. In AEG dishwashers, consumption has fallen from 40 to 15 litres per wash.

Best Practice

- Make, sell or use only machines that are eco-labelled.

See also: Energy label.

Washroom

While cleanliness is important, it is easy to become germ-phobic. This results in large amounts of powerful chemicals being poured into toilets and sinks, in an effort to kill all living organisms.

- *Bleaches and cleaning fluids:* When cleaning chemicals are flushed into the *sewage* system, they can interfere with the bacteria that decompose the waste. *Chlorine bleach* is also dangerous because it can form a dangerous gas if mixed with an acidic cleaner.
- *Air fresheners*: A synthetic smell does not indicate cleanliness, and any strip or cake that gives off fumes may damage health. Lavatory smells can be avoided by opening a window, while effective cleaning rids the air of impure smells. Simple and regular vacuuming, sweeping and washing of floors and other surfaces will keep them free of germs.
- *Aerosols:* Often used in washrooms, these are not a good idea. They use dangerous gases as propellants and are difficult to recycle.
- *Recycled toilet paper:* This is essential.
- *Roller towels:* Thought to be more environmentally attractive than disposable paper towels or hot air dryers (though the impacts are difficult to compare).
- *Cleaning services:* Many offices and washrooms are cleaned and serviced by contractors. In such cases, it is important to find out what materials they are using. Specify what you want used. The cost of changing to environmentally friendly materials should be negligible.

- *Water use:* Companies should try to minimize water use. The washroom consumes a lot of water, which requires more pumping, more electricity and more *greenhouse gases*. Each time the lavatory is flushed, 20 litres goes down the drain. You can reduce the amount of water by restricting the size of the cistern. Using a brick is not a good idea because it can clog the system. A better solution is to convert the existing cistern to dual-flush. This can cut water use by half and save 50 litres of water a day per person. Urinal flushing should also be controlled by occupancy detectors that operate the flush only when someone approaches the urinals. Regulators can also reduce the amount of water flowing from the tap, from an excessive 20 litres per minute to a more desirable eight litres.
- *Energy use:* Organizations can reduce energy by using lights that switch off after a period of time and by reducing the thermostat setting for hot water.

Best Practice

- Use recycled lavatory paper and hand towels.
- Avoid powerful bleaches or toxins in cleaning.
- Avoid the use of synthetic fresheners.
- Reduce the amount of water produced by taps and held in toilet cisterns.
- Check for leaking taps.
- Use less energy by fitting automatic light switches and by turning down the hot water thermostat.

Waste-Derived Fuel: *see Energy from Waste*

Waste, Directive on Strict Liability for Damage Caused by – EU

The EU proposal refers to any significant deterioration of the physical, chemical or biological condition of water, soil or air, but falling short of physical injury to persons or property. Liability for this rests on the person who produced the waste or carried out the preprocessing, mixing or other operation with regard to the waste. This liability continues until the waste has been consigned to a properly authorized disposal facility. The directive introduces the concept of the 'waste eliminator' – the person who carried out the waste disposal, and who can also be deemed responsible. The directive also allows common interest groups (which would include pressure groups) to seek injunctions under the law, and represents an advance for environmental groups. Proceedings must take place within 13 years of the legal party taking action becoming aware of the damage.

Waste Management Industry

According to Ecofin, an environmental investment business, the waste management market of the 12 EU countries was worth more than UK£39 billion in 1994. Spending varies widely. A third of this spending came from Germany, while Britain and France together spent a further third. By 2005, as other EU countries catch up, the market will have increased to UK£62 billion.

The waste management industry is of critical importance to environmental management and the environment as a whole. Poor procedures or housekeeping can result in big problems of pollution.

Impacts

Each sector of the industry has its own impacts. *Landfill* causes a build-up of potentially toxic materials which can leach into water courses. It can also produce odours and cause a build-up of explosive methane gas. *Incinerators* can release dioxins and other hazardous substances into the atmosphere if not properly managed. *Sewage* plants can discharge harmful substances into the sea and rivers if not properly treated. Though politically attractive, *recycling* sometimes uses more resources than rival methods. However, it could become a larger part of the waste management industry, especially as recycling becomes more widespread and is encouraged by legislation and taxes on waste.

Closer legislation will increasingly give a competitive advantage to companies who can invest and who can provide effective controls; and small firms will be less able to compete. This will lead to a concentration of the industry into fewer companies. Toxic materials will continue to be the most controversial part of the industry and perhaps a profitable area, as those who produce toxic material will have to pay a higher price for its disposal.

See also: Landfill; Incineration, Recycling; Waste management; Waste transportation.

Waste Management

The US disposes of the most rubbish: in 1990, each consumer threw away 4.3 pounds of rubbish each day, up from 2.7 pounds in 1960. However, the *content* of the waste can be a more meaningful measure, since the degree of toxicity determines the scale of the impact. Moreover, data on waste should be treated with caution since different countries record their waste differently. In Table 20, both *liquid* and *solid waste* have been combined.

Table 20: Waste Arisings in England and Wales

Waste type	Million tonnes a year
Liquid industrial effluent	2000
Agricultural	250
Mining and quarrying	130
Industrial	
Hazardous	4
Special	1
Domestic and trade	28
Sewage sludge	24
Power station ash	14
Blast furnace slag	6
Building	3

Source: House of Commons Environment Committee, Toxic Waste (1988/89).

In industry, waste is produced from faulty production and trimmings, from *packaging* materials, and from by-products (such as power station ash and blast furnace slag). Depending on the company's processes, the waste can be *organic, paper, metal, plastic, chemical, oil, glass* or other solid materials. It can be in the form of solid, gas or liquid.

Impacts

The disposal of waste usually produces an environmental impact, whether through air pollution in an incinerator, the leaching of toxic liquids from *landfill* into water courses, or the direct discharge of effluent into drains or water courses.

Financial Implications

The cost of waste disposal, already high, is likely to rise as governments seek to reduce the volume of waste being produced and to prevent the creation of *contaminated land*. In the UK, the landfill tax has added to the cost of solid waste disposal.

EU Strategy on Waste

EU strategy on waste involves:

- the prevention of waste at source;
- recycling and reuse of waste;
- the safe and adequate disposal of waste.

The EU aims to cut the quantity and toxicity of waste for landfill, and to reduce the movement of waste, by preventing waste at source and establishing an adequate waste network. It has also established an *eco-label* scheme which is intended to promote environmentally sound products, including those which will lead to less waste.

Legislation

Each country defines waste in its own way. Legislation has been growing around the world, and the EU has issued directives on:

- Hazardous Waste;
- Integrated Pollution Prevention and Control (IPPC);
- Landfill of Waste;
- Packaging and Packaging Waste;
- Strict Liability for Damage Caused by Waste;
- Waste Water.

In the UK, most waste is governed by the *Environmental Protection Act*. Depending on its content, it is also defined as '*special*', '*hazardous*' or '*controlled*', and must be disposed of in specific ways. The courts are more willing to impose heavy fines and prison sentences for waste offences. From 1993 to 1995, as imprisonment first became a legal possibility, the UK courts sentenced five people to non-suspended prison sentences for waste offences. This included operating an unlicensed waste transfer station.

Waste Reduction Strategy

The best ways to reduce the *environmental impact* of waste are in the following order:

1 *Re-use material:* For example, production scrap can often be put back into the manufacturing process. The telephone company BT saved UK£20 million in 1994 by refurbishing pay phones instead of throwing old units away and replacing them with new ones. Faulty hand sets and vandalized cash compartments are now mended and refurbished.
2 *Reduce:* Avoid creating waste in the first place. Waste minimization requires a corporate culture which emphasizes using less.
3 *Recycle* the waste into a marketable product. For example, scrap yards have for a long time recycled copper and other metals, as well as discarded equipment and materials. Recycling bins for glass and paper are now common in plants and municipal sites throughout the West.
4 *Recover:* Where waste cannot be recycled, it should be burnt (through incineration) to recover the energy value.
5 *Dispose:* When all other options have been exhausted, dispose of the waste in an environmentally sound way (*landfill* being the normal choice).

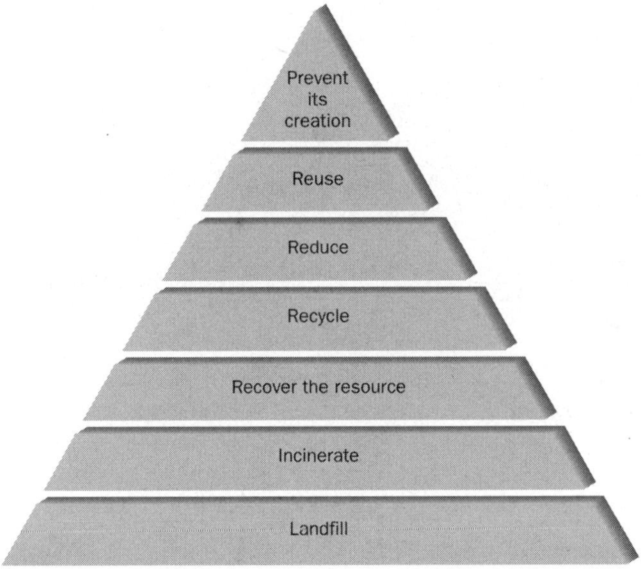

Figure 33: Preferred Methods of Dealing with Waste

Best Practice

- Identify legislation concerning waste disposal. Ensure the organization conforms to it.
- Discover how much waste the organization is producing. Identify the waste by each 'stream' or type. Carry out a 'waste minimization *audit*'.

- Segregate the waste wherever possible. Segregated waste is easier to reprocess or recycle.
- Set annual targets for reducing the volume of waste.
- Set up cross-functional groups to find ways of minimizing, reusing and recycling waste.
- Ask 'what if' or 'why not' questions to assess the effect on emissions, efficiency and economics of changing procedures . British Alcan asked: 'Why not develop returnable packaging?' for its heavy gauge aluminium foil. As a result, its customers no longer have to pay for the disposal of 2000 tonnes of scrap wood, steel banding and plastic film to *landfill*.
- Reduce the amount of consumables (by, for example, using washable cleaning cloths).
- Reduce *packaging* materials to a minimum (especially those from suppliers). Get suppliers to provide returnable packaging.
- Recycle wherever possible. This includes containers, paper, chemicals and oils.
- Train staff to be understand waste disposal requirements.
- Compact *solid waste* in order to reduce its volume and hence the amount of transport required. This can save money where waste disposal costs relate to the volume of waste, not its weight.

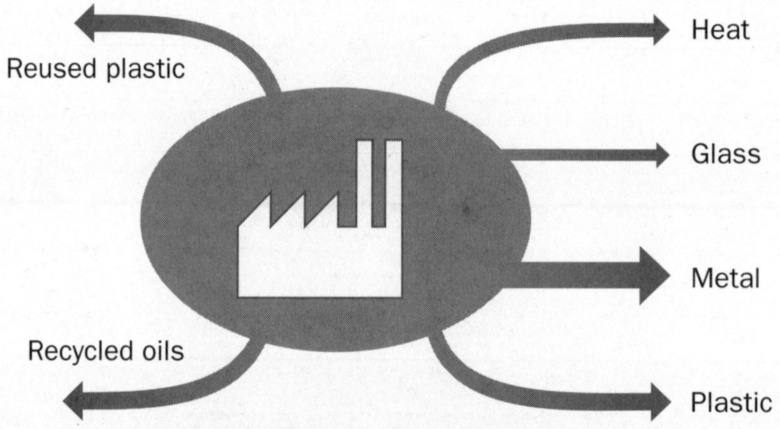

Figure 34: Waste Stream Analysis

See also: Packaging; Solid waste; Take back; Waste management industry; Waste transportation.

Waste Minimization: *see Waste Management*

Waste, Supervision and Control of Shipments – EU

EU regulation concerned with shipments of waste into, out of, and within the European Union.

See also: Basel Convention.

Waste, Transportation

It is tempting to choose a carrier merely on the grounds of the lowest quote. This can be dangerous, as low prices are sometimes achieved only by cutting corners. A good waste carrier is one which:

- is registered (where national legislation – as in the UK – requires it);
- is reliable (delivers on time and offers a quick response);
- is consistent (with the same drivers, same disposal point and same container);
- adopts best health and safety and environmental practice;
- operates professionally – gives advice, keeps paperwork in order, and visits disposal sites.

Legislation

The EU's Waste Directive controls the carriage of waste in member states and makes the choice of a responsible carrier all the more important. National legislation following the *Basel Convention* now prohibits the export of waste outside the EU and the European Free Trade Association (EFTA).

Best Practice

- Ensure you understand the legislation controlling the transport of the organization's waste.
- Make sure that your waste transportation is within the law. This applies particularly to hazardous waste.

Waste Water: *see Liquid Waste*

Waste Water Directive – EU

The Directive 91/27/EEC sets minimum standards for drinking and industrial waste water. It applies to *sewerage* and to waste water from industrial and trade premises and from domestic activities. The directive distinguishes between 'sensitive' and 'less sensitive' areas, the former being places where *eutrophication* is likely to take place. It outlines a monitoring procedure to assess compliance and sets criteria for the design and operation of treatment plants. It sets as a general principle the reuse of sludge where possible.

See also: Water pollution.

Water Act 1989 – UK

The act privatized the UK's water industry and introduced the principle of paying for consents to emit effluent. Under the law, anyone who causes or permits poisonous, noxious or polluting water to enter controlled waters is guilty under the act.

The Water Act was modified by the *Water Resources Act 1991* and the *Environment Act 1995*. The amendments give the *Environment Agency* power to serve an enforcement notice on a consent holder who is contravening any condition of the consent. The notice will specify the action that must be taken to remedy the situation and the timescale involved. The agency can also serve a works notice in cases where pollution is entering 'controlled waters' (rivers, estuaries, etc). The agency may specify the operations necessary to stop the pollution. Failure to comply with an enforcement notice or a works notice is punishable by three months' imprisonment or a fine of up to UK£20,000 or both; or in a higher court a two-year sentence or an unlimited fine, or both may be given.

Licences to discharge into sewers are controlled not by the Water Act but by the Public Health (Drainage of Trade Premises) Act 1937. The sewage companies grant consents for such effluent and their discharges, when they reach rivers or the sea, are controlled in turn by the Environment Agency.

Water Cycle

The principle that water evaporates from the sea, forms clouds, falls as precipitation such as rain, flows into rivers, and eventually reach the sea again. Not all water returns to the cycle. In many places, society is taking so much water for industry and agriculture that rivers are running dry. The water cycle is also relevant to management, because water can carry pollution a long way. Drinking water, marine life and freshwater fish can all be affected by pollution.

See also: Water pollution; Water use.

Water Industry Act 1991 – UK

This act mirrors the *Water Act 1989* and ensures that the same rules are applied to discharges to sewers as to rivers, except that the controlling body in this act is the water company. In other words, the polluter has to apply to the water company for a consent to discharge pollution.

See also: Trade Effluents Regulations 1989.

Water Pollution

Mankind has always used rivers and the ocean to carry away his waste; but the growth of the world's population has meant that waterways are no longer able to disperse the pollution. Rivers foaming with detergents, streams carrying dead fish and beaches awash with human excreta are signs of excessive human pollution and a lack of investment to clean it up.

Despite substantial legislation around the world, water pollution is still a problem. Forty per cent of US rivers and lakes remain unsafe for fishing or swimming. However, things are improving. The number of fish species in the Thames has risen from 20 in the 1970s to 110 in the 1990s. Otters, nearly wiped out by *pesticides* in the 1950s and 1960s, have moved out of the strongholds in Wales and the south-west of England to reappear in parts of the Trent, most of the Severn and east along the Avon as far as Coventry. However, one pollution incident or one summer of over-abstraction can undo years of good work in bringing back lost species.

Table 21: Sources of Common Toxic Materials Found in Water

Acids	Acid manufacture, battery manufacture, chemical industry, steel industry.
Alkalis	Breweries, food industry, chemicals, textile manufacture
Antibiotics	Pharmaceutical industry
Ammoniacal nitrogen	Coke manufacture, fertilizer manufacture, rubber industry
Chromium	Metal processing, tanneries
Cyanide	Coke production, metal plating
Detergents	Detergent manufacture, textile manufacture, laundries, food industry
Herbicides and pesticides (chlorinated hydrocarbons)	Chemical industry
Metals (copper, cadmium, cobalt, lead, nickel, mercury and zinc)	Metal processing and plating, chemical industry
Phenols	Coke production, oil refining, wood preserving
Solvents (benzene, acetone, carbon tetrachloride and alcohols)	Chemical industry, pharmaceuticals

Source: Harrison, (1990) *Pollution: Causes, Effects and Control*, Royal Society of Chemistry

Sources of Water Pollution

Water pollution comes from many sources. The 'point' sources (those which come from a single identifiable source) include:

- *Sewage:* As well as causing odour, sewage is rich in nitrogen, which can cause *eutrophication*. This causes fish to suffocate. In turn, kingfishers and other creatures that eat fish are left without food. Sewage also kills the invertebrates upon which birds such as the dipper feed. Endangered species such as the water vole are likewise dependent on clean water for plentiful prey. Where poorly treated, sewage gets into bathing beaches and its pathogens cause sickness in humans. Sewage companies face stricter controls in many countries. This is reducing water pollution, though much sewage is still only partially treated.

- *Other kinds of organic waste* (in addition to sewage) are highly polluting. This includes the effluent from food waste produced by dairies, breweries and other food processors. For example, milk is extremely polluting. If it gets into a water course it can strip the water of all its oxygen. This kills fish and other river life. Like sewage companies, food processors in many parts of the world are subject to increasing controls.
- *Industrial waste* from all kinds of companies, including chemical plants, textile companies, metal processors, oil companies, and pulp mills. Legislation is gradually reducing the amount of toxic material discharged by the these companies.

Non-Point Sources

Non-point sources are those that cannot be pin-pointed, but their effects can be observed.

- *Oil pollution*, leaking from oil tanks and from spills, is particularly hazardous.
- *Toxic materials* leaking from *landfill sites* are a continuing problem.
- *Agriculture* is one of the main offenders, with fertilizers and silage (both organic wastes) getting into rivers and causing *eutrophication*. Aerial spraying of agricultural *pesticides* is another cause of water pollution.
- *Storm water run-off* contains used motor oil, household chemicals and lawn pesticides.
- *Acid rain* from power stations acidifies lakes.
- *Dumping waste at sea* – especially from ships – is a global problem.

Case Study 41: Sewage Pollution

In the nine months to September 1995, the ten water companies of England and Wales had been convicted 22 times for pollution, mainly connected with *sewage*. One company alone, North West Water, was in court nine times for offences, despite record annual profits of UK £340 million. Between 1989 and 1995, the companies had been prosecuted 157 times for pollution.

However, the Water Services Association pointed out that its members had more sewage outlets and discharge points than any other industry, and account for 75 per cent of all discharges. Despite that, only 23 per cent of serious pollution incidents were caused by water companies.

See also: COD; Drinking Water Directive; Eutrophication; Liquid waste; London Dumping Convention; Oil; Water use.

Water Quality

Water quality is measured by:

- the concentration of pollutants such as *nitrates* and *organic waste* which would cause *eutrophication* – this is usually measured in *BOD*;
- the concentration of other toxic pollutants (such as *heavy metals*).

Measuring Water Quality

A wide range of pollutants in water can now be quickly assessed, using inexpensive electronic meters or by using the services of a laboratory. A regulatory authority may require the organization to keep the levels of pollutants in its effluent below a certain level. The legal consent should not be seen as the ultimate target. Many companies and sewage works set themselves targets that are more rigorous than the legal consent.

Best Practice

- The organization should be aware of water quality limits for any drains or water courses that it uses or borders.
- The organization should have procedures for ensuring that its processes and effluent do not cause water quality limits to be breached.

Water Resources Act 1991 – UK : *see Water Act 1989*

Water Use

Dried up river beds and reduced flows are evidence of a great increase in the use of water by industry, agriculture and consumers. All over the world, more water is being taken out of aquifers and rivers (for irrigation and cities) than is returned. As *aquifers* begin to empty, the water becomes more salty, which then damages agricultural land. The land may also subside: overpumping has caused land beneath Bangkok to subside at a rate of 5 to 10 cm a year. Significant over-pumping has also occurred around Manila and Djakarta.

The problem is acute where one country dams a river, reducing the volume available for downstream nations. Many observers (including the UN) predict that future wars will be fought over water, not territory or oil. This can have implications for ordinary companies: Iraq and Syria have threatened to take action against European companies who are building dams for Turkey on the Euphrates. The dams threaten to reduce the flow of vital water to Iraq and Syria, which have said they will deny the companies any construction work in their own countries and may sue them.

Reduced water flows also cut the amount available to *wildlife*. In the UK, swans have suffered from botulism from silt made poisonous as water levels fall during hot weather.

Cutting the Organization's Water Consumption

Since many organizations' water is metered, and can be a significant cost, it makes sense to minimize water consumption. One hospital reduced its water charges by UK£35,000 a year simply by mending leaking pipes, fitting sprays to taps, and stopping leaking taps.

According to the UK's NRA, forerunner of the *Environment Agency*, England and Wales could save 42 per cent of its water through a range of measures. They include:

- reducing leakage from the water supply system;
- converting toilets to low flush systems;
- making washing machines more water efficient.

This would be cheaper than building new reservoirs and introducing domestic metering.

Best Practice

- Companies should meter their water use to provide comparative information on each department's use.
- Set a target for a reduction on water use. Create a plan to achieve the target.
- *Audit* for leaks in the system.
- Reduce steam losses.
- Recover and reuse process water. This reduces the need for abstracting fresh water.
- Use a regulator on taps to reduce the flow and spread the stream.
- Use dual-flush or low-flush lavatories.
- Use devices which flush a urinal only when they sense it is being used.
- Reduce a cistern's capacity by placing an object in it. Do not use a brick: its particles can block the system.
- Collect rain water on flat roofs. This reduces the demand for water.

WBCSD

World Business Council for Sustainable Development, the successor to *WICE* and *BCSD*.

Welding and Brazing

In welding, toxic smoke is a major impact. In the past, companies used a hood to vent the smoke to the atmosphere. Nowadays, the *particulates* should be filtered to prevent other staff on the site from being affected. This can be done through the use of an electrostatic air cleaner. The cleaner should be of a sufficient capacity and effectiveness that air quality standards are not breached.

Best Practice

- Adopt effective cleaning systems to remove smoke.

See also: Indoor pollution.

Wetlands

Rather disparagingly, wetlands used to be called swamps, bogs or marshes. They are areas of *peat* land which are waterlogged in winter and slightly drier in summer. They are a major refuge for *wildlife*, including many rare species, especially wildfowl. One third of the US's endangered or threatened species of plants or animals live in wetlands. Coastal wetlands are also useful because they act as a buffer against storm water. Until recently, wetlands were seen as useless or even unhealthy places, which benefited from being tamed by drainage and improvement.

Wetlands are found all over the world, especially Australia, Canada, Denmark, Iran, Greenland, Russia and the US. Many have been drained by farmers so as to plant crops and grow livestock. Draining wetlands also allows peat extractors to dig out the peat for garden compost. Developers have also sought to drain the land to enable it to be built on. The Florida Everglades are a two-million-acre (8000,000-hectare) ecosystem, which has been constantly polluted and drained.

In the US, 30,000 acres (12,000 hectares) of wetlands still disappear annually, and the original 200 million acres (80 million hectares) of wetlands have been reduced to 90 million (36 million hectares) today. Only 3 per cent of the UK's wetlands remain: much of it is protected by conservation agreements. The destruction of wetlands has focused attention on the need to stop the sale of peat, allowing wetlands to become waterlogged again, and allowing meadow grasses to flourish.

See also: Peat; Ramsar.

Whales

Many countries now oppose whaling on the grounds that:

- Several species of whale are near extinction.
- Whaling is cruel. Blood is still being pumped to the brain of a harpooned whale even when all other life signs have disappeared.

In 1985, urged by pressure groups, the International Whaling Commission (IWC) enacted a worldwide moratorium on commercial whaling. Australia has a Whale Protection Act, and the USA has a Marine Mammal Protection Act. In 1994, the IWC agreed that commercial whaling would be banned in the Southern Ocean around Antarctica. In 1992 the IWC had also named the Indian Ocean as a sanctuary.

Norway has sought to circumvent the moratorium by killing 425 minke whales for 'science'. It also wants to increase the size of its catch. Japan, another whaling nation, has also violated the sanctuary.

Best Practice

- Ensure that the no products associated with the organization infringe international controls on whaling.

WICE

World Industry Council for the Environment, an organization that includes many leading multinationals, such as AT&T, BP, Mitsubishi and Sony. It merged in 1993 with the Business Council for Sustainable Development (BCSD), which became *WBCSD.*

Wild Birds Directive – EU

The Birds Directive 74/409/EEC on the conservation of wild birds. Requires member states to maintain the population of naturally occurring species of wild birds, while taking account of economic and recreational requirements. It requires member states to designate Special Areas of Conservation (SACs) and Special Protection Areas (SPAs), and to prevent pollution or deterioration of habitats of particularly important species listed in an annexe of the directive.

Wildlife: *see Grounds; Nature Conservation*

Wildlife Trade

Mankind has always traded animals and plants for their fur or hide or for their assumed magical properties, and the legal trade in wildlife is now worth US$5 billion a year worldwide. But with many threatened species now banned by law from trade, a further US$1.5 billion worth of sales are made by smuggling species across national boundaries. Wildlife is sold for specific purposes:

- Chinese medicine, especially aphrodisiacs (such as tiger penises and rhino horn);
- exotic furs, especially cat skins for rugs or clothing;
- reptile skins for handbags and shoes;
- ivory for carved objects;
- live animals as pets or for work (especially monkeys, tropical fish and parrots).

The financial rewards are great, since a clouded leopard coat can fetch US$100,000 in Japan. Penalties are often light and, as in the drugs trade, the use of couriers or 'mules' reduces the risk to traders. Supply of wildlife comes especially from tropical climates, from South America, Africa and East Asia, and from the US. The major markets are Japan, the US and Europe. The US legal trade, worth US$250 million a year, is exceeded by the illegal trade which is worth US$300 million. The main problems caused by the illegal wildlife trade are:

- It threatens to make some species extinct; and the rarer the species, the more it is sought after. Numbers of the northern white rhino fell from 1500 in the 1970s to less than 15 animals in the 1980s.

- Where poaching eradicates a species, local people who dealt sustainably in wildlife lose their income.
- Illegal trade can upset the balance of nature: when a predator such as the crocodile is removed, the *food chain* is altered, with unpredictable results.
- The treatment of animals in transit is particularly cruel. Between 60 and 80 per cent of animals smuggled die in transit. The high prices fetched by each animal makes this level of mortality an acceptable cost for the illegal trade.

Legislation

Trade in wildlife is governed by the international *CITES* convention, while enforcement is the responsibility of the signatory governments. CITES has done much to create awareness of the problem and to protect threatened species. However, the protection of some species (such as the creation of national parks to protect the African elephant) has sometimes caused hardship among local people who have lost their livelihood and sometimes their homes.

See also: Extinction; Ivory; Nature conservation.

Wind Power

The wind turbine's revolving blades create an electrical current, which can be stored in a *battery* or fed into the national electricity grid. Wind power uses an energy source that is free, renewable and infinite. Unlike *fossil fuel* power stations, it does not emit noxious gases and unlike *nuclear power* it does not produce dangerous waste.

Impacts

Yet, despite being a renewable energy, wind power has many critics. Some conservationists oppose wind turbines because they are often sited prominently on hills, especially in national parks, or in areas of high landscape value, and they can be visually intrusive. Detractors also say that the energy produced is unpredictable (the turbines stop when the wind drops) and that each turbine produces so little energy that large-scale and unsightly wind farms are needed to produce worthwhile power. There have also been cases of turbines which have failed to work, having been sited in areas of excessively high wind.

Future wind farms are likely to be sited at sea, where the winds are higher and there are no residents to complain about their appearance.

Case Study 42: The Impact of One Wind Farm

In the Welsh valley of Llandinam, Powys, residents became angry after 193 turbines were built on the hills above their homes. In its planning application, the power company Ecogen stated that the 100-feet (30-metres) high turbines would be inaudible from nearby dwellings. The turbines produce enough power for 23,000 homes. But villagers complain that there is a constant loud droning, like an aircraft engine, and occasionally a thumping noise like a helicopter rotor blade. They say that the noise of the turbines forces them to keep their windows shut at night, and that they ruin the landscape for miles around. The environmental health department of the local authority has monitored the noise, and says that it is not a statutory nuisance, though it is planning to take measures which will reduce the noise by half. Private legal action by individuals has not been ruled out.

The council believes that the turbines would be inaudible anywhere else. It believes that the developers may have underestimated how quiet the area was, set in a deep valley with virtually no wind noise.

See also: Energy; Renewable resources.

Woodfree

A paper which contains no woody impurities. The paper has, nevertheless, been made from wood. A confusing and unhelpful trade term.

Wood Preservatives: *see Timber Treatment*

Wool: *see Textiles; Alkyl Phenol Ethoxylates*

World Health Organization (WHO)

Organization concerned with global health issues. It aims to get agreement and set standards on the quality of air and water, and for the prevention of their pollution.

World Heritage Site

A site designated under the 1972 Convention on the Protection of World Cultural and Natural Heritage. Sites include Stonehenge, England, and the Pyramids in Egypt.

WPZ – UK

Water Protection Zone: an area set up under the *Water Resources Act 1991*. Controls are introduced within the area to prohibit or restrict certain activities affecting water quality. In Wales, the River Dee WPZ controls the storage or use of chemicals. Companies need a consent from the *Environment Agency* and must demonstrate a satisfactory risk assessment.

WQOs – UK

Statutory Water Quality Objectives. Under UK legislation, the government prescribes the quality of the nation's waters, and the *Environment Agency* should ensure that the targets are met. WQOs are made for specific catchments or stretches of water. They stem from the *Water Act 1990* and the *Water Resources Act 1991*, which introduced powers to set these objectives. They provide, for the first time, statutory targets for river quality, and the Environmental Agency has a duty to use its powers to ensure they are achieved.

See also: EQO.

X-Rays

Electromagnetic radiation lying between ultraviolet radiation and gamma rays. X-rays are used in medical diagnosis and the treatment of cancer. They ionize the atoms through which they pass and can cause damage, including cancer. They are also used to detect flaws in structures (such as pipes).

See also: Ionizing radiation.

Xylene

A colourless, toxic and flammable liquid, distilled from petroleum. It is a *benzene* compound and is used as aviation fuel and as a solvent.

See also: VAHs.

Yusho Disease

An illness, first reported in Japan and Taiwan, caused by consumption of food containing *PCBs*.

Zero Discharge; Zero Emissions

The goal of producing no waste, either to air, land or water. This results from a *closed-loop* production system, where process water is reused, where all raw materials are made from recycled or renewable materials, and where the products are readily biodegradable or recyclable. The zero-discharge factory will ensure that its waste materials are reused. For example, spent grain at a brewery can be used as a feed for earthworms, which are used in turn for chicken feed.

A zero-emissions research project is underway at the United Nations University in Tokyo, supported by major corporations.

Best Practice

- Set zero discharge as a corporate goal.

See also: Closed loop; Cradle to grave; Sustainable development; Waste management.

Zero Population Growth

An equilibrium where births match deaths. A goal for preventing population explosion.

See also: Population growth.

Zinc

Though an essential element in the human diet, zinc produces *cadmium*, which is toxic. Impure zinc can contain 2 per cent cadmium, while standard zinc contains around 0.5 per cent. Therefore, zinc production leads to emissions of cadmium.

Zinc is used to prevent corrosion of steel (by galvanizing), and is used in alloys, *paints*, dyes, and in *tyres*. With copper, it forms brass. Zinc sulphide is a phosphor and is used to make television screens and fluorescent tubes. Zinc oxide is used as a paint pigment and in medicines, batteries, cosmetics, and plastics. Zinc is on the EC *Grey List* of hazardous substances for its threat to aquatic life.

Best Practice

- Avoid its use if possible.
- Emissions from zinc smelters must be closely controlled.

Zone of Consequence

The area surrounding a hazardous industrial site. The zone of consequence is the area that would be involved in the case of fire, explosion or the release of toxic substances. The zone (sometimes a kilometre in radius) is especially relevant if the surrounding area contains houses or other businesses. The police will divide the zone of consequence into emergency sectors and will define traffic control points. An incident control point will be set up inside the zone but away from the plant. In the UK, the zone of consequence is associated with *CIMAH* legislation.

Zoos

In recent years zoos have been threatened by:

- television, which offers exciting virtual *wildlife* programmes (which in turn has led to falling number of visitors);
- animal pressure groups, such as Zoo Check, which criticize the conditions in zoos.

Many zoos have responded by reinventing themselves as the saviour of endangered species through their captive breeding programmes. While some zoos are now centres of excellence, too many still exhibit sad brown bears pacing listlessly up and down their restricted enclosures.

See also: Grounds; Nature conservation; Wildlife trade.

Reference Section

In the following section, 400 major entries have been categorised under the following topics:

- Air pollution
- Building management
- Disasters
- Energy management
- Environmental management system
- Hazardous substances
- Industries
- Issues
- Legislation – conventions
- Legislation – EU
- Legislation – UK
- Legislation – US
- Management
- Nature conservation
- Office
- Organizations
- Places
- Substances
- Transport
- Waste
- Water and water pollutants

Only key entries are classified here, and a few of them are listed under more than one category. The '*See also*' section that follows most entries will lead the reader to related issues.

Air pollution

Acid rain
Aerosols
Air pollution
Air quality
Benzene
Carbon dioxide
Carbon monoxide
CFCs
Diesel
Dioxins
Dust and fumes
Indoor pollution
Lead
Nitrogen dioxide
Nitrogen oxide
Ozone
Ozone-depleting substances
Plume
Smog
Sulphur dioxide
Volatile organic compounds
Welding and brazing

Building Management

Building design
Heating
Insulation
Lighting
Sick building syndrome
Washroom

Disasters

Alexander Kielland
Amoco Cadiz
Aral Sea
Bhopal
Camelford: see Aluminium
Chernobyl
Exxon Valdez
Piper Alpha
Seveso
Three Mile Island

Energy Management

Energy
Energy management
Fossil fuels
Fuel cells
Heating
Insulation
Lighting
Solar energy
Wind power

Environmental Management System

Audit, environmental
BS 7750
Certification and labelling schemes
Continuous improvement
Documentation
EMAS
EMS audit
Environmental management system
ISO 14001
Objectives, environmental
Operational control
Performance, environmental
Policy, environmental
Procedures
Process
Programme, environmental
Records
Register of effects
Register of legislation
Preliminary review
Review, management
Statement
Targets, environmental

Hazardous Substances

2,4,5-T
Aldicarb
Aldrin
Arsenic
Asbestos
Atrazine
Cadmium
Carbon monoxide
Chemicals
Chlorine
DDT
Dioxins
Dust and fumes
Formaldehyde
Grey List
Halons
Hazardous substances
HAZOP
HCFCs
Heavy metals
Hydrocarbons
Ionizing radiation
Lead
Lindane
Mercury
Methane
Methyl isocyanate
Methyl bromide
Methyl chloroform
Methyl mercury
Nitrate
Nonylphenol
Oestrogen mimics
Organochlorines
Organophosphates
Ozone-depleting substances
PAHs
Particulate
PCBs
Pentachlorophenol
Perchloroethylene
Pesticides
Phthalates

PM10s
Products of incomplete combustion
PVC
Radon
Red List
Simazine
Smog
Solvents
Tributyl tin oxide
Trichlorophenol
VOCs
X rays

Industries

Aerospace
Agriculture
Airports
Aquariums
Automotive
Banking and finance
Brewing and distilling
Catering and hotels
Cement
Chemical
Construction
Cotton
Defence
Dry cleaning
Electrical and electronic equipment
Electricity generating
Engineering
Filling stations
Financial services: see Banking and finance
Fishing
Food processing
Garages and vehicle maintenance
Gas
Hospitals and health services
Household equipment
IT
Metal
Military
Mining
Motor
Nappy, sanitary protection and incontinence products
Nuclear power
Oil and gas
Paint and pigments
Paper, board and pulp
Photographic
Plating
Printing
Quarrying
Retail
Telecommunications supply
Textiles
Timber industry – temperate
Timber industry – tropical
Toiletries, cosmetics and pharmaceutical Industry
Tourism
Utilities
Waste management
Wildlife trade
Zoos

Issues

Acid rain
Aerosols
Air pollution
Animal testing/rights
Biodiversity
Cities
Contaminated land
Cradle-to-Grave
Dams
Desertification
Energy
Ethical investment
Extinction
Food chain
Fossil fuels
Fur and hides
Genetically modified organisms
Global warming
Greenhouse gas
Incineration
Land-mines
Leg-hold traps
Light pollution
Monoculture
Nature conservation

Legislation – Conventions

Legislation – EU

Legislation – UK

Legislation – US

Management

Nature Conservation

Office

Organizations

International Whaling Commission
IUCN
Shell
UNEP

Places

Antarctica
Aral Sea
Camelford
Chernobyl
Kuwait
Lekkerklerk, the Netherlands
Los Angeles
Love Canal, New York
Milwaukee
Minimata Bay
Rainforest
Russia
Wetlands

Substances

Aluminium
Copper
Diesel
Glass
Nitrogen
Oil
Ozone
Paper
Plastic
Renewable resources
Steel
Textiles
Timber
Water cycle

Transport

Bicycles
Cars
Commuting
Diesel
Distribution, physical
Motor industry
Petrol
Railways
Road building
Sea transport
Travel, business
Tyres
Waste, transportation

Waste

Closed loop
Contaminated land
Controlled waste
Derelict land
European waste catalogue
Green dot
Hazardous waste
Incineration
Landfill
Liquid waste
Microwaves
Organic
Packaging
Packaging and Packaging Waste Directive
Packaging recovery system
Recycling
Refillables
Scrap
Sewage
Solid waste
Special waste
Toxic waste
Waste management
Waste transportation
Zero discharge

Water and Water Pollutants

Black List
BOD
Chlorine
Eutrophication
Laundry detergents
Liquid waste
Phosphates
Reedbed technology
Reverse osmosis
Sea
Storage tanks
Suspended solids
Water pollution
Water quality

Acknowledgements and Sources of Information

I am grateful for the legal newsletters of Denton Hall and Simmons and Simmons. I am also obliged to P J Gait for his comments on the text. Any errors are my responsibility.

The following sources of information were used throughout this text.

- Akzo Nobel
- BBC *Wildlife* magazine
- British Lung Foundation
- British Steel
- British Telecom
- Croner Publications' Annual *Environmental Management*
- Curtis Fine Paper
- CQ Researcher, *Congressional Quarterly Inc.*
- Denton Hall, *Environmental Law* newsletters
- Department of Trade and Industry
- The ENDS Report
- *The Financial Times*
- Friends of the Earth
- *Geography Review* 1994–95 (especially Nick Middleton, Paul Perkins, Philip Hirsch)
- Greenergy
- Green Network
- Green Office
- Greenpeace
- *The Guardian*
- Hewlett Packard
- Keim Paints
- *Kingzetts Chemical Encyclopaedia*
- Layezee Beds
- *Manufacturing Management* magazine
- *Macmillan Encyclopaedia*
- *National Geographic*
- National Power
- National Westminster Bank
- *New Scientist*
- NOR Systems
- *The Observer*
- PA and the Office Toolkit
- Pesticides Trust
- Pilkington
- *Reader's Digest*
- Shanks & McEwan Group, plc
- Simmons and Simmons, *Environmental Law* newsletter
- *The Sunday Times*
- Tarmac (*Tarmac in the Environment* report)
- *The Times*
- UK Eco-Labelling Board

Further Reading

BAA Heathrow (1996) *Environmental Report* BAA, Heathrow

Bureau of National Affairs (1995–7) *International Environmental Reporter*

Confederation of British Industry (CBI) (1992) *Environmental Education and Training*

Department of the Environment (1994) *Biodiversity: The UK Action Plan* HMSO, London

Department of the Environment (1995) *EC Eco-Management and Audit Scheme: a Participant's Guide* HMSO, London

Department of the Environment *This Common Inheritance* HMSO, London

Department of Trade and Industry *Cutting Your Losses* HMSO, London

Elsworth, S (1990) *A Dictionary of the Environment* Paladin, London

Environmental Protection Agency (1993) *Summaries of Environmental Laws Administered by the EPA* Congressional Research Service: The Library of Congress, Washington, DC

Harrison (ed) (1990) *Pollution: Causes, Effects and Control* Royal Society of Chemistry, London

ISO (1995) *ISO 14000 General Guidelines on Principles, Systems and Supporting Techniques* ISO

Lean, Hinrichsen & Markham (1990) *WWF Atlas of the Environment* Hutchinson, London

O'Neill (1993) *Environmental Chemistry* Chapman and Hall, London

Sadgrove, K (1995) in *The Financial Times Handbook of Management: Managing the Environment* (ed Pitman Crainer), London

Sadgrove, K (1992) *The Green Manager's Handbook* Gower Publishing, London

Sadgrove, K (1996) *The Complete Guide to Business Risk Management* Gower Publishing, London

Schott (1992) *World Famous Catastrophes* Magpie, London

Schroeder, H A (1978) *The Poisons Around Us* Indiana University Press, Indiana

Somerset Wildlife Trust (1990–1996) *Nature in Somerset*

United Nations Environment Programme *Industry and Environment* UNEP, Nairobi

Welford (1996) *Corporate Environmental Management* Earthscan Publications, London

David Morgan (ed) (1991) *Hazardous Waste and Human Health* BMA, Oxford